Shaun Considine was born in New York City and raised in County Clare, Ireland. As a writer and photographer, his profiles, reviews and photographs have appeared in the *New York Times*, the *Los Angeles Times*, the *Chicago Tribune*, *Life* magazine, *Newsweek*, *People*, *Vanity Fair*, *Rolling Stone*, the *Arts and Book Review* magazine of the *Independent*, and *The Times* in London.

He is the author of three books, including *Mad As Hell, the Life and Work of Paddy Chayefsky*; *Bette and Joan – the Divine Feud*; and *Barbra Streisand – the Woman, the Myth, the Music*.

BETTE AND JOAN
The Divine Feud

Shaun Considine

SPHERE

First published in Great Britain by Century Hutchinson Ltd 1989
Published by Sphere Books Limited 1990
Reissued by Sphere in 2008
This edition published in 2015 by Sphere

9 10 8

Copyright © 1989, 2008 by Shaun Considine

The moral right of the author has been asserted.

All rights reserved.
No part of this publication may be reproduced, stored in a
retrieval system, or transmitted, in any form or by any means, without
the prior permission in writing of the publisher, nor be otherwise circulated
in any form of binding or cover other than that in which it is published
and without a similar condition including this condition being
imposed on the subsequent purchaser.

A CIP catalogue record for this book
is available from the British Library.

ISBN 978-0-7515-4187-8

Typeset by Hewer Text UK Ltd, Edinburgh
Printed and bound in Great Britain by
Clays Ltd, St Ives plc

Papers used by Sphere are from well-managed forests
and other responsible sources.

Sphere
An imprint of
Little, Brown Book Group
Carmelite House
50 Victoria Embankment
London EC4Y 0DZ

An Hachette UK Company
www.hachette.co.uk

www.littlebrown.co.uk

For the Tuohys and Considines in County Clare
and beyond, and all my friends and the fans
of the indestructible Bette and Joan.

CONTENTS

Prologue

On Saturday morning, April 14, 1973, the phone rang in my New York apartment. On the other end of the line was Bette Davis, calling from her home in Connecticut, to talk about a story I was doing on *The Catered Affair*, one of her favorite films. After discussing the film, I mentioned to Davis, with some apprehension, that I had seen a colleague of hers, Joan Crawford, on stage at Town Hall the previous Sunday night. The news instantly aroused Bette's interest. '*God!*' she said, with that inimitable speech pattern. 'I would have given *anything* to have been a fly on the *wall* at that thing. Tell me, how *did* it go?' Crawford was a little nervous at first before a live audience, I said, but she rallied. 'And?' said Bette. 'She spoke about working with you,' I replied. 'Of course she did,' said Bette. 'And what *did* Joan say?'

Being careful to step around the issue of Bette's explosive temperament (which Crawford dissected), I mentioned that Joan was laudatory, stating that she found working with Davis on *What Ever Happened to Baby Jane?* to be a 'challenge.'

'*Whaaat!*' said Bette, her voice rising in pitch and volume. 'A challenge? That bitch hated working with me on *Jane*; and vice versa. She was a pain in the ass before, during, and after the picture was made.'

Bette went on to discuss the differences between them. 'I was the actress and she was the big *Movie* Star. There is a need for both in this profession, but my dear, at times the woman could be *insane!*' Joan, according to Bette, was also vain, jealous, and about as stable and trustworthy as a basket of snakes.

*   *   *

The following Monday evening the phone rang once more in my apartment. The caller this time was Joan Crawford, who insisted that she be allowed to give her side of the fractious story. Bette was a liar of course. She was also a bitch and a bully who put her through hell during the making of *What Ever Happened to Baby Jane?* and tried to destroy her during the production of their second abortive film, *Hush . . . Hush, Sweet Charlotte.*

A year after my talk with the rival queens, I met Crawford at a New York social function. She was civil, almost cold. She was angry with me, I was told, because I had failed to write about her difficulties with the great beast Bette. But that wasn't my job, my assignment. Furthermore, I wrote nothing because I felt I didn't have the complete facts. One or both of the star ladies was lying about the details given. But certainly I was hooked by the situation. What movie fan wouldn't relish being caught in the crossfire of such living lusty legends? As a journalist I also felt there was a good story here. For years Davis and Crawford went to considerable lengths to downplay or deny that there was any bad blood between them. Now I knew firsthand that the feud not only existed, it was ready to erupt, bursting into full flame at the mere mention of the other star's name.

The cause of it, however, the why, when, and wherefore of their rivalry, which spanned five decades set against the backdrop of Hollywood's most golden era, would take me fourteen years to uncover.

In 1976, the year before she died, I talked with Miss Crawford again, and in 1987, to Bette Davis, specifically for this book. In the interim, extensive research was done; and interviews were conducted with many of the writers, directors, producers, co stars, makeup men, hairdressers – the myriad of people who worked with both actresses over the years. Their recall and insights on the lives and long careers, on the radical contrasts and bitter rivalry between two of the most illustrious and durable legends Hollywood ever created, are documented on the following pages.

PART ONE
1904 to 1945

1

'Bright, ambitious, forceful, impatient, extravagant, self-centered, generous, and stubborn, when one Aries challenges another Aries, they become two battering Rams whose horns are locked.'

Carroll Righter, astrologer to the stars.

They were born under the same sign – Aries (the Ram) – and in the same year, 1908, although Davis would later swear, 'Crawford is five years older than me, if she's a day.'

Their backgrounds were also dissimilar, Davis claimed. She came from upper New England stock, while Crawford's roots were vague, inferior, with the possibility that her parents never married.

Bette's parents came from the small town of Lowell, Massachusetts. Her mother, Ruth Favor, 'resembled a Sargent painting.' Her father, Harlow Morrell Davis, was the son of a Baptist minister and a graduate of Harvard's law school. Possessed of a low tolerance for people, pranks and sentimentality, on their wedding day the groom yelled, 'Damn you! I'll get you for this,' after a guest threw rice at the departing couple. On the 4th of July, their wedding night, Bette was conceived, without plan or desire. Post coitus, her father apparently went into an absolute rage when due to a lack of water at the hotel where they were staying, his bride could not douche. 'Nothing could wash me away,' said Bette, born nine months later between a clap of thunder and a streak of lightning. Her birth, a critic later noted, 'sounded more like an entrance from the wings than the womb.'

Joan Crawford's birth by comparison was tranquil, and somewhat soft-focus in recall, as was the wont of many self-created Hollywood stars of yore. The exact year was said to be 1904, although Crawford preferred 1908, when certificates of birth first went on file in San Antonio, Texas. Her father was Thomas LeSueur. He was French Canadian, a laborer, tall, with dark hair and deep-set eyes, which Joan inherited. Her mother was 'peasant Irish,' and part Scandinavian, with lovely auburn hair and a lack of affection for Joan. 'She worshipped Daisy, my older sister,' she said. 'When Daisy died, mother transferred her affection to Hal, my older brother. When I was born a year later, she didn't care whether I lived or died.' Her father seemed more loving. 'He held me in his arms when I cried, and soothed my pain with soft touches and whispers,' she remembered. When she was ten months old, Thomas LeSueur deserted his family. 'He ran off with a stripper from a Galveston waterfront bar,' said Bette Davis in her memoirs. A second man soon replaced him – Daddy Cassin. He adored Lucille, as she was called then, and she believed for the longest time he was her true father. When she was eleven, he too deserted the family. 'Being abandoned so often traumatized Joan,' said writer Adela Rogers St. Johns. 'She spent the rest of her life looking for a father – in husbands, lovers, studio executives, and directors.' When she found the ideal candidate, Joan felt safe, secure, validated. In time she expected them to leave, to reject her. When they didn't, she grew suspicious, then resentful, and found ways to make them depart.

'Why waste time hating your father, when he had a father who had a father before him?' asked the more pragmatic Bette.

Describing herself as an amiable child, wreathed in smiles, Bette's first word was 'papa.' Her father's affection was minimal, however. 'He despised babies, small children, displays of affection and small talk with *anyone*,' said Bette. A constant smoker and an intellectual snob, he also bequeathed to her his brains and aptitude for self-preoccupation. When she was eighteen months old, her sister, Barbara, was born. Enamored at first, Bette soon asserted her position over the younger child. Finding the baby asleep in *her* crib, Bette lifted her out and dumped her face down on the nearby sofa. 'I like Dolly but I don't want Dolly *here*,' Bette explained. Jealous of her sister's abundant curls, Bette would later give the infant a haircut, leaving her head 'cut in scallops.'

Crawford as a child also experienced sibling rivalry. Small, dark and defiant, she envied the popularity of her brother Hal, who was tall, fair and popular. The contrast between the two was apparent to many who questioned whether they were really brother and sister. Joan had doubts too, telling a reporter years after, 'Mother shacked up with so many men that Hal could have been my half-brother.' Nicknamed Billie because she was a tomboy, she learned to fight at an early age. 'The slightest slur or insult in the school playground and she would attack.'

When she was six, Crawford was introduced to the wonderful world of show business. Father number two, Henry Cassin, operated a Vaudeville theater in Lawton, Oklahoma, where the family lived. Each day after school, Billie Cassin ran to the theater and stood in the wings, watching the comics and dancers perform. 'They were third- and fourth-rate Vaudevillians,' she said, 'but to me they were the most exciting people on earth.' Hooked by the glamour and attention at the theater, she began to skip classes at school until word of her truancy and poor grades reached her mother. When Billie arrived home one evening her mother was waiting behind the kitchen door with what in time became known as 'Billie's stick.' It was a switch, cut from a maple tree. When it was applied rapidly and frequently to Billie's bare arms and legs, it left large, ugly red welts on her skin. She was warned to stay clear of the theater and not to talk to lowlifes; advice that Billie ignored. 'If she told me not to do something, without explaining why, I'd do it anyway,' she said.

'Tell me "*No*, you cannot or should not do this," I would say "*Watch!*" then do it,' said the equally stubborn Bette.

When Crawford was nine she saw her first motion picture, *Little Lord Fauntleroy*, starring her future mother-in-law Mary Pickford. 'I gasped when the picture show began,' she recalled. 'I was immediately captured by the story and by little Mary. I thought she was so brave and beautiful.' But it was the magic of the moving pictures that captivated Billie the most. She had so many questions. Why were the people larger than life? Why could she see them but they couldn't see her? 'They led such adventurous lives,' she said. 'They never seemed bored or sad for too long, and they always had happy endings.' And where did the performers go when the picture ended, she wondered, desperate to go with them. 'Once, when little Mary

looked into the camera and waved goodbye, I wanted to jump up
and yell "Take me with you." I wanted to be her best friend, to
be a part of her life. I really believed if I could be "up there," with
those people on the silver screen, that my life would be perfect too
– that I'd never be unhappy again.'

Bette Davis was about the same age when she saw her first film.
It too starred Mary Pickford. And though she wept at 'its purple
situations,' she had no urge to jump on the silver screen and
exchange places with little Mary. Confident and secure, Bette knew
she was the star of her own universe. 'I always felt special,' she
said, believing that as a child 'the Finger of God was directing the
attention of the world to *me*.'

Christened Ruth Elizabeth Davis, she changed her name to
Bette when she was five; inspired by Balzac's *Cousin Bette*. When
her father ridiculed the affectation she kept the name for good.
Her raucous laugh also offended the man, who offered her one
dollar if she could learn to laugh like a lady. She never collected.
At seven, as she and her mother and sister Barbara left for a
vacation in Florida, her father bid a permanent goodbye to his
family. When told by Mrs. Davis that there was to be a divorce,
young Barbara burst into tears. Bette however laughed. 'Good,'
she said, 'now can we go to the beach and have another baby.'
Years later she would call this her Pyrrhic victory. 'Of course I
replaced my father,' she said. 'I became my own father and everyone
else's.'

When Billie Cassin was eleven her childhood ended. Charged but
acquitted of embezzling gold, her stepfather was forced to give up
his vaudeville theater. The family moved to Kansas City where
they ran a third-rate hotel for transients. When the hotel failed,
Cassin skipped town. His deserted wife found work as an agent in
a laundry, with one room at the back of the shop to house her
family. Forced to choose between keeping her favorite, Hal, or her
rebellious daughter, she chose the boy. Billie was sent to live at
Saint Agnes's, a Catholic boarding school run by nuns. For free
room and board she was expected to work in the kitchen and
dining room. 'The nuns were strict and the other girls were snobs,'

she said. 'They looked down on me and called me a servant.' After two years she left the school. Her mother could no longer afford the tuition, Joan said, although her classmates later claimed Billie was expelled for theft and disobedience. 'She stole money and possessions belonging to the other girls,' one former classmate told the *Kansas City Star*.

From Saint Agnes's, Billie moved back into the laundry, to sleep in a makeshift alcove at the rear of the store. When her mother took in a new lover, Billie was sent to Rockingham Academy, a boarding school outside the city. Again, for free room and meals, she was expected to perform 'light duties.' These included cleaning the fourteen rooms of the academy, and helping to care for the thirty other students, some her own age or younger.

She slept in a room under the stairs leading to the attic. Each morning in winter she awoke at six, broke the ice in the top of her washbasin, washed her face, got dressed, hurried to the other rooms, started the fires, awoke the children, helped the younger ones get dressed, then hurried to the kitchen and dining room to prepare breakfast. After the children had eaten, and the tables were cleared, she had ten minutes to eat, stack the dishes, run to her room, change into her school uniform, and go to class. The procedure was the same for lunch, with a short break after dinner.

When Billie missed her schedule, failed in her duties, or attempted to ask for help from the other girls, she was physically abused by the headmistress. 'Once when I asked a girl for a dustpan, she grabbed me by the hair, threw me down a flight of stairs and beat me with the handle of a broomstick until I was dazed. "I'll teach you how to work if I have to kill you," she shrieked.'

Billie could not complain. Who would listen? Her mother? Her older brother? They were busy with their own misery, and usually took sides against her. Once, when the humiliation and the beatings became too much to endure, Billie ran away. She was found sitting in a park by a policeman, who brought her back to school. The headmistress showed concern and sympathy in front of the law. As soon as the policeman left, she opened the door to the cellar, kicked Billie down the steps, then shut off the light and left her there for the night. Billie never cried. She kept her tears in check,

stored up in a place no one could touch. Years later as a famous
movie star, when called upon to cry on cue for the camera, Joan
Crawford would only have to close her eyes and think of those
early days and the tears would come, 'flowing long after the director
yelled cut.'

In time Billie learned how to please those in authority at Rockingham Academy. She completed her chores with perfection, then
volunteered for more. Her diligence occasionally drew praise from
the headmistress. 'I lived for those words,' she said. 'I also learned
first-hand about hard work and discipline, and about the satisfaction
that comes from a job well done.'

In her youth, Bette Davis was also somewhat of a perfectionist
– in dress and decorum. 'An untied lace on a shoe, or a wrinkle
in a dress, drove me into a fury,' she said. Her standards could
also be unsettling. She was at the circus once. The elephants were
supposed to appear and dance on a red rug. 'The rug was crooked,'
said Bette, 'and that ruined the rest of the show for me.'

At school one Christmas she was chosen to play Santa Claus.
Performing too close to the candles on the tree, her beard caught
fire. Screaming she was quickly wrapped in a blanket. When
they unwrapped the scorched child her eyes remained closed.
'Her eyes!' the teachers and children cried in unison, as Bette
feigned blindness. 'A shudder of delight ran through me,' she
said. 'I was in complete command of the moment. I had never
known such power.'

Joan Crawford, during her final year at Rockingham Academy,
also discovered power. It was not in her dramatic talents, but in
her ripening sex appeal. Her body had filled out, and her face,
with its perfectly formed features, began to elicit looks of lust and
envy from the coed students. Invited to attend a local dance by
one of the older boys, Billie, with her 'natural rhythm and lusty
beauty,' became the proverbial belle of the ball. 'She possessed a
presence and personality that took one's breath away,' said Jim
Miller, a potential suitor. 'Young men would practically line up
on the dance floor to make dates with her.' 'As long as the music
was playing, I kept dancing,' said Joan. 'I wanted that night to go
on forever.'

SEX AND BILLIE CASSIN

She said she caught on to men early in life. When she was four, sitting on the knees of the elderly vaudevillians in her stepfather's theater, she knew instinctively that they had something more on their minds than teaching her the words of the current hit song. She was six or seven she recalled, when by popular request she took off all her clothes for two neighborhood boys. They stripped too, she said, arousing only curiosity as to 'what the extra parts were for.' The answer to that question came when she was thirteen. At Saint Agnes's, she was partial to sneaking out at night to meet boys in Budd Park, a block from the convent. On one of these nocturnal outings, she lost her virginity to a boy from Northeast High School. With time and practice, not to mention her spirit for perfectionism, she became an expert at pleasing boys, and herself. 'When I got the hang of what was going on,' she said, 'I decided I would enjoy myself as much as them, if not more.' At fifteen, attending Stephens College, she was a favorite of the students from the nearby University of Missouri. According to Kansas City historian Fred L. Lee, young Billie was a frequent guest at Phi Delta fraternity parties, 'often or not, ending upstairs.' In her own dorm, it was often noted that after dates 'one boy would drive her home, kiss her goodnight, she'd enter the house, then slip out and drive off with another – to Balanced Rock – sipping from a flask, making love in the back seat.'

'She was the kind of a girl,' said historian Lee, 'who knew what she wanted at an early age, and would do anything to accomplish it. She had no ethical standards at all.'

Joan's sexual pursuits were frequently stymied, she said, when she fell in love. In that blissful condition she was physically faithful, for the duration of the romance. Her first real beau was a tall, goodlooking blond youth named Ray Sterling. 'She said she was in love with me, but she was in love with everyone else,' said Sterling. 'There was a trumpet player in a band at one of the vaudeville theaters. She used to sit up in the front row and heave asthmatic sighs when he glanced in her direction.' She promised another boy, also wealthy, that she would elope with him. Then

she changed her mind, in love with another. 'She hated girls,' said
Sterling, 'because they snubbed her.'

INNOCENT BETTE

She was brought up, she said, as 'a chaste and modest New England
maiden.'

Chaste perhaps, but as a teenager she was seldom timid in her
curiosity or her relationship with boys. In her memoirs she told of
one summer at Cape Cod when she and a girlfriend would stroll
down lovers' lane, shining their flashlights on the lovers parked in
cars. On one of her first dates when working as an usher in a
theater at the Cape, Bette developed her first real crush, on aspiring
actor Henry Fonda. She chased him all over the seaside resort
when he was in the rumble seat with another girl. 'He never looked
at me, never,' said Bette sadly. (Joan Crawford would also pursue
Fonda, gifting the actor with a sequin-studded jockstrap on the set
of *Daisy Kenyon* in 1947. She invited him to model the gift for her,
privately. 'I was carrying her up the stairs for a scene we were
filming,' said the actor. 'When she whispered the invitation, I nearly
dropped her.')

Fonda's recall of the young Bette was somewhat different. He
claimed they met in New York, when she was a teenager. They
were introduced by a Princeton friend, who after an evening on
the town dared the actor to kiss her. 'Well, I sort of leaned over
and gave her a peck on the lips, not a real kiss,' he said. While
returning to Boston by train, Bette wrote Hank a letter. In it she
said, 'I've told Mother about our lovely experience together – in
the moonlight. She will announce our engagement when we get
home.'

'Holy shit,' said Fonda. 'One kiss and I'm engaged. That's how
naive I was, and that's what a devil Bette Davis was at seventeen.'

BILLIE AND BETTE – TWO DANCERS

At seventeen Billie Cassin learned that men could be used to
improve her lot in life. That summer her mother moved into a

more spacious apartment. The street outside their house was filled with automobiles, and their front porch was lined with gentlemen callers, for mother and daughter. Billie only dated the town's wealthiest boys, using them as stepping stones, to escort her to the Kansas City Country Club, and to the Jack O'Lantern night club, where she won her first dancing trophy. Like Bette Davis, Joan found the thrill of the attention and applause pleasing and addictive. She decided dancing would be her life, and her way out of Kansas. 'I had no brains,' she said. 'I failed in school and college. My options for survival were few.' After befriending two girls, a song-and-dance act called the Cook Sisters, Billie auditioned for a night-club tour. She was hired, and that afternoon stole the sisters' theatrical wardrobe and left Kansas. 'She robbed us blind,' said Nellie Cook, who never heard from Billie again but seemed to understand. 'She had such determination and drive, and she was so frightened of failure. She did what she felt she had to do.'

Bette Davis at sixteen also aspired to be a famous dancer, but not in dingy night-clubs or cheap road shows. She wanted to excel in the classical field, by following the exalted steps of Isadora Duncan. During her summer vacation from Academy, she studied with an ersatz Anglo-Indian teacher named Roshanara, in Peterborough, New Hampshire. Rehearsing eight hours a day, she made her stage debut as a dancing fairy in *A Midsummer Night's Dream*. 'My part was small,' she said, 'but I put such grace and dramatic instinct into my movements that I drew considerable attention. My mother was told I belonged on the stage.'

In Boston, after seeing Blanche Yurka in *The Wild Duck*, Bette abandoned her dancing aspirations believing she was destined to become an actress, 'hopefully a great one.' In school that fall she managed to wangle parts for herself in all of the student plays. Mastering the craft of concentration and recall, Bette also practiced a physical technique that would eventually become her trademark. In confrontations, on and off the stage, she learned how to dilate her eyes for dramatic effect. 'I think the child fancies herself a hypnotist,' one critic observed.

*   *   *

In a series of fast-shots, Joan Crawford liked to establish how she jumped from dancing in smokers and stag parties to a featured spot in a big Broadway show. 'A little talent, a lot of drive, and some good luck,' paved the way, she stated. It was also said that holding hands and sitting in the laps of the right men helped enormously. There was a booking agent in Chicago, a nightclub owner in Detroit, traveling producer J.J. Shubert, and a handsome saxophone player named James Welton. He played in the orchestra of the Winter Garden theater where Billie, now known as Lucille LeSueur, danced in *Innocent Eyes*. She needed musical charts, for songs she was learning. The two dated, fell in love, and were allegedly married in the summer of 1924. She moved into his studio, stayed five weeks, then left him. But no public mention was ever made of this marriage then, or later, when as Joan Crawford she had her past carefully processed to fit her promising future.

Agent Nils T. Granlund also knew Crawford during this period. In his book, *Blondes, Brunettes and Bullets*, he described Lucille LeSueur as 'a gorgeous girl, with huge blue eyes, perfect features and ripe, voluptuous lips.' Granlund booked girls into Manhattan clubs and speakeasies. He recalled the day Lucille came to him. Pleading poverty, and the illness of her mother back in Kansas, she said she needed extra work. She was a dancer, she told him, but she could also sing. She had charts for five songs, made up by a musician friend. Granlund sent her to audition for club owner Harry Richman. She was hired on the spot, to perform at midnight for fifty dollars a week. Returning to Granlund's office, Lucille burst into tears. 'She had no money – sob – to buy an evening gown – sob – to wear in Mr. Richman's show – sob.' The agent gave her fourteen dollars and sent her to a dress store on Forty-second Street. She came back with the dress and was trying it on in a corner of the office when the door opened and Marcus Loew, the owner of Loew's movie theaters and the recently formed MGM pictures, walked in. 'Turn your back!' the embarrassed but angry showgirl told the magnate. 'He was quite taken by her modesty and beauty,' said Granlund, who asked Loew to make a screen test of Lucille. She tested three times but was deemed unsuitable for movies. Shortly thereafter, writer Helen Laurenson claimed that the showgirl, eager for more money, displayed her cinematic talents elsewhere – in a series of soft-core porn movies. One of these was entitled *The Plumber*, which featured comedian Harry Green. According to Laurenson, when Joan married Douglas Fairbanks, Jr., she bought up every print of her 'blue movies', with the exception of one copy, which was owned by the The Quiet Birdmen of America, a private club whose members included Charles Lindbergh and one of Bette Davis' husbands.

In October 1924 Nils Granlund introduced Crawford to a visiting MGM executive, Harry Rapf. Granlund claimed he introduced Lucille to Rapf backstage at the Winter Garden. She recalled the meeting took place at Harry Richman's club. Producer-director Joe Mankiewicz said he thought the meeting was held in the bedroom of Harry Rapf's hotel suite. 'She had that extra something,' said Rapf. 'Good looks and a very perky personality.'

'Harry Rapf had a nose so big, it kept his private parts dry in the shower,' said Lucille LeSueur. On December 24, 1924, she received a telegram, offering her a five-year contract with MGM. She boarded the Sunset Limited on New Year's Day, bound for California. 'I was only seventeen, and still wet behind the ears,' she said. 'She was over twenty-one, and already jaded,' said her future rival, Bette Davis.

Bette Davis never had to whore or struggle during her early days of acting. Unlike Joan Crawford, Bette had a formidable ally and financial supporter – her mother Ruth Favor Davis.

A talented but impeded actress in her youth, Mrs. Davis was said to be devouringly ambitious for Bette, whom she described as the more talented and driven of her two daughters. 'Mother had the guts and dreams for her children,' said Bette. 'She fueled my drive.' A single parent, Ruthie worked as a nurse, a housemother, a portrait photographer and retoucher to support and educate her daughters. 'She was a strong, beautiful woman,' said a source who knew her well. 'She could charm the shoes off you one day, then cut you dead the next. Just like Bette.'

When Bette graduated from Cushing Academy and professed her fervent desire to be an actress, Ruthie picked up the family and moved to New York City. She arranged for Bette to audition for the renowned Eva Le Gallienne. Bette, nervous, giggled her way through the audition and was denied admission to Le Gallienne's academy. Undaunted, Ruthie brought Bette to the John Murray Anderson Dramatic School. 'My daughter wants to be an actress,' she told the school's executive director, 'and you've got to make her one. But I haven't a nickel. I'll have to pay you on the installment plan.' The director said he tried to discourage the 'innocent young thing', but the mother was too persuasive.

With fellow students, Lucille Ball, Joan Blondell, Katharine Hepburn, and Paul Muni, Bette studied diction under George Arliss and movement and dance with Martha Graham. She learned how to center her emotions on stage. 'Anguish, joy, hatred, rage, compassion could be conveyed through body language,' said Bette, while working on her own inimitable brand of personal magnetism, style, and star quality, 'all to be defended to my death.'

'We acted in a few school plays together,' said Joan Blondell. 'Once we played nuns in a restoration comedy. Bette always seemed so sure of herself on stage. She was very outspoken and serious about everything. I don't recall her ever having fun or being relaxed outside of class. Of course her mother, Ruthie, was always there, in the background, reminding Bette they had no time to waste.'

'As far as Mother and I were concerned,' said Bette, 'the world would not be a safe place to live until I conquered it.'

2

'The fact that Joan became a star before Bette mattered a great deal. Bette always liked to be first, but Joan's name was established long before hers. That was pet peeve number one.'

Adela Rogers St. Johns

On January 3, 1925, Lucille LeSueur arrived in Los Angeles and registered at the Hotel Washington on Van Buren Place, four blocks from MGM. 'A jumble of makeshift buildings and hastily constructed stage sets', the studio was situated on Washington Avenue, opposite a general store and a gasoline station. When Lucille checked in that afternoon she was asked to make a second, more elaborate screen test, to gauge her dramatic abilities. 'Four basic emotions were called for – anger, puzzlement, wistfulness and allurement.' She was told not to be afraid of the camera. 'It's only got one eye and it can't talk back.' On signing her contract, for seventy-five dollars a week, she was informed she would have to provide her own underwear and stockings, for roles, and if after six months she didn't seem suitable for pictures she would be sent back to Kansas.

The following morning at eight o'clock, Lucille stood in line at Central Casting, waiting to be chosen for that day's schedule of pictures. She never made that day's slate. 'The flashiest and friend-liest girls got picked,' she said. 'Girls who were shy got overlooked.' Adapting to the system, Lucille appeared for three days as an extra in a ballroom scene in *The Merry Widow*; in another picture the back of her head was used as a substitute for Norma Shearer. Described by one writer as 'just one of a truckload of good-looking, ambitious showgirls,' Lucille soon displayed that extra dimension compulsory for starlets who wish to rise above the competition. 'I had the ability to scheme, to finagle, to plan ahead,' said Crawford.

She requested a meeting with Harry Rapf, the man who had brought her to California. Rapf, who had forgotten about the brunette chorine he had met in New York, was married. He suspected trouble when he was told that the new contract girl insisted on meeting with him privately. But Lucille was too smart for common games. She told Rapf she was grateful to him, for bringing her to such a fine studio as MGM, but she felt guilty about the generous salary they were giving her 'for such little work.' The executive was impressed with her conscience, her ambition, and her feeling for 'family', a spirit the soon-to-be mammoth studio was eager to foster. He picked up the phone and called Pete Smith, who was in charge of MGM's new publicity department. Rapf suggested that Smith consider using the new girl for promotion work. Soon photographs of Lucille, jumping hurdles and throwing footballs, appeared in the newspapers. She flashed her sprightly charms at moviegoers in a trailer for forthcoming releases, and at the company's first sales convention in Los Angeles she appeared in a bathing suit with a sash across her breasts identifying her as 'Miss MGM.' In April, the readers of *Movie World* magazine were asked to choose a screen name which best expressed the girl's energetic, ambitious, and typically American personality. The winning name, submitted by a crippled lady who lived in Rochester, New York, was – Joan Crawford.

Even with a new name and the patronage of Harry Rapf, stardom did not come overnight for Joan Crawford. 'It took three long years of working and watching and picking up new tricks,' she said. She haunted the sets and became acquainted with the camera operators and directors. She snuck into the publicity offices to steal photographs, then spent hours studying the stars' looks, experimenting with her own through gab fests with the boys and girls in makeup. She also kept hustling for work. 'If I heard a director or producer had a part that might be right for me, I'd camp on his front doorstep until I got it. I also had a girl watching the back door too.'

Over a sixteen-month period, Joan Crawford appeared in thirteen pictures at MGM. She also acquired the reputation of being a quid-pro-quo girl. Years later when asked if she ever had to sacrifice her virtue for roles, via the proverbial casting couch, Crawford replied, 'Well, it sure as hell beat the hard cold floor.'

Every six months Crawford's contract option was picked up, which meant more money for the struggling starlet. She rented her own home, furnished on the installment plan and decorated by Joan herself. 'It was a nightmare of fringe, lace, tassels and pink taffeta draperies,' she recalled. Once settled, her family came to visit, permanently. Her brother Hal, after seeing her picture in a magazine, arrived on her doorstep from Kansas one day. 'Hi, sis,' said Hal. 'If they can put you in pictures, I'm a cinch.' Her mother soon followed and Joan was obligated to provide room and board for both, and to pay for the bills they ran up in the local department stores. She was also heavily in debt herself, with expenses for clothes, a beat-up car, and fees for an abortionist who allegedly performed two operations on her, one of which landed her in the hospital, resulting in the loss of five weeks' pay.

In the spring of 1927, Crawford met Frank Orsatti. Described as 'an Italianate *Padre-Padrone*' who dealt in real estate and bootleg liquor, Orsatti was a close friend of Louis B. Mayer, the head of MGM production. The rumor was that Orsatti supplied Mayer with liquor and women, invited him to parties in the penthouse of his Los Angeles hotel, and helped the studio boss deal with certain problems. When warned by an associate that Orsatti was 'bad news', Mayer told Myron Fox, 'Look, I've got certain things that have to be done, things that I can't ask people like you to do.' Orsatti, it was said, was quite smitten with MGM feature player Joan Crawford. He bought her an expensive car, then arranged with Mayer to advance her fifteen thousand dollars, so she could buy her first home, at 513 Roxbury Drive, in Brentwood Park, situated between Beverly Hills and the Pacific Ocean, and *away* from her mother and brother. It was here that Joan planned the next step of her budding career. With her energy, beauty, and talent, and with Orsatti's backing, she set out to launch herself as The Jazz Baby, America's symbol of Flaming Youth.

The Jazz Age had already swept across America, but it was Crawford who would 'catch it by its tail, jump on its back, then ride it on to greater glory.' 'I was in the right place at the right time,' she said of her emergence as Queen of the Charleston and Black Bottom in Hollywood. True, there were other flappers before her, such as Colleen Moore and Clara Bow, and prettier competitors on the dance floor, such as Carole Lombard, but it was Crawford who drew most of the attention and the prizes. 'My skirts were a trifle shorter, my heels a little higher, my hair a tad brighter, my dancing faster,' she said. 'Joan had great body tension,' said Carole Lombard. 'She was better than I but she seemed to be working at it, and for me it was all play.' Crawford was the symbol of an era, said F. Scott Fitzgerald – 'the best example of the flapper, the girl you see at smart night clubs, gowned to the apex of sophistication, dancing deliciously, laughing a great deal, with wide hurt eyes. Young things with a talent for living.'

With the loving cups and cash, Joan also acquired a new set of beaus. She 'never dated a boy who couldn't dance', and once more good looks and money were on her list of qualifications. One ardent suitor was Mike Cudahy, the heir to a meat-packing fortune. When Cudahy announced his engagement to Joan, his mother told the press that her son was being used to provide publicity for the star. Furthermore, she was ready to go to court to prevent the marriage license from being issued because her son, at age seventeen was still a minor, 'and he promised me he would remain in school.' 'Horsefeathers!' said Joan, claiming that Cudahy was handsome and divine, but just a little boy. When another Crawford partner, after dancing with her all night caught pneumonia driving home in the cold night air with the top down and then died, Joan, with proper respect, wore a black dress and veil to tea dances at the Cocoanut Grove and the Montmartre for a full week.

During this time, her studio, MGM, took full advantage of the publicity being generated by the starlet in her private life. Commensurate with her popular image, they assigned her roles as a taxi-dancer, a circus performer, a kidnapped heiress, and a gangster's moll in *Four Walls*. She was cast in the latter film as the second lead to the studio's number one leading man, John Gilbert. When the picture opened in New York the critic of the *New York Evening World* had this to say: 'It isn't often that a supporting player manages to steal a picture right from under the nose of John Gilbert . . . But that's what happens in *Four Walls* . . . For Miss Crawford simply walks off with it.'

Full-fledged stardom would come with her next film, *Our Dancing Daughters*.

The accounts of how Crawford got the role differed in the telling. The director, Harry Beaumont, claimed he saw Crawford dancing in a nightclub and told Louis B. Mayer that she would be perfect for the role of Dangerous Diana in his Jazz Age movie. 'That's not true,' said Joan. 'Mr. Beaumont never saw me dance anywhere. I had heard of the picture and I went to the story department late one night and stole the script. Then I went to the producer, Hunt Stromberg, and persuaded him to give me the part.'

The story – that of a wild, self-centered young socialite – was custom-cut for the ambitious starlet. Featured in the opening shot were the lissome Crawford legs, dancing to a silent tune as she steps into her undies in front of a three-way mirror. Segueing to the bar of a country club, we see Joan arrive. She takes a sip from every young man's glass, then, hearing the band warm up, clicks her fingers, shakes her head, and breaks into a wild Charleston on the dance floor. Encumbered by her skirt, she whips it off and finishes the dance in her slip. 'The scene says as much about egotism and sex in the 1920s as John Travolta's disco turn did in the 1970s,' said writer, Ethan Mordden.

When *Our Dancing Daughters* opened in December 1927, Crawford's name was billed under the title. After the rave reviews came in, accompanied by the healthy box-office receipts, her name was lifted above the title. The day of the billing change she was asked to sign a more generous contract with MGM. That night, in lieu of attending a formal dinner at the home of Irving and Norma Thalberg, the new star celebrated alone. 'I rode around town with a small box camera,' she said, 'taking pictures of "Joan Crawford", blazing on the theater marquees.'

BETTE – A SERIOUS ACTRESS

During the time when Joan was firmly placing her black satin dancing shoes on the first rung of stardom in Hollywood, Bette Davis was in the east, still gathering the essentials for the foundation of a serious dramatic career.

Upon graduation from Anderson Academy, she worked for a season at the Cape Playhouse in Massachusetts, then went to Rochester, New York, to work with the George Cukor Repertory Company. Midway through the season she was fired for being aloof with her fellow workers. 'I didn't know ingenues were supposed to party as well as work,' she said. 'She refused dates with the young men,' said actor Louis Calhern, who found Bette 'uppity and unpopular.' 'She wasn't supposed to sleep around, but she wasn't supposed to be Saint Teresa of Avila either,' said Calhern. Equipped with the Aries trait of never forgetting a grievance, Bette would censure Cukor for years to come. 'He had his little circle of admirers,' she said, 'sycophants, if you will. Miriam [Hopkins] was one, Joan [Crawford] came later. They would surround him and adore him. I have always despised that sort of fawning behavior. I was too strong and too talented for Mr. Cukor to mold, and therefore I was released from the company.' Cukor, who described Bette as 'a very interesting actress at the outset, almost maniacal,' had his version of the events. 'She was a stubborn young lady. She liked to disrupt rehearsals by giving her interpretation of the author's thoughts – not only for her character, but for the other roles also. It was useless to argue with her because during the actual performance she would do what she thought was best, frequently giving a different style of performance from the other actors.'

Being fired in Rochester turned out to be provident for Bette. In New York she moved twice as fast to become professionally established. She joined an off-Broadway group on MacDougall Street, the Provincetown Players, and made her debut in *The Earth Between*, the story of a girl incestuously in love with her father. The following day Brooks Atkinson of *The New York Times* deemed her 'an enchanting creature', and one month later she was asked to audition for Blanche Yurka. Judging Bette to be 'a maddening handful', and her mother 'a pain in the neck . . . a weak, silly creature', Miss Yurka nonetheless hired the ingenue to tour with her in *The Wild Duck*. As Hedvig, Bette conquered the critics in Philadelphia and Washington, and in her native Boston her real father visited her backstage. Ignoring her performance, he told her, 'You would make a very fine secretary.'

When the tour with Blanche Yurka ended, Bette played a rebellious daughter in *Broken Dishes* on Broadway. During rehearsals the director found her 'impossible . . . neurotic . . . and emotionally backward.' On opening night the critics said she was 'mesmerizing', 'incandescent', and 'made of lightning'. A week later she was asked by a talent scout to make a screen test for Hollywood producer Samuel Goldwyn. When the test was screened for Goldwyn, he stood up in the theater and screamed, 'Who did this to me?' The producer would be added to her list of old scores to settle, but in the meantime Bette assessed her liabilities. 'I was not prepared for motion pictures,' she said. 'My movements were much too broad. I also had a crooked tooth, of which I was aware, but I had no idea it would stand out like a locomotive.'

Undaunted, she had the tooth fixed and prepared for her next test. 'I had no doubt in my mind that I would be given a second chance,' she said. 'I wasn't a fool. Mother and I knew that talking pictures would soon be very popular. The movie producers would *need* actresses who could talk. Certainly I could do that very well.'

JOAN GOES STRAIGHT

'I had always known what I wanted, and that was beauty . . . in every form . . . a beautiful house, beautiful man, a beautiful life and image. I was ambitious to get the money which would attain all that for me.'

Joan Crawford

Upon the signing of her new contract with MGM, Crawford's salary was raised to fifteen hundred dollars per week, with an upfront bonus of ten thousand. She became a member of Louis B. Mayer's ('Call me Papa') family of stars, which also included Lon Chaney, Buster Keaton, Norma Shearer, and Greta Garbo. Crawford was now entitled to receive all of the privileges and protection that the powerful studio could offer. In Joan's case the latter service proved beneficial. She had already been involved in a few legal skirmishes with stores in Los Angeles. Once she was apprehended leaving a woman's specialty shop with merchandise not paid for; another fashion establishment claimed that Mrs. Anna

LeSueur, her mother, ran up bills that she refused to pay. Joan had already been cited twice by the Los Angeles Police department for speeding, when a third, more serious infraction occurred. She was driving at a rapid pace along Hollywood Boulevard, ignoring the red lights, when she hit a woman crossing the street. Attempting to leave the scene of the accident, she was apprehended by a policeman. Bursting into tears, Joan then tried to bribe the policeman and was taken to the local Hollywood precinct. Allowed one call, she called Howard Strickling, in charge of publicity at MGM. Strickling called L.B. Mayer, who called his friend, the chief of police (who would later be hired to head Metro's security division). Joan was released without being booked, and after Howard Strickling visited the injured young woman in the hospital, with a thousand dollars in crisp, clean bills, all claims against the star and the studio were dropped.

In September 1928 Crawford was not as fortunate in keeping the news of another indiscretion out of the tabloids. That month she was named as 'the other woman' in two divorce cases. One plaintiff told the *Los Angeles Herald* that 'the Venus of Hollywood' stole her husband and she was suing Crawford for damages. Another woman claimed her husband was the recipient of 'expensive gifts' from Joan, and spent long weekends with her in 'motels and resorts, up north.' Both men, one an assistant camera operator, the other, a carpenter, were employed by MGM, and after a consultation with their bosses, they returned to their wives, temporarily.

Joan, as a result, was called before Louis B. Mayer. She was now a star, he told her. She had responsibilities, not only to the studio, but to the hundreds of thousands of young people ('My public,' said Joan) who wrote to her each week. She had a choice, Mayer went on. She could continue to burn herself out, by kicking up her heels with riffraff in speakeasies and hotel rooms, or she could become a bigger star, by practicing selection and discretion in her private life and increased zeal and devotion in her professional one. 'He told her she had to put a lid on it,' said a Metro publicist. 'If she wanted to stay at Metro, she had to behave herself, at least in public.'

Joan was no fool. She knew she was the darling of the Jazz Age, and that, short of murder, her young fans would forgive her anything. But she also knew this Jazz Age thing wasn't going to last forever (Black Monday was just around the corner), so with tears in her eyes she repented at the knee of the great L.B. She told Papa Mayer that she was not only going to be a good girl and a lady from that day forward, but, with his blessing, she intended to become the biggest and brightest star Metro-Goldwyn-Mayer had ever produced.

With this new mantle of responsibility on her shoulders, Joan proceeded to drastically alter her offscreen lifestyle. She quickly dropped her old friends and made new ones, appearing in public with men, 'safe types', who could help her career and contribute to her 'growth as a human being.' She preferred men to women, she said – 'they're smarter and stronger and they seldom want to borrow your clothes.' Director Edmund Goulding was the first to advise Joan to practice restraint in front of the motion picture camera. 'Hold back,' he told her. 'Give the audience just a taste of what you're thinking, not the full meal.' (Goulding would offer the same advice to Bette Davis, who refused it, saying, 'No! I *am* larger than life and that's what my public wants to *see*.') William Haines, a leading man at Metro, was said to be in love 'with the charming Joan', but he was 'as gay as a goose' and he taught her important things like dress and diet and good posture. She gave up smoking and started chewing gum, 'because I heard it was good for the jaw line', and learned how to walk three Metro blocks with a brick balanced on her head. 'That helped straighten my spine,' she said. 'It also threw back my shoulders and firmed up my ass.' Paul Bern was another good friend and major influence. He was an important MGM producer and an intellectual. He wanted to go to bed with Joan. 'He sent me a fur, a coat of ermine,' she said. 'I sent it back. Don't think it didn't take will power. But I kept his friendship.' Bern, who would later counsel and marry Jean Harlow, advised Crawford on what books to read and what parts to play in the future. 'He recognized something in me that other men did not care to see – that I had a brain.'

One night, Bern escorted Joan to the theater. The play was *Young Woodley*, and the handsome young lead, Douglas Fairbanks, Jr., caught Joan's fancy. 'He was enchanting, the epitome of suaveness,' she said. She wrote him a note, asking him to call her sometime. When he called the next day she said she was busy all week, but he could come for tea on Sunday afternoon. At her request he brought along a small signed photograph. She gave him a large eleven-by-fourteen studio portrait. He thought she was 'vital, energetic, very pretty', with two vocal sounds – 'one resonant and professional and one more blatantly flat.' Although at times 'she tried too hard to be what Noël Coward called 'piss-elegant', it was Joan's magnetic dynamism and her 'gracefully muscled legs' that entranced young Doug. She in turn fell in love with his good looks, and his impressive background.

His father was Doug Sr., the world's favorite swashbuckler, and his stepmother was Mary Pickford, Joan's favorite childhood star and the current czarina of Hollywood society.

Doug's talents included writing, painting and the playing of several musical instruments. 'He also had a gay delicious wit, exquisite manners, and so much knowledge,' said Joan. Some suggested she was using the nineteen-year-old lad to further her own twenty-four-year-old social and financial ambitions. 'The money part was a joke,' said a Crawford ally. 'She was making more than him at the time and furthermore when they met he was supporting his mother and in debt up to his elegant ears. As for the talk about her being a social climber, everyone in Hollywood at that time was trying to scale the walls of Pickfair.'

When the press were alerted that the fickle, fun-loving, heart-breaker Joan had finally fallen in love, America took the romance of the Charleston Queen and the Prince of Pickfair to their hearts. The daily coverage and the fan magazine reportage reached epic proportions. 'Many "inside stories" were printed,' said Doug, 'some invented by studio press agents, some by gossipy friends, and some by dear self-dramatizing Billie.'

'I was Billie and he was Dodo,' said Joan. 'We dined together, bronzed on the beach, played golf and tennis, danced Saturday nights at the Biltmore or the Palomo Tennis Club. We were in love and had a language of our own. It went something like "Opi Lopov Yopov" – how nauseating can you get?'

Doug introduced her to culture and social graces. 'I who all but ate my peas with a knife,' she said. 'Laughable, patent nonsense,' said Doug, 'she was a very experienced lady. But one with an inferiority complex, which she used as a whip to spur herself onward and upward.'

'From Jazz to Gentility, Joan Crawford is going to be demure if it kills her,' said writer Ruth Bren in *Motion Picture* magazine. As the romance progressed, the metamorphosis of Joan the lady became more apparent. 'She spoke in a low voice,' said Bren. 'The raucous laughter was gone, her wardrobe leaned towards softly clinging materials, white gloves and picture hats – outfits obviously planned and more suited to the grounds of Pickfair.'

But the gates to the neo-ancestral Hollywood home of Doug Sr. and Mary Pickford did not swing open for Joan Crawford. 'She was gay and giddy and Pickfair did not go in for that,' said one writer. 'What did they think she would do,' asked another, 'wipe her nose on the drapes?'

The accounts of their exclusion from Pickfair were exaggerated, Doug Jr. insisted. He and Joan were never invited to any of the posh dinners, but they did attend for a few screenings, one of which, when the lights came up, found the young man engaged in some heavy necking with Miss Crawford, which brought a stern rebuke from Doug Sr.

'My son's current chorus-girl fling' was how Doug Jr.'s mother described the romance, while his father felt their affair was over-exploited, and that Joan was 'on the toughie side.'

Joan was hurt, of course. Her old image of the carefree thought-less flapper was a bad rap, she felt, a disguise for 'a very lonely young woman.' Dodo knew that. 'Just the other night he said to me,' said Joan to Katharine Albert for *Photoplay*, ' "You know, I didn't change you, Billie. You were always like this, only nobody knew it!" '

MGM naturally sanctioned the romance. L.B. Mayer, pleased that 'daughter Joan' was pursuing respectable pleasure, took advantage of the couple's widely publicized romance by teaming the two in a sequel to her hit picture, *Our Dancing Daughters*. The new movie was called *Our Modern Maidens*, which in turn led to *Our Blushing Brides*. ('What next? *Our Ditsy Divorcees*?' asked one caustic critic.)

Upon the release of the picture, Joan announced her engagement
to Doug Jr. in the social pages of *The New York Times* and the *Los
Angeles Times*. The news and the proper placement, she felt, would
result in an invitation to wed at the home of Doug and Mary.
Their silence was cataclysmic to Joan, who realized that her dream
of a white wedding on the lawns of Pickfair was not to be. So to
save face, just in case her snobbish in-laws planned on boycotting
her wedding in Los Angeles ('They would cheerfully have poisoned
me before I married their fair-haired boy'), she and Doug decided
they would elope to New York.

In late May of 1929, the couple left for New York. At City Hall,
to avoid the press, they ducked in a side door and applied for a
marriage license. Asked for her birth certificate, which would have
proved her true age, Joan claimed it was lost, then pulled a letter
from her handbag. It was from her mother, swearing Joan was
born in 1908. Doug's mother, present at City Hall, swore *her* son
was born the same year, giving the minor the extra year required
by law. ('Had anyone taken the trouble, they could have popped
upstairs to find my birth certificate where it is still filed, showing
the true year, 1909,' said Doug.)

On June 3 the couple were married in the rectory of Saint
Malachy's Catholic Church. At the reception afterward at the
Algonquin Hotel, when the press asked if Joan intended giving up
her career for marriage and motherhood, she replied, 'No, fellas,
not yet. I've got a studio and millions of fans to please.' Those
priorities were also agreeable to the happy groom. 'I am willing
to share her with thousands of girls and boys who adore her almost
as much as I do,' said Doug Jr.

'Oh darling, you embarrass me,' said the blushing Joan.

Upon their return to California, the couple resided at Joan's
Brentwood home, redecorated from 'early nothing' to Spanish
Modern and rechristened El JoDo, an amalgamation of their names,
similar to Pick-Fair. But sanction from the latter estate did not
come until three months after their wedding. 'The only reason we
were eventually invited,' said Joan, 'was because the fan magazines
were ganging up on Mary Pickford, saying how rotten she was to
poor Cinderella Joan Crawford.'

When the coveted invitations arrived, to a dinner honoring Lord and Lady Mountbatten, Joan spent three hundred dollars on her white Belgian lace dress, her matching bag, and white silk shoes. Driving up to Pickfair that night she timed their arrival carefully. As she entered the foyer of the blazing house she could see the guests assembled below in the drawing room. After the butler took her wrap she approached the steps, then whispered 'Wait!' to Doug. From below she could see Doug Sr. stepping forward to greet his new daughter-in-law. 'I think the strap of my shoe has become undone,' said Joan.

'Welcome to Pickfair, Joan,' said Doug Sr.

'My shoe, it's undone,' gasped Joan.

And as Doug Jr., assisted by Doug Sr., bent down to fasten her shoe, Joan's eyes swept down on the crowd below, all fixed in her direction, until she found herself looking into the ice-cold blue gaze of her hostess, little Mary Pickford. Only then, with the Lord *and* young Lad of the manor, literally kneeling at her feet, did Billie Cassin feel relaxed. She raised her head higher and smiled in Miss Pickford's direction.

'What a great triumph for Joan,' said the editor of the *Hollywood Tatler*, commenting on the acceptance of Crawford into the Pickfair family. 'She did it without acting, without pretense, she did it by being herself, by proving she wasn't the wild, reckless creature that gossips had painted her.'

3

BETTE ARRIVES IN HOLLYWOOD

In November 1930, while Joan Crawford was being hailed as the most luminous new star on the Hollywood horizon, Bette Davis was auditioning for her second screen test in New York. She passed this one and was offered a six-month contract, albeit with a minor studio, Universal Pictures.

On the morning of December 13, after spending five days traveling by train, she and her mother, Ruthie, arrived in Los Angeles. The weather was hot, the people unfriendly, and the oft-told tale of her non-reception unfolded. There was no one on hand to meet them at the station. When she called the studio from her hotel room, she was told that their representative had failed to recognize her at the station, whereupon Bette issued her first Hollywood dictum. 'You should have known I was an actress,' she said, 'because I was carrying a dog.'

At Universal, when Carl Laemmle, Jr., the titular head of the studio, got his first glimpse of Bette, he too seemed unimpressed. 'He took one look at me through the open door of his father's office, then closed the door,' she said. Hollywood was a town of reigning beauties, and she 'had as much glamour as a grape.' In the photo studio, when asked to raise her skirt to show her legs, Bette snapped, 'What have legs got to do with acting?' Rejected for two chosen films, she was put to work as a 'test girl', a prop for auditioning actors. Wearing a low-cut gown, she sat on a divan while fifteen men entered the room consecutively, seized her in their arms, and murmured, 'You gorgeous divine darling, I adore you, I worship you. I must possess you.' Then they proceeded to make ardent love, lying on top of her. 'I remained patient,' the serious young Broadway actress declared. 'This was not the grave-yard of my dreams, but just a valley I must suffer.'

Making her debut as the second female lead in a B picture entitled *Bad Sister*, Bette was introduced to the state of the art in making motion pictures, 1930s style. For her first scene, a microphone was stuck between her breasts. To avoid static, she was told not to move, and everytime she turned her head the sound faded, to boom again when she faced front. At a sneak preview of *Bad Sister*, she and her mother sat in the back row of the theater. They cringed as they watched her performance. 'My looks, my acting, everything was piti-ful.' When the final credits rolled, they slipped out of their seats before the lights came up. Embracing each other on the bus back to their rented bungalow, the two wept 'copious tears'.

To her amazement, after the release of *Bad Sister* Universal picked up her option, extending her contract for another six months. She appeared in minor 'goodie-goodie' roles in *Seed* and *Waterloo Bridge*. That September her first full page photograph appeared in *Silver Screen*, captioned, 'little Bette Davis, of the drooping eyelids and sullen mouth, is only nineteen' (she was twenty-one); as Hollywood's leading gossip columnist, Louella Parsons noted that Bette gave a good performance in *Seed*, and might have a chance if she put herself in the hands of a capable makeup man. 'I was not disturbed by her over-beaded eyelashes and an over-rouged mouth,' said Louella.

Determined to be a success in pictures, Davis became avid in her study of the technique of motion-picture acting. She spent evenings and weekends at Pantages and Grauman's Chinese Theater, on Hollywood Boulevard, studying the films of others. Formative influences were Greta Garbo and Ruth Chatterton, but not Joan Crawford. 'This was the period,' said Bette in her memoirs, 'when Joan would start every film as a factory worker. She punched the clock in a simple, black Molyneux, with white piping (someone's idea of poverty), and ended up marrying the boss who now allowed her to deck herself out in tremendous buttons, cuffs, and shoes with bows (someone's idea of wealth). The change of coiffure with each outfit kept Joan so busy it was a wonder she had time to forward the plot.' (Years later when Crawford was cited as being a major influence on the fashions of the 1930s and the 1940s, Davis growled, 'What in the hell did she ever contribute to fashion – except those goddamned shoulder-pads and those tacky fuck-me shoes.')

Aching for a little more glamour herself in 1931 when she was loaned out to RKO Pictures for *Way Back Home*, Bette picked up some beauty secrets from makeup artist Ern Westmore (whose brother Perc worked on Joan Crawford early in her career, contouring her wide, generous mouth, and de-banging her hair). Ern made Bette's small mouth larger, 'extending the length of the lower lip, making it slightly heavier to correspond with the upper lip.' Her best features were her eyes, she said, 'but now with the new lips and hair my face suddenly seemed to come together. I began to think I was rather beautiful, even if I wasn't.'

Cosmetically transformed, Bette was loaned out to Columbia for an eight-day quickie called *The Menace* ('I fainted a lot, as bodies fell out of closets'), and to Capital Films where she played a bootlegger's girlfriend, opposite Pat O'Brien. The reviews for both films were tepid, and in the last month of her Universal contract she was dropped. Disconsolate, Davis and her mother were packing to return to New York when the phone rang and she was asked to test for a picture with George Arliss at Warner Bros. in Burbank. She got the role and a six-year contract which she happily signed.

That first year at Warner Bros., Bette made six films, playing 'ingenues and sweet silly vapid girls.' During this time she was named 'A Star of Tomorrow' by a group of theater exhibitors. The presentation of the award would also provide her first encounter, albeit removed, with the star of the day, Joan Crawford. The story of the evening was re-enacted by actress Joan Blondell. 'There was a bunch of us at Warner's who were chosen,' said Blondell. 'Ginger Rogers had just made *Forty-Second Street*, and Bette and I were cranking out pictures by the hour, it seemed. Anyway, we were voted "Most Promising Newcomers", which meant we got to go to this banquet and have our pictures taken. It was considered good publicity, so we got all dolled up and they put a car at our disposal. The dinner was held at the Ambassador Hotel, where each one of us was supposed to get up and make a short speech over live radio, which was also a big deal. I remember Ginger had already spoken when it was Bette's turn to go up and accept her award. She was just about to speak when we heard these loud screams from the corridor outside the main room. The doors flew open and this absolutely gorgeous young couple entered the room. It was Joan Crawford and Douglas Fairbanks, Jr. The guys from the press and the radio crew fell over each other trying to get to the divine Joan and her equally divine husband. Bette never got to speak, nor did I. Actually I thought it was quite funny; but not Bette. Years later she and I were seated together at a dinner for Jack Warner. Rehashing the old days, I said to her, "Bette, remember the night when Joan Crawford stole the spotlight from us starlets?" And she froze. She acted as if she didn't know what I was talking about. I reminded her of the night at the Ambassador Hotel, until she stopped me. "*Joan!*" she said. "You *must* be hallucinating. That *never* happened!" '

CRAWFORD TAKES ON THE DIVINE GARBO

Of course Joan Crawford did not recall the incident either, or the exact moment in history when she had first heard of 'little Bette Davis'. During the early 1930s Joan had more important things on her menu – namely, the dogged, slavish pursuit of her own career, and the careful refinement of her ever-changing public image. As Mrs. Douglas Fairbanks, Jr., and as an accepted, albeit delayed, member of the Pickfair royal court, Joan was happy at first with her new, respectable role in Hollywood society until she encountered a British journalist at Pickfair, who described her to his English readers as 'the Pickfords' plump young daughter-in-law, with huge hungry eyes, and a rather homely manner.' With that notice, Joan decided some immediate physical changes were in order.

She lost more weight ('I haven't tasted sugar or starch in six months, and I never touch alcohol,' she boasted to another Pickfair guest, George Bernard Shaw, who was not quite sure of just who she was). After altering the shape of her face by having her back teeth removed to give her cheekbones, she had her front teeth, which were spaced and filled with dental cement during her early days of filming, filed down to allow temporary caps to fit over them. The painful procedure, however, infected her gums, which stretched her mouth. When the swelling subsided, it left her with a larger upper lip. Pleased with the extension, she decided to paint in her lower lip, giving the world 'the Crawford mouth', which in years to come, not unlike Bette Davis, would be extended and exaggerated as her will dictated.

The corresponding Crawford hallmark, the imposing wide shoulders, would come courtesy of Adrian, the noted MGM couturier. 'My God,' said the designer, when the semi-clad, wide-shouldered Joan stood before him, 'you're a Johnny Weissmuller.' Viewing her size twelve hips and size forty-nine shoulders, the designer quipped, 'Well, we can't cut them off, so we'll make them wider.' And so the famous Joan Crawford shoulder-pads were born. (Years later Adrian would confess that the padded shoulders also helped to distract attention from another Crawford liability, her big hips. 'To offset her womanly hips, I developed the idea of broad shoulders,' the designer told *Women's Wear Daily*.)

Crawford was always the first to admit that her screen persona was in a constant state of flux in the early thirties. 'I experimented with different styles,' she said. 'When one look didn't work, I dropped it and moved on to another.' Portrait photographer Cecil Beaton met up with the actress during one of her transitional phases. 'She has become one of the most exotic pieces of affectation on the screen,' said the self-invented society lens man. 'It is occasionally most enjoyable to watch her exaggerated Frattellini clown makeup of white face, goggle eyes and enormous persimmon lips.' Noting that behind the mask 'a detective is needed to discern any expression other than surprise,' Beaton regarded the star as 'ordinary . . . childish and uncertain,' and wondered when she would get over her schoolgirl crushes on other female movie stars. 'At one time she was insatiably interested in Miss Dietrich; then the Fairbanks Jr. house was littered with Marlene's photographs and gramophone records. Then she moved on to Lilyan Tashman, followed by the chief of her idols – Greta Garbo.'

But in 1933 Crawford, and most stars in Hollywood, had to

stand in line to worship at the shrine of the sublime Miss Garbo. When Joan first saw the Swedish actress on the Metro lot she confessed, 'My knees went weak. She was breathtaking. If ever I thought of becoming a lesbian, that was it.'

Bette Davis was also quite taken with Greta. 'Oh, Garbo was *divine*,' she said. '*Sooooo* beautiful. I worshipped her. When I became a star, I used to have my chauffeur follow her in my car. I always wanted to meet her.'

Bette never got to meet Greta, but Crawford did. It was Garbo, in fact, who provided Joan with her first class-A talkie, *Grand Hotel*, and, in typical competitive ex-showgirl fashion, Joan would attempt to steal the picture from under the inscrutable one's classic nose.

GRAND HOTEL

The synopsis of the German play came to the attention of MGM producer Irving Thalberg in 1930. It focused on a group of people, of diverse backgrounds, whose paths crossed in a plush hotel in Berlin over a forty-eight-hour perusal. One of the leads, the role of an aging prima ballerina, who is losing her grip on her art and her life, seemed perfect for Greta Garbo. Thalberg arranged to invest fifteen thousand dollars in the forthcoming Broadway production. When the play, followed by a novel, became a huge popular success, MGM made an unprecedented move. They announced they were assembling an all-star cast for their $700,000 movie. The primary cast would be Greta Garbo, John Gilbert, Joan Crawford, Clark Gable and Buster Keaton as Krungelain, the doomed bookkeeper, at the hotel for one last fling before his demise.

The first to drop out of the ensemble was Greta Garbo. 'I t'ank I go home (to Sweden),' she said, a threat she was fond of using whenever scripts, money, or leading men did not meet her aesthetic approval. In this instance it was the choice of John Gilbert as her leading man that upset Greta. The two were lovers, but had recently quarreled, and it was up to Thalberg to tell Gilbert he was out of the picture (whereon the spurned matinee idol went on a prolonged bender, firing several pistol shots at a pair of lovers parked on his property line). Robert Montgomery was then tested for the part of the baron who steals the ballerina's heart and jewels. He looked too young, and the role went to John Barrymore. Clark Gable as Preysing, the corrupt industrialist, was also considered too young and was replaced by Wallace Beery, with Lionel Barrymore taking over for Buster Keaton.

A month before *Grand Hotel* was scheduled to begin production, an article in *Screenland* magazine questioned the choice of Joan Crawford for the role of the slut-stenographer, Flaemmchen. 'Having donned the manner, voice and personality of a great young lady in her private life,' said the magazine, 'it remains to be seen whether she can unbend sufficiently to become the shabby, tragic little Berlin secretary.' A few days later Joan attempted to withdraw from the cast. Garbo had all the glamour and the love scenes, while she had to schlep through the entire picture wearing one dress. Thalberg told her she was a fool to pass up the role of the money-hungry stenographer.

'You said you wanted to be an actress in prestige pictures,' he told her.

'Yes,' said Joan, 'but why must I look so shabby, with only one dress?'

'Adrian will make you *two* dresses, and a peignoir,' Thalberg promised.

'Okey-doke,' said Joan.

On December 30, 1931, rehearsals for *Grand Hotel* commenced on soundstage five at MGM. A long table and chairs had been set out for the principals and the first to arrive was Miss Crawford. She swept onto the soundstage with her dog, Woggles, and seemed upset when she learned she preceded the other stars. 'Her habit of punctuality cheated her of a good entrance,' said director Edmund Goulding. When John and Lionel Barrymore entered, followed by Wallace Beery and Lewis Stone, Goulding distributed the updated revised scripts and called the cast to order. They would read the script straight through, he said. 'But Miss Garbo has not arrived,' said Joan. 'Miss Garbo has been excused from all rehearsals,' Goulding announced.

Joan was crushed. She had mentally rehearsed a little routine for this, her introductory meeting with her idol. Her disappointment turned to anger when she learned that she had no scenes in the film with the great Garbo and that, furthermore, all of the leading star's major scenes would be shot on a separate soundstage, on a set closed to visitors. There would be no intimate chats for Joan, no posing together for publicity stills. As she would intone three times throughout the picture, the elusive Swede 'vanted to be left alone.'

On January 14, 1932, Los Angeles newspapers covered two unusual events. Snow fell in Hollywood, and 'John Barrymore met Greta Garbo for the first time on the set of *Grand Hotel*.' Barrymore had arrived early, before Garbo, who positioned herself by the main gate and waited to pay Barrymore the honor of escorting him to the set. 'Half an hour went by before the situation was straightened out,' said a reporter. After their opening scene, the usually reserved Garbo impulsively kissed her co star. 'You have no idea what it means to me, to play opposite so perfect an actor,' she said. Introduced to a Barrymore friend, Arthur Brisbane, Garbo was shocked to learn that the man was a member of the working press, the editor of *The New York Journal*. 'But I used to work for him,' said Barrymore. 'You? A member of the press?' said the horrified Greta. 'I was a cartoonist,' he explained. 'Aaaah,' she sighed with relief. 'That's better. Much better.'

During the last week in January, the opening and closing hotel lobby scenes of the film were shot on soundstage six. All of the principals, and sixty-five extras were on call to make their entrances and exits through the gigantic Art Deco foyer designed by Cedric Gibbons. To avoid contact with her co stars, Garbo's scenes were scheduled for after lunch, but on the morning of the shoot Crawford called in sick and had her scenes rescheduled for the afternoon. As the director rehearsed the extras, whose shoes had been soled with cork to prevent noise on the marble floors, Garbo sat apart in the spacious lobby, dressed in chinchilla, perched on a little box, eating an apple, her eyes half closed. 'She cut the apple into little pieces with a knife,' said a reporter. 'She would have bitten into it only it would have spoiled her makeup.' Her black maid, Ellen, called 'L-l-l-l-n' by the star, stood nearby, with a napkin and a brown paper bag in her hand, in which the core of the apple would be disposed of when her mistress was through. 'The walls behind Garbo began to move,' said the writer. 'She turned, startled like a deer in the forest. She noticed the walls had wheels. It pulled away. "What ees thees?" Garbo cried. Suddenly from the other side of the walls came the sound of Bing Crosby's voice, singing "Can we talk it over, dear?" Garbo jumped, looked around her. "What ees thees?" she asked again. "Miss Crawford's dressing room," she was told.'

'Nice,' she said.

The door of the palace opened. Joan Crawford put her head out and called to the man who did nothing but change the Bing Crosby records on the phonograph set up for her in the sidelines. 'Put the other piece on, dear,' said Joan, preparing for her appearance in the lobby.

'What other piece, Joanie?' the man answered.

'You know, Ed,' she said,

'What's the scene, Joanie?'

'Oh, kind of gay and bright.'

Garbo, back on her box, looked from one to the other as their voices crossed, then called to her maid.

'What ees the scene, L-l-l-l-n?'

'You walk through the people in the lobby,' her maid answered.

'Then it ees very sad,' answered Garbo.

The director seated on the crane above the lobby asked for quiet, and instructed Garbo that she was to walk from left to right and exit through the revolving doors.

'I valk on my own?' the actress asked.

'Through a crowd of admirers,' the director said. 'Do you wish to rehearse?'

'No,' she sighed, 'I rehearsed it in New York last week.'

During the thirty-five days of filming on *Grand Hotel*, as Garbo remained silent and aloof, Joan Crawford appeared more vitriolic. 'She would arrive late on the set each day, rolling up in her portable dressing room, to the tune of "I Surrender, Dear", played as loudly as the machine could play it.'

The intensity of the feud was enhanced, said the reporter, 'by the fact that whereas Crawford's personality is acquired, that of Garbo is innate, effortless and unconscious. Crawford resents, admires and envies Garbo.'

Of the 275,000 feet of film photographed of *Grand Hotel*, only ten thousand would make the final cut, and according to the *Los Angeles Herald Tribune*, five hundred feet of that, belonging to Joan Crawford, was eliminated at Garbo's request. 'Fearful she might be overshadowed by the dramatics of MGM's vivacious dancing daughter, Garbo demanded that some of Joan's best work be cut,' said the newspaper. Producer Irving Thalberg denied the report: 'not a line or an inch of Joan's work was cut.'

On March 17, Thalberg, his assistant Paul Bern, and director Edmund Goulding, carried six reels of film in three suitcases and boarded a plane for Monterey, California. That evening *Grand Hotel* was sneak-previewed before a regular paying audience. Filling out cards after the preview, 60 percent of the viewers wrote 'wonderful', while 40 percent suggested minor changes, such as making Crawford's role bigger and Garbo less somber and remote. Thalberg agreed with the latter opinion. 'There were altogether too many "mugging close-ups", too many "Garbos and Barrymores", and not enough acting.' He ordered that Garbo be recalled for re-takes,' said *Variety*.

On April 5, the trade paper reported that 'two versions of *Grand Hotel* were now in the can. The re-shot version favored Garbo; the other favored Joan Crawford.' The decision as to which version of the film would be released depended on Garbo. The star's contract with MGM had lapsed and 'the story persists that unless Garbo re-signs, it is MGM's intention to let Crawford steal the picture.' This would have greatly injured Garbo's prestige throughout the country, the trade paper added, 'and greatly increase Miss Crawford's.'

THE GALA OPENING

On a warm foggy evening in late April, the gala opening of *Grand Hotel* was held at Grauman's Chinese Theater in Hollywood. To celebrate the event, black-tie suppers and dinner parties were held at various homes and restaurants throughout Los Angeles, with guests transported by special limousines to the five-dollar top-ticket event at the theater. 'As huge searchlights scraped the low-hung heavens, pots of incense perfumed the air,' reported the *Los Angeles Times*. On hand were five hundred police to protect the two thousand invited guests from the twenty thousand fans lining the streets and the sidewalks of Hollywood Boulevard.

The first to arrive were MGM's top executives – Louis B. Mayer, Nick Schenck, Eddie Mannix, Harry Rapf, and their spouses – followed by the brass from rival studio Warner's, including producers Hal Wallis, Darryl Zanuck and Jack Warner, with their wives. 'Seldom have I seen so many men and women with their own spouses,' said Louella Parsons.

Then the stars appeared – Norma Shearer with Irving Thalberg, Marlene Dietrich with husband Rudolph Sieber, Mr. and Mrs. Clark Gable and Jean Harlow with Paul Bern. Escorted by special bellhops to a desk in the lobby, each guest was asked to sign in at the *Grand Hotel* register. 'Do we need luggage?' the cheeky Miss Harlow asked, as a stampede erupted on the street outside, signalling the arrival of one of the stars on the picture – Joan Crawford. 'Sunburned as a berry, dressed in an electric blue dress, with her hair in the new "bangs style", Joan's eyes sparkled and her voice choked with emotion when anyone spoke to her.' Escorted by her Prince, Douglas Fairbanks, Jr., the star waved to the fans, smiled demurely at the handsome policemen, then signed her name on the shirt-fronts and hatbands of some of the men who mobbed her in the lobby. Greta Garbo was not expected to show, said director Edmund Goulding. 'She has a fear of crowds, a psychosis that is increasing instead of lessening,' he observed.

Scheduled to begin at eight-thirty, the movie was not shown until 11:00 P.M., 'due to the late arrival of limousines, lined up for a mile on the boulevard, choked black with people.' The stalled passengers and celebrities were not bored in the traffic, it was noted, for many of the limousines were equipped with the latest in America luxury – car radios. Throughout the delay they were able to listen to the stage show being broadcast live from Grauman's.

MC of the show was Will Rogers, who, between introductions of the acrobats, dancers, jugglers, dogs and crooners, asked the stars in the audience to take a bow. 'Joan Crawford stood in the aisle, waving and hugging an unidentified Ginger Rogers,' said a reporter for the *Hollywood Tatler*, 'then ran to the other side of the aisle where she embraced Louis B. Mayer.' After the movie was shown, Will Rogers asked the audience to remain in their seats for a special surprise. 'I am going to introduce a lady who is seldom seen,' he said. 'She is going away soon to her own country, but has consented to make this one personal appearance.' As excited whispers of 'Garbo . . . it's Garbo,' swept the theater, Rogers pointed to stage left. 'Miss Greta Garbo!' he said. 'There in the spotlight,' said *Variety*, 'was a woman in a rather dishevelled gown, with long unkempt blond hair. Wearing high-heels she wobbled her way towards center-stage. When she spoke the audience gasped, then giggled. It was Wallace Beery in drag. "I t'ank I go home now," said Beery, which prompted the weary audience to exit the theater.

Two days later *Grand Hotel* opened as a special road-show attraction at the Astor theater in New York. The following day tickets were sold out for two months. 'The most jubilant popular success of talking pictures,' said the *New York World Telegram*, while else-where in the country a heated controversy broke out over which actress, Greta Garbo or Joan Crawford, gave the best and worst performance in the picture. 'Joan Crawford, as the little upstart, contributes the most telling portrait in the whole cast,' said the *Detroit Times*. 'As the conniving stenographer, willing to take any man's dictation, she puts the most subtle irony into an everyday gold digger existence,' said the *San Francisco Evening News*. 'She represents pretentious blankness,' said Herman Shumlin, producer of the New York play.

Garbo in her tutu drew her share of cheers and boos from the critics. 'Sincere and affecting,' said Herman Shumlin. 'Sublime! Accomplished!' said the play's author Vicki Baum. 'As usual Miss Garbo wears that perpetual headache, which once seemed so intriguing in deaf and dumb pictures,' Joan S. Coles wrote in *The Boston Sun*. 'As a dancer she never shows her legs (although Crawford does) and even when she must give a few hops, skips and jumps, to register friskiness, she is not convincing, and of course was never graceful.' 'She dances around the room,' said another, 'and with every gallumping twirl seems in danger of breaking a leg or all of MGM's expensive modern furniture.' When New Orleans reviewer Mel Washburn suggested that Garbo 'was not the actress the world likes to believe she is,' the telegrams, letters and postcards began to pile up on his desk. 'To even suggest that Miss Garbo is not a Goddess, is a crime worthy of capital punishment, I have been told,' he said.

The previous adulation given to Garbo, 'was wormwood in the mouth of Joan Crawford,' Washburn surmised, but her performance in the picture, and the controversy, could establish her as a major popular and dramatic actress. 'Joan is an ambitious woman,' he said. 'She is driven by a deep and compelling need, which will brook no interference, recognize no obstacles.'

'*Grand Hotel* was my first big chance,' Crawford told a film audience years later. 'They told me I wouldn't be able to hold my own with the big boys, against Garbo and the Barrymores. But I proved otherwise.'

4

THE NEW BETTE

'Hollywood in the early days was a tiny place. When a good part came along, there was active scrambling among the women for it. If Bette Davis felt that Joan Crawford got to play, let's say, Sadie Thompson, that would immediately piss off Davis – and vice-versa.'

Joe Mankiewicz

In October 1932, after five consecutive pictures at Warner Brothers and remarkably good notices for her role as the sexually aggressive Southern plantation daughter in *Cabin in the Cotton* – 'Ah'd love t'kiss yew, but ah jes washed mah hair' – Bette Davis was demoted to playing a bit part in *Three on a Match*, with Joan Blondell and Ann Dvorak in the lead roles. 'That's the way Warner's worked in those days,' said Blondell. 'You made one good movie, followed by two or three stinkers. That way Jack Warner kept you humble.'

While her mother, Ruthie, kept dreaming 'that someday Warner's would give me the glorious productions that MGM gave its players,' Bette was told by a good friend that she was 'the victim of a colorless personality.' She would be forever cast in dowdy parts unless she learned to project *joie de vivre*, some pizzazz, on and off the silver screen. It was at this juncture that columnist Louella Parsons noted, 'Bette Davis became just another Hollywood blonde.' Or as the more astute and wicked Hedda Hopper remarked, 'Bette Davis, a serious Broadway actress, has transformed herself into one of the town's leading ga-ga girls, picking up the personality Joan Crawford discarded when she became a lady.'

Bette bobbed and dyed her hair platinum ('Which embarrasses

me when I go home to Boston, because people in Boston don't wear hair that color'), and bought some slinky clothes. She showed up at premieres and nightclubs, sometimes with eight escorts. Stopped twice for speeding, she narrowly escaped death when the engine of her car caught fire and she was trapped behind the wheel. She also learned how to smoke and talk dirty. 'I felt so out of it, at nightclubs and things, I thought maybe if I started smoking I'd look sophisticated. So I started smoking. And then I decided I'd like to swear a little. So I became quite a bad swearer.' 'She had to unlearn everything that she had been taught was proper,' said writer Franc Dillon. 'She had to appear physically flamboyant in order to make her employers suspect she would have glamor on the screen.'

Warner's, a studio known predominantly for its male-oriented gangster and crime pictures, went along with the new Bette. 'They didn't know what to do with strong women,' said Joan Blondell. 'We were used to being cast as the arm piece – the girlfriend, the showgirl, the moll – always as background interest for guys like Jimmy Cagney or Eddie Robinson. Then Bette came along and started yelling for equal time. She was the first one to take on Jack Warner. She had no fear.' Warner, still smarting over the loss of Jean Harlow, who made *Public Enemy* for his studio and then skipped over to MGM to become a star, gave the executive order that Bette Davis was to receive the full blonde-bombshell treatment, Burbank economy style. She posed for studio stills, wearing backless gowns, skimpy playsuits, and in the obligatory swimsuit shots. Later, as first lady of the studio she would deny she had ever posed for cheesecake pictures, but Joan Blondell said, 'Baloney! She did them. We all did them, and were damn glad to be asked. It wasn't as if we ever showed anything; heck, we wore more in those so-called sexy beach photos than they do on Fifth Avenue today.'

With the publicity photos came the press releases, equally synthetic. 'Bette Davis' weight has been insured with Lloyd's of London,' said one bulletin. 'Presently at 107 lbs., if she goes to 120 the insurance company will pay Warner Brothers thirty thousand dollars!'

A pressbook issued during this time gave the following 'Portrait of Bette Davis':

(1) She said she would never bleach her hair but she did.
(2) She can tell a woman's age by her elbows.
(3) She is not interested in Mahatma Gandhi's health.
(4) She loathes scented stationery and has never been to a pawn shop.
(5) She crawls over rather than under a fence, and completely bald men do not fascinate her.
(6) She follows famous murder cases closely and wouldn't spank a baby if she had one.

The new tempestuous Bette was shown on the screen in *20,000 Years in Sing Sing*, with Spencer Tracy. He was a gangster and she was his moll. 'I was good as the moll,' she said. In her memoirs, taking a second swipe at Joan Crawford, Bette described her next film – 'A little gem called *Parachute Jumper*, opposite young Douglas Fairbanks, the Crown Prince of Hollywood, scion of Pickfair, and consort to MGM's Princess Royal, Joan Crawford.'

In *Parachute Jumper* Bette had to learn how to type, chew gum, and 'toss slang' for the role of a nervy, gum-chewing secretary. 'It is very difficult to talk while chewing gum,' she said, but, according to a publicity release – 'Succeed she did, and today she can hold her own with so seasoned an expert as Joan Blondell.'

Fairbanks, Jr., who had scored at Warner's two years before in *Little Caesar*, had an unusual nonexclusive contract with the studio. His salary for *Parachute Jumper* was four thousand dollars a week (compared with Bette's $750), and he was to receive top billing above the title, with Davis below in third place. 'After the planes,' she said.

She was looking forward to working with Fairbanks, however, if only 'to razz him up a little' about his choice in wives and his phony British accent. 'He was still to become Great Britain's last Earl,' she said, 'but he was already saying "profeel", for one's side view.' Before she could dissect his dialect or his lovely wife Joan, Bette was stricken with appendicitis. The studio doctor decreed she could finish the picture so her scenes were rushed ahead, with the doctor, a nurse, and a publicist standing by. When the final sequence was shot, an ambulance was waiting to take her to the hospital, where the operation was performed successfully.

Parachute Jumper, released in January of 1933, was prominently reviewed by the respected critic, Cecilia Ager, although the tone of the notice devoted to the leading lady was somewhat discordant. 'Bette Davis seems convinced she's become quite a charmer,' said Ager. 'Slowly she raises her eyebrows to sear the hero with her devastating glances, then satisfied, she smiles a crooked little Mona Lisa smile. Unfortunately this procedure takes place while Miss Davis is wearing a curious pill-box hat that perches on her head at an angle slightly comic. The hat, and her own self-satisfaction, interfere with the effect.'

At Warner's, in the interim, some good news had come for Bette. At the suggestion of executive, soon-to-depart, Darryl Zanuck, the actress was told that at last she would be given the station she craved. She would star alone, above the title, in her next picture, *Ex-Lady*.

'Daring . . . provocative . . . a modern love story so frank, so outspoken – it tells of a new generation that laughs at wedding bells and yawns at bassinets,' said the film's ad logos.

Ex-Lady, co-authored by Robert Riskin, who would later write the scripts of *It Happened One Night* and *Meet John Doe*, explored a seemingly provocative topic for its day. It told of a woman, a beautiful, emancipated artist, who flouted convention by practicing an 'open marriage'. 'She wanted to wear a wedding ring . . . on certain nights.' Certain to cause a sensation, this film could do for Bette Davis what *Our Dancing Daughters* and *Red Headed Woman* did for Joan Crawford and Jean Harlow. She would be dressed by Orry-Kelly and photographed by Tony Gaudio, and her leading man would be Gene Raymond, who had recently appeared in *Red Dust* at Metro.

Completed in twenty-seven days, a generous schedule for a Warner's picture, *Ex-Lady* was edited while Davis was being photographed and interviewed for advance publicity. Adjusting to the theme of the film, the recently married Bette told interviewers that she didn't wear a marriage ring and that freedom for both spouses was most important. 'Married couples ought not to see each other in the morning until after breakfast,' she said. 'And it is absolutely essential that both husband and wife have close friends of the opposite sex.' In late April 1933, the posters and ad logos for *Ex-Lady* were shipped to theaters. *A NEW TYPE! A NEW STAR! A NEW HIT!* the posters proclaimed. 'As bewitching as Garbo – and as hard to explain,' said one logo, while another gasped in bold print, '*Lots of girls could love like she does – but how many would DARE!*'

In New York, the day before *Ex-Lady* was to open at the Strand Theater there, the management respectfully advised that 'those of our patrons who are over sixty NOT attend this picture of Today's Youth.' For extra hoopla, some elderly citizens were bussed in from the suburbs to picket the theater. Bette Davis, safe in her Manhattan hotel suite braced herself for the storm of controversy, and stardom, that would inevitably follow. But on the scheduled day, on the morn of the reviews and the hoped-for lurid coverage, when she gathered up all of the newspapers from her door, she found that each headline and photograph and entertainment section was devoted not to her but to Joan Crawford and the breakup of her marriage to her Prince, Douglas Fairbanks, Jr.

JOAN DIVORCES DOUG – Story Page 3,4,7,20

Special Photo Insert

On page 27 of *The New York Times* a very brief review of Bette Davis in *Ex-Lady* appeared. 'Downright foolish,' said the reviewer. 'A minor battle of the sexes,' said the Scripps News Service, which pulled a syndicated Sunday news feature on Bette, replacing it with one on Joan Crawford and the tragedy of her marital breakup. 'It was bad timing for Bette,' said Adela Rogers St. Johns, who wrote a series of articles on Joan's popular divorce. 'World War II could have broken out, yet everyone wanted to hear about Joan and Doug.'

'There was an inordinate amount of publicity,' said Doug Jr., agreeing that the brouhaha in retrospect was comparable with the breakup of Elizabeth Taylor and Richard Burton in later years.

'I'm *sick* of it,' said Davis, when she ran into St. Johns on Wilshire Boulevard a week later. 'Day in, day out, that's all we're allowed to read about.'

'Then in a low voice,' said the reporter, 'Bette whispered, "Adela, tell me. *Who* is Joan really sleeping with?"'

THE TRUE STORY OF THE DIVORCE OF DOUG AND JOAN

'Irreconcilable differences' were of course the grounds given for the breakup of the storybook marriage of Joan and Doug. 'It is impossible to put your finger on any one set of circumstances. They had simply gotten on each other's nerves,' said Crawford's best friend, fan magazine reporter Katharine Albert. Certainly it was not because Joan was anything but the perfect wife. During the first year of their marriage she was a veritable hausfrau. 'I cooked, cleaned, polished. I was the little wife who was always home washing and ironing his shirts,' she said. 'In her spare time, when there is such a time,' said Doug in *Vanity Fair* in 1930, 'Joan Fairbanks (is my bosom swelling) covers herself in yarn, threads and needles and proceeds to sew curtains and make various types of rugs. *Entre nous*, they are quite good.'

As their careers escalated, Doug persuaded Joan that they could afford a staff to cater to their household needs. This allowed the pair to partake of the social joys that came with being Hollywood's Golden Couple. They learned French, posed for the famous Russian sculptor Troubetzkody, and were photographed by Steichen in rapt worship of each other on the beach at Malibu. Their dinner parties at home became the talk of many, including Doug's *Little Caesar* co star, Edward G. Robinson. 'I've never been at Buckingham Palace,' said Robinson, 'but I think the young Fairbankses had more service plates, rare wines, and rare lamb than their majesties.' Edward G. adored Joan (and barely tolerated his Warners colleague Bette Davis), but questioned her practice of ending her lavish dinner parties promptly at 9:00 P.M., so that everyone could go home and be fresh for work the next morning. The host Doug Jr., at age twenty-one still robust and alert at that early hour, usually acceded to his wife's demands. 'I would call the Hollywood athletic club and ask for Miron to come and massage us to sleep by 9:30 P.M.,' he said.

Along with being a good wife and a gracious hostess, Joan could also be called the perfect lady. Despite her previous expertise with rough language, as Mrs. Fairbanks the second she embraced a glossary of polite euphemisms. When she spoke of a couple sharing a bed, she no longer said they were 'fucking' or 'making love'. 'She would instead invariably say, "They went to heaven",' said Doug Jr. 'And women's breasts were her "ninny pies".'

TROUBLE IN PARADISE

Doug also, lest we forget, launched his bride in society, making her a mainstay at the royal court of Pickfair. But it was her long days and nights as a lady-in-waiting at the manor that led to the first fracture in their marriage. When Joan, always a quick study, had acquired and assimilated all she needed to know about becoming a lady, she became increasingly bored with dinners at Pickfair. 'The chit-chat at table was vapid,' said Edward G. Robinson. 'After dinner, while the men had cigars and brandies and spoke about politics, the ladies talked about the servant problems, the length of skirts, Bullocks Wilshire versus Magnins, and varieties of roses – whether or not the flowers in a garden should be all white or variegated.' It was the ritual of weekends at the manor that eventually caused the opening rift between Joan and Doug. On Saturday and Sunday afternoons when they visited, it was the custom for Doug Sr. and Jr. to take off for a spot of tennis or golf at their club, leaving Joan alone in the main drawing room, knitting and crocheting, while Lady Mary remained upstairs in the main bedroom, napping. 'One Sunday afternoon,' said one source, 'while Mary napped and the men played golf, a lonely Joan stood at the window, and realized it was Lucille LeSueur or Billie Cassin who was meekly waiting for her betters to drift in and toss her a few leftovers of love.' Reverting to her former self,

Joan said, 'F— this.' She set her jaw, went to the hall phone, and called for her own car.

Another item of dissension between the couples was the disparity in their careers. Equal when they married, Joan's career escalated while Doug's lagged behind, at a pace of his choosing. 'Movies are not the end-all of life,' he said, words of blasphemy to Joan. 'Doug never had to fight his way up the way I had, and had no taste for it either,' she stated. He lacked her discipline and could not understand why they had to be in bed at ten each night when she was working. The tension in their marriage increased when Joan was making *Grand Hotel*. Burdened with the double duty of playing Flaemmchen, her first serious role, and the strain of trying to derail the indomitable Garbo, Crawford would come home and yell at her ebullient and always cheerful husband. 'Don't talk to me,' she would say, only to cry out minutes later, 'For God's sake, say something!'

She was 'a creature of her mood,' Doug wrote in *Vanity Fair*. 'When she is depressed she falls into an all-consuming depth of melancholy, out of which it is practically impossible to recover her. At these times she has long crying spells. When it is over she is like a flower that has had a sprinkling of rain and then blossoms out in brighter colors.'

Doug also had his gloomy moments and neuroses, Joan claimed. 'He might be painting. Suddenly he would think of a suit he hadn't worn in two or three years. Everything would be dropped until I found the suit for him. If we couldn't find it he would go into his closet and throw every suit out in the middle of the floor, until he found the one he wanted.'

While America wept, and sympathized with Joan or Doug, or both because they couldn't make their fairy-tale marriage work, a few jaundiced members of the press and the Hollywood establishment, including Bette Davis, snorted '*Bullsugar!*' The main reason for the split was the extracurricular hanky-panky the pair had been practicing for the last two years. 'Chiseling with an extra girl, with whom he was seen motoring in broad daylight on Wilshire Boulevard,' Doug was said to be busy on his own, while Joan carried on a lengthy torrid affair with MGM's hottest new leading man, Clark Gable.

'Yes, Clark and I had an affair, a glorious affair, and it went on a lot longer than anybody knows. He was a wonderful man. Very simple, pretty much the way he was painted . . . forever the virile, ballsy folk hero.'

Joan Crawford

'Peasants by nature,' she and Gable had a lot in common, said Joan. He was once called Billie (born William C. Gable). Both grew up poor, ignored and uneducated. Both became MGM stars, glamorous, popular, durable; with a shared compulsion about cleanliness. 'He won't take a bath because he can't sit in water he's sat in. He will only shower, and does so several times a day. His bed linens must be changed several times a day. He shaves under his arms. He is so immaculately groomed and dressed, you could eat off him,' said author Lyn Tornabene.

Gable arrived in Hollywood in 1925, the same year as Crawford. They appeared as extras in *The Merry Widow* but never met. Handsome and ambitious, intent on getting launched in pictures, the actor it was said 'accommodated anyone important who could help his career.' Coached by Josephine Dillon, his first wife, and seventeen years his senior – Gable at twenty-four was hired to tour with the Louis MacLoon repertory company, which featured Pauline Frederick, age forty-four, who bought him 'silk shirts and underwear, and paid to have his teeth fixed.' In New York he met Ria Langham, a rich Texas woman, also forty-four, who bought him his first smoking jacket and silk pajamas. Sued by his first wife for desertion, Gable married Langham and the two returned to Hollywood where he opened in *The Last Mile* at the Belasco Theater on June 3, 1930. The good reviews brought him an agent, Minna Wallis. He auditioned at Warners for the second lead in *Little Caesar*, lost the role to Douglas Fairbanks, Jr. but was signed shortly thereafter to a one-year contract at MGM.

Playing a minor role in *Dance Fools Dance*, Gable made an immediate impact on the star of the film, Joan Crawford. She would forever recall the tingle of the moment when he grabbed her by the shoulders and threatened to kill her brother. 'I felt such a sensation. My knees buckled. He was holding me by the shoulders and I said to myself, "If he lets me go, I'll fall down." '

They did not become lovers on that picture, Crawford claimed: she was a star and he wasn't. It would take Norma Shearer to balance the boards for Gable. In his next picture, *A Free Soul*, Norma played a rich, bossy New York socialite looking for cheap thrills. Enter Gable, as a dangerous young gangster. 'A new man, a new world,' she murmured in a come-on to the handsome hood, who proceeded to smack her around and push her into a chair when she mocked his lower-class origins. 'You take it and like it,' he snarled, in the scene that made women swoon and men applaud. 'A new trend in movie heroes was born,' said writer Bill Davidson, 'a breed of rough-hewn gents who assault their women with grape-fruits, knuckles and brawn.'

A Free Soul brought Gable a new contract and the women of Metro, including Greta Garbo and Marion Davies, lined up begging to sample some of his onscreen 'tough kind of loving.' Offscreen, his affection it was said belonged to his respected wife; while the rest of him belonged to Joan Crawford.

In 1931 Joan and Clark made two pictures together, *Laughing Sinners* and *Possessed*. In a *Photoplay* article we learn of the vulnerable state of Joan's heart at this time. 'Already disillusioned with Douglas Fairbanks, because her dream life had failed, she was still fond of Dodo, she was still the loyal wife, but her heart was empty. And to Joan, an empty heart meant she must seek a new tenant.'

Clark also had a 'For Rent' sign hanging out, and not always over his heart. Publicist Billie Ferguson stated: 'He was a horny sonavagun. He seldom let a good looking girl get by his dressing-room door without trying to make a pass at her.' Sitting in a car Gable once tried to fondle Myrna Loy. 'With his wife sitting on the other side,' said Miss Loy.

But it was in Joan Crawford that he found his match. 'Never in his young life had he known such a thrilling and wonderful passion,' said *Photoplay*. 'Joan was aggressive,' said Adela Rogers St. Johns. 'She never played flirty games with men. If she wanted a guy, she let him know it straight out. And Clark was the same way. He didn't believe in poetry or small talk. It was always straight to business.'

The initial phase of their lusty affair was conducted discreetly, in a cottage Joan had rented at Malibu. 'We clung to each other, commiserating on how we were being abused and typecast by the studio,' she said. At the studio they met in the mobile deluxe dressing room that Doug had given her as an anniversary gift. 'In the morning, as soon as Joan arrived on the lot, Clark would go to her trailer,' said Bill Ferguson. 'You could hear them laughing and exchanging banter, followed by shouts and yelps of passion. You had to be a fool not to guess what was going on.' Once Ferguson was escorting a reporter from *The Ladies Home Companion* around the studio. 'We were passing by Joan's trailer,' he said, 'when it began to rock back and forth on its wheels. You could hear these moans and groans going on inside. Then Clark came out, all flushed, followed by Joan. I explained to the nice lady that they were rehearsing a scene for their new picture. Thankfully it never occurred to her to check that they were working on separate pictures at the time.'

> *'I heard rumors that she was seeing someone, and once, when trouble arose between us, I bluffed and said I planned on having a private detective follow her. "Try!" she dared me. "Just try!"'*
>
> Douglas Fairbanks, Jr.

Douglas Fairbanks, Jr. said he was completely unaware of his wife's affair with Gable. He suspected she had a cottage in Malibu, but she wouldn't tell him where it was or how he could reach her. She liked to commune with nature, she told him, and he was grateful that Joan had recaptured her old zest for life. 'Joan these days finds time to do two things she most likes to do – dance and drive,' said the *Los Angeles Herald Examiner*. 'Twice a week she goes to the Cocoanut Grove in the Ambassador Hotel with Doug Jr. and two escorts as a relief if Doug gets tired of dancing. Joan and her party always sit at table 27 and Joan always dances with a gardenia in her hand. She is always the first to reach the floor and the last to leave it. She adores dancing. And driving a car at seventy, to get to work each morning.'

Doug began to notice that his wife went to the studio at least an hour earlier than usual and returned home equally late. 'She even went to work on her days off, explaining that she was so interested in what the others were doing.'

In her autobiography Adela Rogers St. Johns told of one night at the Cocoanut Grove, when she 'stumbled upon' Joan and Clark Gable, behind the bandstand at the club. '*His* wife and *her* husband were sitting outfront at a table, I literally felt stunned,' she wrote.

'I was on my way to the ladies room,' St. Johns elaborated in 1978. 'I *knew* they were somewhere, because I had seen them sitting at the table, then they disappeared. I was well aware they were having an affair; I never wrote about it, because I was very close to both of them. But on this night the club was crawling with press and studio spies, and if Clark and Joan were misbehaving, it would be all over town the next day.

'*Misbehaving?*' Adela laughed. 'When I went looking for them, I found them literally stuck to each other, behind the bandstand. Clark had his back to me and she had her legs wrapped around him, in a position that only a supple dancer like Joan could assume. I yelled something stupid at them. They straightened themselves out, adjusted their clothes. And Joan, when she saw it was only me, said "*Adela! Darling!*" And Clark gave me one of his rogue grins. I was furious with both of them, and told them so. The next day each one sent me flowers, with a note from Joan that read, "I bet you were *thrilled* watching!" And you want to know something? I was.'

In due time Mrs. Clark Gable learned of her husband's flagrant affair with Crawford but instead of confronting Clark, she went instead to his boss at MGM, Louis B. Mayer. The pious mogul, whose main mission in life was to provide wholesome pictures and untainted stars to the public, was *shocked*. He called Gable into his office. Metro stars never cheated on their spouses, he said. He reminded Gable of the morality clause in his contract. The affair with Crawford was finished, Mayer insisted. A meek Gable agreed. 'He would have ended my career in fifteen minutes,' said the future king of the lot. 'I had no interest in becoming a waiter.'

Joan too, faced with a wrecked career, made the ultimate sacrifice. She agreed to keep her hands off Gable. 'Too many wonderful people would have been hurt,' she said. L.B. Mayer, to lower the temptation between the two, changed the casting of their next scheduled film. Instead of Crawford, he cast Jean Harlow opposite Gable in *Red Dust*, and Joan was sent to Catalina Island to make *Rain* for another studio, United Artists.

In July 1932, when *Rain* was finished, Joan and Douglas Fairbanks, Jr. went to Europe. 'It was a last fling – an attempt to revive the thing they saw going – their happiness,' said *Modern Screen* writer Katharine Albert. In London, Joan was mobbed at the theater by fans who tore the clothes off her back. 'I was thrilled,' she said, claiming *that* was the highlight of the trip. Neither England nor France lived up to the movies she had seen. 'She absolutely hated every minute of it,' said Fairbanks. 'She couldn't wait to get back to Culver City. It was like going back to the womb, the only place she felt secure and confident in herself.'

Back home, at MGM, Joan threw herself into work. While practicing her dance routines for the forthcoming *Dancing Lady* musical with Fred Astaire, she was spotted by Ethel Barrymore, on her way to an adjoining soundstage to work in *Rasputin*. Pausing to watch Joan tap-dancing at top speed, grande dame Ethel patted her brow and commented aloud: 'My dear, it's wearing me out just looking at you.'

'Work was the only opiate she had,' said Katharine Albert, who visited the star that spring to talk about her next picture. Joan, pale and thin, having lost fifteen pounds in her anguish, said to Albert, 'Forget my next picture, I've got an exclusive for you. I'm dumping Doug.' The news of the divorce was to be kept a secret by Albert and *Modern Screen*. No one, including Doug, was to know of the divorce until two months hence when the magazine hit the news stands.

'This was a big scoop for *Modern Screen* (and its 3 million readers),' said Ezra Goodman. 'Joan was being loyal to a dear friend.' Katharine Albert wrote up the story and sent it in to the magazine. It was already set in type, ready to go to press, when Doug made the tabloids on his own. He was being sued for sixty thousand dollars by one Jorgen Dietz, said to be a Danish baron. Dietz contended Fairbanks, Jr. stole the 'love and affection, comfort and assistance' of his wife, Mrs. Solveig Dietz. He also claimed that Fairbanks, Jr.

and his manager, in an effort to silence him, 'imprisoned him for four hours in a hotel room without his authority.'

Naturally, this upset Joan greatly. 'It is an outrage,' she told reporters, 'there is no truth whatever in the charges.' It also put her on the spot with the imminent news of her plans to divorce Doug, coming up in *Modern Screen*. 'This was her dear husband,' said Ezra Goodman. 'Should she be a bitch and leave him after this? It would put Joan in lousy with her fans, as a lousy, stinking wife with no understanding. A woman does not do this. A woman stands by her man.' Joan called *Modern Screen* and said she was not leaving Doug. The magazine screamed that she couldn't do that to them. It would cost them a fortune. 'She wanted to play the role of the forgiving wife,' said Goodman. 'Was she to let down her husband or the fan book? She finally decided to let down her husband.'

Joan told Katharine Albert and the editors to let the story stand. She would divorce Doug, and stall the press until their exclusive broke in the magazine. But, two days before the issue went on sale, Joan received a call from Louella Parsons. The columnist was preparing a positive story on Joan and Doug. 'It was a whale of a story,' said Louella. 'I had Joan standing shoulder to shoulder with Doug, staunchly defending their happiness and their marriage.' She called Joan, for quotes to give the column 'punch'. Joan asked for time, begging Louella to hold off, promising that she would have another story for her in a few days. Smelling the scent of her own scoop, Louella minutes later was on her horse galloping to Joan's Brentwood house. She barged in, held Joan's hand, and pulled the news out of her. 'Right under my surprised hostess' eyes,' said Lolly, 'I grabbed her portable typewriter and started banging away on my own yarn, before the competition could arrive.'

The next day the tragic news of the official split between Crawford and Fairbanks, Jr., was on the front pages of the entire Hearst newspaper syndicate. The timing and enormous coverage were beneficial to Joan, but not to Doug – or to Bette Davis, whose first starring picture was released on the same day. 'Everyone wanted to know about Poor Joan,' said Adela Rogers St. Johns, 'how she was holding up. I remember one of her friends, Ruth

Chatterton, had plans to leave for Europe with her husband, George Brent. She told Joan she would cancel her trip to stay with her. Joan of course insisted that Chatterton leave, that she would carry on bravely alone.'

To escape the reporters camped out on her front lawn, Crawford went to Palm Springs with director Howard Hawks, and was later reported to be 'in seclusion' at a private Malibu hideaway. It was there, 'surrounded by the love and laughter of such good friends as Clifton Webb (he called her 'Blessed Joan'), Kay Francis, Ivor Novello, Marlene Dietrich, and Ronald Colman, 'that Joan recovered, casting aside negative thoughts that she would never find true love again.'

'The kind of love I *do* believe in must exist somewhere,' she said, 'or the poets would not have glorified it in beautiful music or a sunset.'

5

BETTE – A BITCH IS BORN

'I wanted to be known as an actress, not necessarily as a star, although that would be frosting on the cake if it should happen.'

Bette Davis

Within a week of its release, *Ex-Lady*, Bette's star debut film was pulled from theaters. 'My shame was exceeded only by my fury,' she said, responding to critics who denounced her for appearing half-naked in the boudoir scenes.

Undaunted, and still determined to launch her as their resident blonde sex symbol, Warner's announced that Bette would co star with William Powell in a glamorous extravaganza called *Fashions of 1934*. Set in Manhattan, against a plot of fashion piracy (Paris haute couture versus New York ripoffs), it would feature Bette who would be dressed in fifteen 'sleek and shimmering Orry-Kelly gowns.' Her hair and makeup would be created by Antoine, a Polish hairdresser imported from Paris to work specifically on this picture. 'Antoine is on the way to the Warner's studio in Hollywood,' said the *New York Sun*, 'there to apply his ideas of hairdressing and makeup, which he declares so powerful a force that it will eventually supersede all methods of conquering fear and acquiring inward strength. Miss Davis fortunately needs neither a change of coiffure nor yet a methods of conquering fear.'

Antoine and *Fashions of 1934* flopped, but Warner's followed rapidly with *The Big Shakedown*, co starring Charles Farrell. The studio now attempted to establish Bette as part of a popular team. They asked the public to find the perfect leading man for fickle

Bette. 'Garbo had her Gilbert, Crawford had her Gable, and Gaynor her Farrell,' the contest declared, 'so let's have your choice. Send us the name of the star you think would be the perfect lover for Miss Davis in forthcoming screen productions.'

Bette said she didn't *want* a perfect screen lover, she wanted a good script, which was á rare commodity at Warner's in those days. 'Jack Warner seldom invested any large amount of money in scripts,' said Joan Blondell. 'In the early thirties his motto was "Let's make them fast, and make them cheap." He seldom bought [the rights] to books or plays. The scripts for most of those gangster pictures and ninety-minute melodramas, were based on remakes or on stories taken from newspaper headlines. I'm not talking against the guys in the story department, but a lot of them were "idea men." The quality writers were over at MGM or at Paramount.'

Davis knew that if she were to succeed she would have to resort to the sneaky tactics used by Joan Crawford during her early days at Metro. She could not rely on studio assignments; she would have to hustle and track down her own scripts. When she raided the Warner files and found nothing worthy of her talents, she began to enquire about parts outside the studio. She learned of two scripts, both potential star vehicles, that had been put on hold for the want of a leading actress. The first of these was *Of Human Bondage* at RKO. It would ultimately establish her name and fix her image as 'the first consummate bitch in Hollywood history.'

> 'Me? I disgust you? You're too fine. You cad. You dirty swine. I never cared for you, not once . . . It made me sick when I let you kiss me . . . and after you kissed I always used to wipe my mouth! Wipe my mouth!'
>
> Bette Davis in *Of Human Bondage*

In the fall of 1933, when the script of *Bondage* was submitted to the ladies in Hollywood they stampeded en masse to get away from the character of Mildred, the guttersnipe Cockney waitress. 'Any number of actresses who had been approached to play Mildred had turned it down,' said the director, John Cromwell. ' "Oh God, no," they would say, "this would ruin my career, to play a bitch like that." Then Bette came in and I felt instinctively that she could do it.' 'I read for Mr. Cromwell,' said Bette. 'Then I read for Mr. Berman [Pandro S., the producer]. I read for any number of people at RKO, including the mail boy. They all agreed. I was Mildred. However, Mr. Jack Warner, my boss, thought otherwise.'

Warner refused to loan her out. He said the part was too vicious, audiences would hate her, it would destroy her career. 'What career?' said Davis. 'I was playing vapid blondes and silly ingenues. For audiences to hate me, they would first have to *notice* me. I needed a role with guts, and Mildred was *it*.' Warner argued that the picture wouldn't make a dime at the box office. He reminded Bette that Joan Crawford had appeared in Somerset Maugham's last film, *Rain*, and it bombed. '*Jack!*' said Bette. 'The reason that *Rain* failed with Miss Crawford is because Miss Crawford *cannot* act her way out of a brown paper bag. *I* am an actress and I will do this picture.'

'Let me think about it,' said Warner.

While Bette was waiting for Warner to make up his mind to release her, a second project materialized, at Columbia Pictures. Director Frank Capra was looking for the right actress to play the part of a runaway heiress in a film called *Night Bus*. Soon to be retitled *It Happened One Night*. The role had been turned down by Constance Bennett, Miriam Hopkins, Myrna Loy, and Margaret Sullavan when writer Robert Riskin suggested Bette Davis to Capra. 'Yes,' said Davis, 'I *was* offered that part. *Before* Miss Colbert. The entire package would have been *heaven*. A good script, a wonderful director, Clark Gable, and *me*. I was absolutely mad about Clark Gable. I admired him *enormously*!'

Director Frank Capra requested Bette, and once more Jack Warner refused to release her. 'He told Mr. Capra that I was tied up for a *year*,' she said. 'Which wasn't true at all. He made me do these *asinine* pictures. In one [*Fog Over Frisco*] I wound up as a corpse in the trunk of a car; in another [*Jimmy the Gent*] I was a last-minute replacement for Joan Blondell. Why I didn't lose my mind I don't *know*. I was angry, but I was a good girl, a very good girl. I wanted to play Mildred. So I had to be nice to Mr. Warner. I pestered him night and day to release me to RKO. I arrived at his office in the morning with the shoe-shine boy. I was there at night when he left to go home. I begged and pleaded, and after six months he finally said, "Yes. Go hang yourself!" '

The part was hers when Bette learned she was pregnant. She would later say her mother and husband persuaded her to have an abortion. The economics and the lost time would hurt her career. 'I did as I was told,' she stated meekly.

'No compromises,' she told *Of Human Bondage* director, John Cromwell. She understood Mildred's nastiness and evil machinations, and wanted to look physically unattractive in the closing scenes. 'No other actress would have dared face a camera with hair untidy and badly rinsed, her manner vicious and ugly,' said Cromwell. 'I was not going to die of a dread disease looking as if a deb had missed her nap,' said Bette.

In her attack on the role of Mildred, the pyrotechnics of Bette's unique and bizarre style of acting – the bulging eyes, the waving of the arms and the zigzag walk – came into full force, although her performance was carefully monitored and controlled by her director. Cromwell, who would later direct Kim Stanley in a quintessential study of a neurotic star, Paddy Chayefsky's *The Goddess*, said he sensed a similar desperation in Bette Davis during the making of *Bondage*. 'She had been in Hollywood for some time. She wanted success. She craved the big time. She knew Mildred would be her last hope, her final chance, and that desperation can be seen in her performance.'

Davis' co star, Leslie Howard, also contributed to her malignant performance. Reporter Vernon Scott said that during the first days of filming, the English actor and his fellow performers, Reginald Denny and Reg Owen, would 'huddle in a corner and bitch about the American girl playing the part of Mildred.' Howard was jealous and indifferent towards her, another reporter stated, and 'that indifference, along with the determination to convince him she was his equal, gave an almost maniacal edge to the hatred she conveyed in acting with him.'

The night the film was previewed in Hollywood, Bette did not attend. She sent her mother and her husband in her place. When they returned their faces were blank and they remained silent until

Bette begged them to say something. Her husband said she gave a painfully sincere performance, and he doubted if it would do her much good.

On June 28, 1934, *Of Human Bondage* opened at the new Radio City Music Hall in New York City. The audiences became over-wrought, bursting into applause when Mildred died, and again when the film was over. 'The reviews were *raves*, every single one of them,' said the triumphant Bette. 'Probably the best performance ever recorded on the screen by a U.S. actress,' said *Time*. 'Miss Davis will astonish you,' said the *New York Daily News*. 'The picture was an immense success all over the world,' said Bette, 'and it brought me my first Academy Award nomination as Best Actress.'

'She was *not* nominated as Best Actress for *Of Human Bondage*,' said Joan Crawford. 'Miss Davis keeps perpetuating that myth. It's incorrect. Check the Academy.'

The nominees that year were: Claudette Colbert for *It Happened One Night*, Grace Moore for *One Night of Love*, and Norma Shearer for *The Barretts of Wimpole Street*.

'There was a *mistake*, a terrible mistake,' said Bette. 'Inadvertently, my name was left off the nominations list. It caused a *tremendous* uproar. The Academy was forced to ask the voters to write in their own choice on the final ballot.'

The voters chose Claudette Colbert for the picture for which Davis had been requested.

'The entire town went for *It Happened One Night*,' she said. 'Everyone said it was a cheat. Jack Warner was also against me. He did not want me to come back to Warners with a swelled head. He sent out instructions to everyone to vote against me. But I made history, of sorts. The next year the entire voting procedure was taken over by the firm of Price, Waterhouse, so the studios could no longer fix the contest.'

BETTE AND JOAN – RIVALS IN LOVE

Back at Warner's, Davis trudged 'through the professional swamp, brimming over with tears of frustration and rage.' In August 1935 the actress was finally given a script and a leading man that met with her approval. The script was entitled *Dangerous*. It was loosely based on another of her idols, Jeanne Eagels, the brilliant, self-destructive actress who died of a morphine overdose at age twenty-nine.

Joyce Heath, her character in *Dangerous*, 'was a drunk, not a doper,' said Davis. 'She was jinxed, self-centered, neurotic. [She cripples her husband in a car wreck on her opening night.] Personally I did not know anyone like her, or like Mildred in *Of Human Bondage*; but I could recognize her ego and devious behavior, from myself and other actresses.'

Her leading man was Franchot Tone. A graduate of Cornell, Phi Beta Kapa, Tone came from a wealthy family and was a member of the prestigious Group Theater in New York. He had talent and East Coast breeding, qualities that appealed enormously to Bette. 'If the truth be known,' she wrote in her memoirs, 'I fell in love with Franchot, professionally and privately. Everything about him reflected his elegance, from his name to his manners.'

But Franchot Tone was already taken, by none other than Joan Crawford.

When Franchot Tone arrived in Hollywood during the Spring of 1933 he told friends he wasn't interested in movie fame, the phony glamor, or superficial parties. He was there for the quick money, to subsidize his Group Theater back east. He intended to take the cash and run, but then he met Joan Crawford.

The two had been introduced before, in New York, when he was the toast of the town, starring on Broadway in *Success Story*, and she was just another visiting Hollywood celebrity. At MGM he was on her turf, in her realm, and Joan, in the throes of her 'painful' split from Douglas Jr., but still eager for some sophisticated masculine company, summoned Franchot to her home for tea. He obeyed the call because he was working with her at the time, playing her brother in *Today We Live*, and he was curious to find out 'if she played the role of the grand star at home.'

Joan did not disappoint the actor. Tea was served from her set of antique silver, complete with scones and a slight English accent. Franchot, for contrast, decided to play along, but from the other side of the tracks. He proceeded to talk dirty, using four-letter words, and Joan, never a slouch when people ridiculed her, laughed, then adjusted her demeanor, lowering her language, with no restraint on expletives.

Mr. Tone stayed for dinner.

She was fascinated with his background, and he was interested in 'the power structure of Hollywood', in which Joan was a leading player. She advised him on his career. She arranged for him to appear with her in a second, then a third picture. She supervised his publicity, ensuring that he be photographed by her favorite, George Hurrell. Interviews were set up for him with her friends. 'I don't think that I'd have any publicity if it had not been for Joan,' he freely admitted. 'Interviewers only wanted to hear about her.'

What Bette Davis and her new neighbour and best friend, Jean Harlow, wanted to know, was what the handsome intellectual Tone saw in the glamorous but superficial Crawford.

Franchot spoke of Joan's '*intelligence de coeur*', her intelligence of heart. 'She possesses a beautiful mind and spiritual qualities that are going to take her to supreme heights,' he said.

He introduced her to the works of Shakespeare, Ibsen and Shaw. 'Sitting on the floor before a great fire in Joan's home, Franchot would read aloud,' said writer Jerry Asher. 'Joan would listen as she worked on one of her hooked rugs, one foot curled up under her.'

'Douglas introduced me to the great plays, and Franchot told me what they *mean*,' said Joan, whose vocabulary was also expanding. 'He taught me words like "metaphor", and "transference",' she said.

'And she taught him words like "jump", and "fuck",' said Jean Harlow.

'*Au contraire*,' Joan could argue: her relationship with Tone was platonic at the outset. 'He helped me recover from my soul sickness over Doug,' she stated.

The physical consummation of their romance came courtesy of the aforementioned Jean Harlow. Joan never liked Jean. She had 'a controlled detestation for the girl,' Douglas Fairbanks, Jr. said in his memoirs, also divulging that at dinner one night, Harlow rested her hand in his lap while announcing she had just become engaged to Joan's good friend at Metro, Paul Bern. Joan overlooked that indiscretion, but later, when Jean began to make cow eyes at Franchot Tone on the set of *The Girl from Missouri*, the star from Kansas City decided it was time to put her territorial brand on the cultured Eastern actor.

On the day she seduced him, she was indulging in her latest passion – sunbathing. 'The best sun is between twelve and two,' she told the readers of *Motion Picture*. 'I give myself an hour on the front of me, an hour on the back and a half hour on each side. Then I feel like a little pig which has been well roasted on a revolving spit.' She had a solarium built for isolated pleasure. It was enclosed, at the rear of of her house. She was in there, revolving, when Franchot arrived for their afternoon culture session. When he was announced by the butler, Joan called out and asked if he would be a dear and fetch her bottle of special suntan oil ('mineral oil, mixed with spring water, a little cologne and one drop of iodine'). Franchot brought the bottle and knocked on the door. On cue, it swung open, to reveal his hostess, gloriously tanned, glistening from every pore, and completely nude. She said nothing. Her eyes were closed. She lay on her back listening to his labored breathing. Then, with perfect timing, she arched one leg, opened her eyes, smiled at Tone and murmured, 'Shut the door, darling and do my back.'

Franchot did not emerge from the solarium until nightfall, the neighbors noted. Not too long after this Crawford had Tone's MGM contract extended and re-negotiated by her agent Michael C. Levee. She got him a raise and a bonus of twenty-five thousand dollars, which enabled the actor to move from his bachelor digs in Santa Monica to a more fashionable, convenient residence, close to her in Brentwood. 'Their backyards almost touch,' said Louella Parsons, who rhapsodized over the decoration of Franchot's house. 'In the bedroom,' said Parsons, 'the chic bedspread of white glazed chintz is set off with red tassels.' All of the interiors were designed by William Haines, with a large assist from Joan. 'Her touch,' said Franchot proudly, 'is everywhere.'

'At the moment, Franchot is Crawford's enthusiasm,' said

Samuel Richard Mook in *Picture Play*. 'And when Joan develops a fondness for a person, said person might as well resign himself to doing nothing else until the fondness has abated – as it always does. She simply smothers you.'

Crawford told Jerry Asher that she had no plans to marry Tone. 'I do not believe in marriage for two people living in Hollywood,' she said. She believed in marriage 'the modern way,' she told Jimmie Fidler. 'You *can* have your cake and eat it. If you nibble at the edges it lasts longer.'

Her liberated philosophy would soon be changed, by rising star Bette Davis.

In September 1935 Franchot Tone had just returned to Los Angeles from location shooting on *Mutiny on the Bounty*. He was told by MGM he was being loaned to Warner Brothers, to play opposite Bette Davis in *Dangerous*. There was no record of Tone's immediate reaction to this news, except for a column quote a few weeks later in which the actor said that Bette was 'a tip-top player to work with'. Bette was also complimentary to Tone. 'He was a most charming, attractive, top-drawer guy. He really was,' she said. During the filming she confessed to Joan Blondell that she had fallen hard for the New York actor. 'I was on the lot doing a picture when Bette came to see me, all soft and dewy-eyed, which was *not* her usual manner, believe me. She was in love, she told me, with her leading man, Franchot Tone. I was amused. I thought she was kidding. After all, she was married to that sweet guy, Ham, the musician. And, furthermore, I didn't think she went in for that sort of thing – for soundstage romances. It's not that she was a Holy Mary; she wasn't. Her career always came first. So I kidded with her, saying that we all get crushes on our leading men from time to time and they passed, although I wasn't one to prove it: I married one [Dick Powell]. Bette got very angry with me. She said, "Joan! I am *not* a school-girl. I don't *get* crushes. I am in love with Franchot, and I think he's in love with me." I said something lame, like "give it time, honey," although I was really thinking, "Boy! If Joan Crawford gets wind of this, there is going to be *war*." '

Adela Rogers St. Johns was at Warner's during the making of *Dangerous*. 'I didn't know Davis too well,' she said, 'but I knew she had a reputation for being tough on her leading men. She hauled off and socked Charlie Farrell over some minor misunderstanding on one picture, and Jimmy Cagney got the brunt of her temper on another. So, when *Dangerous* began and the reports went out that Bette was behaving like a little lamb with Franchot, I suspected something was up.'

Davis and Tone held frequent meetings in her dressing room. The actress explained he was a serious artist and she needed his input on her character. 'Playing an actress,' she said, 'is unlike playing an ordinary woman. All her gestures are a little too broad, all her emotions a little too threatening. Her greed, her insatiable zest for living, her all-encompassing ego make her seem completely pagan, but an articulate pagan, one who knows all the tricks of the trade.'

During the making of *Dangerous*, Joan Crawford suddenly announced her engagement to Franchot Tone. There were no immediate plans for marriage, she repeated. 'Marriage makes lovers just people.' Her relationship with Franchot was one of utter freedom – although, according to Bette, Joan kept Tone on a short leash throughout the filming. 'They met for lunch each day,' she said in 1987. 'After lunch he would return to the set, his face covered with lipstick. He made sure we all knew it was Crawford's lipstick. He was very honored that this great star was in love with him. I was jealous of course.'

But not beaten. She appealed to Franchot's actor's ego. She had Laird Doyle, the writer of *Dangerous*, add new material to his scenes with her. This of course necessitated additional rehearsals, and more private meetings with her. 'She almost drove herself crazy, scheming on how to get Franchot away from Joan,' said Adela Rogers St. Johns, who eventually carried the news of Bette's romantic interest to Crawford.

'Oh,' said Joan, when told of the competition, 'that coarse little thing doesn't stand a chance with Franchot.'

'I mentioned that Bette was a fine actress,' said St. Johns, 'and was going to become a big, big star.'

The latter news apparently intrigued Crawford. She called Adela a few mornings later and asked the writer if she would accompany her to the set of *Dangerous*. 'To my knowledge,' said St. Johns, 'this was the first time Bette and Joan had been formally introduced.'

'We met previously,' said Davis, 'at a party at Marion Davies'.'

'I met many lovely people at Marion's,' Crawford insisted, 'but Miss Davis was *not* one of them.'

At Warner's that day Crawford, the bigger star, was 'her usual gracious self,' said St. Johns, 'while Bette did her best to ignore her, keeping those huge eyes of hers fixed like a bayonet on Franchot.' The visitors stood on the sidelines and watched Davis emote in the scene where she visits Tone in his office and tells him he is a sap to believe she ever loved him.

'You! With your *fat* little soul and smug face. I've lived *more* in a single day than you'll ever *dare* live,' said Bette as Joyce Heath.

'It was a powerful scene,' said St. Johns. 'The contrast in style between her and Franchot was striking. I could sense Joan standing to attention beside me. She knew that Davis could never compete with her sexually, but talent-wise? That was another horse race indeed. And Bette was *the* champion in that field. Joan knew that, and so did Franchot. You could see the sparks flying off him as he worked with Bette. She was the first real actress he had worked with since he came to Hollywood. There was also some talk that he was writing a script for both of them to do. But Joan put a stop to that, real fast. Three days after *Dangerous* was finished, despite her objections to marriage, she took off with Franchot to New York, and the next thing we heard they were married in New Jersey.'

> *'It was Alfred Lunt and Lynn Fontanne who made me change my mind about marriage. They managed to blend their professional achievements so magnificently well with their private life. They inspired Franchot and I to humbly enter the same happy union.'*
>
>   Joan Crawford, 1935

Whatever anger Bette Davis felt when she learned that Crawford had married Franchot Tone, her unhappiness was lifted when Jack Warner told her he had bought the rights to the hit New York play *The Petrified Forest*, and she would play Gaby, the leading female role. In November 1935 filming was already underway, while

Dangerous was being given a fast edit for a December release, to qualify Bette for Academy Award consideration. Another reason for the haste was Jack Warner's desire to capitalize on the success of Franchot Tone in *Mutiny on the Bounty*, released on November 7. The MGM film was a giant hit, with Tone receiving the best reviews of his Hollywood career. The Warners merchandising department were told to feature the actor prominently in the ads and photos for the Bette Davis movie.

'*LOOK OUT FRANCHOT TONE! – You're in for the toughest MUTINY – you've ever faced, when BETTE DAVIS rebels in DANGEROUS*', was one of the popular logos.

Davis, when told of the campaign, said she didn't mind the emphasis being placed on Crawford's new husband. 'Franchot was a swell guy, a really top-drawer person,' she said. 'And at the time I felt the picture needed all the help it could get. It wasn't something I was crazy about.'

The critics felt otherwise. 'Penetratingly alive . . . electric,' said the *Los Angeles Times* of Bette. 'A strikingly sensitive performance, in a well-made bit of post-Pinero drama,' said *The New York Times*. Oscar voters were similarly impressed. In January she was listed as one of the nominees for Best Actress.

Bette wasn't going to attend the ceremonies, she insisted. The nomination was a gesture of sympathy, for being ignored the year before. On March 5, the morning of the banquet, she came down with the flu (a psychosomatic condition used by Crawford on *her* Oscar day), but, bullied by her mother, Bette agreed to attend with husband Ham. She would not get 'gussied up', however. Her hair, back to its original 'mousy brown', had already been permed, and instead of a formal gown she pulled a navy print dinner dress from her closet.

Arriving at the banquet at the Biltmore Hotel with Ham and her mother, Bette found there was no room for them at the studio's front table, where Jack Warner sat with producer Hal Wallis and directors Michael Curtiz and Max Reinhardt (with two films, *Captain Blood* and *A Midsummer Night's Dream*, in the running for Best Picture). Placed at a table at the side of the room, Bette applauded enthusiastically as one by one the major awards bypassed Warner Brothers and went to RKO for Best Script, Score, Best Actor (Victor McLaglen) and Best Director (John Ford) for *The Informer*. Bette was also sure that RKO would pick up Best Actress, for Katharine Hepburn (*Alice Adams*). When D.W. Griffith went to the podium to announce the winner, she managed to smile.

'The winner is Bette Davis, for *Dangerous*,' said Griffith, where-upon Bette felt she was 'going to be very sick.'

Making a short, polite speech, the actress displayed the barest of emotion, although she claimed later that inside she was happy to the point of exploding.

Leading a standing ovation, Jack Warner beamed from table one, while at table two a vanquished Best Actor nominee, Franchot Tone, leapt to his feet as Bette passed by and embraced her. 'Oh God, he was always a gentleman, the tops,' she recalled. Franchot's wife however remained seated, with her back to the Best Actress, until her husband said, 'Darling!' Turning her head, the immac-ulately groomed and spectacularly beautiful Joan Crawford looked up, then down at the Best Actress winner and said, 'Dear Bette! What a *lovely* frock.'

'I was told by any number of people that my outfit was an insult to the Academy,' said Bette. 'One reporter wrote that I wore an inexpensive house dress. That was not true. My dress was simple but expensive, a *dinner* dress. It suited the occasion perfectly, because I didn't feel I deserved to win. So why be a hypocrite about it?'

BETTE DAVIS ALMOST LYNCHED BY ADORATION ON VISIT HERE, read the headline of the *New York Daily News* when the actress went to New York for a visit that April. 'A crowd of five hundred tried to tear down the ropes and get to Davis,' the paper reported. 'Seven cops pushed and shoved, somebody made a pass at somebody else, and only the blonde young actress's calmness prevented much greater excitement.'

Meeting with a reporter in the bar of her hotel, Bette confided she had left some 'minor professional problems' back in California. Anxious for good scripts, she had wanted to play Elizabeth the First, in *Mary of Scotland*, at RKO. But her boss refused to loan her out again. 'So I decided I needed a long rest. And here I am!' she said, not letting the reporter know that she was also refused to do retakes for her new picture, *The Golden Arrow*. And that there was another serious issue at stake. The recent Oscar winner wanted more money, a lot more money, for her professional services. A Warner's press release issued at this time described Bette Davis as 'a very easy person to know. Young, healthy, wealthy and happily married to a person she loves.'

The wealthy part did not amuse the actress. 'When I arrived in Hollywood,' she said, 'I was treated as a poor cousin. I soon learned that you are treated according to your salary scale.'

Although she now lived in Crawford's neighbourhood, Brentwood, in a rented house owned by Greta Garbo, her monthly expenses were enormous. She was the main support of a family that included her mother, her sister, her husband, a maid and a chauffeur. 'I have no savings,' she told a New York reporter, 'no expensive furs or jewelry.' Her salary at Warners was modest, that of a featured player, but she hoped it would soon be adjusted upward, 'commensurate with her importance as an Oscar winner and star.'

To ensure those changes, Bette hired a new agent. His name was Michael C. Levee. He was a respected, astute business man, whose other clients included Cecil B. De Mille, Merle Oberon, Dick Powell, Ben Hecht, and the leading box-office star of 1936, Joan Crawford.

At the start of that year, Bette was making twelve hundred dollars a week, which was considerable for those Depression years but paltry compared with Joan Crawford's annual salary of $241,453. With Joan's representative as her agent, Bette demanded more money and perks. She wanted what Crawford was receiving, and more. 'How much is Joan making?' she asked Levee. 'Does she get free clothes, a car, promotional expenses?' Levee, who preferred to treat such matters as confidential to each individual, was reluctant to release this information to Bette. 'My *God*!' said Bette. 'Everytime Crawford has a headache or a bowel movement she calls Hedda or Louella Parsons, and you're giving me this "confidential". . .?'

While Bette vacationed in New York and Boston, Levee

submitted her new requests to Jack Warner. Along with a large boost in her salary, she asked for approval of scripts, directors and cinematographers; star billing above the title; three months of vacation a year; and the right to do one outside picture a year during her vacation time.

Jack Warner listened to Levee, then sent a telegram to Davis. In essence it ordered the star to 'get back to work' for retakes on her new film. He refused her requests, whereupon Bette instructed Levee to break her contract and place her with another studio, preferably MGM, the home of Greta Garbo and Joan Crawford.

MGM VERSUS WARNER'S

Years later, during the making of *What Ever Happened to Baby Jane?*, columnist Sidney Skolsky wrote that the root of the trouble between Crawford and Davis began with the disparity in their studio backgrounds. 'Joan resembles MGM,' said Skolsky, 'Bette resembles Warner's. The war is between two kingdoms, two Movie Queens, each with an ego that has to be fed with driving activity.'

MGM in 1936 was 'a walled city and fortress', said Skolsky. The studio had more power, more money, more fame than any other picture studio in the world. It also had more stars 'than there are in the heavens', including Joan Crawford, number three in prestige at the studio, behind Garbo and Norma Shearer, but number one at the box office. 'Joan never knew reality when she was toiling within the high white walls of the MGM kingdom,' said the columnist. 'She was protected, pampered, her ego was fed carefully so it would blossom, and at the end of every week there was a pot of gold waiting for her at the cashier's window. There was only one flaw: Joan was completely ruled by the Dictator of the MGM kingdom – Louis B. Mayer.'

Mayer was the Pope, and the MGM girls were medieval chattels. When Joan was unhappy, Mayer met her complaints with promises, flattery and advice. 'If the problem was important enough, he would cry a little. He could turn on the tears faster than any actor. It was said often, but not to his face, that his initials, L.B., stood for Lionel Barrymore.'

'Meanwhile over the hill and into the valley,' said Skolsky, 'there is the Kingdom of Warner's, vastly different from MGM. Called "a plantation," by some, and "the penitentiary" by others, among the peasants there is Movie Star Bette Davis. She had talent, drive and disobedience. She rebelled frequently against the warden, Jack Warner.'

'Warner and L.B. Mayer were alike in one respect,' said director George Cukor. 'Both men loved movies. But Warner was a businessman first. He did not respect talent like Mayer did. ("I'll go down on my knees and kiss the ground talent walks upon," said L.B.) Making the deal, Warner would promise you everything for your picture, then renege on his word if it cost him more money.'

Jack Warner was also not a father figure to his stars, Skolsky stated. But that was all right with Bette Davis. 'She didn't need a father image as Joan Crawford did. Bette was already a papa to her mother and younger sister.'

In April 1936, Davis, who would eventually settle in to become the look and form of Warner Brothers' films, wanted to leave the studio and move to MGM, where she felt she would receive the money, respect and prestigious films that were her due. She soon learned this was not possible. Mayer would not talk to her agent as long as she had a contract with Warner, and that contract, Bette soon discovered could not be broken.

But Jack Warner was willing to be fair. He raised Bette's salary to one thousand six hundred dollars a week, and at her agent's urging she agreed to return to Los Angeles, to begin work on a new film entitled *God's Country and Woman*. She collected on her new salary for four weeks, then refused to begin the picture unless the rest of her demands were met.

'She's a very stubborn young lady,' Mike Levee told columnist Sheilah Graham. 'She told Warner she wanted $3,500 a week, all radio rights and permission to make outside pictures.'

Comparing Bette with his other star client, Joan Crawford, Levee described Davis as 'suspicious . . . impulsive . . . too eager to take charge of everything.' Whereas Joan, in matters of business, deferred to her advisors.

When Levee tried to reason with Bette Davis, advising her to go back to work and meet Jack Warner in an amicable frame of mind, she accused him of kowtowing to the boss. She ordered Levee to step aside, said that she and her lawyer would handle the negotiations. Levee in turn resigned. 'The grief is not worth the commission,' he told Sheilah Graham. When her lawyer questioned her aggressive tactics she fired him also.

On June 20, with new legal counsel, Bette met with Jack Warner, Hal Wallis and two studio lawyers. According to the minutes of the meeting in the studio files, Warner opened by asking Bette 'to be a trouper', to do the new picture at two thousand dollars a week, and with her favorite cameraman, Sol Polito. Bette said no. She stuck to her request for a new contract 'along the lines previously requested.'

'We build stars around here,' said Warner, 'give them every chance. Then they turn around and demand everything.' He repeated his offer of two thousand dollars a week. 'And I'll do better. Six additional yearly options, for another six years, going up to four thousand eventually. I can't top that.'

'That's a six-year contract,' Bette shouted. 'A five-year contract is long enough! And after five years I'll be too damn old to be in pictures.'

'How foolish of you, Bette,' said Jack, 'to believe you'll be too old then. You'll only be thirty-five.'

'Thirty-*three*,' Bette snapped back. And for the moment they laughed.

'*STAR STRIKES! Bette Davis Angry at Producers*', the newspapers reported on July 1. 'I'm ready to quit for good,' she said. 'There are certain things I'm entitled to. And I'm damned well going to get them; or else!'

'It's all being fixed up amicably,' said a studio spokesman. 'Nothing serious at all. She'll be back.'

On a Sunday morning at 12.05 A.M., to avoid being served legal papers, Bette and her husband left Los Angeles, bound for Vancouver. From there they went to Montreal, then on to England, where the actress was scheduled to make two films for an independent producer. Her strategy was inspired by Jimmy Cagney, said Joan Blondell, who told the story of how the feisty little Irish man bested the big studio mogul. 'Jimmy was always complaining about the low salaries we were getting while Jack and his brothers raked in the millions. But we all had firm seven-year contracts and, short of dying, there was no way we could break them. Then Jimmy found a way. One day his wife, Frances, was driving along Hollywood Boulevard and saw Pat O'Brien's name billed above Jimmy's on a movie marquee. She called Jimmy, who had a first-billing clause in his contract. He told Frances to take a picture of the marquee. He sent the picture to Jack Warner and told him he had infringed upon his contract. He quit the studio. They sued. But meantime Jimmy made two pictures for an outside producer, and Warner lost the suit. He begged Cagney to return, which he did, for more money and a cut of the gross profits. When Bette heard of that she decided what was good for Cagney was twice as good for her.'

Bette would not be victorious however. 'I was a woman,' she said. 'I was told I had no right fighting like a man. Jack Warner was determined to teach me a lesson.'

In England, during September of 1936, shortly before Davis was to commence work on her first film for producer Ludovic Toeplitz, Jack Warner had an injunction served on the actress, which prevented her from working for another employer. 'There was a principle at stake,' said Warner, 'whether a highly paid star could dictate to a studio, and make only those pictures that pleased her. If Bette were to win, all the studio owners and executives in Hollywood would get trampled in the stampede.'

When the case went to trial in London that October, Jack Warner was present in court. His lawyer called Bette 'a very naughty girl' and ridiculed her charges of slavery by telling the judge, and the press, that his client was paying the actress two thousand dollars per week. 'With America still locked into the Depression, that princely sum could feed a family of four for a year,' wrote one reporter.

The main issue was not about money, but about better scripts, Davis tried to argue. And to downplay her star image, she appeared for trial each day wearing the same tweed coat, skirt, and sweater, with a matching hand-knit beret. In court Bette attempted to use another 'theatrical' device. Each day she sat with her eyes fixed directly on the judge – trying to stare him into submission, to settle the case in her favor. ('Silly of me, wasn't it,' she said, 'I am not a very good hypnotist.')

The British courts agreed with Warner. Bette's contract was valid. She lost the case.

In November she returned by boat to the United States. 'This is a real sock in the teeth,' she told a reporter. 'I am back to serve another five years in the Warner's jail.'

Getting off the train at Union Station in Los Angeles, she felt a gloomy sense of *déjà vu*. Her reception was the same as when she had first arrived six years earlier. There was no one on hand from the studio to meet her.

'I was back to square one,' she said. 'I had to start all over again. Only this time I was a hundred thousand dollars in debt from the court costs. I didn't beg for parts, but I took whatever they gave me. I was also ostracized by many people. The lesson I learned was a good one. Artists live lonely lives, but they wage lonelier battles.'

6

JOAN TONE

'Even in her bath, Joan Crawford looked as if she were about to make a public appearance, just in case a crowd happened to drop by.'

Radie Harris

In December 1936, while Bette Davis was attempting to rebuild her film career, Joan Crawford for the third year in a row was voted the Top Box Office Star in America. In February 1937 she was named the first Queen of the Movies by *Life* magazine. On the set of her latest MGM film, *Love on the Run*, the fans of *Motion Picture* magazine were given an inside look at the royal treatment bestowed on their favorite. 'She appeared wearing a billowing organdy gown,' said the magazine. 'Two handmaidens held the dress up so the flounces would not get dirty. One girl got her a chair. Another turned an electric fan on her. Another brought her phonograph and started playing sweet music for her. The Queen was very gracious.' Joined by her husband, Franchot Tone – 'full of superiority complex' – he advised her to stop the interview. 'A rug was unrolled from where they were standing, to the door of Joan's portable dressing-room,' said the magazine. 'Mr. and Mrs. Tone strolled along the rug and disappeared into the dressing-room, never to be seen again.'

'Joan Crawford is never the movie star in the presence of the truly great,' said Katharine Albert. 'The renowned conductor Leopold Stokowski has been a visitor to her home. Before him, Joan stands in real awe. And once – when she saw Albert Einstein walking on Fifth Avenue, she was speechless.'

Writer Dale Eunson, who was married to Katharine Albert, spoke about the roles they played in the creation of Joan Crawford. 'We had both worked with Joan from the beginning of her career,' he said. 'I worked in publicity and Katharine wrote for *Photoplay* and *Modern Screen*. Katharine was largely responsible for teaching Joan how to handle the press. She coached her, told her what to say and how to make friends of interviewers.' At one time when the Eunsons lived in Connecticut, Joan called with an emergency. She was getting a divorce. She asked if Katharine would meet her train in Chicago, to brief her on what to say to the reporters in New York. Eunson, who would later write a film (*The Star*), patterned on Joan and played by Bette, commented on the differences between the two. 'Joan was not too intelligent. She wasn't half as smart or as talented as Bette Davis. But Joan developed charm, a wonderful charisma. She knew how to manipulate people with her looks and personality. She was an actress after all, even though later on she often got confused as to what role she was playing in her own life.'

In her life as Mrs. Franchot Tone, the metamorphosis began right after the wedding. Following their honeymoon in New York, the couple returned to L.A., to reside at Joan's home in Brentwood. 'Hello tree, hello house – I'm home again,' said the happy bride, who proceeded to wipe out every trace of El JoDo, by gutting the interior of the house she had shared with Fairbanks, Jr. She changed the decor to Spanish Modern, which captivated Louella Parsons, who said she was enraptured with 'the two mechanical doves that kissed over the doorway everytime the doorbell rang.' There was a new music room, with a false wall built to hide the original stained-glass windows. At the rear of the house, the star told Louella she had installed a formal rose garden and a special area where her beloved dogs could 'do their business' away from the main area.

In *Liberty* magazine, Katharine Albert provided an intimate glimpse of Mrs. Tone at home, preparing for one of her intimate dinner parties. 'In her bedroom,' wrote Albert, 'after badminton, as expert fingers arrange the crisp chestnut curls, Joan reads the most important fan mail, sent by her secretary at the studio. The downstairs maid then appears, asking Madame to put her final approval on that evening's menu. "Clear soup, stuffed lobster, duck and wild rice, endive and chive salad, hot cherries in ice rings – white wine with the fish, champagne with the fowl, coffee, and Napoleon brandy."

' "Check," says Joan.

'The butler then enters. Will Madame select the program for tonight's film showing? Joan selects a newsreel, a Mickey Mouse cartoon, and an unreleased Metro feature.'

In *Carnival Nights in Hollywood*, writer Elizabeth Wilson gave the next installment: the impressive guest list and Joan's entrance. 'The guests are all assembled before Joan appears, pausing first at the top of the stairs. She has the best tan. Barbara Stanwyck the worst (busy working days on *Stella Dallas*). While long and lean Gary Cooper plays with the marble machine in the games room, challenging Una Merkel and Charles Boyer to a game, Cooper's lovely wife, Sandra, talks to Betty Furness and Pat Boyer. Louise Rainer and her husband, Clifford Odets, arrive, and Franchot Tone instantly goes into a huddle with Odets. The two know each other from New York. As Ginger Rogers eyes the food, Robert Taylor and his girl-friend, Barbara Stanwyck, who suffers the torture of the timid, play ping-pong, while Joan Crawford looks on holding a little glass of sherry, which she never touches. She seldom drinks, Joan explains, "it makes me cry." Although a grave girl, bordering on the intense, Miss Crawford always surrounds herself with gay, amusing people. And at the first sound of laughter from her guests Joan snaps out of whatever depressing mood she may be in, and quickly becomes the gayest of the gay.'

THE FIGHT FOR SCARLETT O'HARA

'It was insanity that I not be given Scarlett. The book could have been written for me. I was perfect for Scarlett as Clark Gable was for Rhett.'

Bette Davis

According to Bette Davis, there was never any professional rivalry between her and Joan Crawford. 'Don't be *ridiculous*!' she admonished this writer when asked if the two were ever up for the same role. 'We were two different types *entirely*. I can't think of a single part I played that Joan could do. Not one. Can you?'

In the summer of 1937, Davis and Crawford were in the running for one role, that of Scarlett O'Hara in *Gone With the Wind*. The book had been purchased for her, Davis claimed. 'Before I rebelled and went to England, Jack Warner told me he had bought a wonderful book for me – *Gone With the Wind*. "I bet it's a *pip*," I answered and walked out.'

'That story is just another of Miss Davis' fantasies,' said Joan Crawford. '*Gone With the Wind* was never bought for her by Warner's. I should know, because my studio, MGM, made the picture, and I was the first to be mentioned for the role.'

According to director George Cukor, who worked for two years on the casting of the film, Warner's were asked to bid on the book. 'They turned it down,' said Cukor. 'Jack Warner would not pay the money. Nor would L.B. Mayer. It was David Selznick who put up the fifty thousand dollars for the film rights. When the book became a big success, selling over a million copies in six months, every studio in Hollywood wanted to make the movie, and every actress between the ages of thirteen and sixty-two wanted to play Scarlett O'Hara.'

L.B. Mayer was the first to approach producer Selznick with a package deal. He offered Clark Gable as Rhett Butler, Joan Crawford as Scarlett, Maureen O'Sullivan as Melanie, and Melvyn Douglas as Ashley Wilkes. 'Selznick said he would have to think about that,' said author Gavin Lambert.

While thinking, Selznick spoke to Samuel Goldwyn, who refused to loan out Gary Cooper for Rhett. Then the producer thought of Errol Flynn. 'It was Flynn that prompted Selznick to talk to Jack Warner,' said George Cukor. 'Bette Davis was thrown in as part of the deal.'

Selznick told Warner he would like time to ponder that package too, but in the meantime, with the help of press agent Russell Birdwell, he launched his nationwide door-to-door Scarlett O'Hara talent contest. 'That was pure hype,' said Cukor. 'Selznick had no intention of choosing some unknown for the part. Why should he, when he had the entire female contingent in Hollywood climbing in his window and scratching at his door, begging to play Scarlett?'

Norma Shearer had the part, it was reported, but she gave it up when her fans wrote in and begged her not to play such an unsavory character.

In a preliminary poll, radio-columnist Jimmie Fidler put Bette Davis as number four for Scarlet, with Joan Crawford in fifth place.

'Thousands of people wrote in and said I would make a wonderful Scarlett, with Clark Gable as Rhett Butler,' said Joan. 'Clark and I were a team at that time, having done five or six pictures together. He and I spoke about the book a few times. This was long before he was signed as Rhett. He had some reservations about doing the role, which were foolish, because whatever doubts the people had on who should play Scarlett, everyone agreed that only Gable should play Rhett Butler.'

Crawford, at Mayer's request, went to see David Selznick. 'David and I had made *Dancing Lady* together, with Clark Gable, a few years before. It was one of Metro's biggest grossers that year. He and I had a long talk about Scarlett, but I never tested for the role. David seemed to feel I was 'too modern,' for the part, and I tended to agree with him. He asked me who I thought should play Scarlett. I told him, "Katharine Hepburn would be wonderful; if you could get her." '

Katharine Hepburn wanted the role. She said she was the choice of the author, Margaret Mitchell. But when Selznick asked her to test, she refused. 'You know what I look like, David,' Hepburn told the producer. 'Yes,' he said, 'and I can't imagine Clark Gable chasing you for ten years.' 'Damn you!' said Miss Kate, and that was the end of her bid for Scarlett.

As sales of the book escalated worldwide, the name of Bette Davis began to emerge as the people's choice. 'She was easily the most popular candidate, with forty percent of the vote,' said Gavin Lambert. 'There were as many people against Bette Davis as there were for her – maybe more,' said David Selznick, who spoke to Jack Warner again. Warner renewed his package offer of Errol Flynn for Rhett Butler, Bette for Scarlett, with Olivia de Havilland included as Melanie Wilkes. 'I *refused* to be part of that parcel,' said Bette. 'I wanted to do Scarlett very much, but Errol Flynn was all wrong for the part of Rhett. Gable was *perfect*. I would have done anything to play with him. I was also told at the time that Mister Gable was very much in favour of my playing Scarlett.'

'Clark was not even *remotely* interested in having Bette Davis as his co star in *Gone With the Wind*,' said Joan Crawford in 1973. 'I know that for a *fact*.'

'Gable and Bette Davis? I can't honestly recall if that pairing was ever seriously considered,' said George Cukor.

'Mr. Cukor put thumbs down on me,' said Bette, referring to ancient grievances between the two from their early days in Rochester repertory, when he fired her without proper cause.

'She tells that story repeatedly,' said Cukor, 'knowing full well that the decision was not mine but Mr. Selznick's. Certainly Bette had the talent and temperament to play Scarlett. But in terms of physical type, Joan [Crawford], with her auburn hair and blue eyes, was closer to the heroine Miss Mitchell wrote about. Still, with due respect to both ladies, I don't believe the film would have worked as well with either one. The choice of Vivien Leigh as Scarlett was impeccable. *Gone With the Wind* would not have become the classic it is today with either Bette Davis or with Joan Crawford.'

> *'They called her JEZEBEL – the Heartless Siren of the South.*
> *She asked all, took all, gave nothing.'*

In the fall of 1937, while Metro continued their search for Scarlett O'Hara, Jack Warner had already embarked on his plan 'to steal the wind from producer Selznick's sails.' On October 5, Warner announced that he was going to produce his own Southern saga, *Jezebel;* and to play the leading role of Julie Marsden, the high-spirited imperious vixen of Louisiana, he chose Bette Davis.

'A drama of moss-hung New Orleans,' *Jezebel* surfaced on Broadway in 1934, starring Miriam Hopkins. It ran for forty-four performances, then closed. The film rights had been offered to various studios, including Warner Bros. In a February 1935 memo, assistant producer Hal Wallis recommended that they buy the rights. 'Bette could play the spots off the part of a little bitch of an aristocratic Southern girl,' Wallis stated. But Jack Warner said audiences would never warm to such a rebellious, independent woman, and the story was rejected.

In 1936, when Scarlett O'Hara and the success of the *Gone With the Wind* novel captured the attention of the world, Jack Warner quietly began negotiations for *Jezebel*. In January of 1937, he bought the rights for $12,000, and told Davis she could have the leading role. 'I am thrilled to death about *Jezebel*,' Bette said in a note to Warner. 'I think it can be as great if not greater than *Gone With the Wind*. Thank you for buying it.'

The budget for the film, $780,000, certainly matched Metro's plush mountings and also pleased Bette. Michael Curtiz was assigned to direct, then withdrew, preferring instead to work Errol Flynn on the more expensive $1.6 million production of *The Adventures of Robin Hood*. In his place, director William Wyler was borrowed from Samuel Goldwyn, and at Wyler's urging, his friend and houseguest, aspiring film-maker John Huston, was hired to rewrite the *Jezebel* script.

Early in October 1937 with a 'No Visitors' sign on the soundstage door, cinematographer Ernest Haller tested Bette Davis in color for *Jezebel*. Her skin appeared 'too pasty,' and her lips a 'terrible orange.' 'Technicolor makes me look like death warmed over,' said Bette. It was decided to shoot the film in black and white, with Haller (who, along with *Jezebel* composer, Max Steiner, would later work on *Gone With the Wind*).

To provide an authentic Southern accent, Bette was coached by a philosophy professor from Louisiana State University, who also supervised the plans for the sets. Her period wardrobe was designed by Orry-Kelly. The idea for the scandalous red dress, worn by Bette at the all-white Olympus Ball in 1850, was said to have been inspired by a real-life incident from 1936. At the Mayfair Ball that year, hostess Carole Lombard requested that her female guests wear formal gowns of snowy white. Making a late entrance was Norma Shearer 'wearing a spectacular scarlet gown.' Witnessing her arrival was John Huston, who reportedly inserted the incident during his revisions of the *Jezebel* script. Embellishments to the character of Julie Marsden were added by Bette and director Wyler. For the opening scene where she jumped off her horse and strode into her mansion, she practiced at home with a riding crop, cracking the whip as 'her husband and dogs scurried outdoors.' Her actions had to be perfect, she explained. 'In the scene, as Julie enters her house, she lifts the skirt of her riding outfit with the leather crop. It establishes her character in one gesture.'

On October 25, production began on *Jezebel*. Wyler, tireless and ruthlessly blunt, was described by actress Myrna Loy 'as a sadist'. 'He liked to wear people down, by the number of takes,' said Loy. For the opening shot in *Jezebel*, he made Bette Davis repeat the riding crop scene forty-five times. She had too much energy, he told her. Her gestures were too broad, too theatrical. 'Do you want me to put a chain around your neck? Stop moving your head,' he cautioned her.

In a room of his Beverly Hills home, Wyler had twenty-eight miniature sets of the film erected. Each evening after dinner, he would place the set he was going to work on the next day in the middle of the dining-room table. With a miniature toy camera and miniature actors, he would plan his shots while John Huston spoke the actual lines in the background. Each scene would be repeated, timed with a stop-watch. The following day variations would be added in rehearsals, and then the endless retakes would begin.

'He was a perfectionist and had the courage of twenty,' said Bette, who was pleased by her controlled performance and by the knowledge that she had at last found her creative and emotional match in a man. Wyler, attracted to volatile actresses (including Miriam Hopkins and Margaret Sullavan, whom he married), began a clandestine affair with Davis, which gave the master director the upper hand in dealing with the tempestuous Bette.

The Olympus Ball scene, where the defiant Julie Marsden was forced to dance in her red dress before a shocked virgin-white assembly, took one week to shoot. The estimated distance covered in the endless waltz came to thirty-six miles. Her co star Henry Fonda added to her stress, said Bette.

The role of Jezebel's fiancé had been initially offered to Franchot Tone. He was Bette's first choice, but she was told he was booked solid at MGM, playing back-up to Joan Crawford. William Wyler wanted Henry Fonda, who refused the offer. His wife was pregnant in New York and he wanted to be at her side when the baby was delivered in early December. Wyler assured Fonda his scenes would be photographed in time for him to be released for the birth of his first child (Jane). 'Everytime I see her face, I think of the hell she put me through on *Jezebel*,' said Bette later.

Throughout December and into January, while Jack Warner

howled about the costs of retakes and overtime, director Wyler held steadfast to his creative standards. Bette complained too, but not to Wyler. Wearing slacks under her crinolines, she filmed the final night scenes in a swamp set up on the back lot. The action called for her to wade through the swamp, dart past a roadblock, to eventually reach the bedside of her plague-stricken lover. After the scene was shot five times Wyler said he was not satisfied with the appearance of cold, damp Bette. 'She looks like she merely stepped in a puddle,' he stated. Then grabbing a shovel of wet mud, he threw it at the actress. 'Now we're in business,' the director said.

On January 27, 1938, five weeks and $250,000 over budget, *Jezebel* was completed. That night Bette took to her bed, suffering from bronchitis and nervous exhaustion.

On March 3, the film was screened in Hollywood, with David Selznick in attendance. That night he sent Jack Warner a telegram, stating: 'The picture is permeated with characterizations, attitudes and scenes which resemble *Gone With the Wind*.' Warner replied with a cable of his own, thanking the producer for his 'splendid interest'. A week later *Jezebel* opened at the Radio City Music Hall in New York City. Calling Bette 'one of the wonders of Hollywood', the National Board of Review deemed her performance as Julie Marsden to be 'the peak of her accomplishments.' Described as 'Popeye the magnificent', she appeared two weeks later on the cover of *Time*. The film had 'things that smacked of *Gone With the Wind*,' the magazine said, predicting that it could slow Mr. Selznick's epic down to a breeze, and that the only one who might play Scarlett O'Hara after Bette Davis's performance was Mr. Paul Muni.

'A cheap shot!' said Bette, preferring to ignore all comparison between her Julie and Scarlett O'Hara. Author Margaret Mitchell seemed to agree. 'I liked it [*Jezebel*] so much, but have found so few people who agree with me,' said Mitchell. 'I did not see similarities between it and *Gone With the Wind*, except for costumes and certain dialogue, but I do not feel I have a copyright on hoop skirts or hot-blooded Southerners.'

With the success of *Jezebel*, and befitting her stature, at last, as a bona-fide Hollywood star, Bette moved into a rented estate in Coldwater Canyon, 'with tennis court, swimming pool, wide sunny

patio and porches and plenty of room for the household schnauzers.'
During that summer it was announced she would play Judith
Traherne, the tragic heroine in *Dark Victory*. After playing three
bitches in a row, Bette said she was 'desperate to play a sympathetic
character.' Budgeted at two million dollars, the studio announced
that every effort would be made to add authenticity to the character
of the rich, indulgent society girl who finds peace and humility
when she discovers she is dying from brain cancer. In her column,
Louella Parsons reported that the studio had telephoned London,
to see if Dr. Sigmund Freud, 'probably the greatest psychoanalyst
alive', would come to Burbank to act as technical adviser on the
film. (It is not known if Freud responded.)

Bette was also pleased when she was told that she could have the
leading man of her choice, Spencer Tracy. She and Tracy shared
the same birthday, April 5th. Consummate professionals, dedicated
to the craft of acting, they had worked together once before, in *20,000
Years in Sing Sing*, in 1933. He had been 'fascinated by her odd unpredictable gaiety.' She was attracted to his Irish looks and intensity.
Spencer told her then, 'You know, you could be the best actress in
pictures today. No, I'll correct that. You *are* the most talented.' 'Damn
right,' Bette agreed; 'but who are we against so many?'

She planned to make another film with the actor again. *Dark
Victory* was to be that script. But when producer Hal Wallis tried
to borrow him from MGM, the answer came back that Tracy was
unavailable. He was taken, professionally and privately, by Joan
Crawford, which ultimately led Bette to comment acidly, 'She slept
with every male star at MGM except Lassie.'

JOAN'S SEX LIFE

*Joan and I began at Metro together. She was such a pretty girl. All of the
men wanted to [bleep] her. And most of them did.'*

A fellow MGM actress

Joan Crawford was never a hypocrite about sex. 'I like it,' she said,
'and it likes me.' Her physical conquests, like Catherine the Great,
were said to be in the thousands, not counting repeats.

In Hollywood in the late 1920s, when Joan became a star, many Hollywood women resented her, not only because she slept with their husbands and boyfriends, but because she 'was better in bed than they were.' Douglas Fairbanks, Jr., always a snazzy dresser, was halfway home it was said after his first night with Joan when he realized he was barefoot. 'We were in heat all the time,' said Joan, referring to the first year of their marriage. Then Clark Gable caught her physical attention. He, like Joan, could be 'savage in his lust', although in later years she told friends she preferred to distract him from the bedroom because he 'wasn't too hot in the sack.' ('Pa *was* a lousy lover,' his delectable wife, Carole Lombard, agreed.)

'Thank God I'm in love again,' said Joan when she met Franchot Tone. 'Now I can do it for love and not my complexion.' Tone, it was said, had lots of East Coast culture, but only the basic sexual expertise; exchanges were made. 'He gave her class and she gave him ass, and Tone never went home again,' was a popular rhyme of the time.

Crawford had an X-rated imagination, actress Joan Fontaine believed. Fontaine had a small role in *No More Ladies* in 1935. She recalled one afternoon when the famous Russian actor Ivan Lebedeff paid a call on the star in her dressing room. 'In ten minutes Ivan came pelting out, white of face,' said Fontaine. 'He rushed over to me. In shock, he blurted out, "Poor Joan! She's just told me that after her tragic life with men, she can no longer find sexual satisfaction unless she is tied to a bedpost and whipped!" '

Fontaine said she chuckled, knowing that Joan was inspired by a recent book, *Psychopathia Sexualis*.

Crawford was true to Franchot Tone, in the Hollywood sense of fidelity, which meant that during the production of a movie she could, in the interests of art, surrender herself emotionally and physically to her leading man, or, if it led to better work, to her director or producer. The latter included Joseph L. Mankiewicz, writer and producer of many Crawford films in the late 1930s. Mankiewicz, who was responsible for some classic W.C. Fields repartee, including 'my little chickadee', first captured Joan's unbridled glee when, reading from his script he came to the line: 'I could build a fire by rubbing two boy scouts together.' It was his youth, charm, and intellect, and his ease in handling capricious actresses that led to his producing six of Joan's films, some of them terrible bombs. 'She did what she was told,' he informed this writer. He made her feel relaxed, Joan claimed: 'I was madly in love with him and it was lovely. He gave me such a feeling of security, I felt I could do anything in the world.'

It was Joe Mankiewicz who introduced Crawford to his former college roommate Spencer Tracy. The actor, not yet a star, was cast second to Joan in *Mannequin*, a teary tale of a girl from the Lower East Side (Crawford with an Upper East Side accent) who falls in love with a rich industrialist, played by Tracy. To him the assignment was just another job and Crawford another glamour dame from Metro's assembly line of stars.

True to her tradition of hyperbole, she was far more effusive in her remarks on her current co star. 'He is the finest actor out here,' she told one reporter. 'Everything he does is effortless. I'll certainly have to work hard to keep up with him.'

During the filming it was Tracy who had to work hard, to keep Crawford from heisting the film. Describing her as 'cold-hearted . . . a high-class thief,' he said he never saw 'anyone steal as many scenes as she.' Soon he was enjoying the challenge of upstaging and ribbing her. He told her his favorite actresses were Luise Rainer and Bette Davis. While she fussed with her hair in between setups, he cautioned her: 'Don't bother combing your hair, dearie. Nobody is going to look at it anyway.' Offstage, while she was being made up for the kissing scenes, he chomped on an onion; in their close-ups he stood on her toes.

Joan of course retaliated. She called him 'Slug', and 'a shanty mick'. One day, when he was filming, she had his trailer decorated with colored lights. 'A tribute to your ego,' she told him. She had 'spunk,' Tracy declared.

During the filming of *Mannequin*, Joan came down with pneumonia. When she recovered, at the suggestion of her doctor she visited the Riviera Country Club, 'for the fresh air.' Among the polo players at the club was Spencer Tracy, who helped Joan overcome her fear of horses. He gave her riding lessons. She bought a horse and named him Secret, the status of their affair, in full sprint at this time. Tracy, a Catholic theology major, was said to be 'besotted' with the more sexually aggressive and experienced Joan. They met on the sly (he was married too), at the studio, the club, and at a friend's ranch in the valley. When *Mannequin* was completed, they performed on radio together, and Tracy was set for Joan's next film, *The Shining Hour*. But during the hiatus Tracy started to drink, and the affair turned sour.

'Sober, he was a giant,' she said. 'Drunk, he was vicious, ugly and *mean*.' He lashed out at her acting and ridiculed her attention to 'the phony-baloney stuff,' such as posing and signing autographs for fans. 'She likes to have them follow her when she goes shopping,' mocked Spencer. He unnerved her so while riding at the club one day that she pulled sharply on her horse. Secret stopped short and Joan somersaulted over his head, landing on her derriere. 'No horse could do that to me,' said Joan. 'I climbed back on and rode for forty minutes. The next day I rode again for half an hour. Then I said to the trainer, "Okay, now you can sell him." '

That night she gave Tracy an ultimatum. He had a choice. It was her or the booze. Tracy went for the ninety-proof. The next day she called Joe Mankiewicz and told him Tracy was out of her next film. He was now free to go to Warner's, to make *Dark Victory* with Bette Davis. But Spencer declined this assignment. He said he wanted a break from 'screwy actresses' and went instead to Twentieth Century Fox to work with the all-male cast of *Northwest Passage*.

BETTE'S SEX LIFE

'Sex was God's joke on human beings,' said Bette Davis in her memoirs, which led Joan Crawford to suggest, 'I think the joke's on her.'

When it came to her private life, Bette, unlike Crawford, preferred to keep the important details away from the press. She had been married for four years before most of the public even knew her husband's name. He was Harmon (Ham) Nelson and the two had met during her school years at Cushing Academy.

Tall and quiet, he had worked as a musician in New York while indulging in an ardent correspondence with Bette. In August of 1932, on one of his visits to Los Angeles, her mother pushed for a wedding.

'I was too high-strung, from too much work and no play,' said Bette, 'so Mother insisted I marry Ham and lose my virginity.'

Accompanied by her mother, the couple drove to Yuma, Arizona and were married by a justice of the peace. After the ceremony they drove right back to L.A. That night (without her mother) in a hotel at the beach, Bette had her first sexual experience. She compared it to a powerful drug and was so impressed with the naked body, she later conferred her groom's middle name, Oscar, on Hollywood's highest honor – the Academy Award – which, Bette said, had a similar rear end to her husband.

There were frequent separations for Bette and Ham during the first years of their marriage. While he pursued a career on the road, playing in big bands, she continued her quest for stardom in Hollywood. In his absence she developed an active sexual fantasy life, which led to some heady crushes on her leading men, including George Brent, Leslie Howard ('The only leading lady who didn't sleep with my husband was Bette Davis,' said a presumably grateful Mrs. Howard), and Franchot Tone. The latter, like Gable and Spencer Tracy, had already been taken by Joan Crawford, which led Adela Rogers St. Johns to later comment, 'Bette had the fantasies, while Joan had the actual physical goods in her bed. It's no wonder she despised her.'

Bette's affair with William Wyler was said to be her first official extra-marital excursion. Her marriage to Ham was in trouble at the time. She had grown to loathe the qualities in him she once loved. His career kept him on the road, when she needed him at home. When he stayed at home, playing in an orchestra at the Hollywood Hotel, she asked him why he wasn't on the road, becoming a popular success like Benny Goodman or Harry James. Ham was deep and silent, a New England man, which is why she had married him. But now, as a working star, when she came home from the studio, 'ready to explode,' he didn't seem to comprehend the hell she was going through, which made her scream all the more.

With those odds, it was no wonder, when the director of *Jezebel*, William Wyler, bullied and pushed and challenged Bette Davis, that she fell madly in love with him. 'It was a time of intense work and intense passion,' she said. 'My life would never be the same again.'

Throughout the summer of 1938, as *Jezebel* continued to bring in fresh acclaim for Davis, her affair with William Wyler continued. She said he wanted to marry her. She was apprehensive. Unlike 'poor weak Ham', Wyler was capable of controlling not only her will, but the most important thing in life – her work. 'I was afraid his domination would affect my career,' she said. 'He was capable of taking complete charge and I was petrified. The relationship was tempestuous to the point of madness and I resisted the loss of my sovereignty to the end.'

The actress would later tell her daughter she had another reason for not marrying the director. 'Her biggest concern was that Wyler was Jewish,' said B.D. Hyman. 'She didn't want children who had a Jewish father. When I married my husband that was one of her loudest objections.'

Her eventual break with Wyler came that September, said Bette. He wrote her a letter. It contained an ultimatum. If she didn't marry him then and there, he intended to wed another the following Wednesday. Bette, still angry with him over their latest collision, did not open the letter until a week later. As she read the letter, an announcement came over the radio. That morning in Los Angeles, William Wyler had married Margaret Tallichet, a beautiful young actress he had met five weeks earlier. Naturally, Bette burst into tears. She was unable to return to the studio for several days. She refused to see anyone. 'She realized that not opening the letter was the most serious mistake of her life,' said author Charles Higham. 'It is extraordinary to reflect that her next picture with Wyler was . . . *The Letter*.'

A heartbreaking story, that's for sure, but according to fresh sources, some important details were left out. 'Willie never married on the rebound,' said a friend of the director. 'He was madly in love with Margaret Tallichet and stayed married to her for forty years.' Second, Bette's passion was already transferred to another, to none other than that legendary Lochinvar of the Hollywood skies and bedrooms, Howard Hughes.

BETTE AND THE KINKY TYCOON

Always a lover of dogs, Bette Davis had been asked to be the hostess of a fund-raiser for Tailwagger's, a hospital and shelter for stray canines in Los Angeles. She agreed and told the organization that they should take advantage of her newfound popularity by publicizing the event in the pages of *Life* magazine. The fund-raiser became a black-tie dinner-dance at the Beverly Hills Hotel and with the prestige and exposure of the national magazine behind it, some of Hollywood's biggest stars attended. Other concerned dog-lovers present were Errol Flynn, Randolph Scott, Norma Shearer, Jimmy Stewart, Miriam Hopkins, Joel McCrea, Joan Blondell with husband Dick Powell, and Lupe Velez with husband Johnny Weissmuller. After dinner the guests, led by Bette, were playing musical chairs when a late arrival appeared. It was the millionaire-turned-pilot-turned-movie-producer, Howard Hughes, wearing a rumpled tuxedo.

Since he was a lover of neither dogs, formal affairs, nor *Life* magazine, the presence of the eccentric young man at the well-publicized event surprised many. But Hughes had his motives. He was to the 1930s and 1940s what Warren Beatty would be to the 1960s and 70s. Rich, handsome, and physically endowed, the tycoon was an avid collector of women. Not just pretty women, but gorgeous, talented, famous women. A partial list of his celebrity scores during the thirties includes Jean Harlow, Marlene Dietrich, Dolores Del Rio, Ginger Rogers, Olivia de Havilland, Paulette Goddard, Katharine Hepburn, but *not* Joan Crawford. Howard once expressed his desire to date Joan, in front of her current husband, Doug Fairbanks, Jr. 'He boasted, in his quiet Texas drawl, that he could offer her "a *very* big present" if she went out with him,' said Doug Jr., who never liked him after that. Joan disliked

Hughes for her own reasons. He was indiscriminate, she felt. 'Howard would fuck a tree if it moved,' she said.

At the Tailwagger's party that night, Hughes was introduced to Bette and agreed to pose with her for the *Life* photographer. He apologized for missing the dinner. He was working on a plane, he said, for the government. With that Bette took Howard by the arm and brought him into the hotel's huge kitchen where she ordered a four course meal for his sustenance.

Hughes sent Bette flowers the next day, and called the day after. He asked her if she would be interested in seeing his twin-motored monoplane, in a hangar outside of Los Angeles. She was. On the way home that evening they stopped for supper. She was surprised to find how shy and self-conscious he was. He never made a pass. Driving her home he asked if he could call her again. She gave him her direct number at the studio.

'A bat by night,' Hughes had different moves and strategies for different women. Hedy Lamarr said he had offered her ten thousands dollars to pose nude, for a rubber dummy he wanted to mold and then sleep with. 'Why not sleep with me, the real thing?' Hedy asked. 'Because you are too good for me,' he replied. Another MGM starlet of this period, Lana Turner, said that when Hughes was pursuing her he expressed his 'preference for oral sex.' She politely said she wasn't interested. 'That didn't seem to bother him,' said Lana. 'He'd come to my house just to sit and talk with my mother.'

On his third date with Bette Davis he confessed that his love for her could never be physically consummated. He explained that his recently terminated romance with the haughty and independent Katharine Hepburn had lowered both his self-esteem and his sexual performance. Author Charles Higham said Hughes suffered from 'recurrent ejaculatory impotence'. The condition was so acute, that no cure seemed possible. The challenge to Bette was irresistible.

Their affair was brief but memorable. They met at his hotel for drinks and quiet conversation. During the day Howard would sometimes fly over and buzz her house with his plane, a daring tactic he had also used on Katharine Hepburn. Bette became brave also. She told close friends of her romance with the adventurous tycoon, and that she managed to help him overcome his impotence. For her own dark reason, she also told her husband, perhaps to torment him. One night, according to Higham, while Hughes was visiting Bette at home, Ham was outside, parked in a sound truck on a side street. He had the house bugged. 'After listening awhile to his wife and Hughes struggling to achieve some sort of a climax,' Ham went running into the house. He burst into the bedroom. Hughes swung at him. Bette went into hysterics. Ham told the couple he had recorded their lovemaking and, to cover his grief, plus miscellaneous expenses, he was charging the tycoon seventy thousand dollars for the recordings.

'Deadly afraid of his potency problems being made known to his macho friends,' the *San Francisco Examiner* reported that Hughes considered hiring a professional killer, to take care of Ham, who advised friends that if he were killed, the tycoon would be responsible. So the money was paid, the recordings were destroyed, and Howard's affair with Bette was terminated.

In late September 1938 Davis sent a telegram to the International News Service. She told them that she and her husband had 'decided to take a vacation from each other.' There would be no divorce. 'I am a New England Yankee, we don't believe in divorce,' she said. On November 22 a second telegram was sent. 'There will not be any reconciliation,' it said. 'Harmon will apply for a divorce.' 'Why her husband will sue for divorce was not revealed by the actress,' the news agency stated. 'And she could not be reached to amplify her terse statement.' Bette did not want a divorce. Nelson did. He filed, on the usual charges, 'irreconcilable differences,' making no mention of Bette's adultery.

'He was my first real love,' she stated later. 'I remained in love with him for a long time afterwards, and was bitterly disappointed that I had failed at marriage.'

But consolations followed – professional and financial. Bolstered by her success in *Jezebel* and the imminent release of her second smash film, *Dark Victory*, Bette was the first major star signed by a new aggressive agency called MCA. Its founder, future power broker Jules Stein, would soon make her one of the highest paid stars in Hollywood. In February 1939, along with Spencer Tracy,

Bette also received the town's highest honor, the Oscar, for *Jezebel*. Her victory was twice as sweet the second time around. She said she was never surer of herself professionally. 'I was now a sovereign state demanding my own tithe – a member of the commonwealth. I had never been able to keep my mouth shut, but now mine was a voice that couldn't be ignored.' Her problem with Warner's before was quality. Now she wanted cash. '*No more peanuts*! No more haggling. *Jezebel* was a success and was bringing in the loot. I wanted my share. I *got* it.'

7

JOAN FALLS AND RISES

Letters from fans:
'Bette Davis is one of the greatest natural stars the screen has ever produced. She certainly shows up those beautiful but dumb actresses who are only interested in showing off their shapely limbs, their soulful eyes and carefully coiffured hair.'

Esme Bersach, Topeka, Kansas

A Prayer for Joan – *'It distresses me to see my idol, Joan Crawford, kept down on the lower rung of greatness. I send this prayer that the producers will stop teaming her with Gable and Robert Montgomery in chattering, noisy, fun-loving girlish parts, and cast her with someone like Fredric March.'*

Bobbie Jo Natford, Macon, Georgia

In 1938, while Bette Davis' star was rising, Joan Crawford's was on the decline. Voted number one at the box office the previous year, she had now sunk to below the top forty. It was the fault of her studio, Joan felt. They were not aggressively merchandising her films anymore. MGM put the blame on Joan, and her ever-evolving image.

'From jazz flapper to sophisticated clothes-horse, she's changed her celluloid skin a full half dozen times,' said one publication. 'Her fans are having a hard time keeping track of the many different Joans.'

The trouble began with the star's marriage to Franchot Tone, Metro believed. He screwed up the formula. They had a hot streak going with Joan and her rags-to-riches shopgirl on Park Avenue series. Then Tone told her she had the makings of a great *artiste*, that she could be Bernhardt, Garbo, and Helen Hayes rolled into one. And Joan, obsessed with self-improvement, eager for fresh applause, and always anxious to bury yesterday's persona, went along eagerly with her new husband's plans.

'You can take a whore to culture, but you can't make her think,' said Dorothy Parker, a frequent Crawford-Tone guest in 1935. That was the year Joan had a new clause inserted in her Metro contract. It stipulated that she could get away from Hollywood six months every year. That would enable the Tones to tolerate 'the superficial life you are forced to live here. It wouldn't bother us because we would have something bigger and finer waiting for us in the outside world,' said Joan.

In 1936 Joan told the press that she and Franchot were building a small theater in the east wing of her mansion. This would be used to showcase the couple, in serious plays by Ibsen and Shaw, for the after-dinner entertainment of their friends. 'How *wonderful*,' said Bette Davis, when told of Crawford's plans to play Shakespeare. 'We are all so thrilled that Joan has learned how to read.'

'I'd like to slap their faces,' said Joan when told of the comments on her highbrow aspirations. 'What do they expect me to do? Stay like Peter Pan? Remain the same boring, monotonous person all my life?'

While refusing to let the press photograph her new theater ('Do you allow photographs of your soul?'), Joan did appear with Tone in some home productions, and according to guests she showed genuine talent and promise. Emboldened by their praise and encouragement, she agreed to perform on radio as Elizabeth the First, Bette Davis' favorite historical character, which Joan played *before* Bette, with Franchot Tone as the Earl of Essex. She also played Nora in *A Doll's House*, with Basil Rathbone, and although one worthless critic commented that many of Joan's fans may have been confused as 'to *where* Joan's Nora went, after she slammed the door; to the milliner's or beauty parlor?', the star was content with this brave new step. 'Many of my fans never even heard of Ibsen or Maxwell Anderson before, and now they have,' she said with smug finesse.

'I designed my own hair styles for No More Ladies. *I experimented with braids for formal wear, curls for a gay sequence, maybe a severe coiffure for the difficult parts — wouldn't it be silly to play tragedy in a mass of ringlets?'*

Joan Crawford

That year movie fans got their first glimpse of the new Joan in *The Gorgeous Hussy*. This was her first costume drama. She played Peggy O'Neal, an innkeeper's daughter who became the friend and confidante of President Andrew Jackson. 'Peggy was gorgeous, but no hussy,' said *The New York Times*, and Joan agreed. When Jean Harlow dropped by for a visit (the two were now close friends; Joan frequently gave Jean 'Powders for her nerves'), Crawford took the time to explain her new character. 'She was a remarkable woman, very intelligent, and before her time. She was a *suffragette*.'

'Spell it,' said Harlow.

On the set of *The Gorgeous Hussy*, her co star, Melvyn Douglas, described Joan's mammoth new dressing room. It was the perfect facsimile of a New England house, he said, 'complete with picket fences, grass mats and a steeply sloping roof; built presumably to withstand the weight of whatever northeastern snows might accumulate inside the studio.' Making her grand entrance, in costume, Joan greeted Douglas 'in a gracious and distinctly Southern manner, less as if I was a fellow player than a guest in her home.' This was a surprise to the actor, who had heard stories of Joan 'being a hail-fellow-well-met sort of person whose language was not exactly sanitary.' She remained the perfect lady throughout filming, he stated, but when they met again, for another film in 1938, 'she had again become rough, bluff and hearty.'

Joseph Mankiewicz, Crawford's producer and intermittent lover during these years, also remembered the many personas displayed by Joan. 'You'd have to watch the way she came in,' he told author Kenneth Geist. 'If Joan was wearing a pair of slacks, that meant you could slap her on the ass and say "Hiya Kid. You getting much?" In turn she'd be as raucous as possible. She could come back the next day wearing black sables and incredible sapphires, and by Jesus, you'd better be on your feet and click your heels, kiss her hand and talk with the best British accent you had; but never in any way indicate she was different in any respect from the way she was yesterday because the following day she'd come in in a dirndl or a pinafore and you'd be down on the floor playing jacks with her.'

'That was a telling difference between her and Bette Davis,' said director Irving Rapper. 'Unlike Joan, Bette was seldom affected by the schizophrenia that comes from acting, from playing so many different roles. Bette always had the strength to leave her character behind on the soundstage.'

'I never got lost in a role,' said Davis. 'Actresses who do that are just plain silly. I had no need to escape into someone else's persona. I was always Bette Davis watching herself become the character.'

Although *The Gorgeous Hussy* failed in theaters, Crawford's next venture, playing a frivolous runaway heiress in *Love on the Run* opposite Clark Gable, was a success, and it enabled her to play the grand lady again, in a remake of a Norma Shearer picture entitled *The Last of Mrs. Cheyney*. Critic Cecilia Ager, who had earlier taken Bette Davis to task for her sulky starlet performance in *Parachute Jumper*, examined Crawford's Anglo-enunciation as the British Fay Cheyney. 'It is comforting to see in *The Last of Mrs. Cheyney*, that Joan Crawford has at last attained the manner she's been striving for,' Ager observed. 'Now she quietly looks any actor, no matter how English, straight in the eye, confident of the mastered casualness of her own pronunciation. No more do "beans" for "beens" jut out from her speech naked and terrified; no more do unresolved trimmings distract from the compact and self-contained silhouette of her clothes. Instead of the mark of self-doubt that used to be – now Miss Crawford goes about doing right things, wearing right things, with deafening poise.'

Intent on making two lofty strikes in a row, Crawford followed *Mrs. Cheyney* with *The Bride Wore Red* that same year. Based on the Molnar play, *The Girl From Trieste*, the script was brought to Joan's attention by Franchot Tone. He recommended a director, Dorothy Arznar, who had recently worked with Katharine Hepburn on *Christopher Strong*. Arznar stated she had been signed to do *The Girl from Trieste* with Luise Rainer. 'I was out scouting locations, when

I heard Luise Rainer was suspended, for marrying a communist,' she said. 'Joan would replace her in the movie, which was now called *The Bride Wore Red*. I knew that would be synthetic, but Mister Mayer knelt down, with those phony tears in his eyes, and said: "We'd be eternally grateful to the woman who brings Crawford back." ' With Crawford aboard, the Molnar story was rewritten at Mayer's command.

The lead character was changed from a jaded prostitute who goes straight, to a beautiful but slightly cynical cabaret singer. 'It's the story of a girl who steps on a lot of faces to get to the top,' Joan explained. With sets by Cedric Gibbons, hairstyles by Crawford, and gowns by Adrian, including the ten thousand dollar, thirty-five pound red-beaded title number, *The Bride Wore Red* opened in October 1937.

'Sharp proof of fans' taste was found in its reception,' said the *Los Angeles Times*, 'it flopped resoundingly.' 'Nothing can conceal the underlying shabbiness,' said *The New York Times*, and a short time later Joan Crawford was voted box-office poison by the National Theater Distributors of America.

'How can I be the Queen one year, then washed up the next?' lamented Joan, although husband-mentor-co star Franchot Tone viewed the poison list (which also included the names of Katharine Hepburn and Marlene Dietrich) for what it was – 'bullshit'. The timing was fortuitous, he told his grieving wife: they would revert to their original plan, to leave Hollywood and live part-time in New York, where they could pursue more prestigious work, in the legitimate theater.

'No!' Joan reportedly wailed. 'We made those plans when I was a *star*. I can't move to New York and be a nobody.'

Joan Crawford has started singing opera in her dressing room and the writers next door are threatening to quit.'

Sheilah Graham, 1939

A month after she was voted box-office poison, Crawford's contract at MGM came up for renewal. She was offered a straight one-year deal at three hundred thousand dollars for two pictures. Her agent, after conferring with Joan, passed on the offer. They decided to stall and resell Joan as a brand-new talent – a singing star in the mold of Grace Moore and Jeanette MacDonald.

Crawford could always work her way around a serviceable tune. She told people she began her career as a singer in New York nightclubs. Also, in the first talkie ever made at MGM, *The Passing Show of 1929*, she sang 'I Got A Feelin' For You' (while pounding the soundstage floor with her tap shoes). Again, in 1931, in *Possessed*, in a restaurant scene Joan sang 'multilingual snatches of songs to a trio of dining guests,' prompting a nearby patron to ask, 'Say, what is this? Ellis Island?'

But it was Franchot Tone who deserved the credit for introducing Joan to 'good music'. When they married Joan discovered that Franchot had a well-developed tenor voice. It blended beautifully with her husky contralto. In 1936 their reporter-friend Jerry Asher told her fans in *Modern Screen* that 'From 4 to 6 each day the couple sing for Signor Morando, a teacher of classical music.' The great popular composer Irving Berlin had witnessed a recent lesson, said Asher, 'and came away completely amazed. Stokowski, the famous conductor, was also treated to a recital, and marvelled at their appreciation of good music.'

Joan gave up smoking for singing, resuming her old habit of chewing gum. She also had the walls of her Brentwood music room lined in cork, so her daily vocalising would not disturb the neighbors. 'Sometimes when Franchot writes, Joan plays Bach or sings the Ave Maria,' said Sheilah Graham.

With a little coaxing, Joan could be persuaded to sing at her private dinner parties. Louella Parsons told her radio fans of one magical night at Brentwood 'When Joan thrilled her dinner guests – Gary Cooper, Mr. and Mrs. Fred Astaire, Noël Coward, and Irene Hervey – with a duet from Tosca, sung with Allan Jones and accompanied by the celebrated Viennese conductor, Franz Schuller.'

On the sly, Crawford made several secret recordings at Metro, accompanied on piano by Judy Garland's music teacher, Roger Edens. She carried these disks to New York and played them for the regional leaders of her fan clubs, and for opera singer Geraldine Farrar. Everyone said: 'Go for it, Joan.'

Back in California, Joan recorded three selections with the MGM
Symphony Orchestra, again surreptitiously. She gave these records
to her agent Michael Levee, who made an appointment to see
Louis B. Mayer. Busy toting up the profits from other successful
musicals as *Maytime* and *The Girl of the Golden West*, Mayer took the
time to hear Levee's new singing discovery. 'Who is she?' asked
Mayer, very impressed.

'It's Joanie,' said Levee, whereupon Ida Koverman, Mayer's
secretary, buzzed to say that Miss Crawford had arrived.

Father and daughter embraced in tears. That settled, Mayer
was ready to talk terms for a new singing contract for Joan. But
first, she had a confession to make to L.B. In a moment of madness
the previous evening, while Virginia and Darryl Zanuck were at
her house for dinner, she had played her recordings for the 20th
Century-Fox mogul. Zanuck was thrilled of course, and made her
an offer to join his studio, where Shirley Temple was currently
raking in the cash from *her* musicals. 'But what did you say?' asked
Papa Mayer. 'I told him,' said Joan, bowing her head, 'that my
first loyalty was to my family, to you . . . [head raised] . . . if the
terms are favorable.'

Crawford was given a fresh 5-year contract with Metro, at
$250,000 a year, with twelve weeks off every year, exclusive radio
rights, and a clause specifying that she could be loaned out 'to
major studios only.'

A costly musical extravaganza was announced as her next
picture. Joan would star in the one-million dollar production of *Ice
Follies of 1939*, with James Stewart and Lew Ayres as love interests,
the entire International Ice Capades as back-up, and 6 new songs
composed specifically for her singing debut. On July 31, 1938,
while the picture was in production, the *Los Angeles Times* reported
that "Another edition of the new Joan Crawford series is almost
ready. This, the latest of a dizzying number of metamorphoses,
will show Miss Crawford as a singer of serious music.'

'It's a swell voice,' said another reporter, 'with a range of two
octaves, and a couple of notes at each end to spare. All Joan has
to do is decide whether or not she is going to be an operatic mezzo-
soprano or a torchy contralto.'

'Crawford's singing is going to be as sensational as Garbo talking,' a publicist for the picture told Hedda Hopper, who announced that Joan was scheduled to perform at the Metropolitan Opera House in New York that Fall, when the new movie was scheduled for release.

Unfortunately, the world and her fans never got to judge Joan's musical talent for themselves. In post-production four of her six songs from *Ice Follies* were cut, and on the two remaining her voice was dubbed. 'It was sabotage,' Crawford said. Her singing and years of practice were eliminated because of the threat she posed for the studio's other singing sensation, Jeanette MacDonald. *Ice Follies of 1939* had the same plot and co star (Lew Ayres) as MacDonald's latest musical, *Broadway Serenade*. 'They knew all that when we were going in,' said Joan, 'but then Miss MacDonald heard my singing. She had no idea I was so good. She told Mr Mayer that there wasn't room for both of us at the same studio. Mayer could not afford to lose Jeanette. Her movies were still very popular. Something had to give. Unfortunately it was my songs.'

'It stinks,' Joan told reporters of *Ice Follies of 1939*. She wouldn't talk about the picture, she said, but she had other news for them. With a heavy heart, she announced she was divorcing her second husband, Franchot Tone.

The breakup surprised few. The signs had been scattered around Hollywood for two years. His once-promising film career had been reduced to playing second and third leads to his wife in her starring pictures. In *The Gorgeous Hussy* his part came to twenty-six lines. When he balked, L.B. Mayer insisted that they needed 'an important actor to walk off into the sunset with Joan Crawford.' He did the part but pouted and 'wouldn't speak to me for days,' Joan complained. In the next Crawford picture, *The Bride Wore Red*, he had a co starring role, but it was that of the village postman.

'Sensitive husbands don't like second billing,' said Joan of Tone, who began to drink. 'Vodka zombies,' said Ed Sullivan. Joan said his drinking affected their sex life (and no doubt, her complexion). Once or twice, she said, he beat her up. She loved the guy, and they always made up, *after* Franchot 'knelt before her, made a dutiful recital of his misdeeds and begged for her forgiveness.'

'She humiliated the poor bastard,' said Bette Davis.

It was Franchot's sexual forays that eventually unnerved Joan. She told Katharine Albert that she had followed him one night and found him in the arms of a cheap starlet. 'It wasn't the cheating that bothered me,' said Joan. 'It was the possibility that the girl could blackmail us.'

In June 1938, while she was making *Ice Follies*, Tone moved out of Crawford's Brentwood mansion. Not long after his contract was terminated by MGM. Among the few who rallied to his side was Bette Davis. She called the actor and asked if he cared to work with her in *The Sisters*, due to start filming that month at Warner's. Tone passed once more on Bette. He was moving to New York, to work in the theater he told her. One month later, Joan announced their official 'trial separation'. In September she filed for divorce. In April 1939, a week before the divorce hearing she flew to New York to meet with Tone. They dined and danced at The Stork Club, and appeared very cozy at the opening of Bette Davis' new film, *Dark Victory*, at Radio City Music Hall. Their divorce was still going through, Joan told Walter Winchell; they would be represented in court by proxy. 'This is *our* way of being civilized,' the star added.

'Well, it's all disgusting,' said Florence Foster Parry of the *Pittsburgh Press*. 'It served the purpose of getting the divorce on the front pages again – alongside the collapse of Spain and the push of Hitler.'

Then Joan was told that at least one party had to appear in court or the hearing would be canceled. 'It is appalling,' said Foster Parry in her update, 'that Miss Crawford, with the tears of the Last Reunion scarcely dry, must submit to the embarrassment, the inconvenience, the indignity of a personal appearance in court.'

On the day of the divorce, accompanied by her agent, Joan appeared costumed, wearing a tailored coat and a wide-brimmed hat that, she told reporters, necessitated her being up until three in the morning, 'steaming the brim just right, so it fell over the top half of her face.' She told the judge that Tone had grown 'sullen and resentful,' and the decree was granted. 'No more marriages,' she said to the press gathered in the hallway, emphasizing that she was not removing men and their physical charms from her life forever, because 'Sex is part of what keeps me young.'

'I like Bette Davis. I think she's a real actor, don't you? I never liked Joan Crawford at all. Never. I hate fakes. She was an awful fake. A washerwoman's daughter. I'm a terrible snob, you know.'

Louise Brooks to John Kobal

'It is sad that one of Joan Crawford's biggest disappointments is that she's not in the dramatic category with Bette Davis and Margaret Sullavan. When people say to her: "If you could only do stories like Bette Davis does", Joan sees red'.

A column item in 1938

THE WOMEN

In March 1939 columnist Sheilah Graham reported, 'After three misses in a row, if Joan Crawford doesn't come up with a hit picture soon, she will be joining Luise Rainer in the Hall of Forgotten Stars at Metro.' But Joan at this time had already planned her comeback. For her next MGM picture she intended to forsake music, culture, and tears. She was ready to infringe on Bette Davis' territory by playing her first authentic bitch as Crystal Allen in Clare Booth Luce's *The Women.*

Playing a scheming, hard-as-nails husband-stealer would not require enormous research for Joan, Hollywood believed. It was the news that she had agreed to work with *and* take second-billing to her long-time rival, actress Norma Shearer, that intrigued and delighted all.

In her mellow moments, Joan liked to refer to Norma Shearer as 'Miss Lotta Miles'. The title referred to Shearer's employment as a model for a rubber tire company, during the early days of her career. Norma began in films in 1920 and was already a star in 1925 when Crawford arrived at MGM. It was Norma's friendship, and 1927 marriage to L.B. Mayer's first lieutenant, Irving Thalberg, that led to her prominence in pictures, Crawford declared. 'She doesn't love him, you know,' she told Dorothy Manners. 'She got married for the sake of her career, much like a nun who gives herself to Christ, to fill her inner needs.'

Throughout the 1930s, Crawford complained frequently that because of Norma she was forever locked into the number two spot when it came to good scripts and money spent. 'Big-budget costume meant Norma, low-budget ex-shopgirl, meant me.' Some of the roles she lost to Shearer were Elizabeth Barrett Browning and Marie Antoinette, both popular and prestigious hits that Crawford envied; although she said she was happy she missed out on another Shearer role – that of Juliet in *Romeo and Juliet* with Leslie Howard. 'Christ,' said Joan to her pal, Constance Bennett, after the gala premiere of said film, 'I couldn't wait for those two old turkeys to die, could you?'

In August 1937, when Irving Thalberg died prematurely at age 37, it was said that two of the happiest mourners at his funeral were L.B. Mayer and Joan Crawford. Mayer, because his control and authority had been usurped by the late producer, and Joan because, with Thalberg gone, his widow would no longer have first dibs on scripts at the studio. But she soon found out Norma carried more clout than ever.

The next year, when Joan was desperately looking for a comeback picture, she found out the studio bought the rights to *Idiot's Delight*, which had featured her old friends the Lunts on Broadway. Clark Gable was slated to play Alfred's part and Joan knew she was perfect for the Lynn Fontanne role of the pretentious ex-hoofer stranded in a hotel in Europe on the eve of World War II. When she spoke to the producer, Hunt Stromberg, she learned that Shearer had already requested the part. Joan headed straight for Louis B. Mayer's office. 'The role calls for an ex-chorus girl,' she told the mogul. 'That's *me*! Norma can't sing. Norma can't dance. And furthermore she's cross-eyed.' Mayer explained to Joan what Norma *could* do. In his will, Thalberg left his wife his large bloc of MGM stock. If peeved, she could vote against him. So, to make Norma happy, she would continue to get first crack at all Metro properties. 'Christ,' said Joan, 'she really rode through this studio on his balls, didn't she?'

The lead role in *The Women* also went to Norma. But Mary

Haines, noble wife, was not a part that interested Joan. She wanted to play the bitch. 'When I read the script,' she said, 'my eyes and instincts went straight to Crystal. She was the meat and potatoes of the picture. The rest of the girls were cocktail canapés.' Again L.B. Mayer objected. He told Joan the role was secondary, too small for a star of her stature. 'Listen, L.B.,' she replied, 'the woman who steals Norma Shearer's husband cannot be played by a nobody.'

Mayer eventually relented. Crawford could do the picture, but not at her usual star salary. 'The son of a bitch made me agree to take a day rate. I worked for *pennies*. But that was OK, I had a hunch this role would pay off.'

The director was George Cukor, who said there were 135 speaking roles in total 'and all of them women.' Rosalind Russell was cast as the gossipy troublemaker Sylvia Fowler, Paulette Goddard as the junior adventuress, and Joan Fontaine as Phyllis, the young wife pining away in Reno for the husband she's about to divorce.

The distaff detail encompassed the entire picture said Cukor. 'Everything was female. The books in the library scene were all by female authors. The photographs and art objects were all female. Even the animals – the monkeys, the dogs, the horses – were female. I'm not sure if audiences were aware of that, but there wasn't a single male represented in the entire film, although nine-tenths of the dialogue centered around them.'

The problems in wardrobe and makeup could have been enormous, Cukor said, but 'we ran everything like boot camp. There were specific regulations and schedules everyone had to adhere to. Each department was told to be polite and to accommodate everyone within reason, but at the first sign of star temperament, I was to be called.'

A hundred coiffures were created, with no two being duplicated. Hairstylist Sydney Guilaroff, who was accustomed to working with either Shearer or Crawford, but never both at the same time, solved the dilemma by giving Joan a curly permanent, which left him more time to work with Shearer. 'Norma wore her usual "classic simplicity", do, which took two hours to achieve each morning,' said Joan. 'I was also supposed to have access to Sydney," said Rosalind Russell, 'but he got rid of that by having me wear a hat throughout the picture. At the time I thought it was a divine idea. When I saw the film I realized I was sloughed off.'

Adrian designed the clothes, which included 237 different outfits. 'Miss Shearer alone had twenty-four changes,' said the *New York Herald Tribune*. 'In one scene fifty-thousand dollars worth of real jewelry is worn by three stars. The most expensive is a bracelet and necklace set worth twenty-five thousand dollars, worn by Joan Crawford. Not to be outdone Miss Shearer is said to be wearing the most expensive *item* – a twenty-thousand dollar ring. "If you're any good at mathematics," said Rosalind Russell, "that means this costume junk I'm wearing is worth at least five thousand bucks!" '

At the director's orders, none of the players were allowed to see the costumes designed for the other actresses until they arrived on the set ready to work. This enabled Crawford to get the flashiest outfit – a sexy gold lamé gown with a jewel encrusted midriff. 'May I suggest, if you're dressing to please Stephen, not that one,' said Norma in character to Joan. 'My husband doesn't like circus clothes.' 'Thanks for the tip,' said Joan as Crystal, 'but when anything I wear doesn't please Stephen, I take it off.'

The largest set, designed by Cedric Gibbons, was the beauty salon used in the opening scene. It ran for thirteen hundred square feet, with twenty-seven separate beauty departments occupied by gabbing females. During the filming of these scenes, the traffic of the stars' entourage, despite the director's plan, became congested. 'There were so many personal maids, assistants, and makeup artists on the soundstage,' said a production aide, 'that the completion of the scene resembled a varitable "subway run", as each "crew" hurried to its own victim, to prepare her for the next take.'

The fight scene, with Paulette Goddard and Rosalind Russell kicking and pummeling each other in a bull pen, took three days to film. Goddard complained to *Life* that she had black-and-blue marks over 90 percent of her body, while Russell suffered from a dislocated shoulder.

Joan Crawford too had her trials. She lost eleven pounds in the bubble bath, talking over the telephone. 'It took ten hours to shoot,' she told *Silver Screen*. 'The suds lasted only fifteen minutes under the hot lights. Once, the water began to leak out and the crew had to toss me a towel to clothe myself. It could have been *so* embarrassing.'

In April 1939, during production of *The Women*, Crawford and Norma Shearer appeared in a duel of glares on the cover of *Look* magazine. 'They Don't Like Each Other,' the caption read. As the rumors of 'soundstage snarlings' escalated, L.B. Mayer, furious that anyone would talk publicly of dissension in *his* family, ordered that the set be closed to all press – except for Thorton Delaney of the *New York Herald*. Delaney, who went over the head of publicity, a few AD's, and came away convinced there was nothing to the rumors of gouging, scratching, biting and body checking, which made the production the roughest sport in Hollywood. He met with Shearer and Crawford. 'See, darling,' said Crawford, linking Norma, 'we are close friends.' Norma, gently extricating herself from Joan, said, 'Friends. And professionals.'

'It was like a fucking zoo at times,' Crawford commented later on. 'If you let down your guard for one minute you would have been eaten alive.'

AP reporter Bob Thomas said that Joan herself was not above perpetrating acts of petty malice. During the filming of Norma Shearer's close-ups, she refused to meet Norma's eyes while feeding her the lines. And then there was the incident with the knitting needles. Joan had positioned herself in a chair at the side of the camera. She was making an afghan bedcover, which required large needles. As Norma tried to concentrate on her close-ups for the camera, Joan knitted faster. The loud clicking of Joan's needles distracted Norma. She complained. Joan kept knitting, faster and louder, until George Cukor ordered her off the set. 'She could be a willful, spoiled child,' said Cukor. 'Not that Norma was an angel either. Or Rosalind Russell. I had some tedious arguments with Miss Russell. She wanted to give a different performance to what I had in mind for her character.'

'George and I had some loud arguments,' Russell agreed. 'I saw my character in a different light from him. I wanted to play Sylvia as a brittle sophisticated Park Avenue matron. George wanted me to be loud and exaggerated. Of course he was absolutely right.'

So right in fact, that when Russell saw the first week's rushes of her performance she asked for billing *above* the title, with Shearer and Crawford. When her request was denied, she became ill. 'I let it be known that I was going to be under the weather for quite a long time,' said Russell. Lying in the sun and looking up at the sky when executive Benny Thau called, Roz pleaded ennui. On the fourth day of her strike, when Thau told her that Norma had agreed to her co star billing, the executive asked, 'Do you think you'd feel well enough to come to work tomorrow?' Russell replied 'Hmmmm. I'll make a stab at it.'

Laszlo Willinger was assigned to photograph the stars for publicity stills. He said both Shearer and Crawford had print approval. 'Shearer would look at the prints first and say, "Gee, this is a beautiful picture of me, but I really don't like the way Joan Crawford looks." And then Joan would have her turn, and we'd have the same thing. It's a wonder any pictures of them were released at all.' One morning, Willinger was scheduled to shoot Shearer, Crawford, and Russell for the poster art. 'The call was for 10:00 A.M. I'm there, ready – nobody. It's ten-thirty, eleven – still nobody. Finally Rosalind Russell turns up and says, "Sorry I'm late." I told her, "You're not late. You're the first one here." ' With a crew of ten on hand waiting, Willinger walked outside and saw Norma Shearer's car drive by. 'A little behind her was Joan Crawford, who also slowed down, looked out, and drove on. I thought "What the hell's going on here?" I called publicity director Howard Strickling and told him, "There are two stars outside driving around and not coming in." He said, "Don't you know what they're doing? Shearer isn't going to come in before Crawford, and Crawford isn't going to come in before Shearer. The only thing I can do is stand in the middle of the street and stop them." Which he did.'

In August, fanzine writer Ruth Waterbury said she feared for Joan Crawford's hard performance in *The Women*. 'She is being as brittle and brutal as Bette Davis at her brittle best,' said Waterbury. 'But when we accept Bette Davis with free admiration for this type of feminine piracy, will we like Joan as one?'

In September the critics gave thumbs up to Joan's first turn as a bitch. 'Norma's "good woman" is another bit of typecasting, but Joan Crawford as the husband-stealing chippie deserves high praise,' said the *New York Post*. 'Crawford steals the show from the all-woman cast,' said *The New York Times*. 'She makes you dislike her,' said Wanda Hale of *The Daily News*. 'This may not please some of Joan's adoring fans, but it should make Hollywood sit up and take renewed interest in her acting ability.'

The Women was one of MGM's top-grossing films of 1939 (second in profit to *Gone With the Wind*). The satisfaction for Crawford was enormous. 'It was a double victory for Joan,' said Cukor. 'It provided her comeback, and proved she could indeed act.' It also sent her rival Norma Shearer into retirement, Adela Rogers St. Johns believed. 'Norma never bounced back again. I think she grew tired with the fighting and the jockeying for first place. When Irving Thalberg was alive he protected her from all that. She wasn't like Joan or Bette, who thrived on elbowing their way to the front of the line.'

8

THE 1940s BEGIN

On New Year's Eve 1939, while most of America were celebrating the end of the thirties, a decade of Depression, the New Deal, Labor strikes, and union bloodbaths, a discreet, select group of Los Angeles citizens gathered at the Bel Air home of Ouida and Basil Rathbone to contribute to the British War Relief. Among the stars who responded to the cause were Bette Davis and Joan Crawford. Bette bought two tickets to the Anglo sit-down dinner and dance; Joan, with typical largesse and generosity, bought six. Bette arrived alone; Joan came with five escorts, all male.

Although a tent, with red-white-and-blue-decorated tables, had been set up on the Rathbones' spacious front lawn, a rainstorm came pelting down early in the evening and the guests were moved indoors. Crawford and her five male companions were seated at a table set up in the Rathbones' large California room when Bette entered, carrying her plate of food, a red linen napkin, and her silverware. Joan, spotting Davis, waved and called to her. 'Bette! Bette darling!' said Joan. 'Come join us.' Bette feigning deafness and swinging her famous slender hips, sashayed toward the bar. Balancing her plate, she hoisted herself onto a leather stool, and smiled at the bartender. She ordered a bourbon on the rocks, opened her silver cigarette case, took out a cigarette, and tapped the end three times on the edge of the bar. After lighting the cigarette, she inhaled, then exhaled while surveying the room. Her eyes finally came to rest on Joan Crawford, still seated with her five attentive swains and still trying to get *her* attention. 'Christ! What a *silly* bitch,' said Bette, waving Joan away. Then lifting her glass, she wished the handsome bartender 'a *very* happy New Year.'

On January 14, 1940, a party was thrown in Bette's honor, at the Trocadero night club, where she was proclaimed Woman of the Year by *Redbook*. Two weeks later she was named Queen of the Movies by *Life* (with Mickey Rooney as her King), and a third Oscar nomination (for *Dark Victory*) came in February.

The citation that elicited the most pleasure, and mirth, to Bette, came from yet another source: Hollywood's Press Association, who voted her the Female Actress Best Liked by Interviewers. Appearing in the second spot, was Joan Crawford.

It was Crawford who had always been the pro with the press. From the first time she saw her name in print, in 1925, she was hooked on the extra fame and power that the media provided. She knew their importance. The press became her personal pipeline to all those millions of fans who couldn't eat, sleep, or breathe, unless they knew every last detail of what their idol was doing. And Joan was never shy about giving news, major or minor, about herself. She was available day or night, at work or at play, for reporters and photographers. They were grateful for her cooperation, and thoughtfulness. Through Katharine Albert she learned how to court the members of the fourth estate. She memorized reporters' names, the names of their wives, and other personal data. 'She had a file system,' said a former secretary. 'In it she kept a record of everyone's birthday, important anniversaries, number of children, favorite foods and delicacies, and the topic of conversation last spoken for public consumption.'

In reverse, Bette Davis preferred to keep a cool distance from the members of the press. She was from Boston, she said, and she was brought up to believe a lady's name should appear in a newspaper only when she was born, married or died. But she was also an actress, and at the start of her career in Hollywood, she soon learned that success meant fame, which required free publicity.

In her starlet days she did the essentials – posing for pictures and giving good copy, most of it fabricated by the Warner's publicity staff. After her court defeat in England, and her eventual elevation to stardom with *Jezebel*, Bette announced she was drawing up new ground rules with reporters. She'd talk to the guys and gals of the press room, but she'd do it *her* way. Unlike Joan Crawford and the other stars of the day, she did not want to be briefed on what to say, how to say it, or the detailed background of the people she was to meet. 'Just give me their names,' she instructed. 'I don't have to know who they're married to or what they had for breakfast this morning.' When they met there would be no kissy-kissy either, no false intimacy and promises of eternal friendship after the piece was put to bed. 'I had no time for pleasantries,' she explained. 'I said what was on my mind and it wasn't always printable.'

'I hate ass-kissers and yes-men,' she told *Collier's*.

'I love and respect *all* the wonderful people I work with, regardless of rank,' said Joan Crawford.

'*How to be friends with your ex-husbands*,' said Joan in *Modern Screen*.

'*Friendly divorces are bunk!*' said Bette Davis in *Photoplay*. 'People do not divorce unless they hate each other immensely, unless they are fighting cat and dog, tooth and talon, claw and fang.' Taking Joan to task for her affectionate display with Franchot Tone on the eve of their recent divorce, Bette observed: 'Look what happens after they have made their public declaration of divorce. They go to the Trocadero that night and in a dim corner you find them all wrapped like a pretzel, *avec* photographers. A columnist, the next day, declares it is the dawn of a new understanding, the "birth of a beautiful friendship!" The whole thing is a forced unnatural attitude. You can't tell me that any man who has really loved a woman, or vice-versa, can really be friends again after a divorce. And kidding about it is like tying a pink ribbon on a machine gun.'

(In the same piece Bette asked, 'I do wish somebody would take a week off and define "mental cruelty" for me. The other day I saw where a woman said it was mental cruelty because her husband called her "a little squirt!" I thought to myself, "*Baby*, you should hear some of the things *I've* been called. And for good and sufficient reason too." ')

Due to her frankness and colorful maledictions, interviews with Bette were avidly sought – and carefully read by many, including Joan Crawford. 'She is so doggone honest. She really says what's on her mind,' said Joan.

It was during this period that Joan warmed to Bette. 'She began to talk about her a lot,' said publicist Harry Mines. 'I remember being at Joan's house when she would show Bette's movies, sometimes two in one night.'

'I went through three hankies,' said Joan, giving her reaction to Bette's *Dark Victory*. 'I couldn't stop crying for an hour after the movie ended.'

'Joan always cries a lot.' said Davis. 'Her tear ducts must be very close to her bladder.'

Bette had no time for the likes of Crawford. 'She went out of her way to avoid her,' said Joan Blondell. 'We were all at Marion Davies' beach house one night. I was with my husband, and Bette was with her mother. All was light and gay until Crawford swept into the party. You just couldn't *miss* her in those days. I loved to watch Joan putting on the dog. She was *it*, positively radiant and beautiful and all those adjectives wrapped into one. Bette was dour. When Joan glided towards us, Bette did a quick about-face and exited out the French doors to the beach.'

Adela Rogers St. Johns believed that Crawford wasn't interested in a close friendship with Bette Davis. 'She knew that Bette didn't like her, and Joan, as the world's most popular and powerful star, felt it was her duty to win her over. Certainly she tried hard enough. One day she asked me to arrange a meeting at the grill, in the Roosevelt Hotel, on a Saturday afternoon. I called Bette. She and I were working on a story, so when I mentioned lunch she agreed. Very casually I mentioned that Joan Crawford would be joining us. "*Sweet!*" said Bette. "And what will we talk about? The color of nail polish?" '

GLAMOROUS BETTE

'It seemed to me that each one coveted what the other possessed. Joan envied Bette's incredible talent, and Bette envied Joan's seductive glamour.'

George Cukor

In 1940, the idea of Bette and Joan getting together to exchange beauty secrets was not a remote possibility. This was the year when the new glamorous sophisticated Bette was launched in the pages of *Vogue* and *Vanity Fair*, with extensive fashion layouts and 'makeover tips' also featured in *Photoplay, Modern Screen*, and *Motion Picture* magazines.

The transformation was deliberate on Bette's part. Having portrayed three unattractive characters in a row, in *The Old Maid, Juarez*, and *The Private Lives of Elizabeth and Essex* ('Christ! This will play hell with my love life', she moaned after her head and eyebrows were shaved for the latter film), Bette told a reporter she was ready to forsake art and show the world, as she truly was – young and very attractive. 'While I'm young, I want to *be* young,' she said, flinging her arms outward to express vim and vigor. 'I've proved to myself I can play those older heavier roles. So from now on I intend, and you can tell everyone I said so, to play only young parts in the future.'

With the cash pouring in from her movies, the staff at Warner's were told to do everything possible to glamorize her appearance, as befitted the Queen of the Lot.

George Hurrell, the portrait photographer whose talent captured the luminous charms of Jean Harlow, Norma Shearer and Joan Crawford at MGM, was wooed to Warner's by Bob Taplinger, director of publicity. One of his first assignments was to transform Bette Davis into a vision of beauty and high chic. On hand to assist the photographer were a team of stylists, her own hairdresser, makeup artists, a dresser, and two 'personal shoppers'.

Truckloads of clothes arrived by the hour for Bette's fashion sessions with Hurrell. The racks of clothes included linen suits, cashmere sweaters, cocktail dresses, evening gowns; furs of mink, Baum Martin, a sable, silver foxes, silk culottes and polka-dot lounge-wear; but 'No slacks or swim-suits.'

'Accessories make the costume,' the star declared, making her choice from the boxes of shoes, gloves, hats, scarves, and from trays of rings, bracelets, pins and earrings.

Her hair, which went from platinum to mousy light brown to jet black (for *Juarez*) to bald (for *Elizabeth and Essex*), was now back to its natural light brown texture. Her skin – 'glowing and blemish free', owed its radiance not to sex like Joan's but to a regimen faithfully adhered to by the star. 'I always massage my face with cold cream, while sitting in a hot bath softened with bath oil,' she told *Pageant*. After drying off with a large cotton towel, 'for stimulation, and for daintiness, a brisk rub-down with eau-de-cologne follows.'

'You don't have to be beautiful,' Bette told *Cosmopolitan*, noting that 'Joan Crawford, who is far from beautiful, had maintained and even increased her popularity throughout nearly a decade.' As Lucille LeSueur, Bette went on to say Joan resembled 'a self-satisfied village siren,' but through diet and mental development she had 'swept complacency away.'

Bette neglected to add that her inner glow and extra glamour were stimulated by her desire to please the new man in her life. His name was George Brent. He had stepped in when Spencer Tracy decided not to do *Dark Victory*. 'He was the longest real romance I ever had with an actor,' said Bette. 'I was his girl for years.'

Brent was no stranger to Bette. She had admired him back in 1932 when they appeared together in *The Rich Are Always With Us*. 'I was fascinated and in love with George, but he didn't want me,' she said. 'I had to wait a few years before he felt the same way – when we made *Dark Victory*.'

Their affair lasted through the picture and 'for a long time afterwards.' It was conducted in private, however, because her divorce from Harmon Nelson was not final and because 'gazing adoringly into each other's eyes or dancing cheek to cheek at smart dinner clubs is all right for others, but definitely *not* for me,' said the private Miss Davis.

The discretion suited Brent too. It enabled him to court others, including Marlene Dietrich and Ann Sheridan, whom he later married. (When asked why her marriage to George only lasted ten months, the irrepressible Sheridan replied, 'Brent bent.')

'I often hoped he would marry *me*,' Bette complained, stating that her larger success caused jealousy on George's side. Columnist Hedda Hopper believed the green-eyed monster was in Davis' corner. At the apex of their affair, it was Hedda who said in her column, 'Current gossip is that Greta Garbo is flinging the well-known eye at George Brent. Joan Crawford is also said to have considered him a very personable young man.'

The eventual split came from a beauty poll tabulated by George. When asked by a magazine to name the ten most glamorous women in Hollywood, Brent's list included: Dolores Del Rio, Kay Francis, Greta Garbo, Marlene Dietrich, Joan Crawford, Loretta Young, Norma Shearer, Irene Dunne, Joan Blondell and Margaret Cartew (a starlet at Fox). When Davis, omitted from her lover's roster, heard of this she screamed. 'It was very harmless stuff, but not to Bette,' said Bob Taplinger. 'When she read the list, she had a fit. After all, she had gone to a lot of trouble to become glamorous. She was also having an affair with the guy and she couldn't make his list? It was over for George after that.'

'It wouldn't have *worked*,' Bette subsequently surmised. 'He was an *actor*. I always said I would never marry actors. He was very *actory* – beautiful wardrobe and he'd dye his hair.'

After replacing Brent with Charles Boyer in her new film, *All This and Heaven Too*, Bette had a brief affair with the director, Anatole Litvak (recently estranged from wife, Miriam Hopkins). The two spent weekends at Litvak's beach house in Malibu (the same house where Joan Crawford, as Mildred Pierce, would allow herself to be seduced by Zachary Scott), and during January 1940 Jimmie Fidler reported that 'Bette and the Hungarian hit Ciro's at least twice a week.' It was at the latter night spot, a short time later, that Litvak, intoxicated, appeared with the splendid, also tipsy, Paulette Goddard. 'Sitting at a ringside table, he took out her breasts and kissed them passionately,' Clifford Odets wrote in his Hollywood journal, detailing how the frisky director, banished to the outer sanctum of the bar 'suddenly disappeared, and finally was discovered under the bouffant skirt of Miss Goddard, on his knees.' Hearing this report, and sensing that his intentions towards her weren't entirely honorable, Bette Davis terminated her affair with Litvak, and was seen for a while with Tom Lewis (who would wed Loretta Young), and with Warner's publicist, Bob Taplinger, who sent her 'a gardenia a day.' She also told *Photoplay* that she was hankering for an evening of dancing with Joan Crawford's popular escort, Cesar Romero, but 'Bette was too shy to call him on the telephone.'

In spite of her outward happiness, Bette was inwardly a lonely person, *Modern Screen* decided in September 1940. 'She suffers much and can only bring peace of mind at a great cost.'

She was going crazy because she was living in a house full of women, Bette complained. There was Dell, her maid, 'who took all my explosions with the resignation of a Sicilian who lives in the shadows of Mount Etna.' There was her sister, Bobby, who lived in the shadow of Mount Bette. 'I was always the leader and Bobby was the weak follower,' she said. 'Bobby always wanted to be a star. Some people said she had more talent than I, but she never had my *guts*. She was a bore and a taker. She used to call me "the Golden Goose". When she began to realize that she wasn't going to amount to anything she had a nervous breakdown. It cost me a *fortune* to make her well. When she recovered she ran off and married an alcoholic, without my permission. [As a wedding present, Bette sent the couple a case of liquor.] After the birth of Bobby's daughter, she had another breakdown. It became very tiresome.'

The third and most formidable female in Bette's house was her 'beloved Ruthie'. But she too had changed. With Bette's success, it was Mama who went Hollywood. 'She had done her job and done it well,' Bette told writer Joan Dew. 'Now she was going to rest on my laurels, and rest in elegance. She not only became my daughter, she became a spoiled daughter. She was lovely, fractious, indolent and increasingly self-absorbed. She always spent more than I could earn, and she was indifferent to my daily struggles. I don't think she believed I worked a day once I arrived.'

Added to her pique, the star had become increasingly discontented with the citizens of Hollywood. 'Their values shocked me.

Their serious interests evaded me. The town was awash with outsized egos and rampant flunkies. There wasn't a fistful I could even have a conversation with; and none I respected.'

Bette clearly needed a rest. At her mother's orders, she left Los Angeles for New York. Traveling up the coast, she wandered through New England 'like a ghost in my old haunts.' She ended up at Peckett's Inn, in Sugar Hill, New Hampshire. Dining alone each evening, she became friendly with the handsome young assistant manager, Arthur Farnsworth. They went on drives through the countryside, and he advised her on property she wished to buy. When she left Peckett's Inn, she presented Farnsworth with a plaque for the dining-room wall. It read, 'To Arthur Farnsworth, Keeper of Stray Ladies.' 'That plaque ended up embedded in a rock over a stream in New Hampshire,' said Farnsworth's sister, Mrs. Jon De'Besche. 'They put Bette's panties over it and had an official unveiling with just the two of them.' Not long after, Farnsworth drove across the country to visit Bette. He proposed, a few times. She eventually accepted. 'At last I've found the peace I was searching for,' she said. 'I had my career and the love of a man I respected.' On New Year's Eve 1940 they were married at the home of a friend in Arizona. Bette wore white. Arriving in Los Angeles, the couple were asked to pose for photographers. 'Kiss the bride,' one called out. 'We would rather *not*,' said Bette. 'We are from New England and we don't do those sort of things in public.'

> '*Did you know there were twenty-five thousand baby girls christened with the name Joan this year? Half were called after me, and the others were named for Joan of Arc. Isn't that wonderful?*'
>
> Joan Crawford, 1940

Hot on the comeback trail, Crawford segued from the all-female cast of *The Women* into the all-male cast of *Strange Cargo*. 'Clark Gable, and nine men! I love it,' said Joan, who described her role as 'a singer-tramp, who escapes from a French penal colony with a bunch of convicts who have only two things on their minds – freedom and sex with me.'

Filmed at Pismo Beach and in the 'jungles' of Pico National Park, the location shooting was a first for Crawford. With the exception of some early silent films, she had never worked outdoors before. 'The sun usually makes me squint and cry,' she explained. Another first was the star's decision to go through the greater part of the film without makeup. 'Following the recent naturalised look of Irene Dunne and Bette Davis in pictures, Miss Crawford intends to portray her character without so much as a dab of lipstick, rouge, mascara or eye-shadow,' said a press report. (She cheated in some scenes, Joan later told *Silver Screen*. 'I used vaseline on my eyelids, eyebrows, and lips, to retain moisture. And in one scene in the jungle, using the top of an old tomato can as a mirror, I applied some brilliantine to my hair.')

Wearing one dress throughout the twenty-seven days of filming, Joan was a trouper the director stated. He made no mention of the day in the jungle when Joan, preceded by Gable, passed under a tree with an eight-foot python coiled on a branch overhead. 'That sonavabitch is *alive*!' screamed Joan, looking upward. 'Yes, but its jaws are shut tight with a rubber band,' the director explained. 'What happens if the fucking rubber band snaps?' she asked, and refused to repeat the scene.

In April 1940, when *Strange Cargo* was previewed, Joan attended the showing and experienced 'a definite sense of achievement' concerning her performance. There was one fault with the film, however: in the opening credits the name of Clark Gable came before hers. Her contract forbade this, and she asked that the prints of the picture be recalled and retitled, so that her name was first. Joe Mankiewicz, the producer, tried to explain that Gable had first billing in his current picture, a little epic called *Gone With the Wind*. His immense popularity as Rhett Butler would help them sell *Strange Cargo*, especially if his name came first.

'I don't give a shit about Rhett Butler or *Gone With the Wind*,' said Joan. 'I've got a contract. Either change it or I'll talk to my lawyers.'

Telegrams were sent to Harry Rapf, who called L.B. Mayer, who called Joan. It was such a minor matter, Mayer tried to tell Joan. She had been billed second in her last picture, *The Women*, and she got the best notices. 'That was *different*,' Crawford said. 'I *needed* that role. This time you needed *me*. You asked for Joan Crawford. You got Joan Crawford. And Joan Crawford always comes first on the marquee.'

'I have great admiration for her as an actress, but she's a slut. Her whole life is an act. She is what she is, a cheap flapper who likes to get laid.'

Louis B. Mayer

Strange Cargo, with Joan Crawford in first billing, was banned in Cleveland and Rhode Island for its 'lustful implications in dialogue and situations.' Elsewhere it was an immediate hit, and with this, her second smash hit in a row, the comeback girl behaved accordingly. For a bonus she requested a new, even more lavish dressing room, donating the old one in a public ceremony to the Boy Scouts of America.

Her love life also blossomed once more. She had a lengthy affair with Charles Martin, a journalist. 'He's a real guy. His mouth is wide and boyish and so is his grin,' said Joan, who gifted the writer with a solid-gold watch. When the affair broke up, she asked her friend Katharine Albert to retrieve the watch.

After that 'a veritable platoon' of good-looking young men marched in and out of Joan's Brentwood home and bedroom. 'She was on top again,' said her friend Harry Mines. 'That meant she had her pick of the men in town. It didn't matter if they were married, engaged, or going with someone else. When Joan beckoned they usually dropped whoever or whatever they were doing and ran to her side.'

The list included: Tyrone Power, Johnny Weissmuller, Cary Grant, Tony Martin, and Greg Bautzer. Bautzer was a lawyer, 'tall and husky, with soulful dark eyes, a tanned complexion and a flashy smile.' He was going steady with Lana Turner at the time. Lana was in love with Greg. She gave him her virginity ('I had no idea how to move or what to do,' she said), and he gave Lana her first orgasm ('I must confess I didn't enjoy it at all. I didn't even know what an orgasm was'). Lana knew Joan from MGM where she was an up-and-coming starlet. She also attended some of Joan's

Saturday night get-togethers at Brentwood. 'Those parties were all the same,' said Lana. 'After dinner the guests would be herded into a projection room to watch movies. Joan knitted constantly. During the film you could hear her needles clicking away.'

One day Joan invited Lana to drop by her house alone, to talk about something 'very important'. Sitting in the drawing room, with her knitting, Joan opened with, 'Now darling, you know I'm a bit older than you . . .' which got Lana to thinking: 'She's *quite* a bit older than me.' As Joan rambled on about life's complexities, Lana eventually cut in and impetuously asked her to get to the point. She did. 'Greg doesn't love you anymore,' she told young Lana. 'It's me he truly loves, but he hasn't figured out how he can get rid of you.'

'Get rid of me?' Lana raged. 'Trash is something you get rid of – or disease. I'm not something you get rid of.'

'Baby, I know how you feel,' said Joan. 'Be a dear . . . a good little girl, and tell him you're finished. Make it easier on yourself.'

Lana did break up with Bautzer. She was so upset she eloped to Las Vegas with Artie Shaw, the first of her seven husbands. Joan, as legend tells it, dated Bautzer exclusively for a few days, then dropped him for Jean Pierre Aumont, followed by Laird Cregar, Van Heflin, Robert Sterling, James Craig, and Robert Preston.

When asked her age preference in men, Crawford once replied, 'Oh, anyone over fifteen is OK.' Actor Jackie Cooper was two years past that when he spent some unforgettable moments with Joan. When he was a child star at MGM, his mother was a friend of Crawford's. They exchanged gifts at holidays and visited each other from time to time. When Cooper was seventeen he sometimes dropped by Joan's house, to use her badminton court. One day, hot and sweaty after a game, he was offered a Coke by his hostess, in the pool house. As she poured his drink, the brash young man looked down her dress. He made a remark and she ordered him to leave. 'But I didn't go,' said Jackie. 'Instead, I made a move towards her, and she stood up, looked at me appraisingly, and then closed all the drapes. And I made love to Joan Crawford. Or, rather, she made love to me.'

This performance was repeated eight or nine times over the next six months, Cooper stated. It was always late at night when he would roll his car down his parents' driveway and sneak off to see Crawford. There was never any drinking or drugs, he said. It was all business with Joan. 'She was a very erudite professor of love. She was a wild woman. She would bathe me, powder me, cologne me. Then she would do it over again. She would put on high heels, a garter belt, and a large hat and pose in front of the mirror, turning this way and that way. "Look," she would say. I was already looking. But that sort of thing didn't particularly excite me. I kept thinking: The Lady is crazy.'

One night Crawford announced that the show was over. He could not come back to play. 'And put it out of your mind. It never happened,' Joan whispered, bestowing one last kiss on the satiated teenager.

Cooper would also, inadvertently, bestow something on Joan. At home, he adored his mother and used to call her 'Mommie Dearest'. Inspired, Crawford would soon confer the title on herself.

'Disillusioned with men after three unfortunate marriages, Joan Crawford feels her real happiness lies in being a mother. What a predicament!'

Jimmie Fidler, *The New York Mirror*

By the spring of 1940, Joan Crawford had made the final preparations for a role that her friends and foes agreed she should never play – that of a real-life doting mother.

Her fondness for children, other people's children, was genuine, many believed. As a child herself, in boarding school, she remembered the rare joy she experienced when she read to the smaller children each night and tucked them into bed.

In 1930, when she was married to Douglas Fairbanks, Jr., he wrote in *Vanity Fair* of her sympathy for children. 'She loves to play with a child and adores dolls,' he said. Her acts of generosity toward young people were also well known. Passing through Chicago once she insisted that the baskets of flowers bestowed upon her be sent to the Children's Memorial Hospital. In return she received two hundred letters, all of which were answered along with a personally autographed picture. When she heard that a little boy was born with no legs, and only one arm, she bought him a special saddle so he could play polo. 'You have to admire a kid like that who doesn't cry,' she told columnist Mike Connolly.

Joan of course longed for a child of her own, and she tried repeatedly to have one, she claimed. When she was married to Fairbanks, Jr., she miscarried twice, she said. Fairbanks in his memoirs doubted she was ever pregnant. 'I never quite believed her,' he said. 'She often claimed she had two miscarriages, but I had done some medical snooping that indicated nothing of the sort happened.' The same charade was apparently played with Tone. During her marriage to the actor she stated, she miscarried *seven* times. Yet, in checking for this book not one source recalled seeing or hearing that Joan was pregnant. And the news was never carried in a single column, interview, or story.

Doug Fairbanks, Jr. believed Joan was too vain to become pregnant. 'She frequently voiced her fears that child-bearing might affect her figure,' he said. It would also affect her career, Dale Eunson believed. 'She was too busy and too insecure to take the time off,' he said. Writer Roy Newquist spoke of a rumor that Joan had 'a botched-up abortion' when she was fourteen. Adela Rogers St. Johns claimed it happened later, in California, in 1926.

'Jesus! Look,' said Crawford herself, 'I wanted children desperately. None of the doctors I went to could understand why I couldn't carry full term. One of them, in of all places Tijuana, finally decided I'd picked up something from raw milk when I was a kid, and that's why I aborted.'

In 1938, Joan considered adopting her brother's daughter. Her brother Hal, 'a louse . . . a leech . . . a drunk, who could charm the skin off a snake,' apparently had one redeeming feature. He provided Crawford with her first real-life doll, his child. Hal was a bit player and extra at MGM, a position secured for him by star-sister Joan. When he married, his wife was also employed at the studio, as Joan's stand-in. Their first and only child, a girl, was christened Joan Crawford LeSueur, in honor of her famous aunt. When she was born, Joan would drive forty miles each day to the valley, 'just to watch the sleeping baby for a minute.' A special nursery was set-up in Joan's house, so the girl could visit and stay-over on weekends. 'I raised Joanie-pants,' said Crawford. 'During her first two years she saw more of me than her mother.' When brother Hal and his wife separated, Crawford set her sister-in-law up in a hat store in L.A. so she could still be close to her niece. When the couple divorced, Joan offered to buy the child, whose mother refused. To get away from Crawford's possessive behavior, the mother moved to New York. 'I am heartbroken she is gone,' Joan told Louella Parsons, 'but I wouldn't dream of taking a child away from her mother.'

In 1939, when her chauffeur's wife became ill, Joan insisted that he move his children into her house. 'She frolics on the floor for hours with the youngsters,' said Louella, 'and insists they can stay in her guest room for as long as it takes.' The star was also 'Aunt Joan' to little Tony Stanwyck, to Maria Cooper (Rocky and Gary's daughter) and to Brooke Hayward, the daughter of Margaret Sulla-van and agent Leland Hayward.

It was Loretta Young who inspired Joan to become a foster mother. When the unwed Loretta brought home a little girl (said to be the love child of Loretta and Clark Gable), Crawford decided that she too could adopt a child. Deemed unsuitable as an adoptive parent in California ('based on personal interviews and assessment of her family relationships'), Joan applied to three out-of-state agencies. One in Las Vegas, said to be influenced by a friend, 'the alleged Jewish mafia boss, Meyer Lansky', was the first to deliver. In June 1940 they called Crawford and told her that they had a baby girl ready for delivery. 'None of us knew a word of this,' said Harry Mines. 'She called me one day and told me to come to the house. In the foyer she whispered that she had a surprise to show me. We went upstairs, and there in the brand-new nursery was a baby girl.'

The blonde, blue-eyed baby was called Joan temporarily. Reluc-tant 'to have the child live up to such an enormous burden', Joan experimented with other first names until one day she whispered "Christina" into her crib. The baby smiled and that was the name that was chosen.

DADDY DEAREST

It was a definite plus that Christina was a beautiful child. This enabled Joan to parade the child, and herself, in front of friends and the press. 'I am finding my own lost childhood,' she said gaily, lavishing toys and gifts on the little girl, and having identical mother-and-daughter outfits – dresses, hats and gloves – made up for both to wear in public. Actor Melvyn Douglas, who had been exposed to Joan the grand lady and Joan the natural broad, was now treated to Joan the mother. The performance unfolded during the making of *A Woman's Face* in 1941. 'The little girl would be led on the set at about three-thirty every afternoon, by a real English nanny. The arrival of the child, dressed in a pinafore, patent leather shoes, peek-a-boo gloves, ribbons in her hair, and bonnet, would stop production for about a half hour while everyone gathered in a circle and Joan made a great show of being a mother.'

A second child, a boy, was adopted when he was six weeks old. He would be called Christopher, and to Joan's delight he too became 'blond and beautiful.' To make her perfect family complete, she proceeded to audition various eligible men for the role of Daddy Dearest. 'It would be cruel and selfish of me to let my children grow up without a father,' she said.

Clark Gable was Joan's first choice. Recently widowed when his wife's plane crashed into a mountain, Gable was consoled by Joan night after night in her Brentwood home. 'You've got to stop drinking and crying,' she told him. 'I know, I know,' said Clark. Joan suggested that the only way he could relieve his grief was to move in with her and the children. 'We will fill the void in your life, permanently,' said Joan. 'You mean marriage?' asked the King. 'Yes,' said Joan, and shortly thereafter, at age forty, Gable escaped by enlisting in the Air Force.

Joan was at Columbia Pictures, subbing for Gable's late wife, Carole Lombard, in *They All Kissed the Bride*, when she was introduced to actor Glenn Ford. He was invited to her house for Sunday dinner and was soon 'carried away by the magnetism of Joan.' They dined out together frequently, and on weekends they drove to the beach or had picnics in the country with the children. At home, Joan ran off Glenn's latest picture and gave him 'the benefit of her shrewd constructive criticism.' They would run Joan's films, with no comment from Glenn, for 'he did not feel qualified to speak.' Meanwhile, in the background, little Christina, only two, 'was screaming her head off for Mickey Mouse cartoons.'

As it came to pass, Glenn Ford did not make the grade as daddy to the kids or husband to Joan. One reporter said 'he could not match the maturity, either emotional or mental, of a woman of her experience.' The reality of the situation was that Glenn was classified 1-A by the Marine Corps, and Joan was not at all interested in marrying a serviceman. She let the actor down slowly, however, gradually excluding him from her Sunday night suppers. 'She was grooming him to walk without her,' said *Silver Screen*.

Throughout the summer of 1941, Joan continued to search for the perfect husband, and father figure for her children. A current co star, John Wayne, was considered. He played her chauffeur in *Reunion in France*, and the two dallied sexually until Wayne put the brakes on their mini-affair. ('Get him out of the saddle and you've got *nothing*,' Joan would later sniff to a writer.) Another candidate, (an award-winning director) made the preliminaries. 'I met Joan in New York two years before,' he said, asking that his name not be used. 'She was polite but distant. Then I was signed to a two-picture deal at MGM. I bumped into Joan outside the writers' building one day and she almost blew me away with her charm and friendliness. She asked me to come by for dinner that same night. I accepted of course. I couldn't wait to get there. Sure, I heard the stories, and I envisioned one fantastic night ahead. The first thing that happened when I got there was a trip to the nursery to see the kids. Then Joan offered me a drink. "What will it be?" she said. "I've got ginger ale, club soda, or RC Cola." There was no liquor anywhere to be seen. Then the doorbell rang and this guy came in. The way he looked at me, I knew he was there for a date too. She introduced us, and the doorbell rang again, with *two* guys being ushered in, one of them an actor I knew. When they all trooped upstairs to see the kids, I grabbed my hat and left. I had the wrong impression. I was a square from the East. I thought we were all there for the same thing, and that this was going to be one of those Hollywood parties. A couple of days later I bumped into my actor friend and he told me *nothing* happened. They all had dinner together with Joan. She was sizing each one up. He was the last to leave and made a pass at her. She was shocked. "No!" she told him. "How could you? With the children upstairs?" He told me he felt like a pervert for just trying to kiss her. Later on we found out what the routine was. Joan wasn't interested in any of us as mere dates, she was looking for a daddy for the house.'

With her usual diligence, Crawford eventually found the right applicant. His name was Philip Terry. He too was an actor, 'but a man's man,' said Joan. 'He once worked in the oil fields and drove a truck from California to New York.'

Educated at Stanford, Terry studied acting at the Royal Academy of Dramatic Art in London, which accounted for his British pronunciation of certain words. He was working at Paramount when he wangled an invitation to Joan's house for dinner through Harry Mines. She was impressed with his looks, accent, background and resourcefulness. Since she refused to give him her home number, he copied it down from the hall receiver and called her the next day. He was invited back to a second dinner – a fivesome – 'Joan and four men.' Three nights later she agreed to meet him in a public restaurant. They learned 'they laughed at the same things, and shared the same love for serious works of literature.' For their next date they had dinner on trays in front of a fire at Brentwood, and later Philip cued her lines from the script of her next motion picture, *Reunion in France*. When the film began to shoot night scenes, the studio gateman was 'amazed' to find Mr. Terry arriving at dawn each morning to escort Miss Crawford home. During the shooting of the day scenes, even the cameraman noticed the change in Joan. 'What's happened to your face?' he asked her. 'Something is going on inside you. I've never seen you photograph so radiantly.' Joan smiled and kept her secret. Philip Terry adored her *and* the children. He was handsome, educated, a moderate drinker and smoker (a pipe), and, best of all, he was classified 4-F, ineligible for active duty due to poor vision (he wore glasses off-camera).

Giving their names as Lucille Tone and Frederick Korman, the happy couple applied for a marriage license. At midnight on September 20, 1942, they were married at the home of her attorney in Hidden Valley. Joan wore a suit by Irene, in two-tone beige and a matching pancake hat. The groom wore his glasses. 'He really understands me,' Joan said. 'He doesn't want to change me in any way. Philip loves me as I really am.'

After driving home under a crescent moon, Joan and Philip went to bed at 2:00 A.M. and arose at 6:00 A.M. Their wedding breakfast was . . . milk. At the studio to shoot the final scenes for *Reunion in France*, Joan happily accepted congratulations from Judy Garland, Joe Mankiewicz, Gene Kelly and Louis B. Mayer. 'I never knew such relaxation before,' said Mrs. Terry.

'I knew what kind of a marriage it was going to be when I saw her arrive on the set,' said her co star, John Wayne. 'First came Joan, then her secretary, then her makeup man, then her wardrobe man, then Phil Terry, carrying her dog.'

'There is no feeling of jealousy between us, as to which is the most important,' Joan told a reporter. 'We are now a family and we work for each other.' To wit, the groom stood on the sidelines and gave his new wife his support. 'Just before each scene he looks at her,' wrote a reporter. 'He lifts his hand and says: "Forever!" Joan looks at him and replies: "Forever!" And then they shoot the scene.'

9

THE WAR YEARS

'Stars are not important. You have to be General MacArthur to achieve fame.'
Joan Crawford

A Code For American Girls:
'It should be our duties as American wives, sweethearts and mothers, to unite to avoid any lowering of American morals. The length of skirts or the color of lipstick may be of great importance to some, but these difficult times should put an end to such foolishness.'
Bette Davis

On the afternoon of December 7, 1941, while the Japanese were bombing Pearl Harbor, Joan Crawford was on her hands and knees scrubbing the kitchen floors of her home in Brentwood, Los Angeles. Bette Davis was in bed, at Glendale, recovering from the flu. And Lana Turner was at her house off Sunset Boulevard, preparing for one of her Sunday afternoon record hops. When told three hours later that Pearl Harbor had been destroyed, Lana reportedly answered, 'Who's Pearl Harbor?' (A quote also ascribed to Betty Hutton and Gracie Allen.)

Six months before Hollywood reacted to the war in 'a burst of patriotic enthusiasm and economic shrewdness,' Joan Crawford had rallied to the cause. In July 1941, *The New York Times* reported that she was the chairwoman of a drive to raise money to buy cots for five thousand children made homeless by air raids in London. That Christmas she knitted socks and scarves for British soldiers, and one afternoon she stood on the corner of Fifth Avenue and Fifty-second Street, 'rattling a tin-can for contributions and selling autographs for a quarter.' She raised something like four hundred dollars, said the *Times*.

When Bette Davis heard the news of Pearl Harbor, she said: 'What's the use of going on acting, when your country is at war? But then I felt *that's* what the enemy wanted – to destroy and paralyze America. So I decided to keep on working.'

By October 1942, two thousand seven hundred people or twelve percent of the Hollywood movie industry were in the Armed Forces. Those remaining were put to work, producing the three hundred feature films and countless cartoons, documentaries and short subjects designed to spur the public and spur the fighting men onto victory. At Burbank, within days of the war declaration, Jack Warner was on the phone to the White House, discussing his studio's planned contribution, and his honorary commission in the army. He asked President Roosevelt to start him out as a General, but settled for Lieutenant Colonel instead. 'He insisted we call him "Colonel",' said Ann Sheridan. 'Then the old fart had his officer's uniform tailored by the studio's wardrobe department.' At 20th Century-Fox, Major Darryl Zanuck closed his office, put on his sunglasses, and left for Europe, where the war action was. He would personally supervise and edit the combat footage, from his headquarters suite at Claridges hotel in London. Major John Huston was at Warner's, finishing up *Across the Pacific* with Humphrey Bogart, when he was called to active duty. After tying up Bogart in a chair, surrounded by Japanese soldiers holding machine guns, Huston left a note for Jack Warner: 'Jack, I'm on my way. I'm in the army. Bogart will know how to get out.'

Of the major studios, MGM was hardest hit by the induction of male talent. Among the stars who enlisted or were drafted, were Clark Gable, Jimmy Stewart, Mickey Rooney, and Robert Taylor, leaving sixty-one-year-old Wallace Beery and five-year-old Butch Jenkins to defend the Metro gates. Conrad Veidt was on constant call to play Gestapo heavies, and actor Helmut Dantine was voted the best-looking Nazi. 'There were ugly Nazis too, like Otto Preminger and Alexander Grenach. They were all Jewish,' said director Marcel Ophuls. At 20th Century-Fox, Henry Fonda left his wife and two kids to join the navy, and Tyrone Power said goodbye to 'his wife and a male lover', to join the Marines. At Republic, a stalwart John Wayne was excused from military service, due to family commitments and a badly damaged shoulder; while over at Warner's, many of their top male stars chose to fight the war from within the safety of the Burbank soundstages. Errol Flynn, George Brent and Cary Grant were British subjects and immune from the U.S. draft. Humphrey Bogart had a hearing disability and John Garfield had flat feet. That left Ronald Reagan, who was a captain in the Air Corps Reserves. When he was called to active duty he 'bravely kissed Janie [Wyman] and buttonnose [daughter Maureen] goodbye' and left for Fort Bragg, forty miles from L.A. After basic training, Captain Reagan's eyesight was deemed poor. 'If we sent you overseas, you'd shoot a general,' the examining doctor said. 'Yes, and you'd miss him,' his assistant concurred. So Reagan was assigned to a squadron that made training films, in Los Angeles, not far from the MGM studios, where his group, including Alan Ladd, were known to each other as the Culver City Commandos.

In May of 1942, confident that the war would soon be over, Bette Davis gave the first 'Victory Party', at Mocambo's, a surprise birthday celebration for her husband Farney. For 'the blackout theme', the club was in total darkness and Bette supplied guests with their own flashlight. Special victory cocktails – 'three dots of rum and a dash of Coke' – were served, and each guest got to wear an armed forces service hat of his or her choice.

That winter, as the war in Europe and the Pacific escalated, the stars embraced a new austerity program. There would be no parade, or Christmas trees, or Santas on Hollywood Boulevard that year. Bette Davis, wearing a severe hairdo and a black dress, appeared in a movie short with two fictitious kids, Billy and Ginny, gently explaining to them why they would not be receiving a baseball bat or bike that Christmas. She was giving the money instead to the Red Cross so they could buy food and medicine for their father, 'fighting somewhere far, far away.'

With their men at war, real and pretended, it was up to the women of Hollywood, and their children, to project images of strength and sacrifice to the millions of other war wives, mothers, and children across America. Clothing was scarce or rationed, so

Loretta Young was photographed giving her two sons' outgrown T-shirts, jeans, and underwear to Rosalind Russell (for her son, Lance). At home, Bette Davis had to make do with a two-party line, sharing her phone with a lady in Glendale. ('Of course she hasn't a *clue* as to who *I* am,' said Bette. 'Whenever she tries to listen in to my calls, I deliberately talk dirty. That usually makes her hang up.') Lucille Ball bought a tractor and planted victory corn in the valley. The four Crosby boys organized a paper-string-and-rubber drive in their Sherman Oaks neighbourhood; while Joan Bennett and Paulette Goddard posed shopping with food coupons at their local supermarket in Beverly Hills.

The severe gas rationing affected Hollywood too. Many two-car families now made do with one, and some stars went to work on bicycles. Bette Davis jaunted around Los Angeles, briefly, in a horse and carriage; while Joan Crawford made her shopping rounds on a special motor bike, fitted with bucket seats on both sides, so she could bring the children with her when she went to market. Christina however, was a little testy when it came to coping with the shortage of hired help. 'Our maid and butler left us, to work in a defense plant,' said Joan. 'Christina was asking everyone to wait on her. "Please get me this or that," she would order. I explained to her we had no help and that she had to wait on herself.' Christina adjusted, fast. Standing on a chair by the kitchen sink, she learned how to dry the dishes. She also helped at dusting, wearing special white gloves and an apron embroidered with the words: 'I love Mommy, God and America.' In that order.

> '*The Nazis won't quit, the Japs won't quit, and you won't quit either.*'
>   Jimmy Cagney on a War Bond drive

At President Roosevelt's request, many stars were recruited to donate their time, talent, and charisma to selling war bonds. When called by the White House, Louis B. Mayer gave up his publicity chief, Howard Strickling, for the War Bond Drive. Strickling organized the Hollywood Victory Caravan, a special train carrying stars across America, promoting the sale of kisses and bonds, for defense funds. Among the passengers who embarked on the three-week tour (performing in a three-hour show in eighteen major cities) were Cary Grant, Jimmy Cagney, Merle Oberon, Claudette Colbert, Joan Blondell, Olivia de Havilland, Groucho and Harpo Marx, Betty Hutton, Judy Garland, and Fred Astaire. The tour kicked off in Boston, went on to Washington, and eighteen days later arrived in Los Angeles. 'Our quota was $500 million, but we sold over one billion,' said an exhausted Greer Garson. (The MC of the show, Bob Hope, said this was his first patriotic tour, and he was seriously considering going out on another.)

There were other stars and talents in Hollywood who donated their time to entertaining the armed forces without publicity or comfort. Joan Blondell took her own troupe and performed at 126 Army bases; Gary Cooper sang and danced in the South Pacific; John Garfield went to North Africa and Sicily; and Ann Sheridan went on a grueling four-month tour of India, China and Burma. 'Jack Warner was big on USO tours,' said Sheridan, 'but not too big. He threatened to suspend me when I didn't get back on time from Burma. I said, "Go ahead." He kept trying to get wires and letters through to me, but they'd arrive three weeks later. We didn't know where we were going until we opened our special orders. It was rough! Sleeping on the floors of planes, and living on K-rations. And the heat! I lost sixteen pounds. But I wouldn't have missed it for anything in the world.'

Neither Bette Davis nor Joan Crawford left the mainland during the course of the war. But their volunteer efforts were noticeable. Joan of course made the earliest and grandest gesture. She donated her entire $128,000 salary from *They All Kissed the Bride* to the Red Cross, the organization that had found the body of 'my darling Carole Lombard.' Bette Davis appeared on the Armed Forces Network radio show in Los Angeles and travelled to army camps and hospitals in California, but no farther than a radius of two hundred miles from Burbank. 'Jack Warner wouldn't release Bette for an extended tour,'' said Joan Blondell. 'She was his top moneymaker. It was all right for the peons like Annie [Sheridan] and I to get shot at, but he wouldn't allow Bette to be anywhere near the war action.'

In January 1943 Joan announced she was disbanding her fan club. 'It seemed to me more important things were facing all of us,' she said. In February she announced she had founded a group called *America's Women's Volunteer Services*. The group took care of children whose mothers worked in the defense factories around Los Angeles. In April she was voted the Chairman of the War Dog Fund, raising money to train dogs for the armed forces.

Not to be outdone, Bette joined the Hollywood Victory Committee. But she wasn't too happy with this group. 'They gave permission for actors to appear in camp shows,' she said, 'and the egos and politics abounded.' She really wanted to be the boss of her own group. One day John Garfield came to her in the Green Room at Warner's. He had been thinking about the thousands of servicemen who were passing through Hollywood without seeing any movie stars and Bette instantly agreed something should be done about that. So the two found a building off Sunset Boulevard that looked like two New England barns thrown together. They recruited carpenters, designers, all of the guilds to donate their time. In three weeks the Hollywood Canteen was ready. On opening night Bette had to crawl through a window to get in. They had more stars than the GIs could count: Marlene Dietrich, Gary Cooper, Rita Hayworth. 'Everyone agreed this was the greatest gift we could give the boys,' said co-founder Davis.

Not everyone. Joan Crawford had her own plans to entertain the service men. Inspired by the meet-a-star-over-donuts-and-coffee theme of the Canteen, she decided to throw open her house to the boys for Sunday afternoon picnics. She set up a barbecue and tables on her front lawn and persuaded teenagers Judy Garland and Shirley Temple to act as hostesses and serve hot dogs and soft drinks to the soldiers and sailors. But during the first picnic some of the boys got a little rowdy. One of them spiked the punch, and at evening's end he and a buddy were seen standing beside Joan Crawford's pool, teaching her two-year-old son, Christopher, how to 'piss clear across the creek.'

Joan's Sunday picnics were canceled after that. The star explained that with her Japanese gardener interned in a concentration camp she was having her front lawn ploughed and planted for a victory garden, 'with fourteen different kinds of vegetables, including carrots and radishes.'

QUEEN BETTE

'Bette has played so many meanies on the screen that she has developed a swaggering insolent walk to fit the parts she plays. Let's hope she doesn't adopt the walk in real life. Don't mince. Don't stride like a man.'

Advice from Madame Sylvia in *Photoplay*.

'Show me a great actor, and I'll show a lousy husband; show me a great actress, and you've seen the devil.'

W.C. Fields

Professionally, no other actress in Hollywood could match the accomplishments of Bette Davis during the early 1940s. These were her golden years, when she appeared in one dazzling success after another including *The Letter, The Little Foxes, Now Voyager, The Man Who Came to Dinner* and *Mr. Skeffington*. Among the numerous awards and citations she received, was one dubious honor from the Harvard Lampoon. In one of their annual polls the Harvard students named Miriam Hopkins as 'the least desirable company on a desert isle.' Joan Crawford along with George Brent, was deemed to be 'most qualified for a pension,' and Bette Davis was awarded a special citation for 'having suffered the worst ordeal in *All This and Heaven Too*.'

According to many at Warner's, Bette did not suffer alone during the making of her pictures. 'She put everyone through hell, including some of the toughest stars on the lot,' said a co-worker.

In 1934, Bette had made *Jimmy the Gent* with James Cagney. He was the star of the picture, but Bette couldn't stand his haircut. 'It's cut too close to the scalp and gives me the creeps,' she said, refusing to pose for publicity stills with the actor. 'Jack Warner was giving her a hard time at the time,' Cagney gallantly said in his memoirs, 'so she took it out on all of us.'

In 1941, Cagney and Davis were reunited for *The Bride Came C.O.D.* Made in Arizona, this was her first location picture (as with Crawford, the sun dared make Bette squint). During filming, Bette found some of her lines were changed. She couldn't complain to the producer, because he was Cagney's brother, William. 'I'm sorry

I never thought to fix it so my *sister* could produce pictures,' said Bette to Jimmy. 'Perhaps if I did I could change scripts *too*.' Cutting her lines, and his own, Cagney 'endured many silences from Bette.' She however derived 'enormous fun and satisfaction,' when she got to throw a bucket of water in Jimmy's face, missing her camera mark twice, which meant the splashing scene had to be repeated three times.

'Nobody but a mother could have loved Bette Davis at the height of her career,' said her *Juarez* co star, Brian Aherne. 'Even when I was carrying a gun, she scared the be-jesus out of me,' said Humphrey Bogart, her co star in *The Petrified Forest*.

'It could be marvelous to work with Bette,' a source told author Larry Carr, 'and it could be absolutely hell. Everything depended on her mood at the time. When she was in a good mood, the cast and the crew would relax and filming went smoothly. But when she started her famous tirades – watch out! At such times her behavior was so counterproductive that the picture and everyone with it suffered accordingly. She seemed to thrive on conflict, to want to create turmoil, and when that sort of thing occurred, she was the greatest bitch I've ever known.'

Errol Flynn was obviously not an actor Bette admired. She said it loud and clear that she would not work with him in *Gone With the Wind*. For spite, Jack Warner subsequently put her with Flynn in two pictures. The first of these was *The Sisters*, with Flynn top-billed. 'Why in heaven's name with a title like that is he first?' Bette yelled at Warner, who replied, 'Because *he* is prettier.'

'He was the most beautiful man God ever created,' said Ann Sheridan. 'And a charmer.' 'I like my whiskey old and my women young,' said Flynn. 'Errol was my shining knight,' said his co star Olivia de Havilland. 'Mine too,' said her sister, Joan Fontaine. 'Imagine anyone calling Errol Flynn a Nazi,' said Myrna Loy. 'God! He was never sober long enough.' 'I only know one thing,' said Ida Lupino, referring to Flynn's statutory rape trial, 'Errol never raped any girl. They all raped him.'

On the set of *The Sisters*, Bette Davis complained frequently about the number of 'unauthorized females' who stood on the sidelines ogling Flynn. If she suspected that a continuity girl had her eyes more on Errol than on her clipboard, she would tell the director, then walk off the set.

Flynn was never serious about his craft, said Bette. 'He went fishing and fucking, and paid no attention to his talent,' Viveca Lindfors stated. 'There is no thrill like making a dishonest buck,' Flynn agreed.

In 1939 he was cast with Bette once more in *The Private Lives of Elizabeth and Essex*. She wanted Laurence Olivier as Lord Essex, but without Flynn, Jack Warner told her the film would not be made. Bette relented, then proceeded to supervise the rewriting of the script and overrode the director, Michael Curtiz, on her costumes. Before the picture began shooting, the title underwent some changes. To capitalize on Errol Flynn's bigger draw at the box office it became *The Knight and the Lady*; then *Essex and Elizabeth*. 'You *cannot* give second billing to the Queen of England – or to *me*,' Bette screamed at Jack Warner. 'Either change the title or I'm walking out.'

In her love scenes with Errol Flynn, the idol of millions, Bette closed her eyes and imagined he was Laurence Olivier. Flynn had no complaints. 'She's a far better actress than I could ever hope to be as an actor, but physically she's not my type,' he said. Davis said he almost propositioned her, 'but was afraid I would laugh at him. "You're so right," I told him.'

As Queen Elizabeth, Bette busted his ass in the royal court scenes, said Flynn. He was required to repeatedly walk down 'a seemingly endless carpet' to face Davis, only to find her stand-in on the throne. 'When she finally did mount the throne,' said Michael Freedland, 'she greeted him with a powerful slap across the cheek – a slap made all the harder by the large rings on her fingers.' Flynn, who had once suffered a double mastoid operation, was worried that several blows could deafen, even kill him. He went to see Davis privately, in her dressing room. He asked her to go easy in these scenes. She scorned the idea of holding anything back. 'A slap has to be a slap,' she told the fearful Flynn, whose reaction, he said, was to throw up outside her door.

'Bette is really unable to conceal for any great length of time that she considers herself God's greatest gift to screen acting. She believes that to be a simple fact of life. Oh, she can be disarmingly candid and funny about herself for a short

On the set of *Elizabeth and Essex*, among Queen Bette's usual attendants, was a boy whose sole duty was to follow the actress, holding up an ashtray lest she spill ashes on her expensive costumes. When filming was completed, for his faithful silent service, Bette regally gifted the lad with three coins – not gold but silver – a quarter, a dime and a nickel.

Bette wasn't cheap, said a source who knew her and Crawford. 'If anyone came to either with financial trouble,' he said, 'Bette and Joan were always the first to reach into their handbags for their checkbook. Furthermore they would refuse repayment, no matter how large the sum.'

Being a star made it difficult at times for Davis to relate to mere mortals. 'It was always the small, human things she had trouble with,' said a Warner's publicist. 'Like good morning or hello or thank you. She was also very moody. Somedays she would be very chatty; then others she could wither you with a glance.'

One Christmas Eve, Bette arrived at the Warner's mailroom, carrying a twenty-pound turkey on a platter. It had been cooked and carved personally by the star. 'Merry Christmas, boys,' she said, leaving the bird to be equally distributed by the staff.

END THE WAR! SEND BETTE DAVIS TO THE FRONT was a piece of graffiti scrawled across the north rear wall of the studio lot. When the head of maintenance was called by publicity head, Bob Taplinger, to have the slogan removed, before Davis saw it, he replied, 'But she's already seen it. She called this morning and wanted to know why it wasn't put closer to the main gates.'

'Bette has a lot of mannerisms. I wanted her to be simple and dignified, and not resort to a lot of gestures and accentuated speech and tricks that are just plain bad.'

William Wyler

As mentioned, like Crawford, Davis was seldom forgetful of old slights and injuries. When producer Samuel Goldwyn asked her to play Regina Giddens in *The Little Foxes* she delayed giving him an answer. It was Goldwyn, in 1929 who had vetoed her first screen test, so for *The Little Foxes* she asked the producer to cough up $385,000 for her loan-out services, 'all of which I kept from Jack Warner,' the star said happily.

She was attracted to the character of Regina, the cold and greedy lead, because 'she has the courage to do the brutal things I've always wanted to do and couldn't.' Another draw for Bette was the chance to work once more with her favorite director, William Wyler. Unfortunately for all, this would be their last collaboration. They fought viciously throughout the entire filming.

On the first day Bette walked in with Calamine lotion smeared all over her face. 'What's that for?' asked Wyler. 'It's to make me look old,' she answered. 'You look like a clown. Take it off,' Wyler ordered. They argued over the definition of the part. Wyler said he wanted her to put some humanity into her portrayal. 'This woman was not supposed to be just evil, but have great charm, humor and sex.' Bette was icy to his wishes, Thomas Brady stated in *The New York Times*, 'and each was monstrously patient with the other.'

When one scene reached its eighth or ninth take, Wyler accused Bette of rattling off her lines. 'Her response was cool enough for a Sonja Henie ice-skating spectacle,' said Brady.

Wyler claimed he was trying to get Davis to abandon her usual style of acting. 'When speaking of Miss Davis' mannerisms, he minced around the room flailing the air with his arms,' said another reporter from the set. Bette, afraid that she was being pushed into the background of the film, insisted on playing with emphatic bitchery.

During the filming of an important dinner scene, Wyler criticized her openly, suggesting that she be replaced by Miriam Hopkins. Bette's reaction to this was to walk off the set. She went to her rented home at Laguna Beach and refused to return to work. After a twenty-one-day absence, when she learned she would forfeit her entire salary *and* be liable for the cost of the production, she returned to the Goldwyn studios.

Actor Herbert Marshall, who played her husband, described his final scene with the actress. Stricken by a heart seizure, Marshall was to fall on the parlor floor while Bette remained seated nearby, refusing to help him. As the camera remained on Bette's mask-like frozen face, her dying husband crawled on the floor behind her, dragging himself toward the steps leading upstairs, where his heart medicine was. The actor, who had only one leg (the other had been lost in World War I), said it was no trouble crawling upstairs, 'Because it wasn't me. Once I got out of camera range, Mr Wyler used a double. I was already in my dressing room, changing, when my double finally got to the top of the stairs.'

Marshall was happy to leave the strife of *The Little Foxes* set behind. He checked in shortly thereafter at MGM, where he played opposite Joan Crawford in *When Ladies Meet*. The difference in assignments, between working on a picture with Bette, then Joan 'was like going on a lovely holiday,' said Marshall.

'*A Note to the Girls:*
Joan Crawford has her supply of Spring hats complete − and they're all crownless.'

Pageant Magazine, 1942

Joan was in New York, at a party at Kitty and Moss Hart's, when she met Fredric March. The actor was leaving for Los Angeles the following morning, to appear in *Susan and God* at MGM. 'How I envied him,' said Crawford, who had seen the play on Broadway with Gertrude Lawrence. She longed to play the role of the giddy New York socialite who attempts to introduce God to her upper-crust friends. But, alas, Norma Shearer was set to play the part, until at the last minute she said no. Norma had just turned forty and wasn't keen on playing the mother of a thirteen-year-old girl. Crawford, aided by George Cukor, got the part, and critics called this 'my most important and best-executed role,' she said. One reviewer, Calvin McPherson of the *New York Telegram and Sun*, did say he found it virtually faultless but 'just a bit too heavenly.' Joan bubbled too much, he felt, and she had formidable competition from her Adrian wardrobe. 'She wakes up for a dramatic scene before breakfast and looks like a dress rehearsal of Bette Davis in

The Private Lives of Elizabeth and Essex,' said McPherson. 'In her most penitent scene, her gown is covered with little curlycues of fashion you can't keep your eyes off. It just isn't right for the little gal who is working so hard to give us ART.'

A Woman's Face followed, with Joan appearing for half of the picture with the right side of her face hideously scarred. Set against a scenario of murder, blackmail and plastic surgery, she gave a first-class performance, due largely to the directorial skill of George Cukor. Using the same techniques as William Wyler, who, through intimidation and numerous takes exhausted the kinetic Bette, Cukor subdued the usually ebullient Crawford. In a pivotal courtroom scene, before the cameras turned he made her recite the multiplication tables two by two until her voice faded to a monotone. '*Now*, Anna,' he ordered, 'tell me the story of your life.'

'*A Woman's Face* was a very successful picture for Metro and Joan,' said Cukor. 'She was very happy because it put her in the class of actresses like Ingrid Bergman and Bette Davis. But unlike Ingrid, who loved to work but wasn't obsessed with "career", Joan was never happy being idle. She would finish a picture one day and the next day she was looking for a new script. She was never still for long. It was always "my next picture, my next role." Bette Davis was exactly the same. They only lived for their next role. All that mattered to both was to be up there, on the silver screen, bigger and better than anyone else.'

'Nonsense,' said Bette, taking offence to the 'bigger' part of Cukor's statement. The size of a role was not of paramount importance to her. She could be happy in an ensemble, in 'being one of the team.' If a part was good, and the company was first-rate, she'd do the role.

The production of *King's Row* in 1942 was an example. Bette wanted to play Cassandra, the daughter sexually abused by her doctor father (who also amputated the legs of Ronald Reagan). But Jack Warner regarded the idea as impractical. 'This was one of Warner's most expensive films,' said writer Douglas Churchill, 'and he thought it unwise to add Miss Davis' salary to the budget.' (Betty Field got the role.)

The Man Who Came to Dinner was another ensemble cast. After being hit by a rock during a parade ('People either love me or hate me,' said Bette), the actress knew it was time to change her on-screen image again. She chose the comedy.

She had seen the play in New York, then called Jack Warner, urging him to buy the screen rights for her and John Barrymore. Barrymore would have the lead role of the acidic critic Sheridan Whiteside, and she would play the lesser role of his faithful secretary, Maggie Cutler. 'I wanted very much to work with Barrymore,' she said. 'He did such wonderful things with Katharine Hepburn and Greta Garbo.'

'And Joan Crawford,' she was reminded.

'Joan Crawford? When did Barrymore ever work with Joan?' Bette asked.

'In 1932. In *Grand Hotel*.'

'*Oh*! You are *so* right,' said Bette. 'I always forget that Joan was in that picture *too*.'

Barrymore tested for *The Man Who Came to Dinner*, but at that stage of his career his concentration had been eroded by alcohol, which necessitated his reading his lines from cue cards placed by the side of the camera. Jack Warner, already saddled with Errol Flynn ('too drunk at 4:00 P.M. for his close-ups'), refused to hire Barrymore and signed Cary Grant for the part. When told she would now be working with the debonair Grant, Bette hissed, 'I'd rather work with Jack Barrymore drunk than play opposite Mister Cary Grant.'

So Cary Grant was bounced from *The Man Who Came to Dinner* to *Arsenic and Old Lace* and the role of Sheridan Whiteside went to Monty Woolley, whom Bette found 'bearable.' She didn't like the dog in the ensemble cast either. Rehearsing one scene the Scottie bit her on the nose. 'It was a minor bite,' said director William Keighly, 'but enough for Bette to call a halt to the entire production.' Paranoid about being disfigured, and wearing a large hat and veil to cover her bandaged nose, Bette boarded a train for the East Coast. She spent the entire journey confined to her drawing room; then, recuperating in New Hampshire, she sent daily cables to Jack Warner on 'the de-swelling of her world-famous proboscis.' When production resumed, she said her heart was no longer in the film. 'I stayed out of her way,' said her co star Ann Sheridan. 'I never argued or said "boo" to her. She was the queen, and I did not fancy having my head handed to me on a platter.'

'She was very kind to me, very loyal, very insistent that I be paid a good salary, with all benefits. I remember nothing but good things about Bette Davis.'
                                      Sally Sage, Bette's long-time stand-in

Working with women was never a problem with Bette Davis or Joan Crawford, as long as the women were behind the camera or in subordinate roles.

With their equals on screen there *could* be friction. Crawford, as told, had some stressful working moments with Greta Garbo and Norma Shearer. Davis also encountered some initial agitation working with Olivia de Havilland.

A 'fresh young beauty, with a voice that was music to the ears,' Olivia's star was rising when she was cast as Bette's lady-in-waiting in *Elizabeth and Essex*. The assignment came while Olivia was already hard at work at MGM, playing Melanie Wilkes in *Gone With the Wind*. Ordered to show up at Warner's for rehearsals on *Elizabeth and Essex*, Olivia told the director she would not work until *Gone With the Wind* was completed. The director, Michael Curtiz, 'flew' at de Havilland, who lost her usual calm and proceeded to yell right back. Bette Davis, watching this, said she came 'perilously close to smacking Olivia's face.'

The two became friends on their second film together, *In This Our Life*. They played sisters. Bette was the bitch again. She played Stanley, a Southern vixen, who steals her sister Olivia's husband, marries him, drives him to suicide, then on the way back from his funeral, kills a little boy with her car, blaming the accident on her cook's son, a poor but well-spoken black boy. 'That was a first for black people,' said Bette. 'The negro boy was written and performed as an educated person. This caused a great deal of joy among negroes. They were tired of the Stepin Fetchit vision of their people.'

Olivia played Roy, the older, good sister ('I wanted *that* role,' said Davis), and she and Bette commenced their long but 'peculiar' friendship. Davis became protective of Olivia when she found out the actress was in love with their director, John Huston. She knew

Huston from the days when he worked on the script for *Jezebel*. She also remembered that he was a witness when the reputed great love of her life, William Wyler, married another. As an artist, she said Huston was brilliant, but a bit of 'a macho phony.' He in turn found Bette fascinating. 'There is something frenetic about Bette, a demon within her which threatens to break out and eat everybody, beginning with their ears.'

Bette commiserated with Olivia when her affair with Huston proved to be unhappy. (He was married.) After work, soaking in a hot tub at de Havilland's house as the young actress poured out her troubles, Bette insisted on 'reading favorite passages from the Holy Bible to Olivia.'

When filming on *In This Our Life* was almost completed, Jack Warner told Bette Davis she was a fool: she was letting friendship ruin her performance. She had the best lines in the picture, but Huston was giving Olivia the best camera angles. 'I led her to the projection room,' said Warner. 'I let her see how Huston's manly pulse, beating for Olivia, had ruined her big scenes.'

'When Bette caught on,' said Alex Madsen, 'she came close to tearing out every seat in the projection room, and the next day Huston reshot many scenes he had taken from her.'

Bette later made her peace with Olivia, said Madsen, 'but after that she wouldn't have Huston around driving a truck.'

'The studio was afraid of Bette; afraid of her demon,' said Huston. 'They confused it with over-acting.'

AND THEN THERE WAS MIRIAM

'Miriam Hopkins was a wonderful actress,' said Bette, 'but a bitch. The most thoroughgoing bitch I've ever worked with.'

A Southern belle replete with charm, sex appeal and vanity, Miriam Hopkins was neither a newcomer nor a supporting player when she first worked with Bette Davis. Back in 1928 Hopkins was the star of Cukor's repertory company while Bette was a struggling, soon-to-be-fired, ingenue. Miriam was also a star in films before Bette. In 1933 she appeared in *Design for Living*, the cult classic directed by Ernst Lubistch; then came *Becky Sharp*, the first Technicolor feature, directed by Rouben Mamoulian. William Wyler also worked with Hopkins, using her in four of his films, including *These Three*. He often claimed that two magic words – 'Miriam Hopkins' – could send Bette Davis into a cycle of rage and recrimination.

Miriam was 'nuts . . . certifiably insane,' director George Cukor believed. 'Like most actresses, she was in love with the sound of her own voice. Her ego was so gargantuan it frequently turned and fed on itself. She was *very* self-destructive.'

With blonde hair, blue eyes, and perfect features, Hopkins could 'flirt as naturally as she could breathe.' Her affairs were numerous. 'When I can't sleep, I don't count sheep,' she said, 'I count lovers. And when I reach thirty-eight or thirty-nine I'm fast asleep.' Her staccato speech, nervous energy and infidelity could drive men to distraction. One fevered beau threatened to slit her throat in public. Another, actor John Gilbert, burst into her bedroom one morning and fired a bullet into the bedboard over her head. Instead of screaming or hiding under the covers, Miriam said 'Oh, John!', swept out of bed and took the smoking gun from his hand. Later, using her best friend, the heavy drinker, Dorothy Parker, as a character witness, Miriam applied to an adoption agency for a baby. When the news that the child, a five-day-old boy was ready, Miriam sent her agent to pick him up. She adored the boy, who at age six was enlightened by mother Miriam about sex. 'The worst thing a man could be is a bad lover,' she told her son. When asked what she did when a man was a bad lover, the actress replied, 'I kick him out of bed.'

Miriam loathed Bette Davis for a few reasons. The first of these was *Jezebel*. She had played the role on Broadway and owned the screen rights. She was promised first crack at the role by Jack Warner, but Bette stepped in, played it, and won the Oscar. Then she suspected Bette was having an affair with her husband, director Anatole Litvak. He came home from the studio one night and told Miriam, 'I found a marvelous new script. Bette Davis can do it as a movie; and you can play it on the radio.'

When Hopkins was hired to co star with Davis in *The Old Maid*, Bette commented, 'She'll be trouble, but she'll be worth it.' On the first day of shooting, Miriam showed up wearing an exact duplicate of the dress Bette wore in *Jezebel*. 'It was a grand entrance to end all grand entrances,' said Bette, 'and was calculated to make me blow my cool.' As filming went on, Miriam tried everything to sabotage Bette's performance. 'If I had a long difficult speech, she'd break in with, "Oh, I'm so sorry. One of my buttons came unbuttoned." In one instance this tactic forced me to make twenty takes of a single scene.'

The Old Maid was a big success, and Davis and Hopkins were reunited for *Old Acquaintance* – a story of two girlhood friends who compete as novelists. The picture was to be directed by Edmund Goulding. During a loud and violent argument with Davis, over the cameraman she wanted to choose, Goulding suffered a heart attack, and was replaced by Vincent Sherman. ('Goulding was faking a heart attack,' Jack Warner believed.)

The peace between Bette and Miriam lasted approximately twelve minutes, said Sherman. There were tricks, upstagings, petty arguments and delays, the likes of which he had never seen before. 'I was caught in the middle,' he said. 'I could not show partiality to either actress. It was my job to get the film done on time. Of the two, Miriam was the worst offender, although Bette was not blameless either.'

Hopkins began the battle on camera by blowing smoke into Bette's eyes. During Bette's speeches she would pick imaginary lint off her shoulders, look at her watch, or straighten a painting in the background. Bette in turn allegedly cast shadows on Miriam's face when they shared a two-shot, revised lines in the script, and talked loudly to the grips when Miriam was concentrating on her close-ups. A *Time* reporter told of the squabble over dressing rooms. 'Davis contended that favoritism was being shown Hopkins since her dressing room was slightly closer to the set than hers. To settle this dispute, the assistant director carefully measured the distance between both dressing rooms and the set, made some minor shifts so they were precisely equidistant, and shooting resumed.'

Early in January 1943 *Old Acquaintance* was thirty-six days behind schedule because of rewrites and the combined illnesses of the leading ladies. On January 22, Bette reported ill. The following day Miriam took to her bed. The day after that, when Miriam returned,

Bette was out; Miriam missed the next day. Both actresses were called before Steve Trilling, Jack Warner's executive assistant. He threatened to turn the matter over to the Screen Actors' Guild, barring both from working in films again. With 'tears and denials of any differences,' the stars vowed to cooperate to get the picture finished amicably.

But Davis fully intended to get in one last chop at Hopkins. 'There was a scene in the film where I was supposed to slap her,' said Bette. 'The whole Warner studio knew this was coming up and the morning we shot the scene the set was crowded to the rafters.'

Miriam, however, would not cooperate. 'She wasn't licked yet,' said Bette. 'The most realistic way for an actress to absorb a blow is to be rigid as possible, but Miriam went limp. As I tried to shake her, she was like an empty sack. But she couldn't escape the moment of retribution forever, and at last I got in a perfectly timed swat. I can only report that it was an extremely pleasant experience. Miriam spent the rest of the morning weeping just beyond camera range, in what I assume was one last attempt to disconcert me.'

When *Old Acquaintance* was completed, Miriam Hopkins packed her bags, sold her house in Beverly Hills, and moved to New York. She was through with Hollywood she said. This last experience with Bette Davis had ended her desire to work in films again. (Five years later she would return, as a character actress in supporting roles.)

Bette Davis was also temporarily disenchanted. She vowed never again to work with women (of equal stature). In her next film, *Mr. Skeffington*, she would be surrounded by men, except one minor female role, that of her daughter, and a girlfriend mentioned frequently throughout the film, but never seen on camera. The film was scheduled for production in July 1943. In May, Bette left on an extended vacation. While she was gone her boss signed another major female star to a long-term contract at Warner's. She would prove to be a more formidable competitor and fighter than Miriam Hopkins.

Her name was Joan Crawford.

10

JOAN'S LAST DAYS AT METRO

'The studio no longer cared about us,' said Myrna Loy. 'They kept us locked into our old images while they concentrated on giving the good roles to newcomers. If we complained they had ways of forcing us out, of making us quit.'

After the success of *A Woman's Face*, Crawford wanted to play the part of the deaf and dumb girl in *The Spiral Staircase*, the rights to which she owned. 'No more cripples or maimed women!' said the producer of wholesome entertainment L.B. Mayer, who had previously ordered that no stills of Joan with a scar on her face be released from *A Woman's Face*. Instead, Mayer assigned Crawford to *When Ladies Meet*, wherein she would play the part of a best-selling novelist with 'advanced' ideas on love and marriage.

Playing a writer was a challenge to Crawford. She was working on a genuine characterization of her role, she told reporter J.D. Spiro. 'I'm wearing tortoiseshell glasses. They're very unflattering but they definitely add character.' She was also studying her writer friends. 'They all have one thing in common. They always seem preoccupied, as if their minds were working away off somewhere. Isn't that so?' 'I didn't answer immediately,' said Spiro, 'I tried to look vague and preoccupied. Maybe if we were preoccupied enough someday we might write a great novel. Who knows?'

When Ladies Meet also featured a newcomer to the Metro stable, a beautiful redhead from England by the name of Greer Garson. She had been discovered by L.B. Mayer during one of his periodic talent searches of Europe. Reeking of 'gentility and all round class,' Garson was brought to Culver City to play the headmaster's wife in *Goodbye Mr. Chips*. She was set for the lead in *Susan and God*, until Crawford stepped in and claimed Susan for her own. Reassigned to *Pride and Prejudice*, Garson acquired 'the friendship' of another important MGM executive, Benny Thau, who gifted the Titian actress with a light-blue Cadillac and convinced Crawford that the Britisher had the right level of competent cool to play opposite her in *When Ladies Meet*. Crawford was more than cordial to the newcomer. The two were photographed having afternoon tea, and Greer and her mother were guests at Joan's house that Christmas. By late January however, their friendship had become strained.

The discord had to do with the recent Oscar nominations list. It was a foregone conclusion that Joan Crawford would be nominated, at last, for *A Woman's Face*. But when the names were announced that month, another MGM actress was in her place – Greer Garson for *Blossoms in the Dust*.

'Another British refugee from Hitler,' was how Joan now referred to Garson, and when she was assigned the lead in *Mrs. Miniver*, to be directed by William Wyler, the man responsible for making Bette Davis a star, the air over Culver City turned putrid. 'The ladies are slinging sass, that is rumbling all the way up to the front office, where one of Greer Garson's friends is an important executive,' wrote Sheilah Graham. 'The studio confirms the validity of the feud with fervent and earnest denials.'

It wasn't fair, Crawford told Graham. 'I've kept my part of the bargain with Metro, doing every picture they asked me to. They must keep their part of the bargain too.'

L.B. Mayer tried to mollify the star by offering her two scripts, *Her Cardboard Lover* and *Three Hearts for Julia*. Joan told the mogul to shove both roles (they went to Norma Shearer and Ann Sothern) and she took off for an extended stay in New York.

Joan was really angry this time, her friends noted. She even began spitting at the press. At the Stork Club, after firing a nasty expletive at Dorothy Kilgallen, the star tried to chastise columnist Ed Sullivan for a previous injustice. 'Utterly discourteous' and 'Hollywood's perennial complainer' was how Sullivan described his former favorite. 'It's about time to crack down on wide-eyed Joan Crawford,' he wrote. 'For some years, I've tried sincerely to like her but she strains friendship to a breaking point. She gives the impression that she is some great princess, above and beyond the ordinary rules.' Furthermore, Sullivan believed reporters had always been fair and courteous to the star – 'stressing her good points, playing down her deficiencies. But no longer will this pillar rush to her defense when other movie stars put the blast on her for her insincerity, or for her affectations.'

'I marvel at newspapers,' Joan said in rebuttal, 'who permit journalistic lice to stink up their paper.'

She made up with Sullivan, of course, and with L.B. Mayer. 'There are greater problems facing all of us. We should be fighting *together*, to end the war in Europe,' said Joan magnanimously. She was also out of work, and needed her weekly paycheck for the upkeep of her family, and her five-room house in Brentwood (the seventeen other rooms were already shut down because of the shortage in cleaning help).

Returning to California, Joan met with Mayer. 'He cried and she cried. They're both full of shit,' said John Wayne, who was used as bait to make Crawford agree to star in *Reunion in France*. After bedding down with Wayne, Joan said the story had definite possibilities. She would play a famous French designer who joins the underground to fight the Nazis. She would have *two* love interests, Wayne and Philip Dorn, and a very expensive wardrobe by Adrian ('Dressing like a refugee is certainly not in her contract,' one critic commented on Joan's *haute couture* flight across France). The director assigned to the adventure film was Jules Dassin, who said of L.B. Mayer, 'His hand on your shoulder meant it was closer to your throat.'

Joan's killer instincts were also finely honed during the making of this film. In a scene with Philip Dorn (rumored to have rejected Joan's offscreen sexual advances), the two were walking down a Paris street, when with a flip of her hip Joan knocked him out of the two-shot. Raging at Crawford, Dassin jumped off the overhead camera and threatened to punch her out. 'Go ahead!' Crawford dared him, tearing the hat off her head.

A second dose of Nazi hokum followed. In *Above Suspicion*, Joan and Fred MacMurray posed as American spies on their honeymoon in wartime Salzburg. This would be the film that brought down the curtain on her eighteen-year career at MGM.

By the start of 1943, it wasn't only Greer Garson that was crowding Joan's star spotlight at Metro; the studio had become a veritable galaxy of female talent, some new – including Hedy Lamarr, Lana Turner, Judy Garland, Kathryn Grayson, Ava Gardner – some already established at other studios. 'They brought in Claudette Colbert, Katharine Hepburn and Irene Dunne,' said Myrna Loy, 'and gave them roles that should have been offered to us.'

On March 6, two days after *Mrs. Miniver* swept all the major Oscars, including Best Actress for Greer Garson, Joan Crawford was offered her next picture. It was entitled *Cry Havoc*, about a group of nurses caught in the battle of Batan. 'It should have been called *The Women Go to War*,' said Crawford. 'I turned it down.' She told L.B. Mayer her fans did not want to see her in another war picture, and furthermore she did not look good in a uniform. She asked to be cast as Madame Curie. That part was taken by Garson, Mayer told her, offering her another film, a comedy with William Powell entitled *Heavenly Bodies*, about two astrologers who fall in love. 'It was about a girl who stands around and does nothing,' said Joan. 'I told the studio to give the part to Hedy Lamarr.'

On June 27 Crawford met with Mayer once more. She requested a permanent release. He cried. She didn't. 'It was strictly a business arrangement,' she said. 'There was no loyalty on their behalf. After eighteen years and the millions I made for them, they made me pay fifty thousand dollars for my release.'

Mayer made the emotional statement to the press that his favorite daughter was leaving to pursue other options. But on her last day at the studio he didn't even bother to say goodbye. She drove on the lot, went to her dressing room and unpacked a bucket and cleaning supplies from the trunk. Inside, she scrubbed the kitchen floor and the bathroom. She washed down the walls, vacuumed the carpets, and cleaned the windows. After packing her personal belongings, she was visited by a studio publicist who alerted her to the photographers stationed outside the front gate, waiting to capture her departure. She kissed the publicist and carried her belongings to the car; a few minutes past midnight, she left MGM, via the back gate.

Arriving home that night, as the book *Mommie Dearest* tells it, the crazed and lonely Joan, without a job or a husband, terrorized her kids, then wrecked her rose garden ('Tina! Bring me the axe!'). The story, though vivid and entertaining was a little off in some points. First, Crawford was not alone at the time. Her third husband, Philip Terry was still on the premises. Second, the rose garden was no longer there, having been dug up and replaced by the victory garden a year earlier. And, third, the ousted star wasn't exactly unemployed. Nobody's fool when it came to business, she had already acquired a new agent, Bette Davis ten per-center, Lew Wasserman, who shopped around and was offered contracts for Joan at three studios. She passed on Columbia and Fox ('Darryl Zanuck and Harry Cohn liked to sample the goodies,' she said) and decided to go to Warner's, where the distaff roster of talent was select, but short, with only one formidable rival at the top – Queen Bette – who was battling once more with Jack Warner over money and scripts.

JOAN JOINS WARNER'S

'NO!' said Bette some forty years later when this writer asked her if there was any truth to the story that Jack Warner had brought in Joan Crawford as a backup threat, to keep her in line. 'Jack Warner was a *wonderful* man. He would *never* have done that to me. And, furthermore, how could Joan be a threat to *me*? We were never in the same category. We were different types *completely*.'

Because it was still wartime, and women's pictures were more popular than ever, Crawford, with the help of Lew Wasserman, cut herself in for a good deal at Warner's. She was to receive five hundred thousand dollars for three pictures, to be made over a period of three years, with another three one-year renewal options, with no suspension time added, and all options to be approved by Joan. She would also have pick of the top scripts, with full approval of directors, cinematographers and leading men. She would receive over-the-title billing, with her name to precede stars of equal stature, male or female.

On June 29, two days after she left MGM, Crawford made her

gracious entrance onto the Burbank lot. After she and Jack Warner had lunch in his private dining room, the pair toured the studio and Joan was introduced to some of the writers, producers and directors, the names of whom she already memorized. Joan was given her choice of three dressing rooms. 'For some peculiar reason,' said Bette Davis, 'she had asked for the one next to mine.'

Davis was not at Warner's at this time. While the studio was coming to terms on her new contract, she was spending the summer days in New Hampshire. When she was called by Jack Warner and told that Joan Crawford had joined the studio, Bette evinced mild amusement. 'How *nice* for you, Jack,' she said. 'Are you planning on making some more *musicals* for the war?'

Joan's first film, according to *The New York Times* of July 2, 1943, was to be *Night Shift*, a picture previously slated for Ann Sheridan but postponed many times. 'There were various scripts put in my lap,' said Crawford, 'but one of the main reasons I went to Warner's was because they owned the rights to *Ethan Frome*. I wanted very much to play in that picture.' The cast she envisioned for the classic tragedy was: Gary Cooper as Ethan Frome; herself as Mattie, the young servant he falls in love with; and as Zenobia, the carping wife, who cares for the crippled couple after their attempt at suicide fails, Joan wanted Bette Davis. 'That was my dream,' said Joan. 'When I brought it up to Jack Warner he suggested I move slowly, because Miss Davis also had her heart set on the property, but in the younger role.'

In mid-July, Davis returned to California for pre-production meetings on *Mr. Skeffington*. On her first day at the studio, she entered her dressing room and found a lavish display of flowers. A note was enclosed. It was from Joan Crawford, expressing delight at being at Warner's and asking if they could meet at her earliest convenience. 'Crawford obviously adored her,' said Bette's official biographer Sanford Dody. 'She wanted her approval, but Bette brushed her aside. She had no patience with her.'

Crawford was not dissuaded by Bette's rebuff. She attempted to thaw the cold queen's heart by sending her more flowers, followed by small gifts, a box of handkerchiefs, a small bottle of perfume. 'The safest procedure for Joan was to grovel,' said Charles Higham. 'Anything less abject might not win Bette's imperial approval.' Bette returned the gifts and declined the invitation. There was 'something odd, unsettling, and grotesque about this,' she confided to friends.

Joan's interest in Bette was more than professional, Higham believed. 'This greatest of suffering female stars admired this greatest of actresses sexually, as well as professionally,' he said, stating that Crawford was a repressed lesbian.

'He's full of shit,' said Crawford's foremost fan, and friend, Dore Freeman.

'It is doubtful,' said another Crawford friend, publicist Harry Mines, who frequently arranged dates for Joan. 'If anything she loved men too much.'

'It's possible, anything with Joan was possible,' said director George Cukor.

'How the - - - - do I know if Joan was a dyke,' said Bette. 'I never let her get that close to me.'

In late August, while trying to avoid Crawford, and telling various reporters that she wasn't even aware the actress was on the lot, Davis was to experience a personal tragedy that had all the terror, hysteria and conflict of one of her films. This real-life drama however, could have destroyed her name *and* her illustrious career, if her studio had not stepped in and kept most of the actual details away from the press and the public.

THE DEATH OF A HUSBAND

'Farney and I had a good life together. Classically European in tradition. I believed it would have gone on forever. I will always miss him.'

Bette Davis

Bette's marriage to Arthur Farnsworth, her second husband, was by all outward accounts a serene and compatible union. He was, like her, a 'New Englander', a member of 'Vermont's best families'. His father was a doctor; he was educated at the best East Coast schools; and someday, said Bette, he would 'inherit a lot of money.'

Sharing many of the same interests – a love of the outdoors, an appreciation of good music (he played the violin) – they lived part of the year in California, while she was working, and the rest of their time was spent on their farm in New Hampshire. Bette was reported to be at her happiest there, 'planting trees, walking in the freshly-mown fields, with her sturdy and adoring young husband by her side.'

In Los Angeles, after the war broke out, Farnsworth, an expert flier, was hired as the West Coast representative for Minneapolis-Honeywell. Socially, clad in a tuxedo or tailored tweed suits, he was also a very compatible companion for his star wife at the many Hollywood functions she was on call to attend. 'He was very handsome, well-built, seemingly well-educated and articulate, although most of the time I recall Bette did all the talking,' said Sheilah Graham. From time to time, notably in the spring of 1943, there were also rumors that the couple were fighting and that the marriage was in trouble. 'No truth to that at all,' said Bette. 'We are *divinely* happy.'

In May 1943, after the completion of *Old Acquaintance*, Bette was supposed to go to New Hampshire with her husband, but he went alone, and she travelled south of the border to Mexico, for reasons later explained. She extended her stay in Mexico, then in June she went East, to rejoin Farney. Early in August, after two months on the farm, the couple returned to California, where Bette was scheduled to start work on her new film, *Mr. Skeffington*. Stopped by a reporter at this time, Bette said she was 'very anxious to get back to work. Inactivity at times can drive me *mad*.'

On the afternoon of August 23, Bette said she remained at home while Arthur Farnsworth had lunch with her lawyer, Dudley Furse. They discussed a real-estate venture and signed some papers.

After lunch, walking to his car, Farnsworth suddenly screamed and fell backward on the sidewalk at 6249 Hollywood Boulevard. He fractured his skull and was rushed to Hollywood Receiving Hospital.

When Bette was called, at 4:15 P.M., she immediately alerted her doctor, Dr. Paul Moore, who arranged to have Farnsworth transferred to Cedars of Lebanon Hospital, where X-rays and more comprehensive tests could be made. On arriving at the hospital, Bette visited the unconscious man and, after conferring with the doctors, she decided not to alert his parents. 'If his condition was serious, his famous daughter-in-law would communicate with him,' a reporter for the *Rutland Herald* in Vermont said. 'Two years ago when Arthur was seriously ill with pneumonia, she telephoned or wired everyday,' said the injured man's father.

'All that night, Monday, and through the next night, Tuesday, Bette sat beside her husband, as he lay there, blond, handsome and motionless in the hospital,' *Modern Screen* reported. 'When he moaned she tried to send her voice across the plains of unconsciousness to recall him. Wednesday, without regaining consciousness, Farney died.'

The initial stories said the cause of death was a fractured skull, suffered when Farnsworth stumbled on Hollywood Boulevard. A routine autopsy would be performed, the *Los Angeles Herald* reported on Thursday, with funeral services to be conducted on Saturday at Forest Lawn.

On Thursday evening, in her home, with Farnsworth's flier buddies from The Quiet Birdmen (the group that owned the only copy of Joan Crawford's 'blue' movie, *The Plumber*), Bette toasted her late husband with champagne, 'because that's the way Arthur would have wanted it.' As the toasts were being made, they were joined by some somber mourners – the dead man's mother and brother from Vermont, who arrived too late to see Arthur alive. With them was Bette's lawyer, and an investigator from the district attorney's office. There was possible foul play involved in the death of her husband, Bette was told. The autopsy revealed that he had not died from the fall on Hollywood Boulevard, but from a previous head injury.

'Farnsworth had a blood clot on the right side of his skull, which apparently caused a pressure that made him dizzy and precipitated the fall,' said the *Los Angeles Times*.

'The blow must have been caused by the butt of a gun or some other blunt instrument,' Dr. Keyes, one of the examiners reported.

Arthur's mother, Mrs. Lucille Farnsworth, told Bette that she wanted an inquest to be held. 'My mother requested the inquest because Arthur was involved in secret war work. He was carrying papers in his briefcase, which had something to do with the North Bomb site,' said Mrs. Roger Briggs, sister of the deceased.

The chief coroner, Frank Vance, 'vacationing in the mountains, was reached by telephone.' He said the case warranted a full investigation, and he would return to hold an inquest on Tuesday of the following week.

This news upset Bette greatly. 'It was sheer agony, not knowing what could have caused this terrible tragedy,' she said.

Her agony, it was speculated, was compounded by the guilt she felt. Bette was *not* the devoted wife the Warner's press office presented at the time. Her marriage to Farnsworth was apparently in trouble. She had requested a divorce, and it was also said that she had been involved, albeit accidentally, in her husband's fatal fall.

'I was not violently in love with Farney,' the actress admitted in 1962. 'I loved his loving me and our mutual love of the New England way of life was the tie that finally bound.' In California, apparently the tie became loose a year after their marriage. Although he was strong and visibly robust, Farney it was stated was no match for the tempestuous Bette. She complained that he didn't have the guts to stand up to her. She needed a man to challenge her. 'Like Julie in *Jezebel*,' she said, 'I had to remain in charge, and when the man allowed it, I lost all respect for him. I certainly made it impossible.'

In April 1942, the year before his death, Bette was rumored to be romantically inclined towards a man she had met at the Hollywood Canteen. He may have been the orchestra leader she mentioned in her memoirs. Their affair was discreet but memorable. He wrote a song for her, and fulfilled her favorite sexual fantasy, to be made love to in a bed full of gardenias. 'When the hotel maids were tidying up the next day, what did they think of a wastebasket filled with very wilted gardenias?' she wondered. The affair was 'of limited duration,' she said, 'because we both were married.'

That Fall, while making *Old Acquaintance*, unnerved by the treachery of co star Miriam Hopkins, Bette's old demons surfaced again. 'I never yelled at Miriam,' she said, 'instead I held my anger in until I got home and then I screamed at everyone in sight.' Farney of course, like his predecessor, the placid Ham Nelson, was of little comfort to Bette. 'He didn't care to understand the pressures I was under at the studio, preferring instead to escape my torments by flying off into the wide blue yonder with his pilot-pals.' So, like that other much-misunderstood and tormented star Joan Crawford, Bette was compelled to look outside her marriage for comfort and romantic solace. She eventually found both in Vincent Sherman, the director of *Old Acquaintance*.

'I was not aware of her interest in me during the filming,' Sherman recalled in 1987. 'I had enough trouble trying to get her and Miriam [Hopkins] to behave. On the last day of shooting, a Saturday night, I asked Bette if she would stay late to do some final overdubbing. She agreed – if I would drive her to her mother's house afterwards. It was after ten o'clock, and we stopped at a drive-in restaurant and spoke about the picture. I told her I thought we had something good, that it looked as if we might have a hit picture. I also mentioned how much I enjoyed working with her.'

'I love you, Vincent,' said Bette.

'I love you too,' said Sherman, thinking they were exchanging the usual Hollywood endearments.

'No,' said Bette, taking his hand, 'I *truly* love you.'

'I looked at her,' said the director, recalling the night some forty years ago, 'and I felt chills. You must remember *who* Bette Davis was at this time. She was very attractive, a great actress, and a powerful star. I was a young impressionable director. I had a wife and young baby at home, but the circumstances, and the intimacy of what she was saying, was a very heady thing to ignore.'

Nothing happened on that night, said Sherman. He and Bette spoke for hours. She said that her physical relationship with her husband was over. Farney was a drinker, which made him important. She asked the director about his feelings. He confessed he was strongly attracted to her. 'The movie was finished,' he said, 'so I figured everything would die down.'

But Bette followed through. While he was editing *Old Acquaintance*, she called Sherman and the two had dinner. But again, although romance was in the air, the two remained chaste. 'If I had made a pass at her it would have offended her New England sense of values,' he said. 'Also, it had to be *her* idea.'

At Warner's one day Bette went looking for Sherman and told him that she was taking a vacation, in Mexico later that month, alone, without her husband. She asked the director to join her there. He agreed.

In Mexico that April, four months before the death of Farney,

Bette prepared for the arrival of her future lover. She rested, bought new clothes, and confided in her Acapulco hostess, Countess Dorothy Di Frasso, who, as legend tells it, was somewhat of a crack herself at subversive affairs. American by birth, a countess by marriage, and Dottie to her friends, the rich Di Frasso had a checkered reputation. 'She was a rough sort of woman,' said the genteel Helen Hayes. 'Dahling, she gave the most divine parties,' said Tallulah Bankhead. The men in Di Frasso's life included: Gary Cooper, gangster Bugsy Siegel, and Benito Mussolini. Because of the latter connection the countess was under surveillance by the FBI as 'a fascist agent' at the same time Bette was staying in her house in Mexico. Under those closely watched circumstances, it was just as well that Bette's planned liaison with Vincent Sherman did not take place.

'At the last minute I decided it wasn't wise to go to Mexico,' said Sherman.

'To my chagrin I waited and waited,' said Bette. 'He never came. He stood me up.'

Frustrated but not defeated, the actress knew she would soon see the stalwart young director again. She had already arranged for him to direct her next picture, *Mr. Skeffington*, which was scheduled to begin production that July. But Sherman was busy, directing Ida Lupino in *In Our Time*, Davis was told when she returned to Los Angeles that June. 'I'll wait,' she said, firmly stipulating that without Sherman there would be no Fanny Skeffington in the studio's future.

With the delay in production, Bette decided to go to New Hampshire, to rejoin her husband on the farm. She said their relationship at that point was 'sister and brother', although it was clear to some that the platonic arrangement did not please her spouse. It was at the farm that Farnsworth suffered a fall which precipitated his final injury. According to Bette, he was going downstairs to answer the phone when he slipped and fell on the stairs.

'There was a stairs to a loft in the farmhouse,' said Mrs. Roger Briggs. 'They were upstairs when the phone rang downstairs. He had wool socks on and he fell down and hit the back of his head. Bette was there. He seemed to be all right. We didn't know about it because we didn't see him. This was about two months before the fatal fall.'

The wound apparently healed, although Farnsworth sustained a stiff neck and was a little off balance at times. Early in August, Farnsworth called his second sister, Mrs. Jon De'Besche. 'He and Bette were in New York, on their way back to California when he called me in Connecticut, where I lived. I had a new baby girl and he had always wanted a baby girl. Arthur was very fond of children. He told me he and Bette were trying to have some, but she didn't get pregnant. They were in New York for several days, but he waited until the last minute to call me. I said to him, "Gee, Art, why didn't you call sooner? I would have bundled the baby up and brought her in to see you." He didn't make sense on why they didn't visit. He was fuzzy in his head, from the accident on the stairs.'

It was her husband's 'shakiness' that led Bette to suspect that he was drinking on the sly. 'They all drank a lot,' said Mrs. Briggs, 'but that didn't cause the fall.'

On the train back to California, where Bette would begin production on *Mr. Skeffington*, she told Vincent Sherman she and Farnsworth argued over their marriage. He already knew of her feelings for her director, 'because she told him,' said Sherman. On the train, they fought, and it was said either she hit him or he fell, sustaining a second injury to his head.

'Arthur was a darling guy, but no match for Bette,' a family member recalled. 'He should have left her then. If he had, he would have been alive today.'

In Los Angeles, on the day he collapsed on Hollywood Boulevard, one reporter claimed that Bette was with her husband at the lunch with her lawyer. Another source, writer Hector Arce, said that the purpose of the lunch had 'nothing to do with real estate. Farnsworth didn't have any money ("We weren't a wealthy family," his sister Mrs. De'Besche confirmed. "My father was a dentist and a chiropractor").' The purpose of the lunch was in fact to save money for Bette by having her husband file a joint tax report with her. 'The taxes had to be filed the following week,' said Hector Arce, 'so the forms were signed in the lawyer's office on Hollywood Boulevard, and walking back to their car, Farney became unsteady on his feet again. She accused him of drinking too much at lunch, and she pushed him. He fell sideways, towards the street, and hit his head on the curb.'

'To my knowledge he was alone when he collapsed and hit the back of his head and that was what killed him,' said Farnsworth's sister, Mrs. De'Besche.

'Of course it was an accident,' Arce stressed, 'but it was believed that Bette was indeed there and that she did push him. She had no intention of killing him, and if she was charged she would be acquitted. But if there was a trial the details of their shaky marriage and her infatuation with Vincent Sherman might come out. Her reputation and her career might be seriously affected. Playing a villain on screen was one thing, but in real life people were not as tolerant.'

On Saturday, August 28, services for Arthur Farnsworth were held at the Church of the Recessional in Forest Lawn. At the request of the widow and Warner's publicity department, the press and the public were asked to stay away. 'Rising from her sickbed,' Bette was helped into the church, with Ruthie, her mother on one side, and studio chief, Jack Warner, on the other. The reported mourners included John Garfield, Bette's hairdresser and makeup team – Maggie Donovan and Perc Westmore – and Vincent Sherman. ('No, I didn't attend,' said Sherman, 'I thought it would be awkward.')

The burial would be back East, but the body could not be moved until four days hence, when the official hearing into his death was to be held. And if the ruling was foul play, there would be a further investigation, with charges filed.

Bette wept openly as the 121st and 123rd Psalms ('Farney's favorites') were read in church that Saturday morning. Distraught, when the services were over, she clutched the hand of Jack Warner and asked to speak to him privately. As the other guests filed out, she and Warner remained seated in the front pew, beside the flower-laden coffin. Placing his arm around his number one star, Warner had to bend his head low to listen to her urgent whispers. 'The details of their conversation were not heard by anyone,' said Hector Arce. 'And I doubt if Bette was fool enough to tell Warner about the trouble in her ill-fated marriage, or about her interest in one of his studio directors, especially since Warner could use this as leverage against her at another time. But he must have agreed to use his influence to help her, to get the inquest settled quickly. Certainly he had that power, because look what happened.'

On the following Tuesday morning, wearing the appropriate mourning costume – 'a loose black beret, a black blouse, and black skirt, relieved only by a dull red and green flower pattern' – the widowed actress appeared for the inquest. 'No role of tragedy Bette Davis has portrayed before the camera ever equaled her appearance before a six-man Coroner's Jury when she testified today,' said the *Los Angeles Times.* 'She left glamour behind her when she entered. Her face devoid of makeup, was drawn and tired. She took the witness stand and answered questions briefly in a monotone.'

When asked if she knew of any accident that the deceased might have suffered, Bette told of the incident in New Hampshire the previous June, when he fell going downstairs to answer the phone. 'He was kind of wiggly there for a few minutes and very limp,' she said, 'but he never said anything about it.'

She made no mention of the alleged subsequent fall on the train two weeks before, or of the arguments they had over their marriage. As she talked of the New Hampshire accident, her brow would knit slightly for a moment, said the *Times,* and she would squint a bit. 'He never went to see a physician. Nor did he complain,' said Bette. 'I never thought about the accident until the autopsy, and they asked me if I remembered any previous accident.'

Taking the stand, the autopsy surgeon, Dr. Homer R. Keyes, dismissed this first fall as the cause of death: any injury incurred two months ago would have since healed. Nor was his last fall, on Hollywood Boulevard, responsible. 'A basal skull injury probably caused this man's death,' said Dr. Keyes. 'It didn't result from the fall, but instigated it. Consider the blood in the fracture. It is black and coagulated, not merely purple and partially congealed as it would have been if the injury had been received as a result of the fall. The fracture must have been inflicted about fourteen days ago.'

Bette, 'in an acute state of shock', remained in the anteroom while other witnesses were called. Two gave testimony that they had seen Farnsworth collapse on Hollywood Boulevard. They said he had been alone at the time. Meanwhile her lawyer and a representative from Warner's made some calls. After a recess, the inquest verdict was read. Reversing the examining surgeon's conclusion, the six-man panel decided that Farnsworth's death *was* caused by the accident in New Hampshire, two months previously. There would be no further investigation.

'It is impossible for me to thank individually all the persons who have been so kind to me,' said a greatly relieved Bette to the press. 'We are leaving today to take Farney East.'

> *'Farney was a real charmer, but an alcoholic who was tied to his mother's apron strings . . . and what a mother! Christ, what a cold bitch.'*
>
> Bette Davis some years later

With the investigation over, Davis now had to face the journey east, and the funeral services in Vermont and New Hampshire. Fortified and protected by Ruthie, she and her mother took turns sitting with Farney's brother and his grieving, confused mother, who insisted they visit the coffin in the baggage compartment from time to time.

On Saturday, September 4, the coffin was unloaded in Albany and the funeral cortège drove to Rutland, Vermont, Farnsworth's hometown, where his mother insisted that her son be waked, in an open coffin.

According to author Charles Higham, Bette was 'forced to sit all night by the open coffin . . . and one of Farnsworth's aunts became hysterical and began digging the body out of the coffin.'

That never happened, the deceased sisters claimed. 'I was outraged when I read the stories about the funeral,' said Mrs. De'Besche. 'Most of them were untrue. There was only one disagreement at the wake. Both the minister and I wanted the coffin closed. Bette and my mother wanted it open, so we went along with their wishes.'

An eyewitness in Vermont claimed that during the wake Bette was cool to the Farnsworth clan and only displayed grief when she sensed she was being observed by the press. 'It was a very difficult, very public situation,' said Mrs. Briggs, 'but Bette was absolutely adorable to my mother and all of us. She couldn't have been nicer, more thoughtful or more considerate.'

On Monday, September 6, the funeral services were held at the Rutland Episcopal Church. Immediately following, Bette and some members of the Farnsworth family drove to her farm in New

Hampshire, leaving the deceased and the coffin behind in the Rutland funeral home. 'It was an emotional decision, to have Arthur buried at the farm,' said Mrs. De'Besche. 'They had built the place together and Bette wanted him to rest there.'

In New Hampshire, it was further reported that Bette and Mrs. Farnsworth, suspicious of the details of her son's death, had bitter words. After the blasting of rocks and the leveling of trees, when the deceased was finally laid to rest, 'Mrs. Farnsworth decided her beloved son shouldn't be at Butternut at all but in the family vault in Vermont. She told Bette that Farney would have to be dug up again and shipped there,' said author Charles Higham.

'The remains *were* moved,' said Mrs. De'Besche, 'but it happened much later. [In June 1945, according to the town clerk in Pittsford, Vermont.] Mother felt it would be easier for Bette, because she was married again, and they felt it would be easier for both of them.'

'Bette and my mother were very strong ladies,' Mrs. Briggs added. 'But they had no fight over my brother's death. As far as we know, her marriage to my brother was a happy one, and his death was from a brain hemorrhage caused by the fall in New Hampshire.'

Cloaked in grief, when Bette returned to California in September 1943, she asked everyone to respect her privacy by not asking about the details of her late husband's death and his many funerals.

'She told me he was epileptic,' said Joan Blondell, 'and had fallen many times previously.'

'She told me he was a heavy drinker,' said director Irving Rapper.

After he died they found two empty liquor bottles in his briefcase, Charles Higham stated.

'There was no odor of alcohol on his breath when he was removed to the Hollywood Receiving Hospital,' Detective Sergeant H.R. Johnson and Dr. Paul H. Moore, told the *Los Angeles Times* on the day of his death.

Another popular red-herring story, and one that would be repeated on Hollywood sets for years to come, was that Farnsworth had been seeing another woman. She was married and her husband caught them in a motel and killed him. 'Then they called up Bette and said "He's up in the El Portal Motel. Come and get him",' said script supervisor, Bob Gary.

'No one found out the true story,' said Vincent Sherman.

'The subject [of his death] was off-limits and remained a mystery, because that's what Warners wanted,' said Sheilah Graham. 'You must remember the studios had enormous power in those days.'

'There were certain topics Mother would not go into detail about, and that was one of them,' said B.D. Hyman.

To add to the speculation, in subsequent years, Bette would also vacillate in her devotion to her late husband. 'He was THE most beautiful Yankee,' she told *Women's Wear Daily* reporter Nancy Collins. 'It would have been forever, had he lived. He loved me, he had a good career in his own right, and he certainly had his own identity.'

'It was a tragedy when he died,' she told another interviewer, 'although our marriage was headed for disaster anyway. He used me too . . . he got violent.'

In November, 1943, *Photoplay* writer Fredda Dudley reported that Bette *had* been with her husband at that last lunch, on the day he died. The same month the actress spoke of her emotional guilt, over the accident, to director Vincent Sherman. And three years later her next husband, William Grant Sherry, said he and his bride were walking along Hollywood Boulevard one day when they reached the spot outside her lawyer's office. 'Bette turned white,' Sherry recalled. 'I asked her what was wrong, and she said, "This is where Farney fell that day, after I pushed him".'

Whatever the true cause of his death, the handsome young flier from Vermont had the last laugh at Bette's expense. The joint tax form he signed on the day of his fatal fall, came back to haunt his illustrious widow. The Internal Revenue Service challenged the return a few years later. Her husband had no income for 1943, they stated, disallowing her claim. And Bette was forced to pay sixty thousand dollars in back taxes.

11

BRAVE BETTE

'Once again Bette Davis has faced tragedy with courage and left all bitterness to those of smaller heart and narrower vision.'

A reporter from the set of *Mr. Skeffington*

In the aftermath of her husband's death, Bette said she was fortunate she had her work to return to. Tears were duly shed, but they weren't hers. One co-worker said that production on her next film *Mr. Skeffington* was 'five months of war, sheer hell, with no casualties taken.' And Bette agreed. In those years she admitted that when people disliked her, they really detested her, 'And they couldn't do any more about me than they could about death and taxes.'

As Fanny Skeffington, the most beautiful woman in New York in 1914, the star demanded approval over every facet of the production. She had her friend Maggie Donovan design her hairstyles, 'which gave me the illusion of beauty,' with Donovan's husband, Perc Westmore, creating the makeup. Some forty costumes were created by Orry-Kelly, and Ernie Haller was assigned to photograph the star. 'She began to go to extremes,' said Haller. 'She wanted to look ravishingly beautiful in the opening scenes, and then ugly as sin in the last shots. She had a ghastly rubber mask designed to make her look older. Instead it made her look like something out of a horror movie, but she insisted on wearing it.'

Her ego had also reached monstrous proportions, the producers of the film said. Julius J. Epstein and his brother Philip had written *Casablanca*, the previous year. The success of that classic led to their assignment in 1943 as writers and producers of *Mr. Skeffington*. They quit 'when we found out that Bette Davis had more power than we had.' She did considerable damage to the script. 'She wants her name to be mentioned even when she isn't in the scene, so no one can ever forget for a second she's in the story,' production manager Frank Mattison wrote in a memo to studio executive Steve Trilling. When Bette's temperament and constant demands slowed filming down to a crawl, a second memo was sent by Mattison. 'It sure is tough,' he said, 'to sit by with a show where she is the whole band; the music; and all the instruments, including the bazooka.'

It was Bette's obsession for perfection, coupled with the intense grief she was experiencing for her departed husband, that caused her neurotic behavior, her friends insisted.

'It wasn't grief, it was guilt,' said another source. 'Her sins were catching up with her.'

'Guilty? Bette Davis? Don't be foolish,' said George Cukor. 'She is a star, and all stars learn how to cultivate one very important asset early in their career: a very short memory. They remember only what they want to remember.'

GETTING IT

The main problem with Bette during the making of *Mr. Skeffington* was sex and the lack thereof, said director Vincent Sherman, who at the time was still the object of Bette's persistent ardor. 'She made it very difficult for me,' he said. 'The more I resisted the more impossible she became. She insisted we become lovers. She threatened to have the entire production shut down if I continued to refuse her. I've worked with many actresses, including Joan [Crawford], but no one was as destructive as Bette. That sexual suppression you see on the screen, that nervous hysterical energy was not acting. That's the way she was in real life. The only way I could finish the picture was by having an affair with her.'

Bette wanted Sherman to leave his wife and marry her, but the affair lasted only to the end of the filming, he said. 'I avoided her after that. I refused to return her calls. She tried to make trouble. But Jack Warner didn't care as long as the picture was made. And I already had told my wife, who had a wonderful understanding of what goes on in this business. Then sometime later, after the editing was finished and the guys in the front office had seen it, Bette stopped me on the street at Warner's. "Everyone says the picture is wonderful," she said, "so I want you to direct my next one." I said, "Bette, do me a favor, get another director." And I kept walking, as fast as I could, away from her.'

MEANWHILE BACK AT THE HOLLYWOOD CANTEEN

Neither the loss of her husband, or the affair with Vincent Sherman kept Bette away from her job as chief hostess and president of the Hollywood Canteen committee. Throughout the duration of the war, as long as there were American forces fighting, she said it was her duty to work as hard as she could for the good of the Canteen.

'Only a bare month after the tragic loss of her husband, dressed in a simple black suit and dark snood, her mourning costume relieved by a white orchid, Bette Davis showed up for the first anniversary of the Hollywood Canteen,' wrote Hedda Hopper.

'Mrs. Joe Lewis lost her boy, and a week later she was back washing dishes,' said Bette, making little of her valor. Sitting at a front table at the anniversary party she gallantly signed autographs and postcards for the boys; but refused to dance.

When the star attendance fell off at the Canteen, it was Bette who manned the phones and called up the big names to haul themselves back to the club – 'and not just when the syndicated photographers are present,' she ordered. She also opened the Canteen doors to admit servicewomen – the Wacs and the Waves of America's Armed Forces. But they weren't allowed to dance with the men. That was a duty reserved for the stars and the official Canteen hostesses. Said hostesses also received mimeographed instructions from Bette, 'Hints on how to treat wounded vets.'

'Forget the wounds, remember the man,' the instructions said. 'Don't be over-solicitous, nor too controlled to the point of indifference. Learn to use the word "prosthetics" instead of artificial limbs. Never say, "It could have been worse." And when he talks about his war experiences, *listen*, but don't ask for more details than he wants to give.'

To bring in more cash for the war effort, Bette Davis prevailed upon Jack Warner to contribute his profits from three patriotic all-star films. The first of these was *This Is The Army*, starring Ronald Reagan, George Murphy, Kate Smith and 350 GIs marching on stage in the closing number. The second film, *Thank Your Lucky Stars* had Dinah Shore, Errol Flynn, John Garfield and Bette, in her singing debut. She was originally set to do a scat duet with Olivia de Havilland and George Tobias. But when Bette asked what "scat" meant they gave that tricky rhythmic number to Ida Lupino. Instead she would sing a new song by Frank Loesser and Arthur Schwartz, 'They're Either Too Young Or Too Old.'

Recording the song was not difficult for the star. 'My two former husbands were musicians,' she said, 'and they always complimented me on my musical talent.' It was the dancing that followed the song that caused some worry. She was to do a jitterbug, with full gymnastics that would send the star flying every which way over her partner's shoulders.

On the day of filming, the atmosphere on soundstage eighteen was 'tense'. Bette, wearing a shocking-pink brocaded two-piece gown with long bright-green gloves, arrived with 'a retinue of advisers, well-wishers, and sympathizers, who trailed along, offering maxims, condolences, and banalities.' Sitting down, she was handed a glass of clear spring water and three cigarettes, which she puffed on in succession.

She was introduced to her dance partner, Conrad Wiedell, 'a twenty-four-year-old curly blond – Hollywood's King of the Jitterbugs.' Conrad nervously confessed he had danced with many other stars, including Betty Hutton and Joan Crawford, but meeting Bette Davis was 'like walking into a room where FDR is seated.'

'Go easy on me, kid,' said Bette.

Standing on her mark, Bette lip-synched the song, then sauntered to the middle of the dance floor where she was grabbed by Conrad. 'He swung her clear into the ozone, towards the ceiling, alarming several electricians on the overhead catwalks,' a reporter noted. Then he hurled her to the left, to the right, at a ninety-degree angle, which nearly caused her eyes to pop out. Bringing her back to earth she slammed into his hip and almost stumbled as she tried to stand.'

'Cut!' said the director. 'Let's try it once more.'

'No! No!' said Bette, barely able to stand straight. 'I said one take, and that was *it*.'

Turning to the press she said, 'Show's over, gentlemen. Now get the hell out.'

HELLO JOAN!

In July 1944 Jack Warner announced that the third of his studio's patriotic films was going into production – *Hollywood Canteen*, based on the activities of Bette and her volunteers. The big-budget feature would have sixty-two stars, two big bands, five vocalists, twenty-four dancers, Roy Rogers, Trigger, and . . . Joan Crawford.

> '*Hollywood is tough on has-beens. The invitations stopped coming. My phone stopped ringing. Old friends stopped coming by. If it wasn't for my husband and my family, I would have gone crazy.*'
>
> Joan Crawford

It had been a rough year for Joan. As Bette Davis continued to ignore her calls, Jack Warner threatened to put her on suspension for not working.

After refusing to do the Ann Sheridan reject *Night Shift*, Crawford also passed on *Never Goodbye*, written specifically for her by *Dark Victory* director Edmund Goulding.

'What are you bitching *for*?' she asked Goulding when she vetoed his script. 'You got your fifty thousand dollars for writing the damn thing.'

Joan still had her eyes on *Ethan Frome*, and she asked director Goulding to talk to Bette Davis about working with her. 'I wouldn't go near her with a ten-foot electric pole,' said Goulding, mindful of the heart attack he had to fake on his last visit with the star.

In December 1943 Jack Warner sent Crawford the script of *Conflict*, about a shrewish wife who gets bumped off after her husband (Humphrey Bogart) leaves her for her younger sister (Alexis Smith). After reading the script, Joan told her agent to convey the news to Mr. Warner that 'Joan Crawford never dies in her movies, and she never ever loses her man to *anyone*.' 'Who the hell does she think she is? Bette Davis?' Warner fumed, and sent Joan a telegram in which he ordered the star to 'Come in and go to work,' or she would be put on suspension.

When she received the summons, Joan put on her best star bib and paid a call on the studio boss. Alerted by the studio gateman that she was on her way to see him, Warner ducked out the side door of his office. Warmly greeting the boss's secretary, Joan said: 'Tell Jack he is perfectly right. I should not be getting paid if I am not working. So I want him to take me off salary until we can agree on a suitable script.'

'That really confused the old bastard,' Crawford said later. 'He couldn't threaten or yell at me if I wasn't on salary. Deep down, I think he also respected me. It takes guts to turn down work in Hollywood. The name of the game is always your next picture.'

It also took courage because she had little money. Her funds were tied up in bonds and real estate, she said. So she took out a second mortgage on the house and let the last of her staff, a children's helper, go. Her husband, Phil Terry, had been dropped by RKO and was working in his father's factory. She got up each morning and made his lunch – 'Egg and lettuce sandwich, a piece of cake and a big, juicy pear, which Joan packs herself.' She also continued her volunteer work and wrote a guest column for a fan magazine. 'We can't give you much, only an honorary payment of two hundred dollars,' she was told. 'I'll take it,' said Joan. The column served the main purpose of keeping her name in print before the public, and it also provided upfront seats at the important premieres and top night spots. Her amateur reporter's eye could be keen on these outings. 'Neither Bette Davis, or Joan Fontaine need apologize for wearing long evening dresses at a recent party at Ciro's,' Joan wrote. 'None of us have bought any new formal gowns since the war, so it's fun to take the old ones out of the closet.'

In her column, Joan also shared the news, sad and otherwise, passed on to her by the stars. Hollywood's wartime losses could be deep. Eva Gabor's dog, Misha, had been drafted and killed in action in Europe. Loretta Young lost her maid – not in the war, but at the Hollywood Canteen. (The maid was an aspiring opera singer. She sang at the Canteen one night and left Loretta to join a professional company.)

Joan was also a faithful volunteer at the Hollywood Canteen. 'I was there without fail every Monday night,' she said. She was mobbed on her first visit, and was busy signing autographs when President Bette Davis walked in. 'Hello, *Joan!*' said Bette. 'We need you desperately, in the kitchen. There are dishes to be washed.'

'A very pleasant pile of shit for wartime audiences,' was how Crawford described the movie version of *Hollywood Canteen*. As a Warner's contract star, albeit unemployed, she was asked to appear in the film but balked at first. 'The public haven't seen me in over a year,' she said. 'Playing a bit part might make them really believe I'm all washed up.' Bette Davis and Barbara Stanwyck had already agreed to appear in the picture she was told. 'Oh?' said Joan. 'And what is the billing?' 'It's alphabetical,' she was advised. 'Well . . .' said Joan, ' "C" comes before "D" and "S"; so count me in.'

The producer of *Hollywood Canteen* asked her to do a musical number. 'Nope,' said Joan. 'My musical days are over. I would prefer to do something more dignified. Recite a poem or give a pep talk to the soldiers.'

She would talk, then dance cheek to cheek with an army sergeant (Dane Clark). The day her brief scene was shot, the soundstage was crowded with extras and onlookers, eager to watch Joan Crawford at work. When her scene was over, they mobbed her, asking for autographs. Watching this homage from a distance was the mistress of ceremonies Bette Davis. 'I'll bet you five bucks she paid them to rush her,' she muttered to producer Alex Gottlieb.

Joan Crawford went on record numerous times saying she admired Bette Davis for her talent and incredible fighting spirit. Bette in turn confessed she was 'bored by Joan.' To her cohorts at the studio she often referred to Joan as that mannequin from MGM. 'I mean, nothing could be further from me,' said Bette, 'the clothes, the hair, the constant obsession with image. I have no time for people who spend their time in nightclubs.'

Vincent Sherman commented on the rivalry between the two during this time. 'I think Joan felt that Bette was superior to her. And I was told that Bette made some scurrilous remarks about Joan. "I wouldn't mind her personality," she said, "if only she could act." '

MILDRED PIERCE

In the fall of 1945 Crawford would embark on a film project that would establish her acting credentials and restore her star status in Hollywood. It would also force Bette Davis to acknowledge Crawford's presence at Warner's, and look to her own position as queen of the lot. The name of the property was *Mildred Pierce*. 'It would not only save her, but set her off on a new series of conquests,' said *The New York Times*.

'Kinda hard . . . kinda soft . . . Mildred Pierce. The kind of a woman most men want but shouldn't have.'

Confessions of a gay Cab Driver:
'What Joan Crawford – and most of all Bette Davis – is to me is relief, *a way to relax. I can get out the video, put on a good dress, and watch* Mildred Pierce. *I don't need anything more. That's my food, my sleep, my shoulder to cry on.'*

From the book *Girls on Film* by Julie Burchill

It could have been the story of Joan's life, critics commented later. Mildred Pierce was an ambitious lower-class woman, with a vain, evil, selfish daughter who competed with her mother for the same man.

The book, by James M. Cain, first appeared in 1941. It was not a best-seller, but it did attract the attention of one Jerry Wald, who was to become Crawford's producer and savior for many years.

Wald, a journalist and scriptwriter was described as 'the fastest and smoothest talker ever born in Brooklyn.' His abundant credits at Warner's included two recent successful war films, *Destination Tokyo* and *Objective Burma*, and he was anxious to expand his reputation by breaking into women's pictures.

It was Wald who first suggested to Jack Warner that they buy the rights to *Mildred Pierce*. The story of the 'immoral Mildred,' who uses men to provide the luxuries for her pampered spoiled daughter, Veda, was considered too racy at the time. Wald was told that if he could revise the story so it 'played on a higher level' the studio would have a good chance of getting it past the censors. The producer had the story sanitized, making Mildred more noble, and in February 1944 Warner's bought the film rights for fifteen thousand dollars.

From February to October of that year, seven different treatments and scripts were worked on by six different writers. Screenwriter Catharine Turney worked on two drafts and had been asked to do a third when she was delegated to work on a picture for Bette Davis. 'Wald tried but failed to have me reassigned, because Bette was adamant in refusing to release her writer,' said Turney.

Retitled *Courage* (analogous to *Mother Courage*), subsequent drafts were worked on by Albert Maltz and Ranald MacDougall. On the morning of September 17, 1944, the final script was handed to Jack Warner. His enthusiastic response came that afternoon. He was approving a budget of $1.34 million, with production to start on November 6. The haste of his decision was stimulated by two positive factors, said Jerry Wald. The script, credited to Ranald MacDougall, was first-class. And, by a fortuituous coincidence, two weeks before Paramount Pictures had released a hit movie based on another James M. Cain novel. *Double Indemnity*, the story of a trollop wife (Barbara Stanwyck) who murders her husband with the help of his insurance agent (Fred MacMurray), was drawing popular praise from the critics and public, not to mention the wrath and denunciation from hundreds of church groups around the country.

The timing of the *Mildred Pierce* filming, with the release of *Double Indemnity*, was perfect, and just a tad derivative, some film historians and Paramount executives would later claim. There was no murder in the original book of *Mildred Pierce*, and the incorporation of flashbacks suggested that Wald had altered the plot and inserted those techniques after viewing an early screening of *Double Indemnity*. Not true, said Warner's legal department, claiming the ideas had been in Wald's treatment two years earlier.

THE CASTING OF THE FILM

By late September with the green light from Jack Warner, and a director, Michael Curtiz (*The Private Lives of Elizabeth and Essex*), assigned to the picture, Jerry Wald was still without an actress to play the lead role of Mildred. 'No actress wanted to play the mother of a sixteen-year-old,' said Catharine Turney. Bette Davis would state repeatedly in subsequent years that she never saw a script, although her contract with the studio said she had first refusal on all class A scripts at the studio. Other actresses who passed on the role were Rosalind Russell (signed to an independent deal at the studio the year before), and Ann Sheridan. 'I was offered one of the early scripts,' said Sheridan. 'I didn't like the story. Mildred was too tough, and the kid was an absolute horror.'

It was Jerry Wald who thought of Crawford. He met her on her first day at the studio, when her agent, Lew Wasserman, brought her around to meet the staff producers. Having done her homework, Joan also knew Wald's credits and greeted him as an old friend. 'I was very impressed with her,' he said. 'I said to myself, "Now, *that's* a star." And I made a note to myself to work with her someday.'

With Warner's approval he sent her the script. 'She called me that night,' said Wald, 'whooping with joy. I didn't know about Joan and the telephone then. She considers an hour on the phone par.'

Mildred Pierce would be her comeback role, Crawford decided. 'I was eager to accept this chance to portray a mother who has to fight against the temptation to spoil her child. As I have two adopted children, I feel I could understand Mildred and do the role justice.'

But she had some competition to face. Another actress with an independent contract at the studio was now in the running for Mildred Pierce. Barbara Stanwyck, who had played the steamy blonde killer in *Double Indemnity* and was eager to play another Cain character, read the script and asked for the role. 'I desperately wanted the part,' said Stanwyck. 'I went after it. I knew what a role for a woman it was, and I knew I could handle every facet of Mildred. I laid my cards on the table with Jerry Wald. After all, I'd done a dozen pictures at Warner's by then, including *So Big* and *Meet John Doe*. I'd paid my dues, and I felt Mildred was me.'

Stanwyck also had the support of Michael Curtiz, whose creative influence on the project was considerable. Curtiz, to put it mildly, was opposed to Joan Crawford as Mildred. When Jerry Wald suggested her, the director fumed, 'With her high-hat airs and her goddamn shoulder-pads, she's a has-been. I won't work with her.' His choice was Barbara Stanwyck.

Crawford, when told of Curtiz's reaction, decided her only recourse was to humble herself before the great director. After fifty-six pictures and nineteen years as a star, she told Wald she was willing to test for the part. Early in October, 1944, with a modicum of makeup and her pep personality restrained, Crawford auditioned on camera for Curtiz. 'After the test, which so engrossed him he forgot to yell "Cut!",' said Joan, 'he forgot all about Stanwyck.'

> *'You think now you've made a little money you can get a new hairdo and some expensive clothes and turn yourself into a lady. But you can't. Because you'll never be anything but a common frump, whose father lived over a grocery store and whose mother took in washing. It makes me shrivel up to think you ever conceived me.'*
>
> Veda Pierce to her mother, Mildred

Having secured the main role, Crawford volunteered to test with the young actresses who were trying out for the second lead, that of her nasty, conniving daughter, Veda. 'They auditioned close to twenty girls,' said Crawford, 'but none of them seemed right. It was a difficult role to cast. The part called for a young girl who could act and sing. She had to age from fourteen to nineteen, to be credible as a child *and* as an adult. There was also that combination of sweetness and evil that Veda possessed. I recall one girl who came to see us from Twentieth Century Fox, where she later starred in several of their movies. She was quite good as the younger Veda, but in a later scene, where she was supposed to be a singer in a cheap nightclub, she was hopelessly inadequate.'

A serious candidate for the part of the vile Veda was Shirley Temple. 'Shirley was Jerry's Wald's idea,' said Crawford. 'The idea caused some laughter at first; but not from me. Shirley was fifteen or sixteen at the time, the right age. She had musical talent, and she certainly could act. No one stays on board the Good Ship Lollipop all those years without talent. She had left Fox and was with David Selznick. I believe she had already made *Since You Went Away*, playing Claudette Colbert's bratty daughter, and David was eager to have her do more adult roles.'[1]

Reportedly it was Michael Curtiz who said no to Shirley. 'Vonderful!' he cried. 'And who do ve get to play Mildred's lover? Mickey Rooney?'

'Curtiz didn't want me either,' said Crawford. 'And it could have worked with Shirley. She never got to test, because at the same time Universal sent over Ann Blyth. I was there when Ann came in. She was so lovely that my first reaction was, She's too sweet; she'll never be able to play the bitchy scenes. But we read together and she was wonderful. Then we tested together. Ann was perfect. She was the right age, the right type, and a superb actress and singer. The test was shown to Jack Warner. He agreed, and we were in production within two weeks.'

'Don't do it the way I showed you, do it the way I mean.'
Director Curtiz to Joan Crawford

On December 7, 1944, shooting commenced on *Mildred Pierce*. Within the week Michael Curtiz asked that Crawford be fired. The problem had to do with Joan's revised interpretation of her role. In her winning test for Curtiz her usual look of high gloss had been supplanted by one of low-keyed starkness. For the actual filming, Joan had no intention of appearing dull or dowdy. 'Mike and I wanted to deglamorize Joan,' said producer Jerry Wald. 'We wanted to make her look like she lived in a suburb and bought the cheapest dresses.'

'I went to Sears and bought my dresses off the rack,' Joan later told this writer, failing to add that her dresses were subsequently custom-tucked at the waist with slight padding added to the famous Crawford shoulders.

[1] In her 1988 book *Child Star*, Shirley Temple confirmed that she and her mother 'lit up like beacons' when Warner Bros. suggested she play Veda Pierce. 'Not only does this child seduce and kill her stepfather,' said the enthusiastic Temple, 'she attempts to hang the murder around the neck of her self-made tycoon mother.'

On the first day of shooting she wore one of these dresses for a kitchen scene. Director Curtiz politely asked her to dispose of the shoulder pads. 'Those are *my* shoulders,' Joan cried in half-truth. On the second day, for a scene where she was waiting on tables in restaurant, Joan wore a regulation (but custom-fitted) uniform, plain Red Cross shoes, with full cocktails-at-five makeup and hairdo. This time Curtiz screamed and attempted to wipe the lipstick from her mouth with his fist. Joan, 'gulping down loud dry sobs fled to her dressing room'.

Producer Jerry Wald was called to the set. Curtiz told him to pay off Crawford and replace her with Barbara Stanwyck. Crawford asked that the director be fired and 'replaced with a human being.'

Born in Budapest, director Curtiz was well known for his mala-props. 'Anybody who has any talking to do, shut up,' was one; and on sports: 'You can keep your tennis, golf, and swimming. I'll tell you in two words what I like, polo!' He was also recognized for his lack of finesse when dealing with stars. When he won an Oscar the previous year as Best Director for *Casablanca*, he gave his formula for good pictures: 'Story first, director second, actors last.' 'A no-good sexless son of a bitch,' was how he greeted Bette Davis when they first met on the set of *Cabin in the Cotton* in 1934. By 1939, when he directed her in *Elizabeth and Essex*, she had graduated to 'a stinking no-good bum.' During the first week of *Mildred Pierce* he referred to Crawford as 'Phony Joanie' to her face; and 'the rotten bitch' when her back was turned.

'I had to be the referee,' said Jerry Wald. 'We had several lengthy meetings, filled with blood, sweat, and tears. Then everything started to settle down. Mile restricted himself to swearing only in Hungarian and Joan stopped streamlining the apron strings around her figure and let them hang.'

'He put me through a postgraduate course in humiliation,' Crawford said of Curtiz. 'Then, when he found out I could take it, he started training me.'

During the first four weeks in December, the script of *Mildred Pierce* continued to undergo alterations. Writer Louise Randall Piersall, an early women's liberationist, added a feminist polish; while another studio staff writer, William Faulkner, gave his

Southern male's perspective. Faulkner suggested they change the title to *House on the Sand* (inspired by the sinking foundation of the Malibu house where fornication and murder occur); and he added a scene in which the black maid, Lottie (Butterfly McQueen) held Mildred in her arms during her time of stress and sang the spiritual 'Steal Away'. ('God damn! How's that for a scene?' the Nobel prize winner wrote in the margin of his script.)

Without the Faulkner touches, on December 29, 1944, when Jack Warner threatened to shut down production, the script was frozen. Joan Crawford however still managed to add a few character embellishments. 'There were far more close-ups [for Crawford] than the original script called for,' said cinematographer Ernest Haller. Joan also requested that the age of her character be changed. 'I married Bert at seventeen,' said Mildred, making her thirty-two at the start of the film (the star was close to forty). Mildred was also made 'less conniving . . . less carpy . . . with her lower-class origins underplayed,' and her boozing and teary scenes were kept to a minimum.

A segment that caused considerable anguish to the actress was the fight scene between her and Ann Blyth. In the original script, when Veda tries to blackmail her boyfriend and is stopped by Mildred she turns on her mother and calls her a waitress and a common frump. Joan in retaliation was supposed to turn on her daughter and beat her savagely, then throw her clothes out of an upstairs window. 'I just couldn't hit her,' said Joan. 'I kept looking at Ann's sweet face and I couldn't bring myself to strike her let alone give her a beating.' The scene was revised, reduced to a mean tussle between the two, and three slaps – one administered by Blyth, followed by a double swack from Crawford, who snarls at her daughter: 'Get out of here, Veda, before I kill you.' The confrontation, though softened, traumatized Joan. 'I was terrified of hurting her. I felt sick to my stomach for the rest of the day. Perhaps I was reminded of the physical abuse I suffered as a child.'

Ann Blyth, who would receive an Oscar nomination for her role as Veda Pierce, remembered Crawford as 'the kindest most helpful human being I've ever worked with. We remained friends for many years after the film. I never knew that other Joan Crawford that people wrote about.'

To the cast and crew Joan was equally good-natured. She not only memorized the names of the fifty-six people working on the film, she had her secretary get a list of their birthdays and when possible arranged for a cake and a small gift to be delivered to the set. 'She had a genuine interest in making people happy,' said *Silver Screen*, 'an interest, by the way, which reflects how she has matured.'

'While waiting on the set she knits as she reads, and chews a half stick of gum,' said another publication. 'Her gum-chewing is audible and at times she cracks the stuff between her teeth. She also smokes.' Hopeful that this film would restore her popularity, when asked if she minded the games and infighting that went along with being a star in Hollywood, Joan replied, 'Honey, I thrive on that stuff.'

Watching the daily rushes of *Mildred Pierce*, neither Jerry Wald, Michael Curtiz, or Joan Crawford fully realized they were contributing to a new genre. Photographed in black and white, the look and mood of the film would soon be hailed as the precursor of the Warner's *film-noir* period. 'The first time I heard the words *film noir* was in New York,' said Crawford. 'I was being interviewed by a critic of the "cinema", which, as you might know has nothing to do with the "movies". He kept talking about this *film-noir* style and I didn't know what the hell he was talking about. When it came up again sometime later, I called Jerry Wald and I said "Darling, what is this *film-noir* style they're all talking about?" He explained it to me, which made me appreciate the film even more. I already knew what a terrific bunch of guys we had on that picture. They weren't just artists, they were geniuses.'

It was Ernie Haller, who had photographed Bette Davis in *Jezebel* and Vivien Leigh in *Gone With the Wind*, who was solely responsible for the visuals in *Mildred Pierce*, said Crawford. 'Ernie was at the rehearsals. And so was Mr. [Anton] de Grot, who did the sets. I recall seeing Ernie's copy of the script and it was filled with notations and diagrams. I asked him if these were for special lights and he said, "No, they're for special shadows." Now, *that* threw me. I was a little apprehensive. I was used to the look of Metro, where everything, including the war pictures, was filmed in blazing white lights. Even if a person was dying there was no darkness. But when I saw the rushes of *Mildred Pierce* I realized what Ernie was doing. The shadows and half-lights, the way the sets were lit, together with the unusual angles of the camera, added considerably to the psychology of my character *and* to the mood and psychology of the film. And that, my dear, is *film noir.*'

'Mildred Pierce. Loving her is like shaking hands with the Devil. She gave more in her glance than most women give in a lifetime. Ssssh . . . Please don't tell what Mildred Pierce did.'

In September 1945 Crawford's comeback film was released, to almost unanimous acclaim for the actress. 'Sincere and affecting,' said *The New York Times*. 'A magnificent performance,' said *Life*.

James Agee of *The Nation* found the film 'gratifying', with Joan Crawford 'giving the best performance of her career.' Paying close attention to the James Agee review was another leading actress of that day – Bette Davis.

Bette had a major film released a short time before Crawford's – *The Corn Is Green*. The budget was twice that of *Mildred Pierce*, with Davis recreating the role played by the great Ethel Barrymore on Broadway. Her film was serious art, while *Mildred Pierce* was cheap trash, Davis felt. But the critics, led by James Agee, did not hail Bette as Miss Moffat. Calling Davis 'sincere and hardworking,' Agee said that the actress as the elderly schoolmistress was 'limiting herself beyond her rights, by becoming more and more set, official, and first ladyish in mannerism and spirit, which is perhaps a sin as well as a pity.' ('That shit doesn't know *anything* about acting,' said Bette, 'and furthermore he's illiterate.')

But the audiences seemed to concur with James Agee. They stayed away in droves from *The Corn Is Green*, while *Mildred Pierce* posted a 'Sold Out' sign at all first-run houses. By the end of the year Joan's picture had outgrossed Bette's three to one. More ignominy for Davis would follow.

In December, Warner's pushed both pictures for Academy Award consideration in all categories. When the nominations were released, *Mildred Pierce* received seven, including Best Picture and Best Actress for Joan. *The Corn is Green* received two, with nothing for Bette, who was far from thrilled to be knocked off the annual honors list by Joan Crawford. 'If you value your life,' said Hedda Hopper in her column of January 26, 'do not bring up the name of Joan Crawford in Queen Bette's presence.'

Louella Parsons was also shocked by the monarch's behavior. 'I can hardly believe that Bette Davis is being as rude to Joan Crawford as the spies on the Warner's lot tell me,' she said in her Hearst column. 'Bette's always been swell about extending the welcoming hand to visiting stars and young players,' Parsons explained, telling her readers how Joan went up to Bette's table in the Warner's commissary and extended an invitation to a dinner party. 'While Joan stood there, Bette kept eating and barely looked up, and never invited Joan to sit down.'

'Maybe she had something on her mind,' said Sheilah Graham, reporting the same story.

'I'd hate to think,' said Parsons, 'that such unusual conduct is because Bette, who is the only actress to win an Academy award at Warner's, is not even in the running this year.'

'What a fat silly bitch,' said Bette of the columnist, banning her from visiting her set for two years.

JOAN'S OSCAR NIGHT

The war was over and the dress code for the night was black-tie formal. To accommodate the crowd of 2,048 guests, the ceremonies were held at Grauman's Chinese Theater. Among the early arrivals were Jane Wyman and Ronald Reagan, Myrna Loy, Frank Sinatra, Guy Madison, Diana Lynn, and Bette Davis, who was not campaigning for Joan. '*You* are going to win,' Bette told the candidate from *The Bells of St. Mary's*, Ingrid Bergman. 'I voted for you.' Also present at the ceremonies were Best Actress nominees Greer Garson (*Valley of Decision*), Jennifer Jones (*Love Letters*) and Gene Tierney (*Leave Her to Heaven*). The fourth nominee, Joan Crawford, was absent, at home in bed with the flu and a bottle of Jack Daniels bourbon.

'I fortified myself a little too much,' said Joan, who lost twelve pounds from stress and anguish the week before the show. 'I was hopeful, scared, apprehensive, so afraid I wouldn't remember what

I wanted to say, terrified at the thought of looking at those people . . . I was never good enough for the Fairbanks, Srs., for Mayer.'

She really thought she'd lose, that Ingrid Bergman would win. 'I can compete with a servant girl [Greer Garson], with a tramp [Gene Tierney], an amnesiac [Jennifer Jones] but not with a nun [Ingrid Bergman],' said the nervous nominee.

Wearing a nightgown designed by Helen Rose, Joan listened to the show over the radio, then 'took a deep breath' when Charles Boyer read off the names of the Best Actress nominees. When he announced the winner . . . 'Joan Crawford', she exhaled with a scream that alerted the newsmen on the lawn below her window that she had won. Jumping out of bed, the ailing star then called for her hairdresser and makeup man, on call in the next room.

'The celebration went on all night,' she recalled. 'Mike Curtiz arrived with the award, followed by dear Ann Blyth, whose back had been broken in a tobogganing accident a short time before. The phone never stopped ringing. Eventually we had to take it off the hook. Then, at eight o'clock the next morning, the flowers and telegrams began to arrive.'

That morning the newspaper photos of Joan receiving her Oscar in bed 'pushed all the other winners off the front pages,' said Hedda Hopper. At noon Louella Parsons arrived to congratulate 'Our Own Joan' personally. 'Trailing a black negligee, with her flaming hair high on her head,' the star received Parsons in her library, and the two read telegrams to each other. The messages came from extras (the first year they could vote), carpenters, the switchboard operators at MGM and Warner's and from industry notables. 'I am so happy for you,' said Ingrid Bergman. 'I voted for you and not Greer Garson,' said her old boss, Louis B. Mayer. 'We are all so proud of you,' said her new boss, Jack Warner.

Among the yellow-backed telegrams, some four hundred in all, Louella couldn't help noticing that one was from . . . Bette Davis. 'Isn't that sweet,' said Joan, reading the one-word composition from Bette, 'Congratulations.'

'There is no feud,' Joan told Parsons. 'My heart is too full. Certainly there is room for both of us at Warner's. We may even do a picture together.'

'When hell freezes over,' said Bette, when apprised of this news.

'One comeback performance does not constitute a career,' she commented to a studio publicist that same day. As far as she was concerned, Joan's Oscar victory was a fluke. It changed nothing. She was still the number one star at Warner's. Having recently set up her own production company at the studio, she was geared to make four films in a row, including *Ethan Frome*, *Lady Windermere's Fan* and *The Life of Sarah Bernhardt*. But none of these films would be made; and Joan Crawford, with her Oscar held aloft, would proceed to reap more power and prestige at the Warner's studio. As her star ascended again, Bette's declined. The feud between the two Queens had just begun.

PART TWO
1946 to 1977

12

'To be an actor it is essential to be an egomaniac; otherwise it doesn't work.'
David Niven

In the months prior to Joan Crawford's Oscar victory, Bette Davis had more important things to push around on her professional plate than worrying about the threat to her throne from an outsider. In 1945 Bette had been named the highest-paid female in America. Her salary for the year was $328,000 (compared with $156,000 for Crawford), but due to high taxes she kept only ninety thousand dollars of that sum. On the advice of her lawyer and her agent, to save on taxes and to keep tighter control over her film work, Bette formed her own film production company, BD Inc. She owned eighty percent; her agent Jules Stein got ten percent; and the remaining ten shares were split between her lawyer and her mother. Warner's would continue to finance and release her movies, and Bette the actress would be paid her star salary upfront, but Bette the producer would receive thirty-five percent of the profits after production costs were recouped. 'Maybe now, when she is spending her own money, she'll adhere to a schedule,' said Jack Warner hopefully.

The first picture released under the BD Inc. banner was *A Stolen Life*, with Bette acting opposite herself in the lead roles. Playing identical twins, Bette as Kate the good sister was timid and soft-spoken and wore plain clothes. As Pat, the bad sister, she sneered and smoked, and for her sins was drowned at sea – then replaced in her wealthy home and marital bed, by sister Kate.

Although the film was set in New England, Bette the producer, for time and convenience, decided to shoot the exteriors at Pebble Beach, California, and at Laguna Beach, where she erected an

East Coast lighthouse not far from her home. In the studio, Bette the artist insisted on absolute realism in every aspect. She didn't like the dog that central casting provided for one scene. 'It can't be *any* dog,' she explained to Central Casting. 'When I decide to impersonate my dead twin sister, the dog knows I'm an imposter when he *smells* me. For that we need a dog that can act.'

'She spent an entire day auditioning dogs,' the director, Curtis Bernhardt, recalled. 'Every professional and semi-professional canine in Los Angeles was brought into Warner's. Big dogs, small dogs; poodles, schnauzers, cocker spaniels, collies; they were paraded in and out for her inspection all day long. The street outside the sound-stage was covered with dog-doo. Eventually she picked a wire terrier, but when they got to shooting the scene the little thing was terrified of Bette. He wouldn't go near her; let alone smell her.'

Finding a leading man for *A Stolen Life* was also arduous for Bette. For the role of Bill, the handsome lighthouse inspector, the studio insisted she use one of their contract players. She was given the choice of Dennis Morgan or Robert Alda. Morgan, the perennially smiling matinee idol, was too handsome, and the suave, dark-haired Alda (father to Alan), who had just starred as George Gershwin in *Rhapsody in Blue*, tested but looked too much like 'a Jewish gigolo,' said Bette. It was director Bernhardt who suggested an actor recently discharged from the army, Glenn Ford. Some Columbia footage of Ford was run for Bette. 'Yes! I like *that*,' she said and asked that he test with her. 'There was some resistance from Jack Warner,' said Harry Mines (who had previously arranged that hot romance between Glenn Ford and Joan Crawford). 'Warner didn't want to hire an outsider. So I had to smuggle him onto the lot in the back of my car. Glenn made the test with Bette and she told Warner that she had to have him. So the studio paid something like seventy thousand dollars to Harry Cohn to borrow him.'

Ford was thankful for the chance to work with such a big star as Bette Davis, but not grateful enough to carry their love scenes off-camera. Unlike the seductive and lovely Miss Crawford, the supreme Bette was not successful in establishing a personal rela-tionship with the young actor. He was already romancing another star, MGM dancer Eleanor Powell. 'Bette was very enthused about

Glenn Ford at the start of the picture,' said director Bernhardt, 'but once she found out that he was taken by Powell, she became quite cool and businesslike. She never let him know of her feelings but she made it miserable for everyone else on the set.'

'It was *not* a happy picture. There were many obstacles and upsets to overcome,' said Bette, referring in part to the latest in a series of 'strange mishaps' she suffered during this time.

Cracked toes, rope burns, twisted ankles, cactus needles in her rear – these were a few of the on-the-job travails suffered by Bette Davis during the production of her movies. Two years before, shortly after Joan Crawford moved in next door to her at the studio, Bette was the victim of what she called 'a malicious act.' During the production of *Mr. Skeffington*, someone went to the star's dressing room and tampered with her special eyewash. Due to the glare from the bright lights, the actress was accustomed to washing her eyes out between scenes. Throwing back her head, she emptied the solution in her right eye and immediately began to scream. Her eye was burning. Her makeup man, Perc Westmore, rinsed out the eye with castor oil and Bette was taken to the dispensary. The eyewash, when analyzed, was found to contain a deadly fluid known as acetone. Bette demanded that an immediate investigation be made. But when the head of security asked production chief Steve Trilling if anyone on the set of the turmoil-ridden *Mr. Skeffington* was a suspect, Trilling replied, 'If you were to line up the cast and crew and ask them: "OK, which one of you wanted to kill Bette Davis?" – a hundred people would raise their hands.'

Walking down a street while filming *The Corn Is Green*, Bette was injured again when a small rock fired from a slingshot hit her on the calf of her leg. Shortly thereafter, while Joan Crawford was on an adjoining soundstage testing for *Mildred Pierce*, a second more serious injury occurred. Bette was standing on her mark for a scene when a heavy steel cover from an arc light in the crosswalks above came crashing down and hit her head which was protected at the time by the hat and wig she was wearing for her role as Miss Moffat. To alleviate the tension, one of the camera operators, knowing of the antipathy between the star and Crawford, looked up at the flies and yelled, 'Is that you up there, Joan?'

Bette screamed, 'That is *not* funny!' and walked off the set.

'She suffered from nerves, nausea and severe migraines for weeks,' a production memo stated.

During the making of *A Stolen Life*, Crawford was three thousand miles away, on vacation in New York, when Bette smashed her thumb in a faulty door. This meant an absence from the set for two days – 'during which the bastards docked me for two days' pay.' Driving home on a subsequent evening, a careless driver smashed into the rear of her new car, slamming Bette into the windshield. Her headaches increased. On the set the following week, the process shots for the storm sequence of the film were photographed in a huge water tank on the back lot. For the scene where bad sister Kate was drowned at sea, the star asked for repeated takes. Sitting in a boat in the immense tank as the giant wind machines churned up fifteen-foot waves, Bette when cued was washed overboard. On the third take, however, she failed to surface. Her feet got caught in the underwater wires and as she struggled desperately, 'convinced she would drown in seventeen feet of water,' a frogman was dispatched to find her. 'I thought we had lost you,' director Bernhardt said when the actress finally surfaced. 'Why didn't you dive in and see, you son of a bitch!' a wet and livid Bette replied.

'Bette is outspoken and ninety-five percent honest. There always has to be a margin for untruth. She doesn't like to hide the fact that she likes and welcomes sex. "But it is only work that satisfies," she says.'

Sidney Skolsky.

On October 12, 1945, two months after World War II officially ended, Bette attended a gala party at the studio to welcome Ronald Reagan, Wayne Morris, Gig Young, and others home from the war. The guest list totaled four hundred, and although Bette appeared to be smiling in the photos with the happily reunited families and engaged couples, inside she was suffering from an acute case of the blues. With the war over, she was feeling alone and abandoned. Her last, and lengthy romance – with an Army man she met at the Hollywood Canteen – began to wane when he shipped out without placing a requested engagement ring on her finger. (Shortly thereafter, when the solider was in battle in Europe, Bette dispatched a 'Dear John' letter to him at the front. 'The news upset him greatly,' she said, 'and I was pleased.') To add to her loss, the Canteen was about to close, while another diversion, and steady companion, her mother Ruthie, had remarried that same week. At thirty-nine, with her biological clock ticking away, Bette Davis was indeed the studio's top star and America's highest-paid female, but she had no lover, husband, or children to share the renewed bliss of peacetime with. Resourceful however, and always forward, not to mention impetuous, that void would be filled within thirty days.

On Saturday night, October 20, Bette attended a party at a neighbor's house in Laguna Beach. 'The moment I arrived, a very attractive man brought me a drink and never left my side,' she said. His name was William Grant Sherry. He was tall, well built and soft-spoken. Six years her junior, he was a sailor on leave from the naval hospital in San Diego. 'Weekends I would hitch up to Laguna Beach,' said Sherry. 'I met Bette at the party and we took to each other immediately. We had a lot to talk about, both being from New England. She was interesting, not pretty but attractive and down to earth.'

Bette told the good-looking sailor she was an actress. 'Neither she nor anyone else mentioned Hollywood, and since she was in Laguna Beach, I figured she belonged to the local theater group,' he said. 'The name Bette Davis didn't ring any bell in my mind. She was simply a gal I suddenly had a deep romantic feeling for.'

Discharged from the Navy two weeks later, Sherry went back to Laguna to pursue a career as a fine-arts painter. 'I hoped to see Bette, and I did. She was living there in a simple beach house that I thought belonged to her mother. Nothing indicated she was a movie star, and she never mentioned it. We spent days and most of the nights together.'

'Actually I liked the way he looked on the beach in a pair of shorts,' she told Sheilah Graham when the columnist reported on the romance.

'Three weeks later I proposed to her and she accepted,' said

Sherry, 'but she said she had to go to Mexico on business, and that we would get married on her return. I convinced her we should get married and drive down together as part of our honeymoon. We got our license in Santa Ana. At the wedding the next day I couldn't believe the invasion of newspeople and photographers. I was a little stunned and said to Bette, "Who are you anyway?" She just laughed her hearty laugh.'

On a highway outside Mexico City, the groom soon learned who his bride was. 'We were late getting to Mexico City, because the tires blew out on our car due to the hot roads. We were sitting on the roadside wondering how we were going to get to town when an army of cars filled with police and officials arrived. When they saw Bette, there was much cheering and handshaking. We were transferred to a big limousine which drove us into Mexico City. On the way Bette explained that the Mexican government was using her film, *The Corn Is Green* for their illiteracy campaign. It was then I realized she was more than a local actress. I had to explain to her that I never saw any of her movies and she thought that was a huge joke.'

In Mexico City the couple were driven to a night club, where Bette was given the keys to the city. When they arrived finally at their hotel, her maid from the studio had already prepared their bed in the bridal suite. 'The bed was turned down, with my pajamas lying beside Bette's nightgown,' said Sherry. 'I stood there looking down at Bette and I got very sentimental. It was a beautiful dream. I had a wonderful wife.'

'Oh, Sherry,' said Bette. 'You big sap.'

After their stay in Mexico City, where they dined with the President, Dolores Del Rio and Mary Astor, the couple returned to Los Angeles, where Bette had the studio run off some of her films for her new husband. One afternoon, walking to the Warner's parking lot, a beautiful lady spotted him from the other side of the street. It was Joan Crawford.

'She called across as I was passing,' he said.

'Mister Sherry?' said Joan.

'Yes,' said Bette's groom.

'I'm Joan Crawford and I wanted to meet you,' said the star, taking his hand in hers. 'I want you to come to my home, for dinner.'

'Well, thank you, I'll tell Bette,' Sherry replied.

'Oh, I don't want Bette,' said Joan, 'just you. Come *alone*.'

At home, when he relayed the message to his wife, she laughed. 'Joan does that all the time,' said Bette. 'She always invites the husbands and not the wives.'

'That struck me as kind of strange,' said Sherry, 'and I didn't go.'

> *Joan Crawford weeps openly when the violinist at L'Aiglon plays her favorite classical piece. Lana Turner likes torch songs; Rita Hayworth prefers gypsy songs; and Hedy Lamarr likes waltzes. But Bette Davis has the strangest favorite of all. Recently married, she wants to hear "Kiss me once again" before she even looks at a menu – and she asks for several repeats during the evening.'*
> Elsa Maxwell from Hollywood, 1945

While the newlywed Bette was enjoying the physical and artistic charms of husband number three, Joan Crawford announced that *her* third marriage, to actor Philip Terry, was kaput. The breakup in December 1945 irritated the fanzine writers who were preparing their annual update on the couple's happy marriage.

On their first anniversary, *Modern Screen* reported that Philip had given Joan an expensive wristwatch, decorated with rubies and diamonds, set at the exact hour she met her husband, but with no works inside. On their second anniversary, at Ciro's, Joan was all dolled out in pre-war glamour – a white fox coat, a backless white dinner gown and magnificent sapphire earrings – a gift from Phil, 'who seems to have more confidence and bigger chest expansion,' said Sheilah Graham. On their third year of wedded bliss, *Photoplay* reported that Joan got more jewelry – a gold bracelet encrusted with Siberian amethysts and diamonds. The enclosed card read, 'Dearest, This is the third step on our bridge you have built so well. Love you, forever and a day, Philip. July 21, 1945.'

Eight months later the suspensions to the bridge began to snap. With Joan's comeback in *Mildred Pierce* secured, Philip's career had declined. Despite good reviews as the supportive brother of Ray

Milland in *The Lost Weekend,* the actor found himself relegated to playing leads in such lightweight B pictures as *Torpedo Boat* with Jean Parker. He also made the mistake, it was said, of objecting to Joan's harsh discipline in raising their adopted children.

In *Mommie Dearest* daughter Christina told of the awkward position she was put in at age six, when during her parents' arguments she was forced to choose which movie, his or hers, they should watch on a Sunday evening. Christina, no dunce, picked Joan Crawford's and shortly thereafter Philip Terry left home. He had been a nice man and Christina did miss him. But her mother did cruel things he couldn't seem to prevent. Like the time she tied the girl up in the shower with the door closed. And another time when 'Mommie locked me in a linen closet with the lights off as a punishment.'

'I have no recollection of any of that,' said Philip Terry from his home in Northern California in 1988. 'It was a very long time ago.'

'It's my house! My money! My kids! If you don't like the way I run things around here, then get the hell out,' Christina distinctly remembers her mother saying, and the actor left – with bad timing. His departure from Joan's Brentwood mansion came two weeks before Christmas, upsetting her publicity plans for the family Christmas portraits.

'Yes, he's gone,' she told Louella Parsons one hour after he abandoned her. 'But, Louella dear, I am too upset to talk about it right now.'

She spoke up in court, however. Mr. Terry had kept her a virtual prisoner and criticized every script that was sent to her, she told the judge, who granted the star a no-fault divorce because of the physical and mental anguish she endured. Leaving the courthouse, when asked if she ever intended to hear the wedding march again, Joan had a quick reply. 'Maybe *that's* the trouble,' she said pensively. 'I never had any music at my weddings.'

'The hottest, most popular girl in Hollywood is Joan Crawford. With her Oscar, her new hairdo, her jewels and fabulous wardrobe, she has all the wolves in town howling.'

Ed Sullivan

With the war over, and being a single girl again, Joan Crawford felt it was all right to throw a few gala parties in her home. Her re-emergence as a popular hostess was enthusiastically hailed by Hedda Hopper. 'Her parties were the best,' said Hedda. 'With Joan's flair for the dramatic she would make a production number of tea for two. She'd have gowns flown in from Hattie Carnegie in New York and spend two or three hours on her "toilette". When all the guests were assembled downstairs, you'd hear her voice at the head of the stairs, cooing to her dogs. And down she'd float – "Oh! Are you all here? – Do please forgive me." When told how marvellous she looked she'd twirl her new gown and say: "This? Oh, do you like it" – as if it were a little thing she stitched up before dinner.'

At Warner's, Joan proceeded to tackle Bette in a popularity campaign with the studio's employees. When she won the award for Best Actress she gifted each member of the *Mildred Pierce* crew with Oscar pins and money clips. She also wrote 127 notes of thanks to the rest of the studio's Academy members, presuming they had all voted for her.

When actress Viveca Lindfors arrived from Sweden, she recalled her first day at the studio. Making the rounds of the soundstages, she was introduced to Gary Cooper, then Bette Davis. 'She came over to me and said "Welcome", with no competition only generosity,' said Viveca.

A visit to Joan Crawford's set was next, and Joan outdid Bette in her welcome. She told the talented newcomer she wanted to give her a party.

'A party for me?' Lindfors thought. 'I was stunned, hoping secretly that she was kidding.'

Joan never kidded about such serious social matters. A week later her secretary called Lindfors and said that the party would be the following Sunday afternoon at three-thirty, and that a limousine would be sent to pick her up. Having nothing to wear, Lindfors was told to go to wardrobe and borrow some clothes. She was outfitted with 'a ghastly blue suit.' On the day of the party a chauffeur arrived punctually at 3:30 P.M., and drove the nervous young actress to Joan's home. A maid in black and white opened the door to the ivy-covered English Tudor mansion, and Viveca was shown to the outside garden where she saw the pale blue-green pool, and an enormous pink tent installed for the occasion, 'with individual tables laid all in pink for at least a hundred people.' As the waiters rushed about, setting tables with candles and silver, the hostess appeared 'out of the poolhouse like a goddess, exquisitely beautiful, with her white skin and red flaming full hair; dressed in a black chiffon dress and elegant satin shoes.'

Lindfors said her stomach turned over at the sight of Joan. She felt dull in her dowdy suit. She wanted to run.

'Hundreds of people are coming to meet you,' said Joan, and, one by one, they arrived. Spencer Tracy, Katharine Hepburn, Cary Grant, Bob Young, Gary Cooper, Rex Harrison, Lilli Palmer, Jimmy Stewart, Betty Hutton, Claudette Colbert, Joan Bennett, Ida Lupino, Joan Blondell, Mike Todd, and a twenty-piece orchestra for dancing, with Tony Martin crooning in person.

After saying 'How do you do?' for two hours, and feeling slow and ill at ease, Lindfors sought out Joan and said, 'I want to go home.'

'She looked at me with those enormous eyes of hers, bigger than Garbo's,' said Lindfors, 'and said, "Impossible! We are having supper in the tent in a few moments, and you are the guest of honor." '

Enduring 'a few more deaths,' the actress stayed. Years later she said she could still not understand the situation. 'Was it just a generous gesture by Joan? Or was it a clever move to give a party for a young Swedish star? Or maybe she was just looking for an excuse to give a party.'

TWO QUEENS ON ONE THRONE

Let's Gossip:
'There's a new First Lady out on the Warner lot these days, and she's really getting the red carpet treatment. Name? Joan Crawford. Since her comeback all she has to do is ask and her wishes are granted. She walked off with the lead in Humoresque, *right out under Bette Davis' nose. Bette really wanted that part!'*

Motion Picture magazine, April 1946

'Bad manners, Mr. Boray. The infallible sign of talent.'
Crawford to John Garfield in *Humoresque*

Advancing her popularity and success at Warner Brothers, in 1946 Joan Crawford appeared in a second Jerry Wald film. The script came from Clifford Odets who two years earlier had worked on the life of George Gershwin for *Rhapsody in Blue*. Little of his material wound up in that biomusical, so producer Wald decided to combine his material with the theme and title of a previous Fanny Hurst best-seller, *Humoresque*.

In pre-production, ethnic changes were requested by the front office. Sensitive 'about putting the real Jew on the screen the way they put the Irish Catholic on the screen in *Going My Way*,' Wald told his writer, Barney Glazer, to transform the main Fannie Hurst characters – a dominating 'yiddisha Momma' and her genius violinist son ('an out-and-out little son of a bitch') – to those of an Italian-American family living on the Lower East Side of New York. 'In this outline I am going Italian,' Glazer told Wald in an interoffice memo, 'but do not blame me too much if the Jewish creeps in. It is more a choice between serving spaghetti or gefilte fish; the ingredients I have to cook are Jewish, as Hurst and Odets contrived them.'

A third lead, that of a bored Park Avenue patron of the arts who drinks and preys on young men, was added, making it 'not only the old story of a pushy mother and an artistic devoted son, but the story of a mother, a son, and a dipsomaniac.'

With John Garfield cast as the son, and Anne Revere set as the mother, the role of the alcholic socialite who seduces the Italian prodigy was coveted by a few of the leading ladies at Warner's. 'Barbara Stanwyck was preferred and Bette Davis was a possibility,' said Garfield's biographer, Larry Swindell. 'But then Joan Crawford established her interest in the role and that was that.'

Joan saw the character, not as an alcoholic nymphomaniac, but as 'a woman with too much time on her hands and too much love in her heart.' Nor did she mind if the part was small, 'as long as it was strong, and the billing was large (and first).' Her wardrobe of twenty-five lavish gowns would be designed by her old MGM couturier, Adrian; for research on her character's extensive drinking,

Joan said she intended to study some of her friends. 'I won't be any competition for Ray Milland [in *The Lost Weekend*],' she told columnist Harrison Carroll. 'This girl is a nipper. She drinks for security. She doesn't like to face herself when she's sober. I am borrowing some things from a couple of girls I've observed.'

'What a humble, sweet person she is,' said director Jean Negulesco on day one of production. 'It's just like this is her first picture.'

John Garfield was not as cordial in his introduction to Joan. The talented but moody young actor was a good friend of Bette Davis. They had worked together on one of his first Warner films, *Juarez*, in which he played a 'Mexican schlemiel', and later the two were close buddies, 'both swearing like sailors,' when they ran the Hollywood Canteen. When Bette heard that Garfield was going to work with her rival, Crawford, she coached him on how to behave with the star. 'She thinks she's a *real* big deal,' said Bette, 'so treat her accordingly.'

'So you're Joan Crawford, the big movie star,' said Garfield upon meeting Joan, who held out her hand in introduction. 'Glad to meet ya,' said Garfield, ignoring the hand and pinching her breast.

'Why you insolent son of a—' Joan began, then stopped and smiled. 'I think we're going to get along just fine,' she said, dropping her voice two octaves.

Robbie Garfield, the actor's wife, told *Modern Screen* she wasn't jealous of Bette Davis, Ida Lupino, or Lana Turner, who had recently worked with her good-looking husband on the steamy James M. Cain movie, *The Postman Always Rings Twice*. 'Only one actress worries me,' said Mrs. Garfield, 'and that's Joan Crawford. To me she is the most exciting woman I've ever seen. For a man to work with Crawford all day, and come home to plain me at night – must be an awful let-down.'

To alleviate Mrs. Garfield's fears, Bette Davis called and assured her that Johnny had no interest in 'that mannequin from MGM' (as she still referred to Joan); for safety, she would be on the Warner's lot to keep an eagle eye on the working pair. But Crawford soon won over both her co star and his wife. When she learned that Mrs. Garfield was having problems decorating her new

California home, Joan sent her friend Billie Haines to help with the furniture and drapes, and she picked up the tab for his fee.

On the set, Joan also endeared herself to her co star, by insisting that two of Garfield's big scenes be reshot, with more favorable lighting for the actor. 'I wasn't being generous, believe me,' said Joan. 'In the Carnegie Hall scene, they were supposed to cut from the close-ups of my face and eyes, to a full shot of Garfield playing onstage. My lighting, thanks to Ernie Haller, was wonderful, but the frames of Mr. Garfield were not as dramatic. He looked like just another member of the orchestra standing onstage, playing his violin. In the editing, the dramatic balance wasn't there. I suggested they black out the entire orchestra, giving the illusion he was alone onstage. Then they should close-in to a tight shot of his upper body, and his face, as he played. When they intercut the new shots with mine, it worked much better. In the dubbing, they also raised the level of the music which intensified the power and the attraction between the two characters.'

After that Garfield became Joan's number-one fan, describing her to one reporter as 'a smart tomato'. She told Louella that upon completing knitting a sweater for director Jean Negulesco, she would knit 'something in yellow for Johnny'. When Joan became ill and returned to the set after a week's leave, Garfield went to her dressing room and welcomed her back with a kiss, in front of the unit's publicity photographers. She also showed her serious side to the talented actor. Having been married to a founding member of the company, Joan told Garfield that she had some knowledge of his Group Theater training. She drew him out further on his dramatic techniques and theories. He showed her his copy of the newly translated Stanislavski handbook, *An Actor Prepares*, which inspired Joan to go out and buy six copies, one of which she gave to Bette Davis' close friend, Olivia de Havilland. 'When Olivia later won an Oscar, Joan was pleased,' said Sheilah Graham.

One weekend Joan invited Johnny to play tennis at her club in Beverly Hills. It was here that a friend of Bette's came across the couple leaving one of the private courts, late on a Saturday night. Crawford looked fresh and spry, but Garfield was beat and wilted. 'I was giving Johnny a lesson,' said a jolly Joan. 'Without a tennis racket?' the friend asked with scorn, before dashing to the nearest phone to advise Bette.

'Oh Johnny, not you *too*,' said Bette when she cornered Garfield the next day at the studio, and her friendship with the actor cooled considerably after that.

And then there was the tale told often by Rosalind Russell. Not long after, she and Davis were on the Super Chief, bound for New York, when it stopped in Pasadena to pick up more passengers. Spotting a familiar face boarding the train, Bette rushed into Russell's compartment. 'Guess who just got on the train?' she gasped. 'The cocksucker! Joan Crawford.'

> *'The hottest feud to hit these parts since they thought up Technicolor, is the one between Joan Crawford and Bette Davis at Warner Brothers. Since Joan's Oscar victory for* Mildred Pierce, *she's been getting pretty much of anything she wants at the studio. All of which leaves Davis sizzling.'*
>
> *Motion Picture*, May 1946

Crawford, now referred to by Davis as 'that whore from MGM,' also lost her cameraman during the last weeks of shooting *Humoresque*. Returning to Warner's for her next film, *Deception*, and brandishing her royal prerogative, Bette demanded that Ernest Haller, Crawford's cinematographer be removed from *Humoresque* and assigned to her. 'There was a terrible row,' said *Deception* director Irving Rapper. 'I wanted to use our usual cameraman, Sol Polito, who had worked on Bette's last two pictures, but she insisted on Haller.'

'I was not as young anymore,' said Bette. 'Thirty-nine, to be exact, and I needed special lighting.'

It was sheer spite, said Joan. 'Ernie had worked with me on *Mildred Pierce*, and again on *Humoresque*. When she heard of the wonderful work he was doing with me on *Humoresque*, she said she wanted him too, right away. She went to Jack Warner about it and Ernie was asked if he could work on both pictures. It put a terrible strain on him, but Bette didn't care. In her contract she had a clause that said she could pre-empt any role, or avail herself of any cast or crew member. And certainly if that entailed making my work suffer, she would do it.'

The dueling of the divas continued throughout the filming. In her dressing room, between scenes on *Humoresque*, to sustain the mood of her tragic character, Crawford had been in the habit of playing classical records by Isaac Stern. Her reverie was abruptly shattered one day, when Bette, next door, began playing loud boogie-woogie records on her machine. The 'war of the victrolas went on for days, giving everyone a headache,' said *Humoresque* co star Oscar Levant, until one afternoon, when both stars were on the set, someone (rumored to be Levant) sneaked into their trailers and cut the wires to their machines.

In *Deception*, Bette would also try to compete with Joan on looks and wardrobe. Playing a New York classical pianist kept by a rich man, Davis had a wardrobe designed by Bernard Newman. She had fifteen costume changes, with 'the addition of a sable cape, a fully let-out mink, and a floor-length white ermine evening coat.' Her hairstyles – 'a casual bob and a sophisticated hair-parted-in-the-middle-with-a-chignon-at-the-nape-coiffure' – were designed by Maggie Donovan.

Deception was conceived as a romantic drama to reunite the three stars of *Now Voyager* with the same director, Irving Rapper. Bette as a serious pianist did her usual thorough research. She learned how to play each classical piece and she insisted on recording some of her piano solos, which weren't used. Paul Henreid, adept at lighting two cigarettes at once in *Now Voyager*, was a clod as a cellist in *Deception*. 'His efforts were so crude and hopeless we had to tie his hands behind his back,' said Rapper. 'Then two hands belonging to a professional intrumentalist came out from behind him and played.' The shot took hours to complete, because Henreid couldn't keep from bobbing his head or raising his eyebrows in what he considered to be 'artistic timing.'

There was also some trouble with a scene involving Claude Rains and his cat. Bette had recently lost her beloved dog Tibby. (Laid out in a coffin of brown velvet, filled with gardenias, the dead dog had been taken to New Hampshire, to be buried at Butternut, at which time husband number two, Arthur Farnsworth, was dug up and reinterred in another state). That loss (of the dog) left Bette sensitive to the sight of small animals; so she asked that the cat scene in *Deception* be cut from the script. But the shot was necessary, the director insisted. Claude Rains was to hold the cat under his chin, stroke him, and look evil. 'We must have wasted a week trying to sedate the cat so Claude could hold him without getting scratched,' said Bette. 'They doped the cat until it couldn't move, and when Claude got to the point where he could stroke the cat it was so heavily *drugged* that it looked *dead!*'

The climax of *Deception* was subsequently changed by Bette. Originally, Paul Heinried, crazed with love for Bette, was to kill Claude Rains. 'It was supposed to happen offstage,' said writer John Collier. 'Henreid shoots Rains and goes to prison, while Bette promises to wait for him.' When the ending was shot, onstage, Bette, for a stronger finish, insisted that *she* be the killer. "She was listening to Oscar bells, to another Academy Award nomination,' said Rapper, 'and I was anxious to get the damn thing over and done with, so we did it her way.'

After she pumped four bullets into Rains, Bette, it was said, packed away her gun and went off to chat with Jack Warner about finishing off her real-life nemesis, Joan Crawford. 'It became a knock-down dragged-out fight between the two ladies,' said columnist Jimmie Fidler. 'Bette wanted Jack Warner to boot Joan out of Burbank; and Joan held her contract option over his head. Warner was caught in such a tight squeeze that his balls were turning blue.'

In late August 1947, when the trade paper ads and programs for Warner's twentieth anniversary of talking pictures appeared, Bette's photo, along with Bogart, Flynn, Cagney and others, appeared prominently, together with a list of her entire Warner movie credits. Joan Crawford's name and image, however, were absent, as was any mention of that year's award-winner, *Mildred Pierce*, or the forthcoming *Humoresque*.

On September 21, the *Chicago Tribune* reported, 'There's a honey of a tussle now going on between Joan Crawford and Bette Davis. Warner's wants to postpone Joan's picture *Humoresque* until next spring and release Bette's picture before December, which would mean that Joan would not be eligible for an Academy Award this year.'

On September 24 Hedda Hopper reported that 'the themes of both pictures are the same – about musicians – and both have similar endings. Joan made her picture first, so it would seem fair to release her first.'

'Yes there is a problem,' said Joan, 'and I have no idea why Bette hates me so.'

'I do not *hate* Miss Crawford,' said Bette. 'I hardly *know* her. The decision to release my picture first was made by my boss Jack Warner.'

Joan called Warner. He confirmed Bette's statement. It was the exhibitors who had asked for Bette's picture to be released first. *Deception* was a Davis vehicle, she carried the picture, and the Warner theater owners needed that weight to kick off their fall season. 'Don't bullshit me, Jack,' said Joan. 'Bette can't face the competition. Can she?'

Crawford knew she wasn't in every scene of *Humoresque*, but the picture revolved around her. 'Furthermore,' she told Warner, 'I had my agent call a few of the big exhibitors in Boston, New York, and Chicago. They all said they're dying for a new Crawford picture.'

On October 1, 1946, Dorothy Kilgallen reported the latest round in the battle of the Warner stars. Davis' picture would be released in mid-October, with no definite release date for the Crawford film. 'But you can bet it will be released this year,' said Kilgallen, 'because Joan's contract with Warner's has expired and she won't renew unless the matter is resolved in her favor.'

Jack Warner cursed the feud and the fresh trouble. His studio, closed the previous year by union picketers when 'participants were knifed, clubbed and gassed before police restored order', was facing the threat of a new strike between the unions of the stagehands, carpenters, and cameramen. He didn't need this 'female trouble', from Bette and Joan.

On October 18, *Deception* was released. The reviews were mixed. 'It's like grand opera, only the people are thinner. I wouldn't have missed it for the world, said *PM* magazine.

'Bette is less neurotic than most of her recent assignments. Solid appeal for femme patrons,' said *Variety*.

On October 23 columnist Jimmie Fidler reported that Crawford had been seen dining with Louis B. Mayer. 'There is talk,' said

Fidler, 'that Joan may be returning to MGM, to star in a new picture with Clark Gable.'

With his union problems resolved, Jack Warner made some hasty moves to appease his leading ladies. *Deception* was bringing in good money, so to pacify Davis he bought her a new mobile dressing room. 'It is a beautiful three-room trailer, with a breakfast nook, a separate bedroom and all the latest modern conveniences, including Venetian blinds and a telephone!' said the studio press release.

Warner then met with Crawford and told her he was going to release *Humoresque* in late December, to qualify her for an Oscar nomination. The release, however, was to be limited to one theater in Los Angeles, and it was supposed to be a quiet event (i.e., without alerting Bette) until trade reporter Mike Connolly, invited to a special viewing of the film by Joan, jumped the gun and reported how 'ravishing and controlled' she appeared in the new picture. 'She has Oscar written all over her performance,' said Connolly. 'She and not Bette will be the one to vote for next spring.'

The morning the Connolly item appeared, Jack Warner received a call from Bette.

'Jack!' said Bette. 'Have you read the news?'

'I have not seen the trades yet,' Warner lied, prepared for the worst.

'Not the trades, *Jack*,' said Bette, 'the *Herald Tribune*. Louella's column. She is the first to break the story. I am *pregnant*.'

It was a big scoop, Louella reported that morning, and she virtually had to drag a confirmation out of Bette. They weren't on speaking terms, Louella explained, because she had sided with Joan during the recent Oscar dispute. 'Told by a "little bird" ' (usually her husband, Doc Harry Martin, a proctologist, or 'Old Velvet Finger', as Carole Lombard dubbed him) that Bette was pregnant, Louella called her six times until she made contact. 'Listen, Bette,' said Lolly, 'I happen to know you're expecting a baby. I want to write this good news, but even more than that I want your friendship again.'

'It's true, Louella,' said Bette, 'and I am happy we are friends again.'

'It was a softer, gentler Bette that came to my house for dinner with her husband, a few nights later,' said Parsons in her column the next week. 'Of course, I wanted to talk to her about many things – about the baby, her plans for the future, and her supposed feud with Joan Crawford. But like good women, Bette and I sat back and listened to the war talk of our men, both of whom had served overseas.'

'All is hearts and flowers between Bette Davis and Joan Crawford. They lunch in the Green Room everyday. There could be a shortage of tables of course.'
Sheilah Graham

'If I knew she was going to get pregnant, I could have saved myself the expense of buying her that damn trailer,' said Jack Warner, somewhat relieved that he would not have to deal with Davis for the next nine months. Joan Crawford was cheerful also. With *Humoresque* set to be released the studio could concentrate on pushing her and the picture without interference from mother-to-be Bette. 'I am so happy for you,' Joan wrote in a note to Davis that December. 'If I can be of any help, in any way, please let me know.'

And surprisingly, the 'softer, gentler Bette' responded. 'The feud must be over,' Sheilah Graham reported. 'Joan Crawford gifted Bette Davis with a fancy handbag, set with stones, and matching sandals.'

'No one who spotted Bette Davis and Joan Crawford huddled over their knitting at the Warner Brothers studio, can doubt the depth of their new friendship,' Louella Parsons trumpeted that same week. 'When mother-to-be Bette made a mistake with the little garment she was making, Joan took it from her, unravelled the entire piece and began it anew. As the two top stars laughed and joked together, only the most callous and suspicious of minds could doubt that this alliance is sincere. It is a friendship that will last for a long, long time.'

13

NEUROTIC JOAN

In January 1947, when *Humoresque* was released and doing brisk business at the box office, Joan Crawford made herself available for contract talks with studio boss Jack Warner. For $250,000 per film, she agreed to make two films a year for the next five years. She would have approval over scripts, directors, cameramen, costumers, and co stars; if Warner's failed to come up with suitable material, she could accept outside offers, a privilege requested by but denied to Bette Davis.

With Davis on maternity leave, Crawford now had first call on all scripts at the studio. From the top of the pile she chose *Possessed*, a script that had been tailor-made for Bette. For her performance as a tormented schizophrenic who shoots her lover in a jealous rage, Joan would also receive her second Academy Award nomination.

The director was Curtis Bernhardt, who had worked with Davis on *A Stolen Life*. 'It was not difficult to get along with Bette,' he said, 'provided you knew her moods and the proper time to approach her with ideas. It would be fatal to ask her something at the wrong time.'

Crawford was 'as easy to work with as can be,' Bernhardt continued. 'She was naturally a little subdued because she was the studio's second-ranking star. She threw her handbag at me several times when I called her Bette by mistake.'

Encouraged by the director, Joan undertook extensive research for her role as the hallucinating psychopath who kills the man she loves. She discussed the character with several psychiatrists and spent time in a mental asylum, surveying a patient undergoing electric shock therapy. Her homework ultimately impressed critic James Agee. 'Miss Crawford is at her very best in the mad scenes,' he said. 'She has obviously studied the aspects of insanity to recreate a rather terrifying portrait of a woman possessed by devils.'

The realism affected her emotionally at times, Bernhardt said. 'Bette can snap in and out of a scene quite rapidly. Joan was not as facile an actress. Several times we had to call a break when her hysterics continued beyond the "cut." '

'While making *Possessed*, I wept each morning on my drive to the studio,' said Joan, 'and I wept all the way back home. I found it impossible to sleep at night, so I'd lie in bed contemplating the future. I fear it with all my heart and soul even as I fear the dark.'

'Joan's dark moods affected everyone she worked with,' said Louella Parsons. 'It was frightening to observe the depth of her involvement with the role.'

'She was touching nerves in herself,' said Jimmie Fidler, 'holding a mirror to her own neuroses.'

'Helga, I'm not mad at you. I'm mad at the dirt.'
Joan to her maid, 1947

She had never been on a psychiatrist's couch, and never found the need for one, Crawford boasted to many, but confessed to Katharine Albert that she did possess a few teensy-weensy personal disorders. 'I'm no angel,' she told her writer-friend. 'I have a few compulsions that seem to drive other people crazy. I insist on punctuality, courtesy, and I have a passion for cleanliness.' The latter fixation, shared by Bette Davis, was a constant obsession with Joan. 'She never wore a dress, a hat or a coat that wasn't sent to the cleaners instantly after wearing it,' said Albert. 'I used to wash my hands every ten minutes,' said Joan. 'I couldn't step out of the house unless I had gloves on. I wouldn't smoke a cigarette unless I opened the pack myself, and I would never use another cigarette out of that pack if someone else had touched it.'

'In one scene in *Baby Jane*,' said Bette Davis, 'I was to hand her two vitamin pills. She faked taking them, leaving them in her palm. I said, "Miss Crawford, would you prefer that I hand the whole bottle to you?" "Yes, thank you," she said.'

When she stayed in a hotel, no matter how many stars it had, Joan always scrubbed the bathroom herself before using it. At home, after a workman had installed a new bathtub and toilet, then used them, she had the plumbing torn out and replaced immediately. 'Until Joan discovered she could cover her furniture in plastic,' said Billie Haines, 'there were entire apartments in Los Angeles that had been furnished with almost-new sofas and chairs that had been soiled once then discarded.'

Doing her own housework not only guaranteed sanitized perfection, the task served as a purification of the soul for Joan. Frequently, after a wild night on the town, raising a few drinks and lowering a few male libidos, Joan could purge her guilt the following morning by cleaning her Brentwood mansion from top to bottom. 'She is a woman driven by a great deal of energy,' said writer Ruth Waterbury, who described how 'Joan the drudge' would exorcize her private demons by scrubbing, cleaning and waxing the floors and woodwork of her house each weekend. 'She begins on Saturday morning,' said Waterbury. 'She starts with the kitchen, then the bathrooms, then goes through the library, through the music room, through the upstairs sitting rooms and bedrooms.' Finished by dusk, she then relaxed with a drink and planned her fresh hell for that night.

> *'Love with Joan Crawford might be a strenuous business, perhaps a little difficult at times. But well worth the run.'*
>
> Author James M. Cain

Crawford's obsession for cleanliness and order also permeated her love life. Actor-comedian Jackie Gleason met Joan at a party and went home with her. 'She was neat. Like *real*,' he told columnist James Bacon. 'Minutes after I (bleeped) her – she got up and started making the bed with me still in it.' By the mid-1940s Joan's psycho-sexual games kept pace with the sheer number of her male conquests. 'She had men stacked up to the left and the right of her,' said Adela Rogers St. Johns. 'As new lovers were recruited she shoved the used ones to the rear of the line.'

Like many attractive, promiscuous people, Joan Crawford could be seduced with flattery and attention on a first and second date, but if a man wanted to retain her interest, a challenge or a touch of danger was mandatory. 'She liked men who gave her a hard time,' said Adela Rogers St. Johns. 'If a guy was always available when she called, she soon dropped him.'

'She got bored quite easily and had unpredictable mood swings,' said an agent who was physically enamored of Crawford for a short term. 'At night, alone, she went through different changes. Sometimes she would be this carefree sophisticated swinger, and the next night she acted like a little defenseless girl, all alone in the big world. The changes were OK by me, except it became tiresome to switch along with her. I didn't know who I should be at times – her lover or her daddy. Eventually I told her, "Hey, Joan, I'm an agent, not an actor. I represent actors all day long, and at night I just want to unwind and be myself." She gave me this long hard look, and said, "You're so right, Joe. You *are* an agent, and a good one, but you're also a bore. Now get *out*." '

Fred De Cordova, producer of Johnny Carson's TV show, worked as a dialogue director on *Mildred Pierce* and dated Joan for awhile. 'She certainly knew how to make a man feel important,' said De Cordova. 'Before going out with you, she'd model several outfits and ask you to choose the one you'd like her to wear. She'd lay out her jewelry for you to select. And whatever liquor was your favorite, it was hers too. Some weeks it must have been pretty confusing for her.'

De Cordova and others were only stand-ins for the main man in Crawford's life during this period. He was Greg Bautzer, 'the handsome young attorney who used to open night-club doors for Lana Turner.'

Back in 1939 when Joan had told Lana to hit the road because she wanted Greg, the attorney was no match for the older star; her games of sex and power intimidated the younger man. But by 1946, after a few hot romances with such stalwart Hollywood glamour girls as Merle Oberon and Sonja Henie, Greg was ready to play in the center ring with Joan.

He called her the week after she won the Oscar, but she refused the call. 'George Raft sends flowers daily, but he can't seem to reach her either,' said Jimmie Fidler. Bribing her secretary at the studio, Bautzer learned that Joan was going to Palm Springs for a weekend. He followed, checked in at the same hotel, the La Quinta, and called her from the lobby. 'Look,' said Greg, 'I can't break through that telephone guard of yours in town. You're either busy, or not in, or not talking. But I'm here, you're here. It's a beautiful night. Let's go dancing.'

'They danced until the place closed,' said *Modern Screen*. 'That was their first bond. There were others. Joan loves to swim. So does Greg. He plays tennis. She's learning.'

Bautzer knew how to court beautiful women, the magazine confided. 'He sends her orchids, almost daily. He sends gifts with the flowers . . . a gold bracelet dangling a gold heart and key; a gold cigarette case encrusted with rubies and engraved "Forever and Forever", and a matching lighter that said "Here's my torch and my love." He is always available for her half-hour telephone calls. And don't forget Greg is a lawyer, so he makes the most convincing speeches.'

'Joan Crawford has twenty-six telephones in her home,' reported Cal York, 'and she wears bells on her slippers so her servants would know where she is at all times. She spends as much as four hours a day on the phone and last month when Greg Bautzer was in New York her bill ran to $600.'

Joan gave Greg the gift of a new car, a black Cadillac convertible, Hedda Hopper reported (while Bette Davis surprised 'her fella', husband Grant Sherry, with his own plane – leased – for his birthday). Bautzer was also Joan's special cohost at a formal dinner for two hundred she gave at Le Pavillion, honoring her dear old English chum, Noël Coward. 'It was the party of the year,' said the *Hollywood Reporter*. 'Joan's dear friend Billie Haines converted the restaurant into a small garden of Versailles, with showers of pink gardenias.' 'The menus were printed in French,' said Hedda Hopper. 'Tony Martin and Dinah Shore sang. Jack Benny played his violin and Noël and Celeste Holm did a party number. Other guests included Irene Dunne, Barbara Stanwyck, Robert Taylor, Marlene Dietrich,

Jane Wyman, Gene Tierney, Anne Baxter; and Clifton Webb, who brought his mother. Two of the hostess's ex-husbands, Douglas Fairbanks, Jr. and Franchot Tone, also showed, but Joan only had eyes for her handsome date, Greg Bautzer.'

'Too many teeth,' was Noël Coward's description of Bautzer, but the British playwright said Joan was 'fabulous – I love her dearly – even though all I saw of her all evening was her left shoulder. She turned her back upon me to beam upon Bautzer. Nevertheless, I adore her. My enthusiasm for her increases every year.'

Bautzer's affair with Joan was discussed frequently in Hollywood. He had qualities that attracted and repelled her, she said. He was a man's man. He liked to fight, drink, and gamble. 'Greg loves to gamble on anything and everything. Joan has never so much as placed a two-dollar bet on a guaranteed winner,' said Sheilah Graham. After an all-night poker game, heavily intoxicated, he was driving home when he ploughed into a mailbox and lamppost on Wilshire Boulevard. The next day's newspaper coverage shocked the publicity-conscious Joan. She broke off with him for a while and took up with Lana Turner's ex-husband, restaurateur Steve Crane. Bautzer retaliated by being seen in public with Merle Oberon, whereupon Joan packed her bags and her children and left for New York for four months. A week later, after Bautzer flew to New York and begged for a reconciliation, he and Joan were seen dancing cheek to cheek at the Plaza and shopping at Saks. 'Joan left for New York with four trunks and returned with eleven, loaded with gifts from Greg,' Hedda Hopper marveled.

'These two battle anywhere, any time,' said Dorothy Kilgallen. 'They quarrel in Hollywood and make up in New York. They kiss in the Catskills and feud again at Malibu.'

'Joan liked to be treated rough, and she made sure that Greg obliged her frequently,' said Adela Rogers St. Johns. 'One Saturday morning I ran into her at the Farmer's Market and she pulled me aside. "Look, darling," she said. Lowering her sunglasses she displayed a black eye. I sympathized with her but she wasn't having any of that. "He loves me," she said, showing off the shiner like it was a medal of honor.'

When Greg lunched for two days in a row with Rita Hayworth,

Joan changed her private number again and took up with British actor Peter Shaw.

'It's serious between Joan Crawford and young Peter Shaw,' said Hedda Hopper in February 1947. 'Joan gifted him with a pair of gold heart-shaped cuff links. "He doesn't table-hop. He's completely attentive to the girl he's with," said Joan. "It's Spring and I'm feeling romantic." '

'Joan and the handsome Peter Shaw are serious,' said Mike Connolly. 'He has been on lots of picnics with her and her children.'

'I only have a minute as I'm rushing to meet Joan,' Shaw told Sheilah Graham on March 4, 1947. 'But I did want you to know I may soon be divorcing my wife in England. I am so in love with Joan and I think she loves me too.'

'It sounds like marriage,' said Graham.

'It could be,' he said happily.

Two days later Graham reported that Joan had dropped Shaw and reconciled with Bautzer. 'All I know,' said Shaw dejectedly to Graham, 'is Joan's secretary phoned to say that Joan is still thinking it over and not to feel badly. So you see things may still be in my favor. I've spent every evening with Joan for weeks and weeks. She knows how I feel.'[1]

'Joan Crawford is so much the star her acting spills over into her private life. If she is a mother, she acts like a mother, the best mother in the world. If she is a mistress – which I don't know about – she is the best mistress there is. Everything for her is acting – this is her life, her food, her drink.'

Director Jean Negulesco

In May 1947 Sidney Skolsky reported that Greg Bautzer and Joan Crawford were planning to marry, but a more sceptical Hedda Hopper doubted the ceremony would ever take place. 'Greg would love to marry Joan, but he refuses to live in her house,' said Hopper. 'With two cats, three dogs, and two children already in residence

---

1 Peter Shaw would find more permanent happiness with actress Angela Lansbury, whom he married in 1949.

he may find his honeymoon a little crowded. And separate residences are out of the question. To Joan, her kids come first.'

'To the world I may be Joan Crawford, but to my children I am "Mommie Dearest", and those two words mean everything to me,' Crawford said in 1943 to *Motion Picture* magazine.

'I am an adoptive mother,' she told *Modern Screen* that same year. 'I do not believe that there is such a thing as illegitimate children. But I do believe there are illegitimate parents.'

'Should adopted children be told?' reporter Helen Weller asked. 'Yes,' said Joan Crawford.

'Darling, where did Mummy find you?' the star asked Christina.

'On a cloud of love,' the four-year-old answered.

'And how did you come to live here?'

'Because you loved me more than any other little girl in the world. That's why you picked me out.'

The curse of the word 'adopted' should be removed before children start school, Joan believed. 'It damages if they're not told until they're older, because they can turn on you.'

Although her friends and co-workers would later claim that there was never a sign of child abuse in the Crawford household, there were frequent hints in the press that Joan might encounter trouble when it came to controlling the spirited ids of her two blond children.

In 1945, on an early visit to Joan's house, Louella Parsons said that Christopher was one of the most adorable children she had ever met. 'You just want to bite a chunk out of his little knees and arms. He is the cutest thing. He mutters under his breath when he isn't included in the conversation.'

Visiting a year later, Louella still found the boy to 'be the most loving of all children, but Christina is at the age when she's a bit bossy. So Joan has put her in school even though she is only five.'

Mildred Pierce novelist James M. Cain paid a visit on Joan shortly after she won her Oscar. Sitting in her living room he later described how the star entered the room 'coming in with a swirl of skirts, like a well-bred tornado.' Her son, Christopher, followed, making 'a grinning, correct little bow, as though he didn't really believe in the stuff, but would do it anyway, just to humor his mother.'

Daughter Christina, according to Cain, was 'a prim, smiling little thing' who threw tantrums when she wasn't allowed 'to take part in things.'

'She was a miserable little kid, who deserved to be beaten up,' said Joe Mankiewicz. 'I was there when Christina would deliberately bait Joan,' said author Larry Carr. 'She was a willful and devious little monster.'

'Personally, I think alligators have the right idea. They eat their young,' said Eve Arden as Ida in *Mildred Pierce*.

'If you want Veda to do anything,' said Jack Carson in the same movie, 'knock her down first.'

'I never use soap or shampoo when washing my children's hair,' said Joan for a story on child-raising, 'I wet their hair first and then rub in six whole eggs – one by one – a trick I learned from Katharine Hepburn.'

'She dolled the kids up, trotted them out to be inspected by guests, then told us not to flatter them,' said one actress.

'Don't compliment Christina,' Joan warned her friends. 'A conceited young girl is slated for plenty of trouble.'

As a baby, Christina was promised that she would have everything that Joan had been deprived of as a child. But growing up, the girl became too greedy. At her fourth birthday party, when she opened and tossed her presents aside, she was stopped by her mother. 'I made her take each gift around the room and show it to her guests. I even kept some gifts back. On days when she was especially good I let her open one. Christina must not take things for granted.'

Demanding absolute quiet when she was on the phone, Joan told Carl Schroeder that in the midst of an important call one morning 'my two angels dropped their halos and began to yell at each other. When I hung up I gave them what for. Then I took Christopher on my lap for a session of hugging, because I don't think any child should be disciplined without being left with the idea that you love him very much.'

'She held the children's hands when they were on the operating table, having their tonsils out by Doctor Joel Pressman (Claudette Colbert's husband),' said Sheilah Graham, who then debated Joan's

Joan Crawford, as Flaemmchen in *Grand Hotel*, was one of MGM's hottest rising stars in the early 1930s.

That same year, 'Little Bette Davis of the drooping eyelids and sullen mouth', appeared for the first time in a movie magazine.

Hello Everybody,
Here's your last chance to enter the Joan Crawford Dancing Lady Contest and win a free trip to Hollywood!
See January Modern Screen and don't miss me in my latest M.G.M. picture Dancing Lady.
Joan Crawford

Opposite top left: A casual and captivating Joan Crawford linked arms with Fred Astaire, who made his Hollywood debut in her 1933 movie, *Dancing Lady*.

Opposite top right: As a major, accessible star, Joan received constant and prominent coverage in the leading movie magazines of the day.

Opposite bottom left and right: Bette, a Warner Bros. ersatz sex symbol, continued to toil in third-rate films, until, frizzed and nasty, she played her 'first downright bitch' in *Of Human Bondage*. Her performance brought an Oscar nomination, her first, Bette claimed. 'Not true,' said Joan Crawford. 'Check the Academy.'

Above: In *Dangerous*, made in 1935, Bette fell in love 'professionally and privately' with her leading man, Franchot Tone.

Right: But Franchot belonged to 'Joan of Crawford', who whisked him off to New York for a marriage ceremony before Bette Davis could extend their relationship.

Joan was also adored, professionally and privately, by two other Davis favourites – actor Spencer Tracy, and producer-director Joseph Mankiewicz, on the right.

Clark Gable made 7 films with Joan, and none with Bette, much to her chagrin. 'Bette had the fantasies, while Joan had the reality, in her bed,' one keen source observed.

As consolation for losing out on Scarlett O'Hara in *Gone With The Wind*, Bette played her own southern vixen in *Jezebel*. It brought her a second Oscar and international stardom 'at last'.

Top left: When World War II was declared to save on gasoline, Bette and husband Arthur Farnsworth travelled around Los Angeles in a horse and cart.

Centre left: Not to be outdone, Joan made her shopping rounds in a sidecar and motorbike, driven by third husband, Philip Terry.

Below: *Thanksgiving, 1942* – Bette Davis, the President of the Hollywood Canteen, supervised the dispatch of holiday turkey dinners for the visiting servicemen.

Bottom left: Joan set up her own wartime organization – the American Women's Volunteer Services, which cared for the children of working mothers.

Bette and husband Arthur Farnsworth, photographed at the Trocadero
night club on 20 August, 1943, three days before his mysterious death on
Hollywood Boulevard.

Bette and her mother Ruthie arrive for funeral services of Arthur Farnsworth,
at Forest Lawn Memorial Park, 28 August, 1943.

A short time after the funeral, Bette was back at Warners making *Mr. Skeffington*
and resuming her romantic interest in director Vincent Sherman. At that time, Bette
commented on Joan Crawford: 'I wouldn't mind her personally; if only she could act.'

As Mildred Pierce, Joan Crawford would prove to Bette Davis that she could not only act, she could also take over her throne at Warner Brothers.

tough in-house rules. 'No matter how strict you are kids leave toys behind, or they draw pictures on the wall, bring garden dirt into the kitchen. No one can be perfect all the time, except for Joan. When she takes up swimming she wants to be as good as Esther Williams. When she practices tennis she wants to be good enough for Wimbledon.'

'The image of the mother was all wrong for Joan,' Bette Davis told *Playboy*.

'She should have had puppies, not children,' said Oscar Levant.

'She was a neurotic bitch, she used us only for publicity,' son Christopher said when he was grown.

> *Question – 'Do you ever spank your children?'*
> *Answer – 'Yes Ma'-am – with a capital S. I spank them almost daily. Spare the rod and you have brats, I believe.'*
>
> Motion Picture, 12/44

Christopher as a child could also be willful and devious, said Joan. He frequently baited and irritated her in public. In her autobiography, *Child Star*, Shirley Temple told of the time she invited Joan, her husband, Phil Terry, and the two children to her home. In the bedroom, Christina headed straight for Shirley's closets, and, goggle-eyed, she gasped: 'Look at all those clothes'. 'Those aren't clothes. They're costumes,' Shirley corrected, closing the door to the covetous child. Then Christopher wanted attention. 'Without warning,' said Shirley, 'he drew back his fist and punched her [Joan] in the thigh. Reaching down she slapped him on the cheek. "He struck me," she wailed in defense to husband Terry.'

When Christopher was five, he began to request autographed photographs of his movie-star mother, to give to his schoolmates. 'After the fifth or sixth request, I got suspicious,' said Joan, who investigated and learned the boy was selling them at school for a quarter apiece. Nor was she happy when forewarned the boy insisted on helping himself to an extra piece of candy from an open box on Joan's coffee table. By way of punishment, she made him sit down and eat the whole box, 'then she watched as the boy became violently ill.'

Greg Bautzer told writer Barry Norman of the Sunday dinner at Joan's house when Christopher, left-handed, used the wrong hand to cut his meat. 'Crawford immediately leaned across the table, knocked the food out of his hand and hit him across the face. He started to cry. So I immediately went over and put my arms around him. As I was holding him – we were having a roast leg of lamb – I got it right in my face.'

'I intend that my children grow up to be ladies and gentlemen,' said Joan when anyone questioned her harsh methods. 'Success only comes with order and discipline.' Christmas 1947, when she invited Hollywood writer, Norbert Lusk to her home, she told him that Christina would play the piano while Christopher sang 'Silent Night'.

Then Christina balked.

'I've forgotten,' said the little girl.

'Play it!' Joan commanded.

'I can't.'

'Don't say you *can't*,' the star ordered. 'Don't say you can't do *anything*. Try!'

Christina was stubborn and Joan's temper was rising, said Lusk.

'Let's go to the piano and try,' said Crawford.

'But Mother, I tell you, I've forgotten,' the girl whispered.

'You haven't forgotten this,' said Joan, hitting a note. 'Nor this,' sounding another.

By now Christina had her hand on the keyboard and slowly, tentatively, played 'Silent Night'.

'Be afraid of *nothing*, Christina,' said Joan, pushing her son forward, and lighting the candles for a Yuletide finish.

MOTHER BETTE

Bette Davis answers a fanzine questionnaire, May 1947.

Can you knit? 'Vaguely.'

Play an instrument? 'Afraid not.'

Favorite actor? 'Have many . . .'

Favorite actress? 'Have many . . .'

Favorite hobby? 'Home tidying.'

Do you slam doors? 'Upon occasion . . . doesn't everybody?'
Your ambition? 'To be an intelligent mother.'

She said being pregnant did not make her feel special. Her husband,
Sherry, told her that 'creating a baby is the only creation for most
women. You have been creating for years.' That made Bette feel
much better about her condition.

Her child would be born a Yankee, she declared, so in January
1947 she and William Grant Sherry moved to her farm in New
Hampshire. But the winter became severe and in March the Sherrys
returned to the warmer climate of Laguna Beach.

As the time for the birth grew closer, Bette emphatically stated
that she could not envision any joy in natural delivery. 'Just imagine
Bette in the throes of labor,' said writer Neal O'Hara. 'Not a pretty
picture, I daresay. One imagines her sort of scaring the child from
the womb. "I said, *Out*!" '

When it was discovered that the baby wasn't in the right position,
her doctors suggested that a caesarean be performed. Bette decided
on the day – May Day – and the sex of the child. 'Sherry was sure
it would be a boy, an infant Hercules. I knew it would be a girl because
I did not *want* a male child.' (When Bette and husband number four,
Gary Merrill, decided to adopt a second child, they agreed it would
be a boy. Merrill was overseas when Bette called to tell him she had
found a child, a girl. 'Wrong fucking sex,' said Merrill.)

As willed, a daughter was born to Bette. She was christened
Barbara Davis, but called BD in perpetuity by her famous mother.
'Talk about cosmic revenge,' said Neal O'Hara. 'Even Joan Crawford couldn't have gotten away with *that*. After all, there is an even
higher authority laying claim to the initials, JC.'

BD was a seductress from the beginning, Bette declared. 'For
the first time in my life I became a willing slave to another human
being. I was thrilled it was a girl. I dressed her up and brought
her to the beach when she was eight days old. She was blond and
golden within a week.'

When she was asked to pose for some mother-and-daughter
fanzine photos, Bette declined. 'I am unable to bill and coo publicly
with my child,' she told Hedda Hopper, putting in an obvious dig

at Crawford. 'I did not have her for publicity reasons,' said Davis, 'and I am rather bored with the Mother role – as exploited by some of my cohorts.'

She could not, however, refuse to allow the powerful Hedda to enter her home when the columnist showed up uninvited at Laguna Beach. 'When I walked in Bette was cradling daughter Barbara on her knees,' wrote Hedda. 'Bill Sherry came up from the beach in a pair of bathing trunks. With his tanned and muscular body he looked like a bronze statue.'

Bette told Hedda that she felt 'complete, happy at last.' While husband Sherry painted and swam in the ocean, diving for abalone, she cooked, cleaned, and took care of her robust family. 'She laughs more and broods less,' said Hedda.

Louella Parsons, not to be outdone, also trekked to Laguna to see Bette and her baby daughter. She waxed eloquently about the 'shining Madonna' and her beautiful infant. 'She is blond and plump and tanned, with big blue eyes, the most gorgeous little baby I have ever seen,' said Louella when she just happened to bump into Joan Crawford at La Rue's restaurant the following evening. 'Prettier than my Christina? Cuter than my Christopher?' Joan wanted to know, obviously disturbed.

'Joan became upset with the attention that Bette and her baby were receiving,' said writer Hector Arce, 'so a short time later all heads in the Green Room at Warner's turned in her direction when she arrived one day with Christina and Christopher, followed by a nurse who was wheeling a double pram. When they arrived at their table, everyone watched as Joan reached into the baby carriage and pulled out not one but *two* brand-new babies. She had gone out of state that weekend and adopted two more kids.'

'Well, I think it's *disgusting*,' said Bette Davis when she heard the news of the addition to the Crawford household. 'She buys babies like she's in a supermarket.'

Calling the babies Cathy and Cindy, Joan told the *United Press*, 'I intend to adopt four more. Two boys and two girls. I already have the names picked out. Carol and Cal and Connie and . . . I forget.'

'It's a *hoot*,' said Bette. 'She brands everything she owns with her last initial.' (A dog, Cliquot, and a parakeet, Crazy Crawford, would follow.)

On the weekends, Joan and her 'twins' (they weren't) had their 'gayest fun,' said columnist May Mann in *Silver Screen*. 'When Joan is dressing to go out for the evening, the babies are placed in a drawer on either side of her dressing-room table. As she puts on her makeup the two little girls can play with her jewelry.'

Taking a cue from Davis, Joan put a veto an anyone taking photographs of her new babies. 'You can only shoot the back of their heads,' she told photographer Hymie Fink. Her ban was part fear, part vanity. 'I am terrified that if their natural mother sees and recognizes them, she'll want them back,' she said. 'And anyway, in a few months they'll look different, much prettier, like their real mommie, Joan Crawford.'

'Can Women Trust Each Other?' was the lead to a feature story in August 1947. 'Yes,' said Joan Crawford, adding that the renewed talk of a feud between her and Bette Davis was untrue. 'Why should there be a feud?' said Joan. 'I believe there is a place for every actress in this wonderful business. Certainly Bette and I don't fear each other.'

That same month in Laguna Beach, Bette Davis had grown tired of being a full-time mother. Babies and small children bored her, she said. 'They can't hold their own in a conversation until they're at *least* five or six.' In September she told her husband, Sherry, that she was 'sick of being a fat cow.' She wanted to return to work, and after depositing B.D. with a nurse, she drove to Burbank and asked Jack Warner for scripts. Two came from Jerry Wald, including *Time to Sing*, the story of two retired stage actresses who team up for a tour of summer-stock theaters. The second was *Women Without Men*, about a female prison warden who attempts to rehabilitate a prisoner before she becomes a hardened criminal. For both projects, Jerry Wald wanted Joan Crawford to co star with Bette.

'I know *nothing* of those projects,' said Bette in 1987.

'I knew of the women's prison picture,' Crawford said in 1973. 'It was written by Virginia Kellogg and later became *Caged*, with

Eleanor Parker and Agnes Moorehead. Certainly I wanted to work with Miss Davis, but from what I recall, the studio did not want to put two of their top stars in one picture.'

'Certainly I could understand Jack Warner's position,' said George Cukor. 'Davis and Crawford were both powerful stars at the time. If they collided, World War III would have been declared.'

Irving Rapper agreed. 'I don't believe there was a producer or a director on the lot who was willing to tackle a project starring the two.'

'There is a wonderful story about Kate Hepburn and Ginger Rogers when they were doing the movie of *Stagedoor* at RKO,' Cukor continued. 'Both of them were stars at the studio. Kate already had one Oscar and Ginger was very popular because of the Fred Astaire pictures. When the producer, Pandro Berman, was asked how he intended to handle them in *Stagedoor*, he said, 'It's simple. I told Hepburn she could rule the set from eight to one; and Ginger could take over after lunch.'

It was Katharine Hepburn who picked up a part Bette Davis refused in 1947. The picture was *The African Queen*, with Davis cast as the missionary spinster. 'Are you *out* of your fucking *mind*, Jack?' Bette said to Warner when he announced his plans to shoot on actual locations in Africa. 'If you can't shoot the picture in a boat on the back lot, then I'm *not* interested.'

'They'd have me rocking and bouncing all over the damn boat for weeks,' she explained to Hedda Hopper, 'and I'm much too old for that nonsense.'

Irving Rapper spoke of one other lost role, one that Bette wanted to do that year. With Joan Crawford being touted as a strong Oscar candidate for *Possessed*, Bette planned to regain her dramatic ground by giving a tour-de-force performance as the nation's crazed first lady, Mary Todd Lincoln. The director of the project was Irving Rapper, who met with Bette to discuss the character and the script.

'Mrs. Lincoln would have been a great role for Bette,' said Rapper. 'She was a powerful character in history, the maddest bitch in the White House. She was the first woman to have a black friend [her seamstress] in the White House, and the first wife to influence her husband as President. She uncovered the conspiracy to kill him, and later, after his murder and the death of her second son, she went insane and was placed in a mental institution by her family. My God, Bette Davis could have torn that part to shreds, but Jack Warner at the last minute changed his mind. He said the story was true, but unpatriotic. "I'll be the last man to denigrate a man like Abraham Lincoln," said Warner, and he canceled the picture.'

Without recourse Bette accepted the lead in a film based on the popular best-selling book *Winter Meeting*, about a wealthy New England spinster-poet who falls in love with an ex-naval hero who wants to become a priest. Her director was Bretaigne Windust, who staged *Life with Father* and *Arsenic and Old Lace* in New York. Prior to shooting, Windust and his wife visited Bette in Laguna. 'After dinner,' said William Grant Sherry, 'while Bette was showing his wife our house, Windust spoke to me in the living room. He explained that he wanted to bring out a new quality in Bette for this picture, to make her more restrained and softer. I said it was exactly what she needed at that point. He was a charming, sophisticated man, but Bette would not listen to him when they began the picture. It was half-finished and not going well. There was a meeting with the producer, Heinz Blanke, and he said "the rushes are terrible, what is going on?" Bette said she was doing what the director wanted, but she wasn't. She was overacting. Basically she was a ham, and if not controlled she could be a mess. Her best films were directed by men whose egos were stronger than hers, and she had to give in to them. Windust was too much of a gentleman, and she had to show him she was superior.'

When *Winter Meeting* was released the following April, and flopped ('It was the censor's fault,' said Bette, 'they cut the guts out of the story'), she was already at work on *June Bride*, a sophisticated comedy which would show 'a new Bette', in 'a new look' wardrobe by Edith Head, and 'a new full bouffant hairdo.' 'That was her second mistake,' said a Warner's publicist. 'The times and postwar audiences had changed. The old-fashioned women's pictures and easy comedies were passé. Stars like Crawford, Olivia de Havilland, and Susan Hayward were doing stark dramas like *Possessed*, *The Snake Pit*, and *Smash-Up*, and here was Bette playing parts that Joan walked through back in her heydays at MGM.'

In *June Bride*, Bette was bolstered by a few former Crawford colleagues. Ranald MacDougall, who wrote *Mildred Pierce* and *Possessed*, penned this new script for Bette. Her co star was Robert Montgomery, a steady Crawford leading man of the 1930s. Described as 'smooth and handsome, a thorough gentleman,' by Joan, at her first meeting with the actor, Bette agreed with that assessment. But when Montgomery failed to respond to her 'rather girlish flirting' during the filming, she began to complain that there was 'no chemistry' between them. One afternoon, after finishing a winter's scene in a horse-drawn sleigh, she complained to visitors Lew Wasserman and her husband, Sherry, that Montgomery had misbehaved during the shot. 'Robert still has to prove he's a sexy man,' said Bette. 'He's been feeling around my legs under the blanket all during the take.' The stalwart Sherry, known for his equally strong temper, excused himself and went to the actor's trailer. He knocked on his door. 'What can I do for you?' the polite Montgomery asked.

'You can keep your hands off my wife's legs, for one thing,' said Sherry. The bewildered actor said he didn't know what he was talking about. 'I'm sure you do,' said Sherry. Shaken and confused, Montgomery left for home a short time later and shooting was shut down for the day. That night in Laguna, Bette told her husband that she thought it would be best if he stayed away from the studio for the rest of the picture. 'She seemed rather pleased about the incident,' Sherry recalled later.

In October 1948, Bette, her husband, and daughter, B.D., went to New York for the opening of *June Bride*, and for a one-man show of Sherry's paintings in a midtown art gallery. Prior to the trip, when asked by the Warner's press office where she would prefer to stay, Bette requested 'that the accommodations be comfortable and conservative, within my husband's price range.' When the New York office reserved two rooms for her at the dignified but low-keyed Algonquin Hotel, the actress became upset.

'Bette raised the roof because the studio had been unsuccessful in securing a three-room suite for her at her favorite hotel,' *Motion Picture* reported. 'Her caustic comment was: "I'll bet you wouldn't push Joan Crawford around like this. Imagine putting me into a single room." '

Although the advance trade reviews of *June Bride* were good ('A hilarious laughfest . . . big box-office potential . . . should put Bette back on top,' said *Variety*), some of the major New York critics were not as benign. 'With eyelashes as long as the horse's mane, she conducts herself throughout the film with the grimly competent air of a prison warden,' said the *New Yorker*.

'Neither Bette nor Joan could play comedy,' said director Vincent Sherman. 'They didn't have the flair or the timing of someone like Ann Sheridan. But of course no one at Warner's would *dare* tell them that to their faces.'

June Bride did poorly at the box office and Davis blamed the studio for not properly merchandising the picture. Returning to California, her meetings with Jack Warner grew stormier. 'As a further annoyance to him,' she said, 'I always wore sunglasses, so he could not look into my eyes.

'We could not agree on scripts,' said the star. 'I wanted to play important parts – Mary Todd Lincoln, and Mattie in *Ethan Frome*. Mr. Warner told me that the public did not want to see me in period pictures, that I was "a *modern* woman." Hah! And I fell for that baloney. That's how he got me to do *Beyond the Forest*.'

Flop number three, and the film that would bring about her departure from the studio, was based on a popular book purchased by Warner's in 1948. The lead role, that of Rosa Moline, 'a twelve o'clock girl in a nine o'clock town,' was offered first to Joan Crawford. 'Yes, I saw either a script or the book. It was trash, an endless saga of this woman who wanted to leave her husband,' said Crawford, who opted instead to play the role of the carnival dancer who struts her way through murder, blackmail and politics in *Flamingo Road*.

The script of *Beyond the Forest* was shuffled next to Bette Davis. 'I begged Jack Warner to give the part to Virginia Mayo, who was good at those sorts of roles,' said Bette. Warner also offered King Vidor as her director. 'Somehow they all managed to persuade me that this was going to be a *major*, important picture. And, fool that I was, I *believed* them.'

'What a dump!' was the most quoted line from the film and it summed up her sentiments during the making of the picture. 'Nothing can please Bette Davis today,' Sheilah Graham reported from the set. 'Her cameraman is no good – she's only had him for years. She battles with her director, her producer, her everything. Her nerves are keyed up so high she just has to let off steam or bust.'

In a square dance routine, she missed a few steps. She would not redo them, she told director Vidor. 'The girl I play, this Rosa Moline, she's the type of a girl who could make a few mis-steps in this kind of a dance. How could she be perfect in a dance new to her?' she argued. But Vidor insisted that the scene be done again. 'Miss Davis did not show up at the studio for two days after that,' Cal York reported. 'Tick fever was the reason she gave.' 'She had many excuses for not going to the set,' said husband Sherry. 'Her favorite was laryngitis. One day she sent a note to producer Heinz Blanke saying she lost her voice and couldn't speak. Then, when Jack Warner called to find out how she was, she picked up the phone and started to scream at him.'

'I used to hear her on the phone,' said Marian Richards, the young governess who cared for two-year-old B.D. 'She would be yelling so loud at Jack Warner you could almost see smoke coming out of the receiver. She wasn't going to budge and neither was he. When she hung up she would pace up and down for an hour, cursing him and the studio. The whole house would be steaming and little B.D. heard everything.'

'It was a hopeless situation,' Bette recalled. 'I was supposed to act rotten to Joseph Cotten, to ridicule him as my husband. But I *adored* Joe Cotten. Why should I want to leave him for anyone?' When asked by an interviewer why she didn't coast through the film on star quality as Joan Crawford might have done, Bette replied, 'Oh, I wouldn't do that. Wouldn't? I never *could* do that.'

A week before the film was to be completed, prior to doing a scene where the hysterical Rosa Moline tries to induce an abortion by jumping off a highway embankment, Bette failed once more to show up for work. When Jack Warner called she gave him an ultimatum. 'You want the picture finished,' she said, 'then let me out of my contract.'

Warner, faced with losing the eight hundred thousand dollars already spent, had no alternative but to agree to her demand.

'It was dirty pool on my part,' said Bette, 'but I was desperate.'

HER LAST DAYS AT BURBANK

Although she insisted that she and Jack Warner parted good friends and would 'make many many pictures together in the future,' because she double-crossed the studio boss, Bette lost out on a forthcoming important part.

Director Irving Rapper told the story. 'My agent, Charlie Feldman, owned the rights to *The Glass Menagerie*. Jane Wyman was signed to play Laura, the daughter, and we tested various actresses for the role of the mother, including Tallulah Bankhead and Miriam Hopkins. Then Feldman thought of Bette. He asked me to talk to her because of *Now Voyager* and our friendship. I went out to the back lot, where she was finishing *Beyond the Forest*. As I approached, Bette ran across the road and fell down, dead. King Vidor saw me and yelled, "Cut." Bette looked up and said, "Irving Rapper – wouldn't you know it. This is my last day of shooting and I'm flat on my ass." '

Rapper and Davis went to her dressing room to talk. ' "Well," she said, "it must be *very* important. You're the only one who came to see me today." I said, "Charlie Feldman and I want you to do *The Glass Menagerie*." She looked at me, and after a long pause she said something very humble. "I wouldn't like to step on the toes of Jane Wyman," she said. She knew that Janie had been signed for the role of the girl, and she wouldn't think of taking the part away from her. This touched me so much. This was the Bette I used to know. And I said, "How very nice of you to say that, but Bette, few people remember the name of the actress who played the daughter in the stage play. Everyone remembers Laurette Taylor, the mother." And Bette said, "Oh! My God! Yes, of course." '

Rapper was not aware that Bette had duped Jack Warner and broken her contract. 'Bette was always running around saying, "Oh, Jack Warner loves me. He's a father image," and all that crap. I said, "Will you make a test?" She said – and these are her exact words – "*I'll tell you what let's do.* I'll make the test and if I don't *like* it, I won't do the movie." I thought that was fair, and I went back to Feldman and gave him the good news.'

Feldman called producer Jerry Wald, who met with Jack Warner.

'The next day Jerry Wald called me and said, "Irving, I'm very glad you weren't around last evening when Jack Warner was told that you spoke to Bette Davis about doing *The Glass Menagerie*. He said, "She's leaving the studio tomorrow, and if you or Rapper or anyone else let that cunt back in, I'll fire all of you."

'I was nonplussed,' said Rapper. 'Bette never said a word to me about her leaving. Then when I told her the test was off, she tried to make me feel it was *my* fault. "Oh, Irving," she said, "you just didn't try hard enough." '

Late at night, after dubbing some lines in *Beyond the Forest*, the former first lady of Warner Brothers went to her dressing room and packed her private things in a suitcase. After leaving the bungalow, she locked the door and put the keys in an envelope, together with a note to the studio property manager. The note was her farewell salute to Joan Crawford, whose latest film, *Flamingo Road*, was the studio's top grosser. With her departure, Bette asked that her bungalow, the number-one star dressing room on the lot, be given to her worthy successor . . . 'to Miss Jane Wyman.'

14

LES FEMMES SAUVAGES

'Bette Davis and Joan Crawford top this town's list of "Virile Glamour Girls." They're a little aggressive. They don't purr. They use their own initiative and they put the motion in motion pictures.'

Director Joe Newman

The 1949 release of *Flamingo Road*, with a lascivious Joan Crawford showing off her 'gams' and her wide scarlet mouth clamped shut on an unlit cigarette, pleased Jack Warner, the public, and some reviewers. 'Solid B.O.,' said *Variety*. 'A wrong girl for the right side of the tracks,' said Dorothy Kilgallen, 'and the question never arose that she would cross over those tracks but how she would do it.' As a carnival cooch-wiggler, critic Christopher Vane said, Joan sounded too cultured, 'But the minute she slings a mink across her shoulders, you're right back with the Crawford you know and understand.'

To extend the momentum of tough girl Joan, Jerry Wald, at Jack Warner's request, wrote *The Damned Don't Cry*. The familiar plot showcased the star as a bored housewife who throws off the shackles of domesticity to seek glamour and excitement in the big city. Transformed to a slick model, then to a kept gun-moll, Joan had numerous costume changes, some good, biting lines, and four male co stars – David Brian, Steve Cochran, Richard Egan, and Kent Smith, all of whom were willing to lie down or die at her command.

Offscreen, Crawford's sex life was just as crowded and dictated. 'Predatory and possessive' was writer Barry Norman's description. Joan made the passes and established the rules. Her chosen date for an evening would drive to her house and park his car; then using one of her two Cadillacs (a spare was always on hand in case the other broke down), with Joan behind the wheel, they would drive to a restaurant of her choice. She ordered the drinks, selected the food, directed the conversation, signed the check; then at home, with a 'Wham, bam, thank you, Sam,' she seduced the guy and sent him on his way.

Actor Kirk Douglas had just scored with his first hit picture, *Champion*, when he received a telegram of praise from Joan. It included her phone number and the invitation to call. He called. They made a date for dinner. She mapped out the entire evening, down to the route to the restaurant. He switched restaurants, but back at her house Crawford took charge again.

'The front door closed and she slipped out of her dress, in the hallway,' said Kirk. ' "You're so clean," she murmured. "It's wonderful that you shaved your armpits when you made *Champion*." '

Kirk didn't have time to explain to Joan that he was a blond, with fair hair under his arms. He made love to her on the hallway floor, and afterward she brought him upstairs to see her kids, who were strapped into their beds. 'It was so professional, clinical, lacking in warmth, like the sex we just had. I got out fast,' said the actor.

For industry gatherings, Joan established another set of rules for escorts lucky enough to be seen by her side. Arriving at premieres and parties, when the photographers asked for her picture, her escort, depending on his name quotient, was expected to stand at her side or back to her right and smile, not at the camera but at Joan, adoringly. If she had to give a few words to a radio broadcaster or print interviewer, he would remain by her side, still smiling but *mute*, then accompany her through the theater lobby or nightclub foyer. Once they had taken their seats, he was not allowed to leave her side, even to go to the bathroom, unless she was in comfortable conversation with someone else – and then his absence would be timed. He was also to be on constant alert when her cigarettes needed to be lit, or her drinks replenished. If she agreed to dance with another, he was to jump up, pull back her chair, then remain seated in his own until she returned. Under no circumstances was *he* allowed to dance with another. When she returned to their table, she expected him *there*, ready to jump up and welcome her back with an affectionate touch and a suitable line of welcome. At the evening's end he would drive her home, cater to her physical needs if necessary, then collect his car and depart. She would time his journey home, then place a call to make sure he was there and not in 'some other woman's bed.' If he wasn't home, 'furious retribution would be faced by that escort at their next meeting.'

In the Fall of 1949 attorney Greg Bautzer was still involved with Crawford. Their on-again, off-again affair lasted four years, and Bautzer later described his tour of duty with the star to the London *Daily Telegraph*. 'Her tempestuous almost masculine personality made this office quite perilous,' said Richard Last, who asked Bautzer what it was really like to be the star's devoted vassal, charged with carrying her knitting bag and hidden vodka bottles. 'I still have four scars on my face which she put there,' said Bautzer. 'She could throw a cocktail glass across the room and hit you in the face, two times out of three.'

Daughter Christina recalled Greg as 'boisterous, fun-loving, the most handsome, dashing man alive.' However, she confessed she was often scared of the screaming, yelling, kicking and pounding that went on late at night when Greg stayed over. 'I wasn't afraid for my mother,' she said. 'I was afraid for myself. Mother never seemed to be hurt the next day, and she kept seeing this man.' One time, during the heat of a fight, Joan climbed out on her balcony, yelling for the police. Greg followed, 'calling her dirty names,' so Joan climbed up on the roof, and the neighbors heard everything.

'Both she and Greg have a flair for the dramatic,' Sidney Skolsky reported. 'She threw him out of her house constantly. Once he arrived home with his hands bleeding.'

Another time he fell asleep during one of Joan's Sunday-night movie shows. She told her guests not to wake him and then tiptoed out of the room, leaving him in darkness. 'He woke up at 7:00 the next morning, alone, with the screening room door locked,' said Hedda Hopper. 'The theater had a kitchenette, so he cooked some breakfast, smashed a window and went home. Joan called him later in the day and screamed: "How *dare* you leave my home without washing the dishes?" '

There were many benefits of course to his affair with Joan, Greg admitted. Beyond the obvious, the great sex ('A night with Joan was better than a year with ten others'), she provided valuable clients for his law firm. Through her, he met and handled Joseph Schenck, Jerry Wald, John Garfield, Ingrid Bergman, Jane Wyman, and Ginger Rogers. It was the latter star who caused the permanent split between Crawford and the attorney.

In October 1949 Joan and Bautzer attended a party in honor of Prince Bernhard of the Netherlands. Hosted by Louis B. Mayer, it was held in the Garden Room of the Beverly Wilshire Hotel, with most of Hollywood's royalty attending. Loretta Young wore red taffeta; Roz Russell was in white chiffon; Barbara Stanwyck wore black satin and diamonds; and Joan 'looked breathtaking . . . in green taffeta, with red roses caught up in the folds of the dress.' Greg Bautzer, wearing the white tuxedo and red cummerbund that Joan had given him, looked good enough for Ginger Rogers to monopolize his time on the dance floor. 'Looking divine, they danced every dance, leaving Joan fuming at her dinner table,' Louella Parsons jotted in her notebook.

The story of Joan's revenge on the way home that night has often been told, but it bears repeating. She was driving, of course, and pulling over to a deserted stretch of road, she said to Greg, 'Darling, would you check the rear tire? It feels flat.' Bautzer got out of the car and walked to the rear; as he leaned over to touch the tire, Joan gunned the motor, and the car took off in an earsplitting peal of rubber. She had left him, in his white tuxedo and dancing shoes, stranded on a dark deserted road, somewhere north of Beverly Hills.

After walking the three miles to his home, Bautzer said, the usual procedure would be to send flowers the next day and beg for Joan's forgiveness. This time around he didn't bother. He stayed away from her for a month; then he began to date Ginger Rogers in public. The first time they bumped into Joan, she cut them dead. The second time they met, she threw names in their faces that reportedly 'mortified Ginger.'

'I am sorry that Joan and I didn't remain friends,' said Bautzer the lawyer. 'It upset me greatly when she took her business to another firm.'

'Bette most admires men who dominate her — yet, she always marries men she can dominate.'

Sidney Skolsky

'Davis, like Crawford, liked to create scenes. They enjoyed provoking men to violence. When satisfied they would yell "Cut." But real life can't be controlled as easily as the movies and they sometimes suffered for their little dramas.'

Adela Rogers St. Johns

The same month that columnists reported on the parting of Bautzer and Crawford, the news flashed that Bette Davis' third marriage was also on the rocks. She was said to be heartbroken. 'Aries are the most romantic fools on earth,' Davis mourned, claiming the man she had loved and married turned out to be a fortune hunter *and* a wife beater. 'I was told that before he married me he told some of his Marine buddies that he intended to marry a wealthy woman,' she said. 'His mother also warned me not to marry Sherry, because he had a violent temper. On our honeymoon in Mexico he pushed me out of the car on an open highway. In our hotel room he threw a trunk and almost killed me.'

Other acts of violence were reported by Bette. He pushed her down a flight of stairs, then knocked her out with a flying ice bucket. Yet some friends from that period seemed to recall a different William Grant Sherry. Irving Rapper visited the couple from time to time and recalled that Sherry was a 'quiet sort of chap, very much in love with his wife and child.' Rosalind Russell, who bought one of Sherry's paintings, remembered him as 'a talented artist, soft-spoken always and very polite, not at all the bully type.'

'It was fascinating to watch this couple at dinner parties,' said Sheilah Graham. 'Sherry looked pleasant, but he opened his mouth only to eat, never to talk, because Bette carried that end of the ball herself.'

Born in East Hampton and raised in New York, where his father was a carpenter for the Theater Guild, Sherry was often described by Bette as an ex-boxer, but his professional time in the ring was limited to one fight at Madison Square Garden. 'I was looking at guys who were becoming vegetables,' he said. 'I wanted no part of that, so I quit boxing and became a physiotherapist.' While recuperating from a war injury at the San Diego Naval hospital, he became a medical illustrator and was asked to join a clinic in Philadelphia, but opted instead to pursue a career as a fine-arts painter in Laguna, where he met Bette. 'I never told any Marine buddies that I wanted to meet a wealthy woman,' he said, 'because I was never in the Marines. I was a Navy man, and I never had any buddies. And my mother never warned Bette not to marry me, because they never met until the day of the wedding.'

Bette said that Sherry's dedication as an artist fell short of hers, and his frustration had a frenzy that terrorized her.

He had a ferocious temper, Sherry, an established artist, said in 1988. 'But she enjoyed making me violent. She would keep after me, criticizing me in public and needling me at home. She would push me until I eventually exploded. But I didn't do half the things she said I did.'

What about the time she said he threw her down the stairs?

'That never happened.'

And the ice bucket that knocked her unconscious?

'That never happened.'

And the traveling case he threw at her in Mexico?

'Yes, that happened. It was a small trunk. I was unpacking and she had been at me all afternoon about some silly thing. She kept needling and needling me. I kept telling her to be quiet, and she wouldn't, so I picked up the case, which was on a stand, and I threw it at her. She was standing in the doorway with her hands on her hips, and when she saw the case coming she ducked. It took a big chip out of the doorjamb and scared the daylights out of her. But it did shut her up for a while.'

He loved his wife dearly, he said, and he believed the feeling was mutual. Then he was told that she had married him only so that he could give her a child. 'She had three abortions when she was younger, but she never told me that. Now she was getting older, and wanted a child, a healthy baby. I was a good candidate. I didn't drink or smoke. I was in excellent physical shape, and she liked my background. I was also crazy about her.'

'His adoration of me, quite naturally, excited me,' said Bette.

'We had a lovely marriage at the beginning,' Sherry continued, 'but after the baby came everything changed. She didn't seem to want me around anymore.'

'He wanted to be indispensable to me and that of course was impossible,' the star insisted.

'She used to call me "a goddamned puritan" because I didn't like her drinking and swearing. "I can outdrink and outswear any man," she said. I didn't doubt that, I replied, but what an unladylike thing to brag about. Another time she told me, "I've always been able to put men under my thumb, but I can't you." I said, "Bette, why don't you stop trying and maybe we can have a decent marriage?" '

'I think Bette quickly grew tired of Sherry,' said director Curtis Bernhardt. 'I remember a party once – it was some studio shindig. Sherry had been placed at her table – the star's table. She said he had no right to be seated next to her, and she ordered him and his place card to another table. He was ready to kill. When she danced with a man, Sherry broke in and she refused to dance with him.'

'That sounds like something that happened another time,' Sherry recalled. 'There was a big party that MCA gave for all its top stars at the Beverly Hills Hotel. I wasn't allowed to be at the head table, where all the big shots, including Bette, sat. I was at a side table, with Alan Ladd and his wife. Ladd kept saying, "Where's your bride?" I said, "She's over there with the big shots." Then, when the music started playing for dancing, I went over and said, "Bette, I'd love to dance with you." In front of all these people, she said, "I'm *not* dancing with you." So I just reached down around her waist and lifted her right out of her chair and brought her to the dance floor. She tried to get away from me, but I held her tight and kept dancing with her until the music stopped. Then I let her go. She went running and yelling from the dance floor, through the place, to the ladies' room. I went after her, and Joseph Cotten reached up, grabbed my arm and said, "When you catch her, punch her right in the mouth." '

On October 19, 1949, three months after she left Warner Brothers, and three days after *Beyond the Forest* opened to disastrous reviews,

Bette Davis sued for divorce from William Grant Sherry. Charging extreme cruelty and physical abuse, she asked the judge to issue an order to restrain him from doing bodily harm to her and her daughter.

When the suit was filed, Bette gained the sympathy of the public and the press, until two renegade reporters questioned the seriousness of her accusations. Columnist Dorothy Kilgallen said she had met William Grant Sherry a few times, and he didn't seem to be capable of Bette's charges. Reporter Arthur E. Charles also wondered how innocent poor Bette was in the matter. 'Any amateur student of human nature, analyzing the obvious things,' said Charles, 'must see in Bette Davis' off-screen face the evidences of her long reign as Empress of Burbank. Her mouth, drawn full on the screen, is tight and narrow. Her eyes are wide and cold and queenly. She is as likely as not to raise her hands in a sweep and expect to find a cigarette in her fingers, her wish anticipated. This is okay around a movie set but hardly the thing in a man's own home. If Mr. Sherry had been the brute he was, Miss Davis would certainly have had a number of broken fingers by this time.'

There would be no splitting of community property, Bette's lawyer declared, because Sherry had signed an agreement before the wedding ceremony stating that, if and when the marriage ended, he would make no claims on her property. 'In other words, Bette Davis could try it out, and if it didn't work, it wouldn't cost her anything,' said Arthur E. Charles.

'That's not entirely correct,' said Sherry. 'I never signed anything until after our daughter was born. Bette asked me to sign a paper saying I wanted nothing from her, that I was in love with her, not her money. I was happy to do that, because I loved and trusted her.'

In late October 1949, after the divorce action was filed, and without the former protection of Jack Warner and his publicity guards, Bette learned that she was being portrayed by the press as a shrewd, aggressive, less-than-battered spouse. Refusing to be cast as the heavy in her private life, she decided to change her divorce plans. Sherry wanted a reconciliation ('I loved her and my child; divorce was never my idea'), and she agreed to drop the suit if he would renounce *his* sins, publicly. 'I told her I would do anything to preserve our marriage,' he confessed to the *United Press* on October 24, 1949, 'I asked her to call off the suit so I can go to a psychiatrist whom I can talk to and who really knows about the mind. My temper is hooked up with the war, I think.'

At dinner at Lucey's restaurant with the editors of the mass-circulation magazine *Photoplay*, Bette held Sherry's hand while he repeated his confession. 'It was Bette who saved our marriage. She had the intelligence to give me the help I need.'

'I was willing to do almost anything so we could stay together as a family,' said the artist later. 'I did have a bad temper, although now I know she caused everyone who had anything to do with her to lose their temper. But I didn't want to lose her or the baby, so I agreed to see this man, a Dr. Hacker, who treated all the big movie stars in Beverly Hills. I took a psychology test with his woman associate, and apparently I upset her. She showed me an ink blot and asked for my response. I told her it reminded me of a kidney operation I had sketched in the hospital. She stared at me and said, "You mean to tell me that picture doesn't remind you of a woman's vagina?" I said, "If it did, I'd have nothing more to do with women." '

Sherry's treatment continued for a few months. 'I liked Dr. Hacker. I told him my problems, and he told me his. He had one movie-star client who thought someone was watching her house all the time. He went over to talk to her one night and the cops arrested him. They thought he was the imaginary prowler. After a while I said to him, "Listen, doc, when is something going to happen here? When am I going to get rid of my bad temper?" He said, "Grant, there's nothing wrong with you. You're just a red-blooded American man, married to the wrong woman." '

In January 1950, still married to Sherry, and five months after she had left Warner Brothers, Bette made her first independent film, *Payment on Demand*, at RKO studios. Her co star was Barry Sullivan, and according to Dorothy Kilgallen and Sheilah Graham, Bette became romantically involved with Sullivan. On the last day of shooting, in late March, when Bette failed to come home, her husband went to the studio and made a shambles of the set when 'he found his wife being extravagantly attentive to the actor she was co starring with – and not a camera was turning,' said Kilgallen.

'It was the end of the picture, and they always have a party,' Sherry explained. 'Nobody outside the cast was invited, which was OK with me, but Bette didn't come home. It was late, around midnight, and I thought, something's wrong. I called the studio and they said, "No – there's nobody on the set – it's all closed." So I figured she started drinking and fell asleep in her dressing room. I decided to go and get her. When I got to the studio, I went to her dressing room. There were two parts to it – a living room in the front, and then the dressing area in the rear. Well, the lights were on in the front and it was dark in the back. So I called out Bette's name. She came out from the back holding a glass of whiskey in her hand. When she saw me she said, "Oh . . . hi." And then Barry Sullivan came out behind her. They had been sitting in the dark, and I don't think anything was happening. I wasn't angry either. I said: "OK, Bette – come on, we're going home." She said, "No, I'm not going home." I picked up her mink coat and put it around her shoulders and repeated, "Let's go." She took if off, threw it on the couch, and said, "No. Leave me alone." At this point Barry Sullivan stepped in and said, "Come on, Grant, have a drink." I said, "No thanks, Barry. It's late. You better go home too. Your wife will be waiting for you." I was trying to keep the whole thing calm. But Bette started getting louder, saying she was never going home, and I reached for her. Barry came closer and put his hand on me and said, "Look here, just take it easy. I don't want any trouble with you." I told him there was no trouble, to mind his own business, that she was my wife and I wanted to take her home. At that point he put his hand on me again, and went to push me. I was in terrific physical shape at that time, and I took a swing at him. I wasn't thinking of hitting him, but I did. His back was to the open door and when I hit him he went flying out the door and across the street, and he landed in a bunch of tulips.'

With that, Bette ran out the door, screaming. The studio police arrived and pointing to Sherry, she yelled, 'Take him! Arrest him!'

'There were three of them,' said Sherry. 'My temper by then

was very hot and I warned them: "If any of you guys want to come near me, you're going to get hurt." One of the policemen was trying to get behind me and I turned and told him to get back with his friends, that I was taking my wife home. Then Bette started screaming again: "Call the city police!" "Oh, sure," I told her; "make a big thing out of this, so it'll be in the papers tomorrow." And she decided not to do that. She eventually agreed to come home with me. Her car and her chauffeur were still there, so she said, "I'll leave with him." That was fine with me, but I told the driver, I would follow them, and that he better not try to shake me. "If you dare to turn off, anywhere, before we get to our house, I'll ram my car right into you," I said. He looked at me, and Bette said, "He'll do it, he'll do it." So he drove off. I followed, and we went straight home.'

ALL ABOUT EVE

'*There goes Eve. Eve evil, little Miss Evil. But the evil that men do – how does it go, groom? Something about the good they leave behind – I played it once in Wilkes-Barre.*'

Bette as Margo Channing

'*Never in the history of motion pictures has an actress been so perfectly cast.*'

Gary Merrill

Early in March, when *Payment on Demand* was in its last week of filming, Bette Davis received a call from Darryl Zanuck. He wanted her to read a script about a brittle ageing Broadway actress who competes with a conniving young ingenue. The writer was Joseph L. Mankiewicz, who had once romanced and produced 'some very bad Joan Crawford pictures.' After *All About Eve*, however, he would be referred to by Bette as 'a genius, and the man responsible for the greatest role of my career.'

'A vicious, absurd little man,' was Mankiewicz's description of Darryl Zanuck, who tried to impose his casting ideas on the writer-director of *All About Eve*. Zanuck's first suggestion for Margo Channing was his top star, Susan Hayward, who at thirty-four was considered too young for the 'over-forty' lead character. Zanuck then suggested a package: Marlene Dietrich as Margo, Jeanne Crain as the sweet but evil Eve Harrington, John Garfield as the director Bill Sampson, and Jose Ferrer as the venomous critic Addison De Witt.

Mankiewicz argued that Jeanne Crain lacked 'the bitch virtuosity' for Eve; and the script was too literate for Dietrich, who 'poses beautifully but cannot really speak.' He insisted on testing Anne Baxter for Eve, and Claudette Colbert was signed to play Margo Channing. 'Claudette could have played it beautifully . . . bitchily, icily, with a great elegance – a piss elegance, if you like,' the director believed. When Colbert missed a step in her home and broke a vertebra in her back, he considered Gertrude Lawrence as a replacement. Mankiewicz sent the script to her lawyer, who asked for changes. Miss Lawrence would not drink or smoke in the movie, and in the party scene she should sing a song on the order of 'Bill', the Jerome Kern classic. 'I said that had already been done in *Showboat*, said the director, 'and thankfully, a short time later Bette Davis was signed as Margo.'

> *'Margo Channing was not a bitch. She was an actress who was getting older and was not too happy about it. And why should she be? Anyone who says that life begins at forty is full of crap. As people get older their bodies begin to decay. They get sick. They forget things. What's good about that?'*
>
> Bette Davis, 1973

With only ten days before production commenced, Davis was fitted for her Edith Head costumes by night. 'It was such a rush, we made a mistake on her dress for the cocktail party scene,' said Head. 'It was too loose around the neckline, so Bette pulled it down over her shoulders and she wore it as if it was designed like that.' On Sunday she made comparative makeup tests with Fox actor Gary Merrill who thanked her for coming in. 'For this part I would come to the studio seven days and nights a week,' said Bette.

While the rest of the cast flew on the company plane to San Francisco for three weeks of filming at the Curran Theater, Bette went by train, accompanied by her secretary, her three-year-old daughter, B.D., and the child's governess, Marian Richards. At the station, Bette was not overjoyed when the photographers started snapping pictures of the young governess. 'I was wearing sunglasses and my hair was the same color as Bette's,' said Marian. 'When we left the train they rushed up and began to photograph me. I said, "No, please, you're making a mistake. That's Miss Davis back there, in the fur coat, carrying the baby."'

> *'I admit I may have seen better days, but I am still not to be had for the price of a cocktail – like a salted peanut.'*
>
> Margo Channing

Arriving at the Curran Theater for the first day of filming, Bette flew to Joe Mankiewicz in vocal distress. 'I was told by three or four people very close to her that the night before she had a scream-ing fight with her husband,' said Mankiewicz. 'She was on the lawn in her nightgown – she and this artist husband of hers. She screamed so loud at him that she broke a couple of blood vessels in her throat. It gave a husky quality to her voice. She said to me, "Oh, what am I going to do about it?" I said, "Honey, we're going to keep it."'

When she had been signed for *Eve*, Mankiewicz said he had been warned by 'countless directors' that Bette would try to destroy him, but from the start of production he found her 'intelligent, instinctive, vital, sensitive – and above all, a superbly equipped professional actress.'

Outwardly, Bette was just as complimentary about the director, but under the surface lay a few negative doubts. She was the star of the film, but Anne Baxter as Eve Harrington had more lines and scenes. 'I was through in three weeks, but poor Anne had to work the entire schedule of ten weeks,' said Davis in mock sympathy. She also suspected that Joe Mankiewicz favored Baxter. 'When you work on a film with other actresses, and one thinks the director is having an affair with the other one – then there's going to be some sort of conflict,' said Davis' secretary, Vik Greenfield. 'There was no love lost between Bette and Mankiewicz. Years later we were at Sardi's one night when Bette gave Glenda Jackson an award. Mankiewicz was there also and Bette was so cold to him. I didn't know why, because the man had coaxed such a brilliant performance from her as Margo Channing. Then, a short time after that we went to see Anne Baxter in *Applause*, and when we were backstage, Bette came right out with it. She asked Baxter if she had an affair with Joe during the making of *All About Eve*. "No," said Baxter. "I always thought you did," said Bette.'

The entire cast of *All About Eve* were 'first-rate', said Bette, with only one bitch in the bunch – Celeste Holm. A class act, and winner of an Academy Award for *Gentleman's Agreement*, Miss Holm annoyed Bette by giving her 'a cheery good morning' each day. 'Oh, these *terrible* good manners,' Bette snapped eventually. 'I never spoke to her again after that,' said Holm.

The work process was 'like a delightful group therapy session, with Mankiewicz as the psychiatrist,' said Anne Baxter. George Sanders as the acidic Addison De Witt had 'a low energy level' and had to be pushed and prodded into his Oscar winning performance. When George's current wife, Zsa Zsa Gabor, arrived on the set one day and announced, 'I must haff George to go shopping,' Mankiewicz politely informed her, 'We're making a fucking picture, honey.' And Marilyn Monroe, in her major debut as Miss Caswell, the decorous but dim-headed starlet, was 'just another chorus girl.' She had only two lines to deliver in the San Francisco theater lobby. 'Tell me this,' she asked George Sanders, 'do they have auditions for television?' 'That's all television is, my dear. Nothing but auditions,' Sanders replied. 'She got it right, after ten takes,' said Gary Merrill. 'When she left, we all wondered what was going to happen to that dumb blonde.'

In San Francisco, Bette Davis had her own car and chauffeur, who doubled as a bodyguard. 'He was a great big black guy, and he'd chauffeur B.D. and me around,' said Marian Richards. 'He also had a picture of Grant [Sherry] in his pocket, so he'd know if Grant showed up. Bette didn't want him in San Francisco. She already had stars in her eyes because she was falling for Gary Merrill.'

Merrill, the fifth-billed actor in the film, played Margo

Channing's love interest, director Bill Sampson. On the first day of shooting the actor from Maine established his mettle with Davis. Rehearsing on stage at the theater, Bette whipped out a cigarette from her silver case, put it in her mouth and waited for Merrill to light it. He refused. 'And why *not*?' Bette enquired. 'Because I don't think Bill Sampson would light Margo's cigarette,' said Merrill. After pondering this, Bette nodded her assent. "You're quite right, Mr. Merrill. Of course he wouldn't." '

The actor soon became a comfort to Bette during filming. 'I was miserable, utterly,' she said, referring to the recent troubles with her husband. She welcomed the attention and humor of her co star, Merrill. 'Would Miss Davis like coffee? A cigarette? A sandwich? Someone murdered?'

'He's from New England,' Bette marveled, 'a beachcomber, and an individualist. He doesn't care what anyone thinks of him. I envy that. I care a great deal what people think of me.'

Akin to their characters, Margo and Bill Sampson, Bette and Gary soon discovered they were deeply in love. 'I was irresistibly drawn to her,' said Merrill. 'My first feeling, of compassion for this misunderstood talented woman, was quickly replaced by a robust attraction, an almost uncontrollable lust. I walked around with an erection for three days.'

It was evident to all that Bette's spirits had lifted also. 'She is having fun again,' said Cal York in his column. 'She plays records on the set and dances the Charleston for the entertainment of the cast members.'

She and Merrill 'formed a kind of cabal,' Celeste Holm told Kenneth Giest, 'like two kids who had learned to spell a dirty word. It was not a very pretty relationship, as they laughed at other people together.'

Her marriage to William Grant Sherry was over, and she was filing for divorce, Bette told everyone – except her husband back in Laguna. 'Grant sent her a letter on her birthday,' said Marian Richards. 'In it he said he loved her very much and would do anything to make their marriage work. She read the letter out loud in front of her guests at a party. She thought it was the funniest thing but no one laughed. Everyone felt it was cruel.'

'Infants behave the way I do, you know. They carry on and misbehave – they'd get drunk if they knew how – when they can't have what they want. When they feel unwanted or insecure – or unloved.'

Margo Channing

When filming was completed in San Francisco, Bette returned with the troupe to Los Angeles, but not to Grant Sherry. While her husband awaited the return of his wife and child in Laguna, Bette went into hiding in Los Angeles. 'We stayed at various houses in Beverly Hills, producers' houses, directors' houses,' said Marian Richards. 'We were on the run from Grant. Bette used to call us "the molls". There was B.D., her sister Bobby, the secretary. We went from place to place. Once we stayed at Katharine Hepburn's house, while she was out of town. Bette was terrified that Grant would find her. One night she woke me up at two o'clock in the morning and insisted that we go to the kitchen so she could cook for me. When she got nervous she liked to cook. After a few drinks the actress side of her would appear. "I wonder if he's going to come after us and kill me?" she would say, playing these big dramatic scenes which I thought were hilarious. There was also a certain amount of guilt involved in her behavior, because Gary Merrill stayed over some nights. They would come down together for breakfast in the morning.'

Merrill was married also, for eight years, to an attractive blue-eyed blonde called Barbara Leeds. Attending a party in Malibu one night, 'in an alcohol daze,' the actor told the other guests that he'd marry Bette Davis 'if she'd have me – not exactly the sort of thing to say in front of one's wife.'

Divorce proceedings were instituted by Merrill's wife the next day.

William Grant Sherry wasn't as easy to dislodge. When Bette's lawyers told him she wanted a divorce, they suggested he go to Las Vegas for the separation. He refused. 'I knew nothing about Merrill and I didn't want a divorce,' he said. To force him to reconsider, Bette immediately sold their Laguna Beach home and his studio. She also closed out their joint checking accounts. 'I was left with no money,' he said. 'I had to move into a smaller house down the street. It was a shack where her sister Bobby had lived. If you drove a nail in the wall to hang a picture, it went through to the other side. Weeding outside one day I found a strange-looking wire and traced it up to the attic. Bette had the place bugged. There were microphones placed in the ceiling over the bedroom. She was doing the same thing her first husband did when he found out she was having an affair with Howard Hughes.'

'I am so afraid that Sherry is going to crash his plane and kill himself. He is so distraught at losing me,' Bette told friends.

'He will not let her go,' said Louella Parsons. 'Bette tells me he wants the glitter and the attention he commands as her husband. Terrified and living on sedatives, she goes nowhere without a body-guard.'

'I fully intended to contest the divorce,' Sherry stated. 'I didn't want to give up my daughter. One day, when I went to visit her, Bette had two Marines posted at the door to her house in Los Angeles. They told me I couldn't see my daughter; I pushed them away. B.D. would visit me with Marian, her governess, then when she went back to Bette she would break out in hives. Bette and Merrill had already started fighting over other things, so it wasn't a happy time for B.D. My lawyer suggested that I get evidence that Bette was shacked up with Gary, but I didn't want to do that. I agreed to the divorce. Sometime later an old friend of hers told me it was a good thing I made that decision, because Bette had planned on having two men swear they had sex with me, that I was a homosexual. I couldn't believe this was the woman I had loved and married.'

'My divorce from Sherry cost me a bundle,' said Bette. 'For the first time in my life, I had to pay alimony to a man.'

'She owed me money,' said Sherry. 'She had closed down my studio and cleaned out our bank account. Her lawyers told me they couldn't make a cash settlement because Bette was broke, that she would give me monthly payments. I refused because I didn't want Bette to call that alimony. Her lawyers pleaded with me. Bette swore she would never say it was alimony, but that's exactly what she told the press. She also said that I had planned on kidnapping B.D., by running off with her governess Marian. Well Marian was the best thing that came out of the entire mess. When she visited with B.D. I used to watch her with my child. She was a beautiful caring girl, and after the divorce I asked her out, but she said "no." '

'He wasn't my type,' Marian Richards said in 1988. 'I was only twenty-two at the time, and he was thirty-six. I was still with Bette, although I wanted to quit as governess for over a year. "Stay with me through one more picture," she would make me promise. I loved B.D. but I wanted to get out and see something of the world. Then after she divorced Grant he asked me out again. We began to date. There was never an affair. And we never tried to steal B.D. When Grant proposed I accepted. As I was packing to leave Bette's house, B.D. put her little shoes in my case. I told her we couldn't take her with us. She was such a sweet child. It was a shame she was exposed to so much unhappiness, to so many angry people who weren't meant to be together. Grant and I then moved to Paris where he studied art. We have been married all these years, with two children and three grandchildren, and he has never been the monster that Bette said he was. She wasn't so terrible either, not to me. She could be thoughtful and kind and very funny. But she was a star and she had to feed that ego constantly. She didn't want anyone to be stronger than she was. She had to be on top constantly. She had to always be able to say "Well, here I am, Bette Davis. Famous and powerful." To be anything less than her image, to ever appear soft and forgiving – well that was a weakness to her.'

'Bill's thirty-two. He looks thirty-two. He looked it five years ago, he'll look it twenty years from now. I hate men.'

Margo Channing

In July of 1950 Bette Davis and Gary Merrill were married in Juárez, Mexico. Driving cross-country in Bette's black Cadillac convertible, they honeymooned in a tent on Westport Island in Maine, where Bette cooked for her new husband over an oil heater.

That October *All About Eve* was released.

'The wittiest, the most devastating, the most adult and literate motion picture ever made,' said *The New York Morning Telegraph*.

'A thoroughly convincing theatrical first lady, given to spats, rages, and drunken maunderings,' said *Time*, 'she commands sympathy and admiration.'

'Magnificent! For the first time in her unaccountable career she remembers her part, not her insincere, artificial thespian self,' said the *Dallas Morning News*. 'She remembers also, that other actors are in the show, not merely to feed her lines and hold her sables.'

On November 9 a gala invitational screening was held at Grauman's Chinese Theater in Hollywood. The word-of-mouth on the film's harsh depiction of actresses had spread through the town, and every female star of stature had requested an invitation to the showing. Attending were Lana Turner, Ava Gardner, Joan Fontaine, Jane Wyman, Susan Hayward, and Anne Baxter. Bette Davis posed for photographs in the forecourt of the theater, but wouldn't enter the theater. 'My husband, Gary Merrill, is in Germany,' she explained, 'and I promised him I would not see the picture until he returned.'

For the post-performance party at Ciro's night club, the star arrived with her mother, Ruthie. 'It was Bette's night of triumph,' said Louella Parsons. 'It was heartwarming to see the great and the near-great of Hollywood line up to pay her tribute.'

Sitting in a front banquette of the club, with Clifton Webb and Jane Wyman at her feet, Bette felt a curious sense of *déjà vu* as a commotion erupted at the front entrance. She looked up in time to catch the late arrival of another female competitor. Framed in the doorway, wearing a red brocaded gown under a full-length white mink coat, stood Joan Crawford, posing for pictures. As she made her regal way toward the main banquette, Bette muttered an 'Oh Christ!' under her breath. It wasn't Joan's attendance or tardiness that upset the *All About Eve* headliner, it was her rival's choice of escorts. On Joan's arm was Vincent Sherman, the man who directed Bette in *Mr. Skeffington* and spurned her offer of marriage. He was now professionally and sexually involved with the glamorous Crawford.

'I met Joan in the spring of 1949, when I came back from London after making *The Hasty Heart*,' said Sherman. 'I was assigned to direct her in a picture called *The Damned Don't Cry*.'

During the preproduction meetings on *The Damned Don't Cry*, Joan began to come on to the cultivated, virile director. 'On day one I looked at her, and said to myself, "No way am I getting involved with this one." She looked like a lot of trouble,' said Sherman.

On location in Palm Springs, Crawford had her director placed in the motel room next to hers. 'I was put off by that,' he said. 'She came on too strong . . . almost whorish.'

Joan then trasmitted her patented charm and generosity.

'She was very hard to resist,' said Sherman. 'Even my wife, who met Joan at a party at her house, liked Joan. Unlike Bette, who tended to ignore or confront women, Joan went out of her way to be nice to my wife. She took a real interest in her. On the way home the night of that party, my wife remarked, "There's something there. Underneath the movie-star façade there's a human being that I could probably like." Then she turned to me and said, "Vincent, are you having an affair with her?" "Yes," I answered. "Just be careful," my wife said.'

Sherman directed Joan in two consecutive movies – *The Damned Don't Cry* and *Harriet Craig*. Their affair continued and reached the open ears of Bette Davis. 'I was told that Bette was furious when she heard I was seeing Joan,' said Sherman. ' "How could he have anything to do with that woman?" she said. I knew nothing about the animosity between them. Although later I wondered if Joan hadn't deliberately pursued me, to get what Bette couldn't.

'Crawford always looked up to Davis as "someone who was superior," ' said the director, 'but in terms of ability and, I guess, in terms of background. Well, the truth was, there wasn't any great difference. Bette didn't come from any highfaluting family either. In my opinion, they were sisters under the skin.'

In December 1950, both Davis and Crawford's names appeared on many of the year's Best Actress lists. Bette led all the honors for her magnificent romp as Margo Channing in *All About Eve*, while Joan was cited for one or the other of her two Vincent Sherman films, *The Damned Don't Cry* and *Harriet Craig*. In January 1951 both were voted Most Popular Actress by *Photoplay* and each agreed to attend the Gold Medal ceremonies in February. On the morning of the *Photoplay* awards party, the Oscar nominations were released. *All About Eve* received an unprecedented total of fourteen nominations, with Bette Davis and Anne Baxter cited as Best Actress. Joan Crawford, who had expected a nomination, was not mentioned. That afternoon she became ill and canceled her appearance at the *Photoplay* awards dinner that night.

But Bette attended. Wearing a black cocktail dress and a flowered hat, she showed up at the party with Gary Merrill. Happily quaffing champagne she accepted kisses and congratulations from former co star Ronald Reagan and his new wife, Nancy; and from Jane Wyman and her new beau, attorney Greg Bautzer. At one point in the evening's proceedings, waving her cigarette in the direction of an adjoining table, Davis asked: 'Who *is* that little boy seated between Ann Blyth and Elizabeth Taylor? He keeps staring in my *face*?'

That was Joan Crawford's nine-year-old son, Christopher, she was told. He was accepting the award that night for his mother.

'How *sweet*,' said Bette. 'And *where* is Joan?'

'At home, ill,' the answer came.

'Oh,' said Bette, 'something *fatal*, I hope.'

15

THE FABULOUS FIFTIES

'It was a terrible decade for Hollywood. The old studio system as we knew it began to crumble. Actors with long-term contracts were let go. They worked in independent films, on television, or they went out of their minds.'

Bette Davis

'I was never questioned because I was never involved. Franchot swore to that when he took the stand. He was deeply involved and was questioned for months by all committees. Now does that answer your duped question? I need no retractions – want no retraction or involvement in this whole messy uprooting of filth on peoples' pasts.'

Joan Crawford

In 1951, in the wake of strikes, riots, and the destruction of lives and careers by the McCarthy witch hunts, the power and autonomy of the major Hollywood studios were eroded further by severe economic sanctions and structural changes. Ordered by the Justice Department to divest themselves of their large theater chains, MGM, Warner's, Fox and the other studios could no longer book their own pictures into their own theaters. Exhibitors were now free to purchase their features from independent distributors, or from the growing European market, where film production had boomed during the postwar period.

Another serious encroachment on box-office revenues was from a new form of domestic entertainment – television. As the purchase of TV sets quadrupled in two years, with 'a box in one out of every five homes,' the attendance at movie theaters dropped drastically. To recoup their losses and save on overheads, the studio radically trimmed their employee ranks. Rosters of talent were examined then slashed. The contracts of many actors, writers, directors, and producers were either broken or not renewed. Scores of talented personnel were discharged and dumped on the open market.

Bette Davis was one of the first to feel the economic pinch. In March 1951, when *All About Eve* failed to provide her with a third Oscar (Judy Holliday won for *Born Yesterday*) and no other scripts materialized, she went to England to work in a film entitled *Another Man's Poison*. The job came via Douglas Fairbanks, Jr., actor-producer, and ex-husband of Joan Crawford.

'I had a production company with a man called Daniel Angel,' Fairbanks said in 1988. 'We made one picture, in which I appeared, the name of which I can't remember. When this second script came along, my partner said, "You must know Bette Davis from your Hollywood days. Could you possibly ask her if she's interested?" Well, of course, I did know Bette, but not very well. She was never at the house when I was married to Joan, but we worked at the same studio in the early 1930s, and we made one picture together [*Parachute Jumper*], which I have conveniently forgotten most of. I do remember that she was very professional, if not always agreeable. She always did as she pleased and she was very good at her job. So, when the script of *Another Man's Poison* came along, I approached her. She apparently liked the story and wanted to know if her husband, Gary Merrill, could play the male lead. I said yes, because he is a very good actor and the part seemed right for him.'

Bette asked to be directed by Irving Rapper. 'That was a dirty trick that was played on me by Bette's agent, Lew Wasserman,' said Rapper. 'He sent me the script and after I read twenty pages I called Wasserman and said, "This is terrible." He said, "Well, Bette Davis doesn't think so. It's going to be her next picture, and it's going to be a great box-office hit." So he got me to agree to do it, but eventually I learned this was just an excuse for Bette and Merrill to get a free honeymoon in England.'

On arriving in Great Britain with Gary Merrill, her personal maid, a secretary, a nurse for their two children (including newly adopted daughter Margot), Bette got piqued at the Fleet Street press when they called her husband 'Mr. Davis' and described her as 'a middle-aged matron.' 'She threatened to catch the next boat back,' said reporter David Marlow. 'She made dark hint about "putting a stop to this kind of treatment of American stars by the British Press." '

'You must remember that most of England was still destitute after the war,' said Douglas Fairbanks, Jr. 'They did not have the means or the inclination to indulge anyone.'

'We tried everything, foul means and fair, to win her confidence,' said screenwriter Val Guest.

'Miss Davis is not winning any new friends or admirers during her dinner breaks at the Walton-on-Thames film studios,' a writer for *Picture Show* magazine stated. 'While the rest of the cast and crew make do with soup or fish and chips the American star dines on sirloin steak, which is flown over daily from the States for the film star's consumption.'

'Yes, that was an unfortunate occurrence,' said Fairbanks, Jr. 'She did have her own food flown in, but once it was brought to Bette's attention that meat was still rationed in England, she took her meals alone in her dressing room.'

One evening the Merrills dined at John Gielgud's house, arriving as Ralph Richardson was departing. 'He's been a favorite of mine for years,' said Merrill, scrambling out of his car to meet him. 'Why *didn't* you bring your autograph book?' said Bette. Another weekend, they visited Vivien Leigh and Larry Olivier, at their Notley Abbey estate. When the Oliviers, hung over from the night before, made their late appearance, they 'bounded in with Peter Finch and Noël Coward and headed straight for the bar.' Later, resting on the patio of the abbey house, when Miss Leigh drifted by, wearing a large hat and carrying a basket of flowers, Noël Coward dryly explained, 'She's doing her gardening bit.'

Bette Davis could be jolly, with 'a toilet sense of humor,' said Britisher Val Guest. She was frequently loud and boisterous, especially during the long cocktail hour she and Merrill shared in their hotel suite. The manager of the sedate hotel in which they were staying had frequent complaints from other guests about the nocturnal fights between the couple. 'It was very embarrassing when I had to explain to her why we were moving them to another hotel,' said Douglas Fairbanks, Jr.

*   *   *

'This is the weirdest, most unrelieved, and at times the hammiest bit of goings on this side of a wake,' said a reviewer when *Another Man's Poison* was released, in January 1952. 'They were so *right*. It was a lousy less-than-B picture,' said director Rapper, who had hoped to make amends with another film with Bette Davis. 'Hal Wallis visited me in England and told me he purchased the rights to *Come Back Little Sheba*,' the director recalled. He also mentioned that he wanted me to direct the film. Back in Los Angeles I was told that Daniel Mann, who directed the Broadway version with Shirley Booth, was signed. That was all right. Things change. Words are said, then forgotten. But then I got a call from Hal Wallis' assistant, Paul Nathan, who said, "Hal wants you to make a test of Bette Davis for *Come Back Little Sheba*." I was confused. Where was Danny Mann? I called up the boys at MCA and they confirmed that Mann was about to be signed, but he had never worked with Bette before, so I was being asked to go behind his back and test her for the role. I said no. The next morning Bette called me. She never said hello. "So you don't think I could do the part?" she began. I tried to explain the situation, and told her it had nothing to do with whether she could play the part. "You could do anything," I said. She persisted. I said, "Well, I don't see you playing a defeated woman." "Go to hell!" she said and hung up. When Hall Wallis gave the part to Shirley Booth, whom he wanted in the first place, Bette blamed me again for her loss. She never forgot it either. With time her rage grew stronger. Some thirty years later she went on the Johnny Carson television show and tore my reputation apart. She said I never did anything for her. She remembered the loss of *The Glass Menagerie* and *Come Back Little Sheba*, which were *never* really hers in the first place, and she preferred to forget that I directed her in one of the most romantic films of her career, *Now Voyager*.'

'My idea of a movie star is Joan Crawford, who can chew up two directors and three producers before lunch.'

Shelley Winters

'I saw Shelley Winters in A Place in the Sun. *She gave a very moving performance, which surprised me, because Shelley is not a sensitive girl socially.'*

Joan Crawford

By 1952 the Hollywood studios were preparing to launch their first defense against the competition of television. To combat the lure of the small box, each major studio announced plans to make bigger and better films, to be photographed in 3-D, CinemaScope, VistaVision, Todd-AO, and with stereophonic sound. At Warner's, *House of Wax*, a horror film, shot in 3-D 'by a one-eyed director' (Andre De Toth), became a top grosser, but the new medium did not impress durable star Joan Crawford. 'I like people coming out of the screen, but I prefer they do it with their talents and not special effects,' she said.

'Anyone who appears on TV is a traitor,' Crawford stated when Bette Davis made her three-minute debut on the Jimmy Durante TV comedy show. Joan had her own way of combating the new medium. As the movie screens became larger, so did the Crawford features. 'The mouth got bigger, the eyebrows got thicker, her face began to resemble that of a man, her father,' said one writer. Her roles became equally macho. In *This Woman is Dangerous*, she played the tough mistress of a killer and the mastermind of his holdup gang. The story inspired novice TV comedy writer Neil Simon to offer the synopsis as audition material: 'Joan Crawford plays the mistress of a murderer. He gets caught and is fried in the electric chair. She promises to wait for him.'

This Woman Is Dangerous would be the last of three Crawford pictures directed by Vincent Sherman. When it ended, so did their romantic relationship. 'That was stormy, to say the least,' said Sherman. 'Joan threw me out of her house many times, for various reasons. After one battle, she called my wife and said "Hello dear, I am sending your husband home to you." My wife said: "Thank you, Joan." And we remained good friends.'

In February 1952 Crawford asked that her contract with Warner Brothers be terminated. 'They were grooming Doris Day to take over the top spot,' she said. 'Jack Warner asked me to play her sister in one picture [*Storm Warning*]. I said, "Come *on*,

Jack. No one could ever believe that I would have Doris Day for a sister." '

Warner gave that part to Ginger Rogers and Crawford went to RKO Pictures to make her first independent film – a first-rate thriller entitled *Sudden Fear*. Offered two hundred thousand dollars as salary, she agreed to put the entire sum in escrow in exchange for forty percent of the profits and coproducer status. The latter title ensured her approval of her leading man. To play the young actor who marries then plots the murder of his older, playwright wife, Joan wanted Marlon Brando.

A year before, Crawford had been at Warner's when Brando arrived to make *A Streetcar Named Desire*. Her first impression of the newcomer matched that of her good friend, Vivien Leigh. Both agreed that Brando was an ill-mannered slob. But after attending the premiere of *Streetcar*, and watching Brando in animal action as Stanley Kowalski, Joan dropped her reserve and joined the caravan of feverish Hollywood women who were openly lusting for the mumbling, muscled, T-shirted genius. The morning after the premiere, Joan sent Marlon a telegram, praising his performance and inviting him to park his motorbike on her front lawn sometime in the near future. He ignored the telegram. When she signed on for *Sudden Fear*, she sent another telegram, followed by phone messages to his service, but again Brando did not respond. Joan, the coproducer, then went through the regular channels, submitting the script to his agent. The agent passed it to Brando who sent back word to Joan that he wasn't interested 'in doing any mother-and-son pictures at the present time.'

After that crass rejection, Marlon made it all the way to the top of Joan's 'active shit list', and another newcomer, Jack Palance, was signed to co star in *Sudden Fear*. But his working relationship with Joan was also stormy. She argued that Palance wasn't handsome enough for a star of her glamorous stature. Also, like Brando, he was a method actor, and she objected to their style of realism. In one kissing scene she was shocked when Jack shoved his tongue down her throat. 'He kisses me like I'm his wife,' she complained to the director. But the chemistry between the two worked on the screen. At the first preview of the picture, Joan's special guest,

Louella Parsons, predicted that *Sudden Fear* 'would be a big money-maker and bring another Oscar for Joan.'

Other columnists agreed with Parsons' prognosis. In a piece devoted to the widespread unemployment and paranoia sweeping through Hollywood, Walter Winchell reported: 'While many female stars in Tinseltown are scrambling to find work in movies or television, Joan Crawford, with the smell of a new hit movie, *Sudden Fear*, on her hands, is lining up jobs for the next three years. She's putting all offers right next to the requests for dates, from every eligible male on both coasts.'

When asked by a movie magazine to name her favorite male sex symbols for the 1950s, Joan began with Clark Gable. 'His magic has not dimmed with the years,' she told *Silver Screen*. William Holden was tops too, she felt. 'He's a dream. He isn't flashy – he doesn't seem to have sex appeal, but brother he's got it. In fact I like Holden so much I'm putting him on the list twice.'

In 1952, her list led off with Kirk Douglas – 'Kirk's got it. He knows it and he knows you know it,' Joan said, and put Burt Lancaster in the next spot, because 'Burt is perfectly proportional . . . and never shows off.'

In June of that year Joan was in New York, taking in the new plays, when she spotted that town's newest sensation, Yul Brynner, on stage in *The King and I*. After sweeping backstage to pay her respects to Gertrude Lawrence, Joan asked if she could be bold enough to ask for an introduction to Brynner. Yul, the bare-chested Mongolian sex symbol, fixed his hypnotic brown eyes on Joan and said, 'An honor! A privilege,' then kissed her hand.

Acceding to her request for a photograph, Yul sent a large portrait to her hotel the following morning. The pose showed the smoldering gypsy star, sitting cross-legged on the floor, naked and semitumescent.

An appreciative Joan called Yul within the hour, and their affair began that afternoon, in his dressing room. He was married, so they were discreet. She became a frequent visitor backstage, and they sometimes dined in her hotel suite after his show. It was here that Yul taught Joan how 'to play the balalaika guitar and other Russian instruments.' She was on her way back to Los Angeles when she stopped in Chicago to change trains. While shopping at Marshall Field's, she looked at her watch then told columnist Tony Weitzel, 'It's four-thirty in New York. My darling Yul is between shows. I must call him.' On his day off, Yul flew to California for a twenty-four-hour visit with Crawford. 'It was a f—k date,' said writer Carl Johnes, 'but Brynner was exhausted from the trip and when he got to Joan's, he fell asleep, which infuriated her.' When Sheilah Graham reported that Brynner had separated from his wife, Joan denied she had anything to do with the breakup. 'No one can break up a happy marriage, unless the crack is beyond repairing,' she said astutely. Then, just as suddenly, Yul cooled the romance. 'After flooding her with flowers and attention in New York, he hinted he was the pursued,' said Walter Winchell. 'Nothing of the kind,' said Joan. It was she who dropped Yul, only to pick him up again when he came to L.A. to make the movie version of *The King and I*. In her memoirs, daughter Christina told of the night she opened the front door at home and 'gasped' when a half-naked, bald-headed gypsy man stood there. 'Say hello to your Uncle Yul,' Joan instructed the girl.

> *'I love the new poodle-cut hairstyles for women. I saw stripper Lili St. Cyr wearing one in her act at Ciro's. I went out the next day and got the same style.'*
>
> Bette Davis

> *'Those new poodle hair-dos are not for elderly women. I think they look better on dogs and teenagers. I should know, I have one of each.'*
>
> Joan Crawford

There were no feature-film scripts awaiting Bette Davis when she returned to California from England in July 1951. That September, Gary Merrill was given the lead in a Fox episodic drama, *Phone Call from a Stranger*. Reading the script, Bette volunteered to play the supporting role of Marie Hoke, an invalid. The role was budgeted at fifteen hundred dollars for a minor actress, but Bette, for three days' work, had the salary upped to thirty-five thousand dollars. 'The producers got back more than that in publicity alone – the "Star playing a bit part",' said Gary Merrill.

Six months passed before another job materialized for Bette. In July 1952 she returned to 20th Century-Fox to play in a small independent film, *The Star*. The story was about a shallow, alcoholic, former Hollywood star who tries for a comeback. 'They can't put *me* out to pasture,' said the movie's lead character. 'Why I'm an institution. Girls talked like me, imitated my makeup, my hair. I was a *star*. I *am* a star.'

'That was one of the best scripts ever written about a movie-mad actress,' said Davis. 'Of course you know whom it was written about, don't you? . . . Joan Crawford.'

The writers were Katharine Albert and Dale Eunson, long-term friends of Crawford. Albert was Joan's favorite fan-magazine reporter. She was given the exclusive scoops on the star's marriages and divorces from Douglas Fairbanks, Jr. and Franchot Tone.

In 1939, Albert also wrote a novel, *Remember Valerie Marsh*. It was about 'a tough, ambitious, frank, sexual little tramp from Oklahoma who became a star.' That was based on Joan Crawford, Albert's husband, writer Dale Eunson, confirmed, but the couple's friendship with the star did not go into deep freeze until the summer of 1952, when the second Crawford-inspired story, *The Star*, went into production with Bette Davis.

The idea for the movie came from *Mildred Pierce* producer Jerry Wald. He met with writers Albert and Eunson one day and said, 'You two know Hollywood very well. Why don't you do a story about a star who has fallen on hard times and goes to her own auction sale?'

'That was our starting-off point,' said Eunson. 'Once we had the script written, we tried to get the film made with Lucille Ball. But her movie career had never taken off, and we couldn't raise any money on her.' (Lucy, weary of trying to become a star in movies, then made a pilot for a CBS TV comedy series which would play for the next two hundred years.)

Contrary to reports, Joan Crawford was never approached to play the role in *The Star*. 'Frankly, it was a little too close to her, which is one reason Bette liked it,' said Eunson with a laugh. 'Bette could play Joan Crawford to the hilt.'

'Oh, yes, that *was* Crawford,' Bette told *Playboy* in 1983. 'I wasn't imitating her, of course. It was just that whole approach of hers to the business as regards the importance of glamor and all of the offstage things. I *adored* the script.'

Prior to production, Bette met with the writers and suggested some changes. 'She came to us and said there was just one scene that she thought was a cliché,' said Eunson. 'It was the scene where she's locked out of her apartment by her landlord. She felt it had been done a great deal. Not knowing Bette too well, or how to handle her, but feeling the scene was absolutely necessary, I sat down and wrote her a note. I said it *was* a clichéd scene, but it had never happened, as far as I know, to a movie star – to be locked out of her house before. I sent the note to her, and at seven o'clock the next morning I got a telephone call from her. "Dale, you are absolutely right," she said. "From now on I intend to keep my big mouth shut." ' Another scene, written specifically with Crawford in mind, had minor input from Bette. After being evicted and jailed for drunken driving, the star, desperate for a comeback, auditions for a character role in a film; but, upon reading the script, she decides to audition for the younger, ingenue part instead.

Wearing heavy lipstick, makeup, and exaggerated gestures, Bette as Joan Crawford flirted lewdly at the camera; then exiting the set after her test she bestowed the familiar Crawford 'Bless you!' on the crew. Rehearsing the scene, Bette conferred with the writers. 'You know,' she said, being careful not to mention Crawford by name, 'when *these* people say "Bless you" once, they say it several times. So if it's all right with you I will repeat it a few times as I leave the set.'

'I often wondered if Joan knew the movie was about her,' Davis asked this writer, years later.

Crawford knew, and she apparently planned her revenge carefully – not on Davis but on her good friends Katharine Albert and Dale Eunson.

The Eunsons were the parents of a lovely daughter, Joan, who was named after her godmother, Joan Crawford. At the age of fifteen, as Joan Evans, the Eunsons' daughter was signed to a contract by Samuel Goldwyn. She subsequently appeared as the lead in *Roseanna McCoy*, and in *Our Very Own*. The beautiful teenager had a promising career until 1952, when she met and fell in love with a young man, Kirby Weatherly, a car salesman. At seventeen she was too young for marriage, the Eunsons felt, and they appealed to Joan Crawford to talk some sense into her goddaughter. In mid-July, while *The Star* was in production, Crawford invited the young couple to her home. At midnight she called the Eunsons and gave them the happy news: 'Dear Katharine and Dale,' said Joan, 'I want you to be the first to know. Joan and Kirby were married at my house tonight.'

'She set the whole thing up behind our backs,' said Dale Eunson. 'She called the judge, and the press. She didn't invite us to our own daughter's wedding. We were both very angry and heartbroken.'

The following morning, when the Eunsons arrived on the set of *The Star*, Bette Davis was reading about the wedding in the paper. Sympathizing with the parents, she told them they should go to Crawford 'and scratch her eyes out.'

During the remainder of filming, the writers became good friends with Davis, whilst terminating their twenty-five-year-old relationship with Joan Crawford. 'Our daughter was close to Joan for a while, and her marriage became a lasting success, but Katharine refused to speak to Crawford again,' said Dale Eunson in 1988. 'Then, sometime later, after Katharine had died and I remarried, I heard from Joan. She had once met my second wife, Berenice, also known as Binks, at a party. Binks disliked her enormously. But when we married, Joan sent us a letter. This was the first time I had heard from her since *The Star*. "Dear Dale and Binks," the letter said, "I am so happy that two of my best friends are married. Love, Joan." Naturally I laughed, because this was the kind of senseless thing that Crawford would do.'

'A Scoop from Louella Parsons – December 1952.
Two of Hollywood's most durable stars – Joan Crawford and Bette Davis – will be seen on Broadway next season. Bette will appear in Two's Company, *and Joan will do Norman Krasna's play,* Kind Sir, *with Charles Boyer as her co star.'*

' "I am returning to Broadway, to refine my craft." That's what Hollywood actors always say. But that's a bunch of BS. No one leaves movies for the stage unless they can't get work; and I'm no exception.'

Bette Davis

For three thousand dollars a week and ten percent of the house receipts, Bette agreed to return to Broadway in a song-and-dance revue entitled *Two's Company*. 'Certainly I'll sing, it's a musical, isn't it?' said Bette, who described her range as three octaves and 'somewhat masculine in tone.' Staged by Jerome Robbins and directed by Jules Dassin, the revue would include twenty-two original sketches, including one featuring Somerset Maugham's famous character Sadie Thompson. Her interpretation, however, would veer from the original stage portrayal by her idol, Jeanne Eagels. It would be closer to the cinematic performances of Gloria Swanson and Joan Crawford. 'I am doing a burlesque of the part,' said Bette, 'with lots of Swanson and Crawford touches. You'll be able to see my makeup and hear the clanging of my jewelry down on Fourteenth Street.'

Joan Crawford also announced her return to the Great White Way – in a straight play, a comedy written by Norman Krasna. In November 1952, while Bette was in Boston in tryouts for *Two's Company*, her rival flew to New York to read onstage for Krasna and director Joshua Logan. She was electrifying, said Logan. 'It was as though she had been on stage always. She read two acts, then the third, and we offered her the role on the spot.'

'Oh no,' said Joan, turning down the job, 'never. I just wanted to know whether or not I could do it, for my own satisfaction. I could never play a long run on the stage. I'd be bored to death. But thank you for letting me make the experiment.'

'This was a new experience for me,' said Logan, 'planned frustration.'

On December 15, after playing two months of tryouts on the road, *Two's Company* with Bette opened at the Alvin Theater in New York. 'The ovation I received was heartwarming,' she said, 'but the reviews were bloodcurdling.'

'She bumps, grinds, struts, kicks and shimmies,' said the *New*

York Daily Mirror, while the *Times* compared Davis' return to the stage 'with much the same kind of awe that might attend the spectacle of Eleanora Duse deciding to play comic Bobby Clark.'

In January, as *Two's Company* continued to play to respectable houses, the movie of *The Star* was released. The reviews for Bette were excellent. *Newsweek* found her Joan Crawford-inspired performance to be 'an acute, frightening picture of a woman possessed with her past career and legend, self-accusing and humble at times, but then again utterly callous to the ordinary and wonderful business of human relations.'

'In February, Davis received her tenth Oscar nomination for the role – but placed one slot ahead of her for *Sudden Fear* was Joan Crawford.

'I am *honored* to be in the same company as Julie Harris [*The Member of the Wedding*] and Shirley Booth [*Come Back Little Sheba*],' said Crawford, ignoring the other two nominees, Susan Hayward [*With a Song in My Heart*] and Bette Davis. She claimed she had not seen Bette's picture. 'Of course I had heard she was supposed to be playing me,' she said years later, 'but I didn't believe it. Did you see the picture? It couldn't possibly be me. Bette looked so old, and so dreadfully overweight.'

In March, when the major Hollywood studios said they couldn't afford to subsidize the cost of the annual award ceremonies, the Academy accepted a bid from NBC television. On the night of March 19, 1953, the shotgun wedding of the movies and TV was held. The first telecast of the awards was transmitted from two theaters, one in Hollywood and one in New York. Nominee Bette Davis had planned to host the New York segment, but the week before, she checked into New York Hospital, to be operated on for osteomyelitis of the jaw. Nominee Joan Crawford was present in Hollywood, but, ever loyal to the movies, she refused to appear on TV as a presenter. 'If her name is called as Best Actress, that's a different ballgame,' said Dorothy Kilgallen. 'I'll be thrilled to accept,' Joan agreed.

The award went to Shirley Booth for *Come Back Little Sheba*.

From her hospital bed, Bette said her loss was doubled, 'because *Come Back Little Sheba* was offered to *me* first. But I turned it down. Because I didn't want to take the part away from Shirley Booth.'

Had she won for *The Star*, she might have been offered other scripts, Bette lamented. With *Two's Company* already closed on Broadway, at a loss of $320,000, the actress checked out of the hospital, packed up her three children (including recently adopted son Michael) and moved to Maine with husband Gary Merrill. Announcing her retirement, Bette said that at last she could indulge in a dream she had harbored since childhood. She could now become a housewife and mother. Settling in a big white clapboard house by the ocean, Bette called the place 'Witch-Way,' because 'a witch lives there, and we don't know which way we're going.'

> *'Hitler's diaries were released today. It turns out that he too dated Joan Crawford.'*
>
> TV host Johnny Carson

At the start of 1953, Joan Crawford, age forty-nine, had no intention of retreating or retiring to the country. When her share of the profits from *Sudden Fear* came to more than three hundred thousand dollars, she decided to plough a good portion of that back into the maintenance of her career. Television and Cinemascope be damned, she was an old-fashioned movie star and she intended to keep her name suspended in lights for as long as her talent, energy and cash held out.

To launch the new year, Joan and decorator Billie Haines cohosted a black-tie dinner dance at her home for Mr. and Mrs. Stanley Marcus of Dallas. With guests seated eight to a table on the badminton court and around the pool, the hostess, 'shimmering in diamonds and a short white strapless chiffon gown,' greeted each one of her 150 guests, while her teenaged daughter Christina watched from an upstairs window, worrying about when her mother was going to pay her long overdue school bills.

A week later, Joan showed up in black satin and emeralds at the Marion Davies party for Johnny Ray, and while a jealous Fernando Lamas fought with Lex Barker over Lana Turner ('Why don't you take her outside and fuck her in the bushes?' an angry Fernando told Lex), Joan, adept at being quoted in any situation, said she felt embarrassed for hostess Marion, and that she honestly believed it was time for the overactive Lana to take a rest in the romance department.

'Look who's giving advice,' Lana could have replied, for Crawford was hardly on a sabbatical from sex that year. Socially her name was linked with Kleenex heir James Kimberly and with director David Miller, while *Silver Screen* said that Joan was 'seeing a lot of Jennings Lang these days. The popular agent appears to be completely recovered from the gunshot wounds incurred when Walter Wanger, husband of Joan Bennett, fired on him one evening in a Beverly Hills parking lot.'

Crawford also had a short fling with the notorious gigolo-playboy Porfirio Rubirosa. The former Dominican Republic diplomat, known as 'Rubi the Swordsman', was often described as: 'priapic, indefatigable, and enormously proportioned.' He liked to excite a woman beyond control. 'Rubi was sweet,' said his second wife Doris Duke, 'but we weren't married more than a few hours and he was already diddling the maid.' As a wedding gift from Doris, Rubi received a check for five hundred thousand dollars, a house in Paris, a string of polo ponies, a plane, and three sports cars. Thirteen months later he left Duke and went in search of new and wealthier women. In Argentina he dallied with Evita Perón; in Mexico it was Dolores Del Rio. When he reached Hollywood, he said he wanted to meet the luscious Lana Turner, but she was already busy shedding fiancé Fernando Lamas for Tarzan and husband-to-be, Lex Barker. Rubi then tried Ginger Rogers, but she was in France; until someone suggested Joan Crawford. He called, visited, and since she was no slouch in the bedroom herself, it was said that the lusty pair cleared the birds out of the trees in and around Brentwood for the first few days and nights of their lovemaking.

For a break one night, they went dancing. Joan also arranged for Rubi to meet some Hollywood producers. With time to spare he toyed with the idea of becoming a big movie star. She got him a minor role in a Western, but having no work visa, he lost the job, so as consolation the couple drove to Palm Springs for the weekend. It was there that the playboy made the mistake of telling Crawford that she was stingy, compared with his ex-wives. In their ten days together, all that Joan had given him was a silver cigarette

Happy at last – Bette holds daughter B.D. at her christening in 1947.

Joan meantime showered her daughter, Christina, with love and attention. (Another Crawford lover, Otto Preminger, is on the right.)

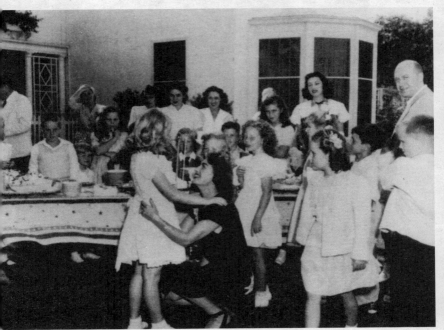

By 1960, although her film career had declined, a regal and glamorous Joan Crawford found new popularity as the Queen of Pepsi Cola.

While Bette Davis, less alluring but a more versatile actress, segued into playing such character parts as Apple Annie in *A Pocketful of Miracles*.

Together at last – in May of 1962, Crawford and Davis signed the contracts for the classic horror film, *Whatever Happened to Baby Jane?*

Still smiling, the two stars posed at a welcome-home luncheon, with studio boss Jack Warner, and director Robert Aldrich on the far right.

The violence begins: Bette as Baby Jane delivers the first blow to her long-time rival, sister Blanche.

During the vicious kicking scene in the hallway, Bette's foot wasn't supposed to touch Joan's head. But it did, deliberately gashing her scalp, Joan claimed.

In the follow-up scene in the bedroom, a vengeful Crawford wore special lead weights under her robe, which caused Bette to sprain her back when she carried her across the room.

During the filming, Crawford took some time off to promote her autobiography. Bette also had a book released at this time. 'Poor Bette,' said Joan of her rival's memoirs, 'she's had such an unhappy life'.

'You mean after all this time we could have been friends?' Bette asked Joan in the climactic scene of *Baby Jane*. The moving on-screen reconciliation did not affect their real-life feud however.

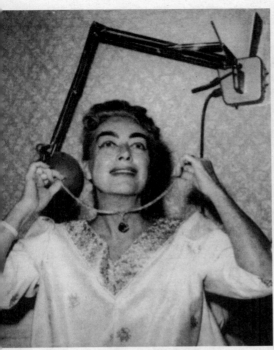

In the hospital in Los Angeles, while rallying from her mysterious illness. Joan showed off a sapphire necklace and hospital gown by Christian Dior. 'She was a very sick girl,' her hairdresser said, defending Joan's actual illness. 'She was sick all right. Sick of Bette Davis,' said another witness.

When *Sweet Charlotte* was eventually finished and released, a victorious Bette Davis toured theatres with Crawford's replacement, Olivia de Havilland. 'I'm glad for Olivia,' said Crawford, 'she needs the work'.

In a rare moment of camaraderie on the set of *Baby Jane*, the two most durable legends of the silver screen, share a laugh. 'We will never see their likes again,' said celebrity columnist, Liz Smith.

case from Cartier and a gold money clip, with no cash attached. Unperturbed, the star told the gigolo not to worry his macho head over such paltry matters. She had something unique and priceless already on order for him. With visions of a new car or a yacht on his mind, Rubi made love to Joan that night and the next morning when he woke up there was a small box and an envelope placed on the table beside the bed. Opening the box first, he found what appeared to be a hand-knit scarf or muffler. The enclosed note explained that it wasn't a scarf or muffler, but a 'cock sock', perfectly measured and knitted by Joan. In the letter, she bade a fond farewell to Rubi, explaining that she had been called back to Los Angeles on some urgent business. She hoped that he would call when he was in town again, and signed the letter, 'Amor, etcetera . . . Joan Crawford.' On calling the front desk, Rubi then learned that the star had checked out, leaving him, the great lover, stuck with the hotel bill. (Rubirosa would of course recover his losses. The following month in Deauville, France, he met Barbara Hutton, who bestowed $3.5 million in cash and gifts on him in the fifty-three days of their marriage.)

JOAN AND THE UNIVERSAL BEEFCAKE BOYS

'Recently I heard a "wise guy" story – that I had a party at my home for twenty-five men. It's an interesting story, but I don't know twenty-five men I'd want to invite to a party.'

Joan Crawford, 1953

In New York, Joan met a business executive, Milton Rachmil. He was the head of Decca Records, owned by MCA, and he was about to be transferred to Los Angeles, to take over production for Universal Pictures. The studio connection interested the star. Once considered a minor, Universal had recently moved into television production and had increased their output of regular feature movies. When Rachmil arrived in California, Crawford gave a party in his honor. He in turn invited her to tour the studio, where she met some of the writers and producers. On her own the star also introduced herself to the Universal corral of young male contract players. The emphasis here was on the word 'young' because, according to one agent, 'Joan had already exhausted the older members of the Screen Actors' Guild, and was working her way through the junior division.'

By then, Crawford had her own production company, and as a producer 'she acted no different from any man in town. She used her executive position to purchase scripts, and to sample the talent in town,' said Adela Rogers St. Johns.

According to the agent, when Joan saw an actor she liked she set up a preliminary meeting at the studio. If pleased, she followed through with an invitation to dinner at her house. The procedure was always the same. After the main course, Joan would lead her guest upstairs to her bedroom, for dessert.

'I barely got out of there with my virtue intact,' said teenage idol, Eddie Fisher.

Tony Curtis was in the hot-male-newcomers stable at Universal. 'He was one of the sexiest and best-looking,' Joan told *Modern Screen*. 'Usually when a guy has his kind of face and sex appeal you can't touch him with a ten-foot pole,' she said, 'but Tony has a refreshing humility and gentleness.'

She invited Tony for dinner at Brentwood. But he showed up – with his bride, Janet Leigh, whom Joan chose to ignore for most of the evening.

At Universal, Jeff Chandler was being groomed as the studio's answer to Burt Lancaster and Kirk Douglas. The previous year he made Joan's list of popular male pin-ups in *Screenland*. 'Jeff was purely male; without resorting to any of those muscle barbell distortions that ordinary "body beautiful" boys indulge in,' said the star.

Jeff, in a pre-parlance of the times, 'took a meeting' with Joan at Universal, then dropped by for dinner. He returned a second and third time. Married, he soon became separated from his wife and moved into his own apartment. Joan was a frequent visitor. She picked out his furnishings and his clothes, making sure every-thing he bought complemented *her* wardrobe. Although they were seldom seen on dates in public, Jeff was always in the background, alone, at whatever function Joan attended. To wit, some fanzine items: 'Joan Crawford, in strapless white net and all gorgeous diamonds showed at the premiere of *Moulin Rouge*. Also there were Tyrone and Linda Power, Robert Wagner, Debra Paget and Jeff Chandler, stag.' 'Enjoying Edith Piaf at Mocambo was Zsa Zsa Gabor and husband George Sanders, Robert Wagner and Terry Moore, and Jeff Chandler, recently separated from his lovely wife, Margery, was seated at the same table as Joan Crawford, who looked breathtaking in blue.'

Eventually Sidney Skolsky blew the whistle on the secret affair. 'Joan Crawford needs a real cool romance, and Jeff Chandler isn't it,' the columnist wrote.

'It's over,' Joan told Jeff.

'But I love you,' said Jeff. 'What do we care what some crummy columnist says?'

'*I* care; and my fans care,' said Joan. 'They would be *so* disappointed in me if I was seeing a married man.'

Exit Jeff, and enter Rock Hudson.

In 1953 at Universal, Rock Hudson was still a year away from hitting the big time with Jane Wyman in *Magnificent Obsession*. But Joan, after seeing an early cut of *Captain Lightfoot*, told Milton Rachmil, 'That guy has got it. He's a combination of Gary Cooper and Robert Taylor.' Hollywood lore said that Joan, with her normal enthusiasm, sent Rock her usual telegram. A dinner meeting at Brentwood followed, but on this night, perhaps heeding a rumor that Rock was gay, Joan changed her routine. It was a warm California evening, so after dinner they sat outside, drinking brandy by the pool. She entertained the bashful actor with stories of his favorite Metro stars, Garbo, Harlow, and his idol Clark Gable (whose lopsided grin, Rock had borrowed for some of his early movies). Then the star suggested they swim in her heated pool. There were brand-new trunks in the poolhouse for her guest to wear, and as he swam she sat nearby, nursing her drink and watching the magnificent Rock as he cut through the water. Afterwards she suggested he shower and change, so they could go dancing. The story told, true or fabled, is that Rock was back in the poolhouse, taking a shower, when the lights went out. Suddenly he felt the warm, naked body of Joan Crawford beside him. 'Sssh, baby,' she whispered, 'close your eyes and pretend I'm Clark Gable.'

In March 1953, with no man left at Universal to conquer, Joan decided to marry the boss, Milton Rachmil. The ceremony was scheduled for Las Vegas. On the morning of the wedding, according to daughter Christina, 'they left her house together in the limousine because they both had studios to report to before leaving for Las Vegas. On the way to work they had a fight over who was going to be dropped off first. That was the end of the marriage plans. Guests were called and the party in Las Vegas was canceled.'

It also temporarily shelved Joan's plans to work at Universal. But she still believed that she was a big star and able to call her own shots at the major studios.

> *'You have to be self-reliant and strong to survive in this town. Otherwise you will be destroyed.'*
>
> Joan Crawford, shortly before her own decline

It was the success of *Sudden Fear* that made Joan too cocky, some people said. In January 1953 after she had agreed to play Karen Holmes, the adulterous army wife in *From Here To Eternity*, she overplayed her hand in contract talks with Columbia Pictures. Her agent had already secured the cash (a hundred thousand dollars and a percentage of the gross) and top billing for Joan. In the all-star cast, she would come second, after Montgomery Clift but before Burt Lancaster (Frank Sinatra, begging for a comeback, would come fourth, below the title). Joan would also receive full perks. These included a first-class suite on the ship to Hawaii; her own house on the island; and her screen wardrobe to be custom-made by Sheila O'Brien, her personal designer. Reportedly it was a fight over the clothes that led to the star exiting the picture. But executive producer Jerry Wald said Joan's main objection concerned the script. She wanted her part beefed up, with less emphasis on the army and Pearl Harbor and more on her. 'Fuck her,' said Harry Cohn, using the excuse of the wardrobe as an out, and the role went to Deborah Kerr.

That March, Joan landed a two-picture deal at her old studio, MGM. At $125,000 per film, her first project would be *Torch Song*, which was described by one critic as 'a technicolored musical version of *All About Eve*, with all of the female characters rolled into one.'

With a soft name and a hard heart, Jenny Stewart, Crawford's character, was an ageing, neurotic, compulsive, arrogant Broadway star who bullied her staff and co-workers. 'She's tough because she's really lonely at heart,' said Joan, who added that she was thrilled because she would be doing her own singing in the movie. 'You may not know this, but many years ago in this same studio, I made some recordings of my singing,' she told one young scribe. 'They were never released because my boss, L.B. Mayer, thought I was a threat to Jeanette MacDonald. Well, dear Jeanette is gone now, and so is Mr. Mayer, so audiences will finally get a chance to hear me sing, and I don't mind saying I am very happy about that.'

After losing ten pounds and undergoing slight surgical improvements, Joan boasted to MGM costumier, Helen Rose, 'The face and the breasts are new, but my ass is the same – as flat and as firm as a twenty year old's.' Described by one critic as 'a drag Queen let loose on film,' she had her hair dyed apricot-orange and styled in 'a brutal page-boy.' Her onscreen dialogue also matched her rigid appearance. 'People will only do what you want if you hit them first,' said Joan as Jenny; later snarling, 'You get paid a lot of money to dance around that leg,' to a terrified chorus boy.

Her off-camera lines were also unfriendly, a Metro publicist recalled. Welcomed back to the studio after her ten-year absence, Joan strolled around the lot and was introduced to the current crop of players, including Debbie Reynolds, Bobby Van, and Anne Francis. 'Lovely *children*, but where are the stars?' the established legend snapped.

The role of the blind pianist in *Torch Song* was played by British actor Michael Wilding, who had recently been signed to MGM on the strength of his marriage to the studio's hottest commodity, Elizabeth Taylor. Joan, at forty-nine, was not taken with Elizabeth age twenty. 'Princess Brat' was how she referred to her co star's wife, and one afternoon when Elizabeth drove up to the outdoor filming in her pink Cadillac convertible, leaving a twister of dust in her wake, Joan suggested to Michael Wilding that he put a harness on his young wife. When Elizabeth persisted in visiting her husband on the indoor set during filming, Joan had a security guard put at the soundstage door barring Taylor from entering.

Elizabeth, for all her youth, managed to pitch a few *bons mots* at the older star. 'Michael is making his first and last picture with Joan Crawford,' she told one reporter, while another learned how fortunate her husband was to be playing a blind man in his first American role. 'That way he doesn't have to look at Joan Crawford throughout the entire movie,' said Liz.

In years to come Joan would get the opportunity to retaliate against Taylor, but that season she had a more provocative newcomer to challenge – Marilyn Monroe.

JOAN AND MARILYN

'Monroe was like Crawford. She had an affinity for the camera. There's a lot of her type around today. They're not actresses – but creatures of the camera.'
                                                                    Joe Mankiewicz

'There's nothing wrong with my tits but I don't go around throwing them in people's faces.'

                                                      Crawford on Marilyn Monroe

In 1953 Joan was once again voted Favorite Actress by *Photoplay* and Marilyn Monroe was named Fastest Rising Star. At the awards dinner the two stars clashed, and while the press reported that the inter-galactic confrontation was their first meeting, the ageing movie queen and the blonde starlet had been introduced before, under private circumstances.

Author Fred Guiles claimed the two met in 1947 in a church – Saint Victor's in Los Angeles – when Monroe was making *Ladies of the Chorus*. Attorney Greg Bautzer said that Crawford was with him when they first met Marilyn at the home of Joseph Schenck – an old-time producer and patron of aspiring starlets (including Joan in her younger, hungrier days). Bautzer's story was that Crawford was with him when they spotted the provocative young starlet, dressed in a tight tan skirt and white angora sweater, standing in line at Schenck's buffet table. Taking the initiative, Joan approached Marilyn and said sincerely, 'You're very pretty, my dear, but you don't know shit about clothes.'

During that evening, Joan also extended an invitation to the struggling actress to dine at her Brentwood home. Marilyn, a long-time fan of Crawford, said she was thrilled to accept the invitation. She was also eager to meet Joan's adopted children. But on the chosen night, when she arrived at Crawford's home, there wasn't sight or sound of the Crawford children. Furthermore, Joan never served dinner. She served a drink to Marilyn, replenished her own, then, without much ado, she brought the girl upstairs, 'to see what a real star's wardrobe looked like.'

Marilyn reportedly 'gasped' when she saw Joan's dressing room, 'which was bigger than most people's living room.' The walls were stacked with shelves and plastic color-coded boxes containing shoes, gloves, hats, and handbags, while underneath hundreds of dresses, coats, and evening gowns were hanging on multiple racks. A special room nearby held her furs, including minks and sables, some seventy in number. 'Try one on,' Crawford told the impressed starlet, who reached for the white-fox stole.

In her bedroom, Crawford presented Marilyn with a box. Inside was an expensive brand-new black cocktail dress, in Monroe's size. 'Take off your things and try it on,' said Joan. 'If it's not OK, I'll send it back tomorrow.'

'Oh!' the breathily excited Marilyn whispered, then slipping out of her clothes, the nubile young beauty sent the semi-intoxicated Joan into a state of cold sobriety. Underneath her street dress, Marilyn wasn't wearing a stitch of underwear.

'Oh!' said Joan, her eyes widening and her temperature rising, as she began to experience the full impact of seeing the naked, exquisitely formed body of America's future sex symbol.

It has been said that what transpired between Crawford and Monroe that night was more than a mere fashion show. Some also believed that Joan's intentions were strictly philanthropic. 'Joan was very generous to newcomers,' said Vincent Sherman, 'although I remember when we were at Columbia there was a girl who was always hanging around her. We often wondered about her.'

'Mother had lesbian proclivities,' said daughter Christina, revealing how, when Joan was drinking she sometimes wanted to sleep with the children's nurse.

Actress Louise Brooks also decreed that Crawford was 'one of

those girls who went back and forth'; while director Joe Mankiewicz
said he thought that Monroe was attracted to her own sex.

'I often wondered about Marilyn,' said publicist Harry Mines.
'But Joan? We were very close friends. I never saw it, and I doubt
it seriously. She liked men too much.'

Author Fred Guiles claimed that 'at another brunch, and with
the hostess slightly drunk,' Crawford made a sexual pass at Marilyn
and the friendship ended. 'Marilyn, who saw nothing wrong with
lesbianism, recoiled more from shock than offense,' said Guiles.
Supposedly Joan's grudge began then, and it grew in proportion
to Monroe's growing popularity, eventually exploding publicly on
the night of the *Photoplay* dinner.

Among the other stars gathered for the awards dinner in the Crystal
Room of the Beverly Hills Hotel that evening were John Wayne,
Maureen O'Hara, Susan Hayward, Doris Day, Lana Turner, and
Lex Barker. Arriving late, making 'a grand entrance, wearing a chiffon
gown of muted grays and blue, with real diamonds in her hair, was
Joan Crawford.' Seated at her table were Gary Cooper, Grace Kelly,
Rock Hudson and his date, Mamie Van Doren. 'In no time at all I
realized that Crawford was on the way to becoming blind drunk,'
said Van Doren. 'Every so often she'd knock back a slug of her drink
and look around the room malevolently.'

'Whole goddamn place is full of newcomers if you ask me. Right,
Rocko?' said Joan to Rock Hudson, 'with whom she tried to flirt,
but it only made her look like she had indigestion,' said Mamie
(who confessed in her memoirs that *she* made it with Rock, later
that night, on the kitchen floor of her parents' home in the valley).

Fixing her eyes on Mamie, Joan spat out, 'Pretty new faces with
nothing going on behind them. Pretty few fuckin' real stars here.'

Meanwhile, on the front dais, 20th Century-Fox boss Darryl
Zanuck sat with an empty seat beside him, reserved for the Fastest
Rising Star – Marilyn Monroe, who was still at the studio, being
sewn into a gold-lamé dress by designer William Travilla. ('To be
thin enough for the dress, she went on two high colonics,' the
designer confided.)

Finally wriggling in two hours late, wearing the skin-tight gold-
lamé gown ('It was just the kind of dress I'd hoped my studio would

make for me,' said Mamie wistfully), Marilyn 'swayed sinuously' down the long room to her place on the dais, while gasps and wolf calls filled the air.

'It was like a burlesque show,' said a horrified Joan Crawford to Associated Press reporter Bob Thomas. 'The audience yelled and shouted, and Jerry Lewis got up on the table and whistled. But those of us in the industry just shuddered.'

Marilyn was a cheap joke who flaunted sex in people's faces, Joan went on to say in the lengthy wire-press interview. 'Kids don't like her . . . and don't forget the women. They're the ones who pick out the movie entertainment for the family, underneath it all they like to know all actresses are ladies.'

Crawford's comment on Monroe made every newspaper across the United States. It was also picked up by the radio and TV news reporters, the foreign press, and the important weekly news magazines. The dispute went on for days as the pros and cons from the media added more fodder to the fire. Crawford was accused of being jealous of the younger, sexier Monroe. Others applauded Joan as a brave and responsible arbiter of Hollywood's morals. 'Her loyalty to Hollywood goes above and beyond the call of duty,' said Edith Gwynn. 'She was following the normal middle-age trend to conservatism,' said Bob Thomas, who believed that Joan enjoyed the controversy and the wide publicity her criticism generated.

Marilyn, who cried all night after the attack from Crawford, was reportedly 'so embarrassed that she did not go outside her apartment for a fortnight.' Yet, like most celebrities in times of contention, the distressed sex symbol did manage to drag her gorgeous self to the phone, to talk to Louella Parsons, who was also willing to 'open her vitally important column so Marilyn could express her agony.'

'At first all I could think of was "Why should she select me to blast?" ' Marilyn whispered. 'She's a great star. I'm just starting. The thing that hit me the hardest is that it came from her. Along with Bette Davis and Katharine Hepburn, Miss Crawford was one of my favorite actresses. I've always admired her for being such a wonderful mother – for taking four children and giving them a fine home. Who, better than I, knows what it means to care for homeless little ones?" '

16

'I'll never know why Joan Crawford didn't keep her real name. Joan Crawford was a Lucille LeSueur; she certainly was never a Joan Crawford. You could believe that a Lucille LeSueur would strap her adopted children to the bedpost, but a Joan Crawford would have to be sitting in the solarium sipping Pepsi with Caesar Romero.'

Mercedes McCambridge – *The Quality of Mercy*

Putting Marilyn on hold, as soon as Crawford finished *Torch Song*, she went over to Republic Studios to make her first talking western – *Johnny Guitar*. Her director was Nicholas Ray. Married to Gloria Grahame, he met Joan when she and Grahame made *Sudden Fear*. Not long after, Ray and Joan were an item (and Grahame, no slouch in the allure department, began to date her stepson, Tony Ray, whom she later married).

Crawford and Nick Ray were scheduled to make a film called *Lisbon* at Paramount. The script of *Lisbon* had 'no balls,' said Joan, and when Ray landed a deal at Republic Pictures for *Johnny Guitar*, he induced Crawford to play the main role.

Johnny Guitar was not the usual shoot-'em-up western, but an existential, allegorical Trucolor parable, with two women as the leads. Joan would play Vienna, the ambitious owner of a saloon who, in pursuit of urban commerce, wanted the railroad to come to town. Her opposition, Emma Small, a bitter, sexually repressed cattle owner, was against the railroad and against Joan, whom she tries to lynch.

Crawford had two actresses in mind to play Emma. 'She wanted Barbara Stanwyck or Bette Davis,' said Nick Ray. 'I agreed with her. Either one would have been fine. Except Herbert Yates, the boss at Republic, was a cheap son of a bitch. He was famous for making cheap pictures. The only way he got Crawford to come to Republic was because he made *The Quiet Man* the year before. That won the Oscar and made a lot of money, although John Ford had to sue Yates to get his profits. When I told him Joan's suggestion of using Stanwyck or Bette Davis in the second lead, Yates said no, the budget wouldn't pay for two stars. I had to go with someone lesser-known, thereby cheaper. When I told Joan that, she said, 'Well you better get someone who can hold her own with me, or the picture won't work.'

Ray got actress Mercedes McCambridge, who won an Oscar in 1950 for her portrayal of Sadie Burke, the sharp, tough assistant to the redneck politician in *All the King's Men*. The talented McCambridge said she had a certain edge over Joan Crawford when they first met. She had recently married Fletcher Markle, an orchestra leader. He was a very attractive man, who had received a pair of gold cuff links from Joan shortly before eloping with McCambridge. 'He had picked me. So there, Miss Crawford, so there,' said Mercedes to herself with a smirk, when she met Crawford for wardrobe tests on *Johnny Guitar*.

Joan was smirking too, when she gave supporting player McCambridge the shabby side of the wardrobe test slate. While she was outfitted in expensive gabardine jodhpurs and silken shirts, Crawford decided that Mercedes would wear 'nothing but a heavy black, slightly modified nun's habit, throughout the whole film.'

In makeup, Joan also insisted that Mercedes' hair be dyed jet black, to contrast with her own warm russet-brown ('Also a dye job,' said McCambridge), and during a break in the color tests, when Mercedes sat down, the star stood by her side, then, after bestowing a truly sensational Joan Crawford smile, slipped out of one of her shoes, lifted her bare foot and placed it firmly up against McCambridge's stomach. Looking like 'a flamingo in a splint,' with one foot on the floor and the other in her co star's navel, Crawford instructed McCambridge to examine her 'funny little feet.' They had grown from a perfect model size, $4\frac{1}{2}$, when she was sixteen, she said, to a huge $5\frac{1}{2}$, from '*all* that dancing in *all* those films.'

'Good heavens,' Mercedes cried, yet to learn that Crawford's feet were actually a size seven, in leather boots, and would soon dance a tarantella on her head and spirit.

Arriving on location in Sedona, Arizona, with thirty pieces of luggage and twenty-nine cases of vodka, Joan became fast friends with most of the men in the company, and none of the women. On the first day of shooting, during a scene with her co star, Sterling Hayden, Crawford spied his wife watching from the sideline. 'She ordered my husband to take me off the set,' said Mrs. Hayden. 'Sterling refused, saying: "If she leaves, I leave too." '

Describing himself as 'not too bright . . . but a decent enough guy,' Hayden confessed he was an actor only for the money, which enabled him to indulge in his first love, ships and the sea. On the set, he did not endear himself to Joan Crawford when, comparing her with Bette Davis, the lead of his last film, *The Star*, he said, 'Listen. I'll say my lines and kiss any actress my paycheck says to kiss; whether I like 'em or not.'

> *'I've never seen a woman who was more like a man. Looks like one, acts like one, and sometimes makes me feel I'm not.'*
>
> A cowboy in *Johnny Guitar*

Joined by her son Christopher, Crawford wrote home to columnist Hedda Hopper that she and the boy were thriving outdoors and that they had become 'real tough cowboys.' Shooting in a place called Oak Creek Canyon, with the red dust blowing into their eyes and teeth, and the sand biting into their flesh, Mercedes McCambridge said, 'Everybody looked like Margo in *Lost Horizon* . . . everybody but Joan.'

Crawford never got on a horse except for her close-ups, and those scenes took hours to light. 'When you are as big a star as Joan Crawford was in those days,' said Mercedes, 'you don't allow anybody to photograph you outside. Not in harsh light, and only in long, long, long shots. If you are a cameraman and you think you are going to get any closer than the length of a football field to take pictures of Miss Crawford, in anything but elaborately diffused interior light, you had better get out of show business, and a few of them had to.'

In her memoirs, Joan referred to the unnamed McCambridge as a friend of Sterling Hayden's and 'a rabble rouser.' She of course did her gracious best to be charming. 'I was always friendly,' she said. 'I asked her to my dressing room for tea.'

'She told me she never wanted me in the role,' said McCambridge. 'She wanted Claire Trevor, and then she threw me out of her dressing room.'

On the set, when the crew applauded Mercedes McCambridge in a difficult outdoor scene, Crawford watched from a nearby hill-side, and the trouble intensified. 'I tried to be friends with Miss Crawford,' said Mercedes. 'Five times I went to her dressing room and five times she ordered me out.'

'Joan was drinking a lot and she liked to fight,' said Nick Ray (who lost an eye in a barroom brawl in Madrid ten years later). Describing the star as 'very attractive, with a basic decency,' Ray said he was personally involved with her during the making of the picture. 'That only added to the problems, because McCambridge and the others didn't like it.'

'He spent his evenings with her, and left orders not to be disturbed,' an assistant told the *Los Angeles Mirror*. One evening an important message arrived for Ray. The assistant director approached Crawford's cabin and 'overheard a wild argument between the two.' The door opened suddenly and Ray stalked out. He came face to face with a raging Crawford. 'The next day the assistant director was off the picture.'

When a reporter for the *Arizona Republic* wrote about the erratic behavior of Crawford on the set, she retaliated by having a letter signed by the crew and printed in the rival newspaper, the *Phoenix Gazette*. The letter was a loving epistle. 'If there is a more cooperative, charming, talented, understanding, generous, unspoiled, thoughtful, approachable person in the motion-picture business, we have not yet met him or her,' it read.

When news of the fracas reached columnist Erskine Johnson in Hollywood, he called Mrs. Sterling Hayden, who said that Crawford had abused Mercedes McCambridge so badly 'that the poor kid had to be hospitalized.' McCambridge when asked about her hospital stay, said she was suffering from 'Crawforditis.'

After reading Erskine Johnson's story, Joan called the columnist at home.

'Is this Erskine Johnson?' she asked.

'Yes it is.'

'This is Joan Crawford,' said the star. 'And you're a shit.'

Joan then called columnist Harrison Carroll, with a quote on McCambridge. 'I wouldn't trust her as far as I could throw a battleship,' she said. That same night, when director Nick Ray refused to take sides in the dispute, Joan threw him out of her cabin. At midnight, roaring drunk, she went to the movie company's wardrobe truck. She gathered up McCambridge's costumes, then, screaming 'They stink!', she scattered them along the Arizona highway.

'I now know what it takes to become a movie star, and I want none of it.'
                                                    Mercedes McCambridge

In Arizona, the final scene with bad woman Emma Small, crashing through a wooden railing and falling to her death two hundred feet into a canyon, was filmed. 'I really don't remember whether Joan's gun killed me or whether I just fell off a balcony,' said McCambridge. In California a week later, the reaction shots of Joan, set against a canvas sky and a scenic backdrop, were done at the Republic ranch in the San Fernando Valley. Accompanied by her retinue of ten, including one director, two assistant directors, script man, secretary, costumer, wardrobe lady, makeup man, hairdresser, 'and a propman who carried sweat spray and spirits-of-ammonia ampules' (to make her cry, because 'Noble leading ladies like Miss Crawford don't kill people easily, even bad guys like me,' said McCambridge).

In Los Angeles, Crawford received some bad news. *Torch Song*, her big musical, had been edited and scored but without Joan's vocalizing. Her singing voice had been dubbed by India Adams, 'in a voice so husky it could pull a dog sled.' On the night of the Hollywood premiere, Joan showed up and spoke in the lobby with guests Marlene Dietrich and Butch Romero. At the postpremiere party at Chasen's, with the photographers present, she spied Mercedes McCambridge across the room and rushed over to embrace her. When asked about the feud, McCambridge shrugged and said: 'Some days it's on, some days it's off. I guess this is one of the off days.'

Torch Song flopped, as did *Johnny Guitar*, released the following May, in 1954. Reviewing Joan's Trucolor Freudian western, Bosley Crowther of *The New York Times* said, 'No more femininity comes from her than from the rugged Van Heflin in *Shane*. For the lady, as usual, is as sexless as the lions on the Public Library steps, and as sharp and romantically forbidden as a package of unwrapped razor blades.'

'Miss Crawford went thataway,' another critic observed. 'She screeches nastily and Mr. Hayden gallumps around morosely. Let's put it down as a fiasco.'

'It *was* a mistake,' said Crawford. 'During the filming I never knew what in the hell the script was about. It was full of metaphorical double meaning, which in terms of entertainment means that the audience is going to be bored out of their skulls.' ('Don't talk to *me* about any of that "New Wave" or "existential" crap,' said Bette Davis agreeing with her rival. 'If a story doesn't have a beginning, a middle, and an end, then it just *ain't* a story.')

'*Johnny Guitar* was a hit in France,' said Nicholas Ray. With a dubbed soundtrack ('in which the cowboys call each other "Monsieur" '), Francois Truffaut, calling Ray 'an auteur in the best sense of the word', said the film was 'phony . . . a hallucinatory Western,' but he was captivated by the image of Crawford in a white dress, playing the piano in the cavernous saloon, 'with a candlestick and a pistol beside her.' The film was made to order for the star, just 'as *Rancho Notorious* was made by Fritz Lang for Marlene Dietrich,' Truffaut wrote, but of Crawford's patriarchal rigid beauty he noted: 'She has become unreal, a phantom of herself. Whiteness has invaded her eyes, muscles have taken over her face, a will of iron behind a face of steel. She is a phenomenon. She is becoming more manly as she grows older. Her clipped, tense acting, pushed almost to paroxysm by Ray, is in itself a strange and fascinating spectacle.'

JOAN GETS LYNCHED BY THE PRESS

'Miss Crawford has a remarkable gift for public relations. She knows by-lines I've never heard of. A reporter will say something nice about Joan, and pretty soon a pleasant note or a small present will arrive for the writer.'

John O'Hara, *Collier's*, 1954

When Crawford and Davis were the queens of MGM and Warner's, the powerful press offices ensured that when their majesties spoke to the media, their words were never questioned. Those that dared refute what the stars said were duly chastized or denied future access to the entire royal duchy. So most of the Hollywood press played professional ball, churning out coverage that was fluffy and flattering.

With the breakup of the studio system in the early 1950s, the stars lost the protective barrier that existed between them and the press. Bette Davis learned that in divorce from artist William Grant Sherry, when she tried to paint him in colors more violent than he deserved. 'Bette Davis could be very moody, and difficult. She was always fighting with someone, and she never forgot a wrong,' said Sheilah Graham. 'But Joan Crawford was a pro. She knew we had a job to do and she was always good copy, so we tended to look the other way when it involved her drinking or having affairs, especially with married men. In those days most of our editors were married men, having affairs all over the place.'

But by 1954, as television continued to make deeper economic cuts into the advertising revenues of the once powerful print media, more sensational news stories were needed to boost circulation. The private lives of stars, no matter how sacred, were no longer considered off-limits to interviewers and reporters, and Crawford, 'Saint Joan of the Fan Mags', was one of the first to be burned at the tabloid stake.

In March 1954, a month before the opening of *Johnny Guitar* an enterprising reporter named Roby Heard of the *Los Angeles Mirror* called Republic's press office and said he wanted to do a story on Crawford, to break when the movie opened. It was to be part inter-view and part overview of Joan's long, illustrious career, the writer informed.

Crawford gave the interview, the 'overview' was expanded, and the piece was scheduled as a series.

'I am thrilled,' said Joan, granting Heard access to members of her family and to her friends.

'The son of a bitch never told me he was going to put a knife in my back,' the star soon complained.

'JOAN CRAWFORD – QUEEN or TYRANT? The Star Thrives on Feuds', was the headline of the nationally syndicated story. Offering their help in the dissection were Marilyn Monroe, Jack Palance, Mercedes McCambridge, Greg Bautzer, Gloria Grahame, Nick Ray, Joan's mother and brother and her ex-servants. (Not quoted were Bette Davis, in retirement in Maine; and Joan's children, who were possibly too young for telephone privileges.)

Opening with Joan's long-ago 'dog-eat-dog' fight with Norma Shearer, reporter Heard jumped to her more recent diatribes against Marilyn Monroe.

'I criticized Marilyn Monroe as I would criticize my own daughter,' said Joan. 'No comment,' said Marilyn. 'Jealousy caused Crawford to attack Marilyn. She should develop benevolence towards other human beings,' said Marilyn's former coach, Natasha Lytess.

Joan was also 'tactless and cruel' to Gloria Grahame during the making of *Sudden Fear* the previous year. 'They hated one another,' said a cast member. 'Gloria was always late for work,' said Joan. 'Sometimes we didn't even know where she was.' 'If I was sleeping and had a dream, and if Miss Crawford appeared in my dream I always woke up screaming. That went on for months after we worked together,' said Grahame. Joan's behaviour on *Sudden Fear* was 'the talk of Hollywood,' an 'unnamed' columnist confided. 'Once in the presence of the entire company, she berated David Miller [the director] and slapped him in the face.'

She also abused Jack Palance. 'Look, I don't want any more squabbles with Crawford. I have my future to think about,' said Palance, adding, 'She's difficult. Unless she's handled properly she's lots of trouble. She's a woman and has to have her way in everything.'

'She hates all women,' said Mrs. Sterling Hayden, 'except for those who can help her. If I ever see her again I'll probably strike her in the face.'

'It is apt to be necessary to step on people on your way to the top,' Joan's mother, Mrs. Anna LeSueur, believed.

'I have the same driving force. But those of us with talent and ambition must develop tolerance, must make allowances for people less gifted,' said former silent star Theda Bara.

'Dear Theda,' said Joan. 'No one knew she was still alive.'

'I haven't seen my sister in more than five years. For personal reasons I must refrain from saying why,' said Hal LeSueur.

'Ask Joan why we stopped going out together. No comment from me,' said Greg Bautzer

'Ask Miss Crawford why she abused a *Johnny Guitar* actress so badly the player had to travel twenty-eight miles across the desert to enter a hospital,' Mrs. Sterling Hayden suggested.

'Over the years she has built up so much power in the industry that she knows she can lord it over the little people,' said Mercedes McCambridge. 'Everybody is afraid of her. She destroys those who oppose her.'

'I quit after two weeks,' an ex-servant in Joan's household told the reporter. 'She made me take off my shoes when I entered the house so I wouldn't get dirt on the rugs.'

'Let's not be too critical,' said *Johnny Guitar* actor John Carradine. 'After all she was the star of the picture.'

'She is our one really great star,' said actor David Brian. 'I don't see her very often. She's a very busy woman.'

'I've only seen her twice,' said actor Rory Calhoun, 'once at a party and once as she drove her car – and I'll never forget her.'

'As a human being, Joan Crawford is a great actress,' said Nicholas Ray.

'I've had all I want to do with working with Miss Crawford, and I don't care to continue the contract,' Sterling Hayden concluded.

'I'm still glad I worked so hard to give an important part to Mr. Hayden, in spite of his feelings towards me. Bless him,' said Joan.

After the 'smut series' appeared, Crawford blamed the negative coverage for besmirching her name and putting her on unemployment for a year. She lost numerous roles, she claimed, including that of Georgia Elgin, the alcoholic's wife in *The Country Girl*, when in fact that part had been given to Grace Kelly in January, six months before the articles appeared.

When the movie offers stopped, Crawford considered joining the enemy – television. She offered herself and an old script about a schoolteacher, Miss O'Brien, to CBS, but they turned her down. A second concept for a series was sent to Joan by Hedda Hopper, who received this reply: 'Hedda Dear, I think it's a brilliant idea, for an unknown, or someone who's done a couple of pictures, but certainly not for a star. God bless – and thank you again for your belief in not only a devoted friend, but, as Billie Haines calls me, an iron reindeer in a Victorian garden. My name, however, is still Joan Crawford.'

> *'Her career was on the decline, her love life was shit, she was getting old, losing power. When you're in a situation like that, your nerves give way. I felt sorry for her, not the kids.'*
>
> Reporter Arthur Bell

That summer, while Bette Davis was content playing 'Mother Merrill' in her maritime retreat in Maine, the cracks in the façade of tenacious star Joan Crawford began to widen. Unemployed and near-broke due to bad investments, she attempted to fill her days supervising her fan patrol, the faithful Crawford disciples who came to her home to address and stuff envelopes with thousands of eight-by-ten photographs and mimeographed news sheets, which were sent to other fans to retain their allegiance while she was off the silver screen. At night, no longer invited to the 'A' events in Hollywood, Joan stayed at home, where, 'spurred on by alcohol and seized by fits of madness, she stormed through the house screaming obscenities,' daughter Christina reported. At fourteen, the girl claimed she was on frequent call to carry her mother to bed after she had passed out drunk in various rooms of the Brentwood mansion. Sober, Joan subjected the bewildered teenager to many acts of mental torture. She threw Tina's tight toreador pants (bought without Joan's permission) into the incinerator, made her do messy housework ('Mother never scrubbed floors. I did, and so did the fans'); for her birthday she gave Christina a box with a single earring inside, the other earring would come at graduation time if Tina got good marks, her mother promised.

Christina admitted she could be a maddening handful at times. When she was nine, she said, she caught on to Joan's publicity game of using her and the others for display purposes only. It was then she started 'tuning out' on Mommie Dearest's silly requests. 'Mother could no longer control our every thought, gesture and move,' said the girl. When she was 'not yet ten years old,' she became an expert bartender, taking 'secret delight' in making drinks too strong for her mother's boyfriends, 'just to see what effect they'd have on them'. At eleven and a half Christina made love to an older boy in a stable at school, and told others, until the word reached Joan. Arriving at the school in a station wagon with her secretary to pick up the expelled youngster, Joan was drinking vodka from a plastic glass. On the way home she needed replenishments, and the helpful girl volunteered the name of a liquor store in the vicinity. Joan slammed on the brakes, sending Christina 'sprawling half-way into the front seat, the secretary nearly into the windshield, and mother's drink all over the floor. She slapped me across the face and yelled: "You always know where to find the boys and the booze, don't you?" Then she slapped me several times again.'

At thirteen, Christina said, *she* finally put her foot down. She refused to call any of her mother's boyfriends 'Uncle': 'It would be plain "Mr." from here on unless I particularly liked them or they lasted more than a couple of months.' But by the summer of 1954 Crawford's love life was non-existent; it had vanished along with her career. When fan-magazine writer Jane Wilkie visited the star, she was ironing a dress. Holding up the steaming iron, Joan commented wryly, 'That's the hottest thing that's been near my ass in months.'

Saturday nights were the worst, she told director-friend Vincent Sherman, when she didn't even have a man to have a hamburger with.

'Come on now!' Sherman told her. 'You're Joan Crawford. There are hundreds of guys in this town who would drop everything to take you out.'

'*Actors*!' said Joan with disdain. 'Who only want to get their pictures taken having dinner with Joan Crawford at Chasen's. Or guys who only want to brag to their buddies that they went to bed with Joan Crawford.'

That summer, to escape the frustration and boredom of staying at home all day waiting for the phone to ring, Joan began to take off on long drives, alone. Wearing sunglasses, a head scarf, slacks, and a raincoat, she would cruise up and down the highways in northern California, stopping at diners and truck-stop restaurants along the way. She dropped Louella Parsons a line from one stop, telling her about the fascinating characters she bumped into. 'I might write a script about life on the open road,' wrote Joan. At first these jaunts were day trips, but eventually they became two- and three-night layovers. 'I call my babies [the twins], every night,' she told Parsons. 'Then the next day I drive on to a new location.'

Without mentioning her name, one publication printed that the star was often seen intoxicated, in the company of 'unsavory male companions', leaving and exiting highway motels. *Joan Crawford and the handsome bartender* was the heading for a story in *Confidential* magazine months later, but by then the star had stopped her wandering ways.

The desultory road trips apparently ended one gray rainy morning when Crawford woke up on the floor of a strange motel with a sore jaw and a badly bruised eye. During the night she had either been beaten or had fallen down drunk, then rolled by one of her gallant highwaymen. Her watch and the cash in her handbag was gone, but she found her car keys intact, tucked into a side flap of her raincoat, and she made it back to L.A. safely that afternoon.

After that unpleasant incident, the star never patrolled the highways again. And she was seldom seen out at night in Los Angeles without her secretary or a friend for company.

'We were driving home after dinner one night,' said Vincent Sherman. 'As we passed Grauman's Chinese Theater, there was a big premiere going on. Kidding, I said to her, "Hey, why weren't you invited to that shindig?" Joan looked out at the lights and crowds, and said, "Fuck 'em. I'll be back." '

*   *   *

She kept her word of course. Durable, tough, tenacious, the word 'comeback' was invented for stars like Joan Crawford and Bette Davis.

The jobs were minor at first. For ten thousand dollars, Crawford agreed to act as a hostess that November, shaking hands at the opening of a hotel in Las Vegas. Some critics thought the actress was demeaning herself, but writer John O'Hara defended her employment. She was worth every penny, O'Hara believed, because Joan was an authentic celebrity, always punctual and glamorous. 'There are, of course, actors and actresses who would gladly supply the oil if they could be sure Joan would be boiled in it,' said the author. 'I am not an actor and I am very fond of her.'

In December, Crawford landed a one-picture deal at Universal. Old boyfriend Milton Rachmil offered her a low-budget suspense thriller called *Female on the Beach*. Checking in at the studio, Joan made her customary showy entrance. Wearing white shorts, a white shirt, a black bow tie, and black high heels, she drove onto the lot in her white Lincoln Convertible. Carrying her two white miniature poodles, she headed for costume fittings and gave the once-over to the starlets gathered in the Universal wardrobe room. 'She surveyed the room imperiously,' said the resident blonde sex symbol, Mamie Van Doren. 'It was obvious that she was checking out the young ingenues to see who her new competition would be.'

Zeroing in on Mamie, Joan said, 'You have such a sweet face. You look like a doll.'

'Thank you,' said Mamie ('liking her in spite of myself').

'Have we met before?' Joan inquired.

Mamie tried to remind her they had, at the *Photoplay* awards two years before, when Joan was drunk and attacked Marilyn Monroe.

'Really?' said Joan. 'I don't remember it. I would never forget a face like yours, dear.'

Female on the Beach was the story of an older, wealthy widow and a young good-looking beach bum who was out to kill Joan with love or a blunt instrument. To play the beach bum, Joan requested Tony Curtis. He was twenty-nine, the right age, but Rachmil told her he photographed too young for the role. Audiences would feel queasy if they saw the young Tony in bed with the older Joan. Jeff Chandler was only two years older than Curtis, but with his prematurely graying hair, and 'wearing skintight pants and bathing suits,' he appeared more compatible with the aging star.

'You're about as friendly as a suction pump,' said Joan in character to her former boyfriend in the opening scene.

'I don't hate women,' said Jeff. 'I just hate the way they are.'

'I wish I could afford you,' murmured Joan.

'Save your pennies,' Jeff advised, grabbing her in his arms.

She bites his wrist (the script read). He rips her dress off. Her eyes dilate. She clutches her breasts protectively. He kisses her brutally. She goes limp, then slowly her arms, as if moved by a will of their own, go gliding around him, her fingers dig greedily into his flesh.

'Just once,' the lonely but worldly-wise widow sighs, 'just once, love me a little.'

When 1955 dawned, Crawford's personal fortunes rose considerably. She signed a three-picture deal with Columbia. Her first film would be *Queen Bee*, in which she played a ruthless, depraved Southern woman who dominates and destroys those who loved her. ('That wasn't any acting job on Mother's part,' said Christina. 'It was exactly the way I knew her at home.')

In the Spring, Joan found true love again. He was Alfred Steele, the President of Pepsi-Cola. 'Not one of her usual glamour boys,' Steele was portly, older, but a powerful take-charge man. 'He loves me even without my makeup; and in the sack he's a *tiger*!' said Joan happily. On the night of May 9 they flew to Las Vegas in his Pepsi jet and got married.

Back home, Joan told daughter Christina that Steele was too fat, wore glasses and was hard of hearing in one ear, but he was a nice man, and she instructed the girl to introduce herself. 'When I tried to kiss my new father,' said fifteen-year-old Christina, 'Mother slapped me and pushed me up against the wall. "Damn it," she said, "I got my man, you go out and get your own." '

For a honeymoon the couple sailed from New York to Capri,

where they were serenaded at night by the villagers. In Rome and Paris the rich Mrs. Steele bought new wardrobes for her children ('But our school bills were *still* not paid,' Christina whined). Stateside, the press were told that the Steeles would have two homes, his town house on Sutton Place, New York, and her mansion in Brentwood. In August the couple flew to Los Angeles so Joan could begin work on her second film for Columbia. As Mrs. Alfred Steele, she soon let Hollywood know that she was no longer hustling for jobs, or publicity. Invited to a cocktail party for a trade-paper columnist, she sent a magnum of champagne with her regrets. She explained that, as a working star and executive's wife, her schedule left no time for 'fun socializing'. Writer Bob Sherman was hired as dialogue coach on her new film, *Autumn Leaves*, and he recalled meeting with the star at that time. 'Bob Aldrich (the director) asked me if I'd go out to Crawford's house on a Sunday afternoon, to go over lines with her. When I got there, I was ushered through the white living room, with the white couch and white pillows and white rugs. At the back of the house, two little girls were dressed in their white crinoline dresses, playing with two white French poodles. Mister Pepsi-Cola [Al Steele] was standing by the Greek white pool area, with two white pool houses on each side. And then I saw Joan. She was lying on a white chaise longue, wearing sunglasses, having a manicure and a pedicure while dictating letters to a secretary sitting on one side. She patted a chair on her other side and I sat there, reading lines to her whenever she had a moment to spare. She was playing the "executive-actress" to the hilt.'

Accompanied by her secretary, Crawford arrived at the studio in a long black limousine. Wearing her daytime pearls, she gave dictation as they cruised through the lot. Suddenly Joan spied a familiar figure exiting from one of the buildings. She instructed the driver to slow down and follow. As the car drove alongside, the glamorous Joan lowered her window and called out to the matronly figure walking along the street.

'Bette? Is that really you?' said Joan.

'Hello, *Joan*,' said Bette Davis, at Columbia to make a film called *Storm Center*.

'Darling,' said Joan, 'can we give you a lift?'

Bette kept walking.

'I got married,' said Joan.

'*Good*!' said Bette.

'Can I give you a call?' said Joan.

'*No*,' said Bette and without a hint of goodbye, she turned a sharp right, into a cul-de-sac and disappeared into the side door of a soundstage.

Settling back in her limo, Joan turned to her Pepsi stenographer and said, 'Do you know who that was?'

'No,' said the stenographer.

'That was Bette *Davis*,' said Joan.

'No,' said the stenographer with surprise.

'Yes,' said Joan, quite pleased, 'and she looks old enough to be my mother.'

17

'BLACK YEARS' FOR BETTE

'I went back to work because someone had to pay for the groceries.'
                                                    Bette Davis, 1955

In 1954 Bette and Gary Merrill's three-year-old adopted daughter, Margot, was diagnosed as retarded. Refusing to return the child to the adoption agency, the distraught couple enrolled the girl in a special school in Geneva, New York. Later that same year Merrill's contract with 20th Century-Fox was canceled, and in February 1955 Bette went back to work. 'They're all fatter and richer and stupider than ever,' she said of the people in Hollywood upon her return, yet she did accept the work and the fifty thousand dollars that Darryl Zanuck offered, to repeat her role as the older, more imperious Elizabeth the First in *The Virgin Queen*.

Her co star, Richard Todd, was a shy, competent actor, but another British import, the fresh sultry Joan Collins, was not to Bette's liking. 'She can speak correctly,' said the plump and almost bald Bette, 'but she can't act for shit.'

'I had been warned that Miss Davis did not take kindly to pretty young actresses and she lashed out at me a couple of times,' said Joan.

In August, when she went to Columbia Pictures to play a librarian in *Storm Center*, Bette bumped into Joan Crawford, and also had a very unpleasant experience with the head of the studio, Harry Cohn. Known for his antipathy toward women of talent but unconventional looks (openly berating actresses Judy Holliday and Kim Stanley), Cohn admitted he liked sexy women with 'good tits and a keister.'

Earlier that month, when Crawford checked in for *Autumn Leaves*, the studio boss welcomed her to his office. Over drinks, he said he was willing to forget their differences of the past (he fired her from *From Here to Eternity*; and she, at Ciro's, criticized his eating habits with: 'My dogs have better table manners.'). He admired her style and talent, Cohn said in his office that day, and she had guts. During this spiel, the mogul stood up behind his desk, and placing his hands in his trousers, he commenced to play a very active game of pocket pool. They were going to make some hit movies together, he promised. Racking up an impressive lower score, he moved closer to Crawford, until she stopped him in his tracks. 'Keep it in your pants, Harry,' she warned the mogul. 'I'm having lunch with Joan and the boys [his wife and young sons] tomorrow.'

When Bette arrived at Columbia, she was assigned the star dressing room. One night, after shooting, she was sitting at her makeup table cold-creaming her face, when the wall next to her swung open and Harry Cohn walked in. Without looking at her, he 'made an obscene gesture,' until Bette screamed, 'How dare you come in here. Get out immediately!' Harry fled. The next day, when she told the story to her producer, her ego was deflated. Cohn wasn't looking for sex with her. He was on the prowl for Kim Novak, whose current dressing room she occupied, and who had been moved to a larger suite without notification to the boss.

That fall, Bette realized another early dream when she went to work at Crawford's old studio, MGM. 'Unfortunately,' she said, 'the studio was no longer the symbol of glamour and grandeur; nor was I.' For her role as Aggie Hurley in *The Catered Affair*, she padded her body, powdered her arms (to make them appear heavier and older), subdued all of her familiar mannerisms, and gave what she considered was 'the most unappreciated but self-satisfying performance of my career.'

When the picture was completed, Bette and Gary Merrill, intent on putting some harmony into their marriage, bought a black Mercedes SL 190 'with red leather seats,' and drove to Florida for a second honeymoon, without the children or an entourage.

Joan Crawford also traveled extensively that year. In August, accompanied by husband Alfred Steele, she went to England with forty-two pieces of luggage. Her traveling wardrobe, with a change for every three hours, included five fur stoles, one full-length mink, half a dozen jeweled sweaters, thirty-six pairs of shoes, four suits, twenty-five cocktail dresses, twenty daytime cotton dresses, and twenty-five Jean Louis evening gowns – ten of which were old but were rehemmed to accommodate the new shorter styles.

Sweeping up to the Dorchester Hotel in a long black limousine, the couple were followed by three white Pepsi vans atop of which was Joan's luggage, with each piece embossed J.C. At a press conference in the Oliver Messel suite, the star told the reporters she was there to make a film entitled *The Golden Virgin* (changed to *The Story of Esther Costello*). She was the star and coproducer. Mindful of the latter responsibility, and of her new position as the wife of an important cost-conscious company executive ('My darling Alfred Steele. Stand up and take a bow, dear'), she had gone over the film's budget and cut some of the expenses to the bone. The original budget for her movie wardrobe was seventy thousand dollars. 'But after countless grueling hours of conferences, she whittled it down to a measly forty thousand dollars, by such drastic measures as leaving the mink off the bottom of one dress and having a coat lined with velvet instead of real seal.'

At a 'Hello London' party held at the Les Ambassadeurs club, Joan asked that her guests wear either ballerina or full-length gowns. 'She herself wore a gown of her own creation – an aquamarine silk organza, embroidered with green and blue sequins, short in front and long at back.' Flanked by old friends, Sir Laurence and Lady Olivier, Mr. and Mrs. Steele greeted such guests as Noël Coward, Marlene Dietrich, John Gielgud, Dame Edith Evans, Helen Hayes (who came straight from the set of *Anastasia*), and Rita Hayworth, who arrived stag, wearing no makeup or jewelry, yet she was asked to dance every dance, 'and at the evening's end she waltzed off with the boyfriend of the much younger starlet, Joan Collins.'

Notable no-shows from Crawford's party were Ingrid Bergman, who pleaded fatigue from *Anastasia* filming; and Sir Laurence's current co star in *The Prince and the Showgirl*, Marilyn Monroe, who sent a telegram explaining that at the last minute she had come down with the flu.

Marilyn would annoy Joan further when the two stars were invited to meet the reigning British monarch, Queen Elizabeth the Second. 'The Queen is a lady, and expects to meet other ladies, but most of today's actresses can't even act politely,' said Joan when Marilyn, Anita Ekberg, and Arlene Dahl failed to attend the afternoon rehearsals for the Royal Command performance. 'That night,' said Joan, 'as Her Majesty came up the staircase, Monroe's hairdresser was still doing her hair. And the girl didn't even know how to curtsey.'

When *Esther Costello* was completed, Crawford and Al Steele hit the Pepsi trail, logging over 125,000 miles, opening bottling plants from Denmark to West Germany to South Africa. Back in New York, they bought two penthouse apartments at 32 East Seventieth Street and proceeded to convert them into a duplex, reducing sixteen rooms to eight, including Joan's spacious geranium-pink bedroom, with an open fireplace and a special custom-built closet for her 300 pairs of shoes. To help with the one-million-dollar renovations, the star sold her house in Los Angeles. At a Pepsi stockholders meeting, a 'gadfly' voter questioned the cost of the apartment to the company, and he was told that Mr. Steele had been advanced a loan of $387,000, which he was to return at 6 percent interest. When the voter asked to talk to Mrs. Steele, Joan Crawford rose, took a bow, then ordered the stockholder to 'Make it brief, boy.' When he asked how many shares of stock she owned, Joan snapped, 'It's none of your business. Besides I owned them before I married Mr. Steele.' As another stockholder insisted on making critical comments about the management, Joan was heard to murmur, 'Shut up, shut up.' 'If anyone attacks my husband, I bristle,' she told *Variety*.

On Thanksgiving night, when Pepsi sponsored the TV special *Annie Get Your Gun*, starring Mary Martin, some last-minute changes were made in the commercial messages. Miss Martin had been asked to deliver the end-of-the-show holiday greetings, but she was bumped and replaced by Joan Crawford. Sitting beside her husband and her twin daughters, in front of an open fireplace in their penthouse apartment, Joan wished viewers across the nation the happiest of times. 'It was an ideal arrangement,' said the star's third but unseen daughter, Christina, referring to her mother's new role as the official Pepsi spokeswoman. 'It enabled her to play "movie star" again, to throngs of adoring fans.'

Christina it seemed also had a yen to become famous during this time. After a year of college, she dropped out and decided to become an actress in New York. She got her own apartment, with furniture supplied by Joan Crawford. But Tina did not appreciate her mother's decorating or her help in getting media coverage for her aspiring career. Booked on the Jack Paar TV show through Joan's influence, Tina was radiant during the first few minutes of her interview, but got visibly miffed when Paar asked too many questions about her famous mother and not enough about her own anonymous eighteen-year-old self. The next day, after complaining to Joan, she was told to go out and make it on her own. Crawford also forbade her to use her established surname. 'You're cruel. You're hard. You want me to suffer,' Tina yelled at her mother in front of a reporter. 'You're right, dear,' said Joan, 'I *do* want you to suffer. I want you to struggle and fear and worry the way I did. I want you to fight every step of the way, because when you suffer you don't forget. That's what it takes to become an actress, a star, something great; and not just a personality.'

Crawford's fifteen-year-old son, Christopher, also appeared in the news that year, when he and three other boys were arrested in Greenport, New York, after a wild three-day shooting spree with air guns. They shot out a hundred windows in private homes, at streetlights, and at two girls, who received facial injuries. When informed of the incident, his mother got hysterical. Al Steele told a reporter that the boy was 'morally insane,' and that he had been living at the home of a psychiatrist in Greenport for several years. 'The other three Crawford children are "all jewels," ' said Mr. Steele.

When Christopher was sent to a reformatory, Joan broke the news to her grieving twins. 'Your brother didn't live up to society's expectations,' she explained, 'and society has a way of taking care of these things. When he learns to behave the way he is expected to behave, he'll come back home.'

*   *   *

Early in May 1959, after a barnstorming eight-week tour through the United States, opening new plants and attending conventions, Alfred Steele and his wife returned to New York to repack for a vacation in Bermuda the following Monday. On Saturday night they watched TV together, played a hand of gin rummy, then went to bed. The following morning, when Joan arose, she found the bed empty. Her husband was sprawled out on the bedroom floor. 'She ran over to him, crouched down and touched his forehead,' said a movie magazine. 'She felt his pulse then put her hands to her face and began screaming. Tears were running down her face. It was more than ten minutes later before she became calm enough to go to the telephone and call a doctor.'

At fifty-seven, her husband had died of a heart attack. 'He had drunk too many cocktails, eaten too many banquet meals, flown on too many jets,' said the Associated Press. 'It was the combination of too much work and too many pep pills,' said *Variety*.

Joan arranged the funeral, down to the exact seating in the limos. Two days later she met with the Pepsi board. They told her they were appreciative of her efforts on behalf of the company. She would be receiving her late husband's death benefits, including a partial pension, but her days as a spokeswoman were over. They also asked that her late husband's estate repay his outstanding personal loans as soon as possible. Wearing a black hat, veil, and black gloves, Joan listened calmly to their requests, then, after peeling off one glove, and the other, she placed them in front of her. Regally lifting the veil of her hat, she then told the board, 'Don't fuck with me, fellas. I've fought bigger sharks than you.'

'My husband loved me for my spirit and soul and he'd come back and haunt me through eternity if I didn't go on now with happiness and joy,' Joan told Louella Parsons that evening. She also confessed to the syndicated columnist that she was flat broke. 'I haven't a nickel. Only my jewels. His company did not reimburse me for the half million dollars I spent on the apartment.'

'It was a sob story that would have brought tears to a glass eye,' said Louella, who printed the entire confession, in an attempt to shame the giant corporation.

Within a week, Pepsi announced that Joan had been elected to fill her late husband's position on the company's board of directors. She would be receiving forty thousand dollars annually for the next five years, her own office, a secretary, and the use of the Pepsi plane which would be redecorated in colors of aquamarine, turquoise and brown.

'I told myself, "Why stay home and mope? Pick yourself up and be the glamorous person you're supposed to be,"' said Joan, announcing that she would return to California to appear in Jerry Wald's *The Best of Everything*. It was only a cameo role, but Crawford would receive sixty-five thousand dollars and her customary star privileges. On the days she appeared, the set was cooled to fifty degrees, which caused the stars of the film, Hope Lange and Stephen Boyd, 'to do an Irish rhumba to keep warm.' Reporter Charlotte Dinte described a tense shooting scene between Joan and Hope Lange. Joan, as Amanda Farrow, waspish editor, was to leave junior editor Hope's office and close the door behind her. They shot the scene once, then twice. On the third try, Hope interrupted. 'Would you mind letting me close the door when you leave?'

Joan stared at her. 'No. You can't. It's my line and my exit. I close the door.'

'But I don't know what to do with my hands,' Hope argued.

'Again there was a pause,' said reporter Dinte. 'Again Joan's eyebrows raised. And then this icy voice, at which top directors, famous leading men and wealthy producers have all trembled, said loud and clear: "I suggest you find something to do with them, dear.'

Much to Joan's chagrin, the director, Jean Negulesco, sided with Lange, and the scene went to her. Negulesco also cut a subsequent sequence between Crawford and model-actress Suzy Parker. 'That scene was the reason I took the movie,' said Joan. 'It was set late at night in Amanda's apartment. She had been drinking. She was all alone in life. No man, no family, just a career. Certainly I knew a few things about that predicament, and I gave it everything I had.'

'I have just come from the Actors' Studio, where I saw Marilyn Monroe. She had no girdle on. Her ass was hanging out. She is a disgrace to the industry.'
Joan Crawford to photographer Eve Arnold

'I should have never come back to Hollywood! I hate all of you! And Apple Annie most of all! I must have been out of my mind to come back here.'
Bette Davis, 1961

In 1959 Bette Davis sat for a year in Hollywood without working. 'Oh yes,' she recalled, 'I had a chance to go to Mexico, to play Burt Lancaster's *mother* [in *The Unforgiven*]. I turned it *down*. I'll be damned if I play Burt Lancaster's mother after thirty years in the business.'

The following year, after Helen Hayes rejected the role of bag lady Apple Annie in *Pocketful of Miracles*, the part went to Davis. On the opening day she posed in costume, serving strawberry cheesecake to the producer-star, Glenn Ford, and his co star, Hope Lange. A week later Sheilah Graham reported the first signs of discord on the set. 'You could hear a pin drop when Hope Lange asked to have the dressing-room next to Glenn Ford's – because the lady in that room was Bette Davis!'

'Mr. Ford wanted his girl, Hope, next to him,' said Bette, who moved to the smaller trailer, then blasted Ford for his 'bad manners and lack of professionalism.'

Trying to make amends, the actor-producer gave an interview saying he had always been grateful to Bette for giving him his start in pictures, with *A Stolen Life*, in 1946. He was now repaying the favor by putting her in this picture, hoping it would be a comeback for her. 'Who is that son of a bitch that he should say he helped me have a *comeback*!' Bette raged in reply. 'That shitheel wouldn't have helped me out of a *sewer*!'

The filming went downhill after that, said director Frank Capra, who regretted not trying to understand Davis better. 'I didn't see that she needed consolation and reassurance after so long away. That she was in fact vulnerable, living on her nerves. She'd only become a monster to take care of herself in a monstrous business.

Underneath she was a neurotic woman, deeply afraid and uncertain of everything except her own genius.'

She was coming out of a bad cycle, she said later, the end of her ten black years. Her marriage to Gary Merrill was almost finished. He fell out of love with her when she became a housewife, she believed.

'That's nonsense,' said Merrill in 1988. 'I gave her the best ten years of her life. But she was never a playmate, she would never play golf. She never wanted to leave the house.'

Photographer Phil Stern recalled staying with the couple in Maine. 'Bette asked me to work on the Edward Muskie campaign. My wife and I stayed in their house, and Davis was never still. She was a fanatic about cleaning. She went around all day with a rag in her hand, dusting the lamps and the furniture. She drove everyone crazy.

'You're not Harriet Craig,' Gary Merrill would yell at her, 'so sit down for chrissake.'

Bette had a compulsion to create her own dramatic scenes, Merrill continued. 'When she decided to become "the little woman" she threw herself into it with energy, wanting everyone else to play their part in her drama. When that didn't happen, her short circuits would blow everything apart.'

Gary was a good actor, but 'a lazy son of a bitch,' said Bette. And when he drank he had an explosive temper.

So did Bette, he stated. 'After a few martinis (*in vino veritas*) the shouting matches began. The noise level was so intense I'm surprised we could speak the next day.'

There were *some* laughs, the pair agreed. He hated birthdays, so she surprised him once with a party and a prop cake. Across the top she had inscribed, 'Fuck You.' And they had fun with the kids and the animals, which included dogs, cats, chickens, a horse, a burro, a goat in heat, and some pet sheep which eventually ended up on the dinner table. 'The children named the sheep but weren't upset when the time came for lamb chops or mutton stew,' said Merrill. 'They would say, calmly, "I wonder if we're eating Mark or Luke." '

Merrill frequently beat her up, Bette complained.

'Bullshit,' said Merrill.

He had a cute trick in wintertime, she insisted. 'Gary took delight in pushing me out of the car into a twenty-foot snowdrift in the middle of the night. Then he would drive off screaming with laughter.'

'That happened only once,' said Merrill. 'We were walking along a snowy road one day and had an argument. I don't remember what it was about, but she kept screaming in my face. She slapped me, so I pushed her into a snowbank.'

'He was a natural character, always up to some prank,' said Phil Stern. 'Once we were at the airport in Maine and he spotted William Buckley dressed in a suit and tie, standing at a pay phone. Gary was carrying this walking stick, and he went up and poked Buckley in the ass. "Hey, William Buckley, you big fucking faggot," Gary yelled at him, then poked him again. Buckley turned around, red livid with anger. He called for the police. A security guard came up, and when he saw it was Gary he said, "Mr. Merrill, behave yourself." They all knew him.'

At home, the children were not immune from their parents' rages. 'Bette was apt to take her frustrations and disappointments out on Michael,' said Merrill. 'In retaliation, I used B.D. as a target for my discontent.'

'All my husbands beat me. I don't seem to bring out the best in men,' said Bette, finally separating from Merrill in the spring of 1960. The split was amicable, she insisted.

'If a man is willing to give up his house, control of his kids, and everything else, divorce isn't much of a problem,' her ex-spouse claimed. 'I let go of all of it.' He did retain visitation rights to his son, Michael, and B.D. He was dropping them off at Bette's house in Los Angeles when an upstairs window 'flew open with a bang.' Sticking her head out of the window, Bette saw Gary's lovely companion, Rita Hayworth, and commenced to scream and yell, 'using language a hardened sailor would have thought music to his ears.' She kept it up for about five minutes, Merrill recalled. 'I thought, "Isn't that just like Davis! She wants everything her way. She doesn't want me, but she doesn't want me to be happy with anyone else either!" '

He yelled right back, of course, 'but the shit had hit the fan.'

The next day Bette went to court and tried to have his visitation rights revoked. 'If you fight me,' she warned the actor, 'it will be the dirtiest fight in history.'

Merrill fought. 'If I didn't she would tell the kids for the rest of their lives that their father didn't give a damn about them.'

Bette had Merrill followed by a photographer, who took pictures when he was with son Michael. In court, Bette produced the pictures and told the judge that Gary was a drunk. He had committed acts of violence and was 'having an affair with a woman to whom he was not married.'

Hayworth's name was mentioned, and the details of their unconventional romance came up in court. The couple were often seen walking around Beverly Hills with no shoes on. They had an open brawl at Au Petit restaurant in front of Rita's eleven-year-old daughter, Yasmin, Bette's lawyer said, providing a witness. 'I heard Rita screaming Bette's name at Gary and then the punches came. It was awful,' Jean Louis the owner of the restaurant testified in court.

On that evidence, Bette demanded she be given full custody of her son, with visitation rights of one hour every Christmas for Merrill.

The judge refused her request. 'I am starting a campaign to do away with *all* men,' said Bette to Hedda Hopper.

'My son, Michael, showed up at my door one day,' said Merrill. 'When Bette couldn't have full custody of him she packed up his things and said, "Go live with your father." She later abandoned our daughter Margot. She stopped paying for her care in 1965. Maybe I did fall in love with Margo Channing, but Bette shattered all my dreams.'

'Talk about life imitating art,' said *All About Eve* creator Joe Mankiewicz. 'Bette came up to me very drunk at a party two years after the divorce and she said, "Mankiewicz, you son of a bitch. You never told me the sequel." '

Throughout the winter of 1961 Bette and Joan were both living in New York, in the same East Side neighborhood. The two never met because each was busy indoors, dictating her memoirs to a professional writer. That summer, in need of more money, Bette decided to return to the Broadway stage. She heard of a new Tennessee Williams play – *The Night of the Iguana* – and solicited a part. The lead of the refined traveling spinster was already taken by the accomplished British actress Margaret Leighton which meant that Bette would have to take the secondary role of the boozy, bossy landlady, Maxine Faulk. 'None of us had originally thought of her for the part,' said literary agent Audrey Wood. 'Who could have expected her to subordinate herself to a character role that was nowhere near the equivalent of the leads she played in her halcyon days at Warner's?'

In signing up, Bette did not consider her role as peripheral. She demanded top billing and the star dressing room at all theaters. In Rochester, when the play opened, the performances were rough but the audience and critics seemed receptive. The following morning, when the reviewers gave most of their praise to the incandescent Miss Leighton, Bette checked out of her hotel and was taken to a hospital in a wheelchair. 'It seemed our co star had fallen backstage, the night before,' said Audrey Wood. 'Why this hadn't come out sooner, or why she had attended the opening night party, ostensibly in good physical shape, I cannot explain.'

Bette traveled by limousine to the next performance stop, Chicago, where she immediately found fault with director, Frank Corsaro. Censuring his theatrical training she insisted he be barred from rehearsals. 'He stayed out of the theatre,' said Tennessee Williams, 'but remained in Chicago. But Bette complained she could sense his lingering presence in the city, and said that he must be sent back to New York and "that goddamn Actors' Studio, which had spawned him." '

During the previews in New York, Bette, with newly dyed red hair, appeared for some performances and missed others. 'That happened so often that customers buying preview tickets would ask, with justification, "Is Miss Davis going to be playing in this performance?" ' said Audrey Wood.

She did show up for opening night, December 28, 1961. Making her entrance on stage Bette was greeted with an ovation from her fans in the balcony. She halted the play, turned to them, and raised her hands above her head, in a classic prizefighter's gesture.

The following morning she hit the canvas again, ko'd by the big-league critics who found Margaret Leighton to be poignant and magnificent. 'She reaches new levels in her illustrious career,' said Howard Taubman in *The New York Times*. Bette as Maxine, 'freshly widowed but not exactly shattered by grief, made much of her shocking flame-colored hair and her unbuttoned shirt that shows the flaccid flesh down to her waist,' said the *New York World Telegram*.

Throughout her protracted absences, co star Margaret Leighton had remained patient and kind to Bette. After the New York reviews, Davis turned on Leighton, calling her 'a bitch . . . so congenial . . . she makes me *sick*.' Fellow actor Patrick O'Neal was also frequently tongue-lashed. In retrospect, Audrey Wood realized that Bette should never have taken the part. 'Maxine, her character, is offstage for long periods during the play. When you have been a great film star, it must be difficult to sit backstage in your dressing room, with nothing to do but to wait for your next entrance.'

Early in January, one night after the show, there was a knock on Bette's dressing-room door There was a lady to see her, she was told.

'I don't know any,' said Bette.

She strode to the door and pulled it open; standing there, dressed in sables and jewels, was an angel of mercy, a savior come to rescue her from this rotten play with an exciting new film project.

The woman in the doorway was Joan Crawford.

18

WHAT EVER HAPPENED TO BABY JANE?

'I made a picture in 1934 too. But the studio didn't want to show my film. They were too busy giving a big build-up to that crap you were turning out.'
Baby Jane to sister Blanche

The project began with Bob Aldrich, producer and director of *Apache*, *Vera Cruz*, and *Autumn Leaves*. The latter starred Joan Crawford in 1955, and since then the director said, she pestered him to find another project for them to work on. 'She said she wanted to work with Bette Davis,' said Aldrich. 'I could never see them working together in anything. Then I read *Baby Jane*.'

The book, written by Henry Farrell, told of two sisters, former movie stars, who lived together in a dank forbidding mansion somewhere in Hollywood, bound to each other by mutual hatred. 'There was never a thought of doing the picture with anyone but Joan Crawford and Bette Davis,' said scriptwriter Lukas Heller. In July 1961, while filming *Sodom and Gomorrah* in Rome, Aldrich instructed his agent at William Morris to buy the film rights to the book for $17,500. That October he sent a first draft of the script to Joan Crawford. A week later she cabled him: 'When do we start?' In January, Joan visited Bette backstage at the Royale Theater on Broadway.

At that meeting there were no show-business kisses or embraces exchanged between the pair. 'Let's make this quick, Joan,' said Bette curtly, 'I'm going to the country in five minutes.'

Joan told Bette that 'at last' she had found the perfect film script for them to do together.

'*Together*?' said Bette with pursed lips and brows raised to her hairline.

'Yes, dear,' said Joan, 'I have *always* wanted to work with you.'

'I looked at her,' said Bette, 'and I thought, "This woman is full of shit." '

Joan gave Bette a copy of the book. Bette took it to the country, read it, and thought, 'Well, it could work, you know. It's all there. Phony Joan and Crazy Bette.'

In California that same month, when the script was completed, Aldrich mailed it with a letter to Davis. 'I took a lot of time composing a letter that was arrogant, but I thought it was necessarily so,' he said. 'I wrote "If this isn't the best screenplay you've ever read, don't see me." '

Bette replied that the script was OK, and she'd meet with Aldrich.

'She had only professional questions,' he said.

The first question was, 'What part will I be playing?'

'Jane of course,' said Aldrich.

'Good,' said Bette, 'I just wanted to be sure.'

The second question was of a more personal nature. Bette knew that Aldrich and Crawford had worked together before, on *Autumn Leaves*. She also knew that Joan had a habit of developing 'a meaningful relationship' with her male star or director, to give her a certain power. 'I did not know, or care, if she was the sexual athlete others have described,' said Davis. 'I just wanted to be sure there was no partiality involved.'

'Have you slept with Joan?' she asked the director.

'No,' said Aldrich. 'Not that I haven't had the opportunity.' (Joan tried to seduce Aldrich during production of *Autumn Leaves*, he told his dialogue director, Bob Sherman. 'She would sit in her dressing room at Columbia forever, drinking,' said Sherman. 'Sometimes she'd sleep there overnight. One night she called Aldrich in for a conference. She came on to him but he backed away at the last minute because he didn't want to be compromised. He told me he didn't want her to have anything over him, anything that he couldn't handle.')

Davis agreed to do the picture, with a few stipulations upfront. She wanted first billing, and more money than Joan. 'I offered both actresses a piece of picture plus some salary,' said Aldrich.

'Joan accepted, but Bette's agent held out for more than I could pay.'

Eventually a deal was struck. Davis would receive sixty thousand dollars in salary, plus ten percent of the worldwide net profits. Joan would receive less money upfront – thirty thousand dollars – and fifteen percent of the net profits. The film would be shot over a six-week period in Los Angeles in the summer of 1962, and both stars were assured of approval on costumes, makeup, and cinematographer.

With Bette and Joan set for the lead roles, Aldrich attempted to secure financing and a distributor for the picture. 'Four major studios declined to even read the script or scan the budget,' he said.

'I wouldn't give you one dime for those two washed-up old bitches,' said Bette and Joan's venerable old boss, Jack Warner.

To make the package more attractive, Aldrich considered adding a third name to the cast – that of Peter Lawford. He would play the part of Edwin Flagg, the overgrown mama's boy whom Baby Jane hires as her accompanist. Lawford accepted the part, then withdrew two days later, due to 'family' concerns. He felt the effete character might reflect badly on his real-life role as brother-in-law of the current President of the United States, John F. Kennedy. Aldrich then signed an unknown, twenty-six-year-old Victor Buono (which would bring the actor an Oscar nomination), and the package was offered to Seven Arts, a small independent company owned by an Englishman, Elliott Hyman, with Ray Stark as a vice-president. Hyman told Aldrich he would finance the film 'on very tough terms, because it's a high-risk venture. But we feel it should be made by you, and with Davis and Crawford.'

In February 1962, after the financing was secured, Jack Warner agreed to distribute the film, but he would not allow it to be made at his studio. His soundstages were tied up in production, primarily with the big-budget musical *Gypsy*, starring Rosalind Russell and Natalie Wood. For their comeback, Joan Crawford and Bette Davis would have to hike it over to the Producers Studio, a ramshackle lot reserved for B westerns on Melrose Avenue.

'Joan and I have never been warm friends. We are not simpatico. I admire her, and yet I feel uncomfortable with her. To me, she is the personification of the Movie Star. I have always felt her greatest performance is Crawford being Crawford.'

Bette Davis

'So I had no great beginnings in legitimate theater, but what the hell had she become if not a movie star? With all her little gestures with the cigarette, the clipped speech, the big eyes, the deadpan? I was just as much an actress as she was, even though I wasn't trained for the stage.'

Joan Crawford

That spring, while Bette played out her last weeks in *The Night of the Iguana*, Joan flew to Los Angeles and rented an apartment on Fountain Avenue, in a building owned and occupied by Loretta Young. On April 9, for renewed visibility, Joan got herself booked as a presenter on the Oscar show, in a major slot, the Best Actor category. On the day of the event, she arrived at the Santa Monica Auditorium at three in the afternoon, to supervise the placement of a wet bar and lavish buffet outside her dressing room. That evening she stood in the wings and corraled the (big) winners as they left the stage. Rita Moreno, winner of the supporting award for *West Side Story*, recalled her encounter with Joan. 'I was in tears coming off the stage when suddenly I found myself locked in the arms of this woman in diamonds. It was Joan Crawford. "There, there," she said, clutching me to her bony bosom, "I'll take care of you." One of the show's coordinators wanted to take me to the press room, to talk to the media, but Joan wasn't having any of that. She wouldn't let go of me. She took me to her dressing room, so we could be photographed together. A week after she sent me a thank-you note. It said, "Dear Rita, It was so thoughtful of you on your night of triumph to take the time to stop by my dressing room. Love, Joan." I thought, To take the time? She would have torn my arm from its socket if I tried to break away from her.'

'People couldn't see the chemical combustion of these two ladies who were so different. They act differently and they think differently. Their attitudes are so

different. You'd put them in a room and you know they've got to – in terms of theater – explode.'

Robert Aldrich

On May 9 Bette and Joan met in Hollywood to sign their contracts. Sitting at a table and posing for pictures, Bette managed to grab the best position. She sat in the far right chair, which meant that when the photo captions were read, from left to right, her name would be first. Joan, wise to this old trick, then stood up *behind* and to the right of Bette, ensuring that her name would be first in those shots.

When the actual signing of the contracts commenced, by mistake Joan was given Bette's contract. The error was quickly rectified, but not before Crawford's eagle eyes noticed that on page one, in addition to Bette's sixty-thousand-dollar salary, she was to receive six hundred dollars per week in living expenses. Two days later, at Joan's insistence, a new clause was inserted in *her* contract. It said that in addition to her salary she would receive fifteen hundred dollars per week for living expenses. Furthermore, if production on the film exceeded six weeks, she was to receive the same amount in overtime as her co star.

With Crawford to contend with and her own comeback to ensure, Davis moved into an expensive house in Beverly Hills and leased the flashiest car – a blue Cadillac convertible with a white top and white leather upholstery. The Beverly Hills house, rented in advance by daughter B.D., had a projection room, volleyball court, hillside gardens, a pool, and a pool house. Inside was a sweeping curved staircase, huge bedroom suites, and sliding glass doors everywhere. 'I must have been going through a Hollywood phase,' said B.D., who was fifteen at the time. 'Oh B.D.,' said Bette, 'not another one.'

Strolling by the pool, going over her lines for *Baby Jane*, Bette would frequently pause to admire her statuesque teenage daughter B.D. lying by the pool, acquiring a golden tan. 'Look at her!' said Bette. 'Great face, great body, and *smart* too. If I had a *fraction* of what she's got I'd be married to a millionaire and be miles *away* from this f---ing town.'

Meanwhile, in North Hollywood, Joan was preparing for her role as a cripple, by learning how to navigate in a wheelchair. 'I had to push myself around, wheeling myself back and forth,' she said. 'The exercise with the chair made me as firm and hard as a brickbat. I weighed only ninety-one pounds, the thinnest I was in years.' A Korean service veteran, a paraplegic injured in an air crash showed her how to get herself in and out of bed. 'He taught me how to hoist my body into the bed first and then lift each leg, and how to fall out of the chair – straight forward, and then roll over.'

The two stars met with costume designer Norma Koch a month before production. A concerned Joan told Bette, 'I do hope my color scheme won't interfere with yours.'

'Color scheme?' said Bette. 'I haven't a speck of color in any dress I wear. Wear any color you want. Besides, it's a black and white film.'

It was fun and a challenge to outfit Bette as Baby Jane, Norma Koch recalled. 'There were two distinct changes for Bette's character. As Jane, the sloppy housekeeper, when she was slouching around the house, drinking and being miserable to her sister, I tried to come up with the sleaziest outfits possible. Then as Baby Jane, when she was planning her career comeback, I designed grown-up versions of dresses of what a little girl would wear. They were supposed to be extensions of the child star she once was.'

The outfit that Bette wore in public, when she drove to downtown L.A. to place her showbusiness ad in the newspaper, 'had to be big Jane's idea of sexy,' said Koch. 'The dress had a see-through top, which clearly showed her grayish-white brassiere straps. It also had chipped pearl buttons down the front. I deliberately made the dress a half size too small, so she would look like one of those old chorus girls coming apart at the seams.'

The accessories were equally tawdry – a black waist cincher, a black velvet beret with a zircon clip, an old fox fur piece she pulled out of the closet, and for her feet she wore the classic Joan Crawford 'chase-me fuck-me pumps.'

'Yes,' said Koch with humor, 'the shoes were the final touch. We tried various styles with the outfit – some with stiletto heels, some were slingbacks; then someone, I'm not sure if it was Bette, said, "Why not get a pair of those old ankle-strap shoes, the ones Crawford used to wear in the forties?" We found a few pairs in the wardrobe department at Warner's. I'm not sure if they were Joan's, but they fit Bette perfectly.'

Crawford was also responsible, unknowingly, for Bette's outrageous platinum curls in the movie. After Davis had tested in the original blonde wig for *Baby Jane*, Bob Aldrich asked for a private word with Joan's personal hairstylist, Peggy Shannon. 'He had a problem with the wig,' said Shannon. 'Bette's hairdresser brought in this Shirley Temple-style wig from Max Factor. It didn't look right. Bob knew I had spent years at MGM, so he said to me, "Peggy, you worked on all those old musicals at MGM, can you help us out? We're desperate." That evening I went over to Metro and found this long platinum-blonde wig. I took it home and styled it, with curls and ringlets at the nape of the neck. The next day I brought it to Bette. She put it on, looked in the mirror, and in a loud voice said, "It's the NUTS! I love it!" She wore it through the entire picture, and she never knew that it was an old wig of Joan's – one that Miss Crawford wore in an early MGM movie.'

Norma Koch, who would win an Oscar for her *Baby Jane* costumes, admitted there were some slight wardrobe problems with Crawford. 'She wanted to wear her own negligees and dressing gowns. The negligees were low-cut and revealing, nothing an invalid or recluse would wear. I managed to talk her out of that by saying they were too lovely and new, that her character should only wear clothes that looked dated. After all, she was crippled, and her sister, Jane, hated her so much she wasn't about to go to expensive stores to buy clothes for her. Joan agreed on that, and then we discussed the day wear. The dresses she wanted to wear were short. They were supposed to show off her famous legs. But again I explained that her character had been in a bad automobile accident and, having been an ex-movie star, Blanche was vain and would never want to show off her disfigured legs. She went along with that, and I designed two high-necked nightgowns for her, a peignoir, and a flowing monk's-robe type of dress, which Joan insisted on wearing with a belt to show off her waist.'

When it was her turn to test her wardrobe for *Baby Jane*, Joan gave a full performance. 'The camera was on a track,' said Bob Gary, the script supervisor.

'Aldrich wanted to see how every costume photographed and what the makeup looked like. You started full-shot – then you dollied in from head to toe. By the time the camera got to Joan's face, she was crying. She was wearing the dress she was supposed to die in at the beach, so she must have concentrated on that, and the tears began to fall. She is the only person I had ever seen who cried at her own wardrobe tests.'

'The bitch could cry on demand,' Davis commented to Judith Crist.

Early in July, while rehearsals were under way, Jack Warner took advantage of the growing media interest in the teaming of Bette and Joan by hosting a welcome home luncheon for the two stars at Warner Brothers.

'The son of a bitch wouldn't let us film in his studio, and now he wants to give us a luncheon?' said Bette.

'Yummy,' said Joan. 'What should I wear?'

On July 18, at noon, wearing a colorful print dress, with her auburn hair rolled back in a chignon, Joan, flanked by Bette – also looking swell in a flowered hat, three gold bracelets, pearls, and two diamond sunburst pins attached to the scooped neck of her black silk-and-linen suit – entered the Trophy Room at Warner's accompanied by their former boss. All three Hollywood legends beamed broadly as the flashbulbs popped and the assembled press applauded this happy 'family' reunion. This was Bette's first visit home in fourteen years, and she was 'overwhelmed with emotion to see Papa Jack.' 'I can't exactly call you my father, Mr. Warner,' said Crawford, 'because I give that credit to the late Louis B. Mayer. But you are my second father.'

Talking to reporters, the two stars were ultra-careful to avoid even a hint of calumny toward each other. 'I have been waiting for twenty years to work with Miss Davis,' said Crawford.

'It's a good script and we expect to do good things with it,' said Davis. Of her character, she explained, 'It takes guts to hurt some-one. This woman minces no words. She's full of hate.'

Joan agreed. 'This is wonderful for me. I usually play the bitches. Now I can sit back in my wheelchair and watch Bette do it.'

'ALL RIGHT Blanche Hudson! Miss BIG FAT MOVIE STAR, Miss ROTTEN STINKING ACTRESS! Press a button . . . ring a bell . . . and you think the whole WORLD comes running. Don't you?'

Bette as Baby Jane

On Monday, July 23, filming on *What Ever Happened to Baby Jane?* began at the Producers Studio on Melrose Avenue. The call was for 9:00 A.M., and, at fifteen minutes to, Crawford arrived with her entourage – her hairdresser, makeup man, secretary, maid, junior agent from William Morris, and chauffeur, who carried a portable cooler filled with ice and bottles of Pepsi.

Bette Davis arrived alone.

Their dressing rooms were exactly the same size, placed at catty corners, at exactly the same distance from the soundstage. Bette's was to the right of the stage door; Joan's was on the left. After inspecting her trailer, Joan asked the studio carpenters to put in extra shelves and lights for her secretary, who would be answering the fan mail while her mistress emoted. 'Bette stood in the doorway of her dressing room, watching all this activity,' said photographer Phil Stern. 'When the carpenters left Joan's trailer, they passed Bette and asked if she wanted anything done. "Thank you, *no*," said Bette, in a voice loud enough for Joan to hear. "Dressing rooms do *not* make good pictures." '

Then the bestowal of gifts from Joan began. 'She had a deep and gnawing need to be liked, loved, admired, appreciated,' said Bette. 'She could be touchingly generous. She brought gifts for me to the set and presented them in front of the crew.'

Bette did not reciprocate. In a note thanking Joan for the gifts, she asked that she discontinue the practice: 'because I do not have time to go out and shop.'

In front of the cast and crew, the stars were 'painfully polite' to each other, said script supervisor Bob Gary. 'They were very careful how they behaved.'

Each star was a professional, said the director's seventeen-year-old son, Bill Aldrich, whose duties included knocking on the doors of their respective dressing rooms and saying: 'We're ready, Miss Crawford. We're ready, Miss Davis.' 'They were never late and they always knew their lines. Each one intended to outdo the other by being cooperative, because they needed this picture, and so did Bob Aldrich.'

The first scenes were done on stage two, in Blanche's bedroom. In the opening takes, director Aldrich told Davis that she was coming on too strong as *Baby Jane.*

'Who'd *cha* expect,' Bette shot back, 'Ann Blyth?'

Joan complained that the parakeet perched on her shoulder was pecking at the makeup on her face. 'It's a sign of affection,' the bird's trainer told her. 'Then we'd better find one that hates me,' the star snapped back.

During the first week, Bette Davis took her lunch breaks at Lucy's, a restaurant across the street from the studio. 'She would cross the street in her makeup and stop traffic,' said Phil Stern, 'so after that she stayed in the studio and ate with the rest of the guys.'

'Mother liked to be thought of as "one of the boys",' said daughter B.D., 'but that too was a performance.'

'Crawford could also be very cordial at times,' said Phil Stern. 'She wanted to show she could be a nice person too.'

Crawford would 'yell and scream,' said continuity girl Adelle Aldrich, 'and so did Davis, but afterwards she would teach me my job. I was only eighteen years old at the time, and that was my first job, to make sure things matched in the shots. My dad had told the ladies to give me a hard time. They both would question me very hard. Davis did it with great fondness. She was a wonderful teacher, and I'll forever be indebted to her. But Crawford was quite evil about it.'

At nightfall Joan departed as she had arrived, with an entourage. 'She had all kind of characters around her,' said Stern. 'There was her maid, her social secretary, her manager – this entire entourage would follow her. Then you'd see Davis – she's stepping over the cables on the floor – going home, alone.'

'Hollywood expected an eruption when Joan Crawford and Bette Davis got together for What Ever Happened to Baby Jane? *But it turned out to be love in bloom.'*

                                        Hedda Hopper

'Yes, I know. Everybody believed we would kill each other. But we fooled them. We were tempted to hang a sign on the set, saying, "Sorry folks, we're getting along beautifully." '

Bette Davis

'There is *no* feud,' Bette told Mike Connolly of the Hollywood *Reporter* after the first week of filming. 'We wouldn't have one. A man and a woman yes, and I can give you a list, but never two women – they'd be too clever for that.'

There was an implied test of strength between the two women, but 'they had to play that game of denying there was any competition between them,' said Bette's daughter B.D. 'Mother's favorite line at the beginning of the picture was, "We're just two professional dames doing our jobs." It was beneath them to compete with each other. Both felt so superior that they couldn't acknowledge their hatred let alone express it.'

On their first free Saturday evening, Bette and Joan had dinner with columnist Hedda Hopper at her home. 'The three of us were dressed in black,' said Hedda. 'As we sat down to dinner, I said we looked like three black-widow spiders.' For cocktails Bette made do with Hedda's scotch on the rocks, but Joan produced her own flask of hundred-proof vodka from her handbag. 'I say if you're going to have a drink, have what you want,' she declared.

The filming was going beautifully, they chorused.

'Joan is wonderful, she's going to win all the awards,' said Bette.

'No, no,' said Joan, 'Bette has Oscar written all over her performance.'

She had to concentrate very hard on getting into character every day, Bette admitted.

'I'm aware of that,' said Joan. 'You didn't say good morning to me for a full five minutes today.'

'I get absent-minded,' said Bette. 'And sometimes that can be mistaken for something else.'

Then there was the problem of the name-calling, said Joan.

'*Oh?*' said Hedda, alert and ready for some good old-fashioned nasty dish.

'Yes,' said Joan to Davis, 'you flip when they call you Bet, just as I do when they call me Jo-ann. I was amused today when you told someone: "If you called me Bette, I'd like you much better." '

'Yes,' said Bette, 'it can be tedious.'

Caught in the middle of this Girl-Scout debate, Hedda tried to liven up the proceedings by asking which star had top billing in the picture.

'We tossed a coin and I won,' said Bette proudly.

'She comes first,' said a smiling Joan. 'She plays the title role.'

A few cocktails later, after the trio had discussed Hollywood today ('A ghost town,' said Joan; 'It's been taken over by the agents,' said Bette), the two stars freshened up for the journey home. 'When Joan reached into her purse and began to apply lipstick, Bette immediately followed suit, applying lipstick to *her* mouth,' wrote Hedda. 'Then Joan exited first, in her chauffeur-driven car, while Bette called her secretary.'

AP reporter Bob Thomas was also treated to an act of sweetness and compatibilty between the two. 'A convincing performance,' he called it. 'The display of felicity persuaded everyone, perhaps even themselves. But it couldn't last. Inevitably, the spirit of competition entered into everything. They competed in their interviews, in their performances, in their relationships with the cast and the crew.'

By week number two, although the two stars were still pros in front of the camera during the day, at night their fangs began to show.

'My dad had to spend an awful lot of time trying to keep them happy,' said Bill Aldrich. 'But he never took sides. Luckily he had worked with some very tough guys in his time, so he played it right down the middle with the two ladies. He was just as tough as they were. Otherwise I don't think he would have survived.'

When the director arrived home at night, Crawford would call. 'Did you see what that (bleep) did to me today?' Joan would say. As soon as he hung up, the phone would ring again. This time it was Bette calling. 'What did that (bleep) call you about?' she would ask.

'Mother was on the phone to Aldrich for at least an hour every night,' said B.D. 'She would come home, take off her makeup, then, with hair flying all over the place, she would sit in her giant bed, in her master bedroom, with her papers all around her, and the phone. We would have to bring her dinner to her on a tray, then she would call Aldrich. She'd rehash everything that happened on the set that day that Aldrich had to apologize for – all the slights she suffered that were unfair – and the terrible things Joan had done to her, which he would have to prevent her from doing the following day. Then she'd go into discussing the next day's scenes and how they were really going to fix Joan tomorrow. And I always had this funny image of Joan Crawford calling Aldrich and saying the exact same things.'

'First one, then the other,' said Aldrich. 'I could rely on it every night. They were like two Sherman tanks, openly despising each other.'

Bette felt that Joan was deliberately trying to upstage her by not adapting to the pace of her performances. While she barked out such character lines as 'You *miserable* bitch!' Joan would respond with an air of heavenly grace, as if she were performing in a sweet Noël Coward drawing-room play.

'Bette had a certain tempo to her lines,' said Bob Aldrich, 'which Joan wouldn't respond to. She had her own, softer rhythm, which meant that when she came off her lines and Bette came in, Bette would have to slow down.'

'This is not a fairy tale, for chrissake,' Davis said to Aldrich at one point. 'Can't she at least snap back at me?'

'I will try, dear Bette, I will try,' said Joan the movie star.

'Oh, brother!' said Bette the actress.

'Crawford never reacted to anything,' said Lukas Heller. 'She sat in her wheelchair or in bed and waited for her close-ups. As the camera got closer, she would widen those enormous eyes of hers. She considered that acting.'

According to Aldrich, there were also some problems over the makeup the two stars wore for their roles in the film. Bette went to extremes with her cosmetic application. 'I wanted to look outrageous, like Mary Pickford in decay,' she said. 'It was my idea to wear the ghastly white base, scads of black eye shadow, a cupid's bow mouth and the beauty mark.' It was Crawford's hairdresser, Peggy Shannon, who suggested that Bette add more layers each day. 'I had worked with the extras in those Technicolored musicals at MGM,' said Shannon. 'We would give them these gorgeous faces. They were so in love with the way they looked, they never washed their faces. You would see them days later walking down La Brea Avenue with the original makeup still on. Each day they just added more. I told Bette that. She loved the idea. "Yes," she said, "that's it! I'll put it on with a shovel every day." '

As Bette became more hideous, Crawford insisted on improving her looks. When her original makeup tests were done, she fought with Bob Aldrich. 'She loathed the makeup he suggested she wear,' said Joan's makeup artist, Monte Westmore. 'He wanted Joan to be horrendously ugly, like Bette. For the test, I had to put huge lines under her eyes and the shadows on her face made her look like she had jowls. She looked rotten, like she had been on dope. Having been a glamour queen all her life, it upset her enormously to look like that. That was his concept, and we tested that way, but Joan would not approve the tests. So a compromise was reached; they met each other halfway.'

'Miss Crawford was a *fool*,' said Bette Davis. 'A good actress looks the part. Why she insisted on making Blanche look glamorous, I just don't know.'

'I am aware of how Miss Davis felt about my makeup in *Baby Jane*,' Crawford said in 1973. 'But my reasons for appearing some-what glamorous were just as valid as hers, with all those layers of rice powder she wore and that ghastly lipstick. But Miss Davis was always partial to covering up her face in motion pictures. She called it "Art". Others might call it camouflage – a cover-up for the absence of any real beauty. My character in *Jane* was a bigger star, and more beautiful than her sister. Once you've been as famous as Blanche Hudson was, you don't slip back and become a freak like Miss Davis preferred to see her character. Blanche also had class. Blanche had glamour. Blanche was a *legend*.'

'Blanche was a *cripple*,' Bette Davis argued. 'A recluse. She never left the house or saw anybody, yet Miss Crawford made her appear as if she lived in Elizabeth Arden's beauty salon.'

*   *   *

Ernest Haller, the cinematographer, had photographed Bette in *Jezebel* and *Mr. Skeffington*; and Joan in *Mildred Pierce* and *Humoresque*. On *What Ever Happened to Baby Jane?* he was told to forget the past: to photograph the characters, not the stars. 'If I lit either of them this way ten years ago they'd have my head,' he said. When asked on the set to choose his favorite star, the cinematographer diplomatically replied, 'In terms of sheer beauty, the most lovely face I ever photographed was Hope Hampton.'

According to the movie's editor Michael Luciano, both stars saw the rushes for the first few days, then stayed away.

'Why do I have to look so damn old?' Crawford said after viewing the early dailies. 'It's like I have a grandmother playing my part.'

'She started crying and crying that first week,' said Vik Greenfield. 'And Bette in exasperation finally said, "Joan, if you're so unhappy with this film, I'll play your part and you'll play mine." With that, Crawford broke down again and wept: "I can't play *her*. She's twice as ugly." '

Bette also sobbed when she first saw herself as Jane. Then she complained there were too many flattering close-ups of Joan.

'There were far more close-ups than the script called for,' Ernest Haller agreed.

'Mother had a tendency to find many things wrong,' said B.D. Hyman. 'She became so hysterical at the rushes she stopped going. But she never stopped complaining about Joan and her tricks.'

B.D., who had a small role in the film, had her own memorable encounter with her mother's rival. On the first day she was introduced to Joan Crawford, the star pulled back her hand 'as if I were diseased.'

Pointing to her twin daughters, Cindy and Cathy, who were sitting quietly on the sidelines wearing matching outfits and knitting, Crawford asked B.D. not to talk to the girls, ever. 'They have been carefully brought up and shielded from the wicked side of the world,' said Joan, 'and you obviously have not. I don't want your influence to corrupt them.'

B.D.'s mouth 'fell open.' When she repeated the tale to Bette, the star raged. 'How dare she pull that crap with me. I'll kill her. That bitch is loaded half the time.'

Joan spiked her Pepsi with vodka, Davis claimed. 'She had that bottle by her elbow every *minute*. When one was finished her secretary would bring her another. Everyone *knew* what was in it.'

'She used to drink "white water" on *Autumn Leaves*,' said Bob Sherman. 'It was a paper cup filled with vodka. She'd start drinking it after noon and continue throughout the day and night.'

'Bob Aldrich liked to drink Coke out of a paper cup,' said Phil Stern. 'When he had a case of the stuff brought in, Joan had a Pepsi vending machine set up. Every time his back was turned, she used to throw out his Coke and replace it with Pepsi. One day when they were casually going over the script, out of nowhere he said, "Furthermore Joan, I'd appreciate it if you'd stop filling my goddamn paper cup with Pepsi." '

But Pepsi was good for you, Joan told everyone. 'It helped indigestion and irregularity, and it was good for tired feet.' Taking her slippers off she would demonstrate, rolling the Pepsi bottle under each foot twenty times. 'It relaxes the tootsies and keeps your ankles thin,' she claimed.

'You hang around that woman long enough,' said Bette, 'and you'll pick up all *kinds* of useless shit.'

GOODBYE, NORMA JEAN

Although she was careful about saying anything nasty about co star Bette during the making of *Baby Jane*, Joan Crawford was not shy in chastising two other leading ladies of the day – Elizabeth Taylor and Marilyn Monroe.

In June, when 20th Century-Fox laid off two hundred workers, due to the thirty-million-dollar production costs and delays on *Cleopatra* and *Something's Got to Give*, Crawford felt it was time for her to rap both stars on the knuckles again. 'Miss Taylor is a spoiled, indulgent child, a blemish on public decency,' said Joan.

'It gets worse and worse with Marilyn,' said director Billy Wilder. 'It used to be you'd call her at 9:00 A.M. and she'd show up at noon. Now you call her in May and she shows up in October.'

Crawford it seemed had been quietly seething at Monroe since November of 1960, when Clark Gable had died. His heart attack, two days after the completion of *The Misfits*, had been brought on by the grueling hot sun in Nevada, and by Marilyn's chronic lateness, Crawford believed. So when the blonde star was fired by 20th Century-Fox in July of 1962, Joan was delighted. 'I was proud to be a part of this industry when Marilyn was fired,' she told Joseph Finnigan of UPI. 'I don't think she has a friend in this town, because she hasn't taken the time to make any. And the same with Liz. She's a taker, not a giver. She deserves the same as Marilyn, but nobody has guts enough to fire her. But she'll get it. Liz can get what Liz wants only for so long.'

On Sunday morning, August 4, Crawford was at home, immersed in her weekly ritual of facials, manicures and hair tinting, when the phone rang. It was answered by her maid. The caller was a reporter from the Associated Press. He spoke of Marilyn Monroe, who earlier that morning had been found dead in her bed. Her body was on the way to the city morgue, and the reporter wanted a quote from Joan. Gesturing wildly to her maid to hang up, Joan immediately called George Cukor, who had worked on Monroe's recently aborted Fox film, *Something's Got to Give*.

'Joan came to my house that evening,' said Cukor. 'She was in bad shape. She had been drinking. She was very angry. I thought at first she was angry at me. She kept saying, "Damnit, George, this shouldn't have happened! Something should have been done!" I felt she was being a hypocrite, as were many others in town. People who were nasty to Marilyn when she was alive, with good reason perhaps, were now gathered in a weeping circle. Eventually I said to Joan, "What is this? You never liked Marilyn." '

Joan answered, 'Yes! You're right. She was cheap, an exhibitionist. She was *never* a professional, and that irritated the hell out of people. But, for God's sake, she needed help. She had all these people on her payroll. Where the hell were they when she needed them? Why in hell did she have to die alone?'

'I hate this fucking picture, but I need the money, and if it goes over I'll get a nice percentage of the profits.'

Joan Crawford to writer Roy Newquist

As filming of *Baby Jane* continued, embellishments to the characters and plot were added by both stars. While Blanche was being starved to death by her evil sister, Joan lost weight in some areas of her body. As the hollows in her cheeks grew deeper and her waist grew smaller, her breasts became larger. 'Christ!' said Bette. 'You never know what size boobs that broad has strapped on! She must have a different set for each day of the week! She's supposed to be shriveling away, but her tits keep growing. I keep running into them, like the Hollywood Hills.'

Famished from hunger, in one scene Joan was to wheel herself to Bette's bedroom where she finds some chocolates hidden in a drawer and proceeds to gorge herself. Averse to chocolate, Joan, prior to the filming of the scene, had her maid wrap 'tiny chunks of chopped meat' in the candy box. Unaware of the substitute, Bette Davis, during a break in filming, reached for one of the fake bonbons, popped it into her mouth, began to chew, then gagged.

'Christ!' said Bette.

'Protein, Bette, protein,' said Joan. 'It's good for you.'

'Balls!' said Bette.

In the script another unsavory item was added to the invalid's menu. 'By the way, Blanche,' said Bette in the setup, 'I was cleaning the bird's cage when it escaped and flew away.'

That day, for lunch, Joan was served the dead bird, laid out on a bed of pineapple rings.

Columnist Sidney Skolsky said it was Bette who suggested the next *entrée*, and contributed the teaser line, 'By the way, Blanche, there are rats in the cellar.'

'I am not sure if it was in the original script,' said writer Lukas Heller.

'Bette proposed that, instead of a dead parakeet, they substitute a dead rat,' said Skolsky. 'Aldrich called the prop man, and a rat was found.'

Crawford, unaware of the switch, lifted the silver serving cover and 'screamed loud and clear, then fainted,' while Bette cackled loudly in the background.

'When I was at the Plaza Hotel in New York some months later, I gave a big cocktail party,' Bette told this writer, 'and I asked them to serve the pâté in the shape of a rat. When my guests lifted the serving cover, they were *horrified*. I laughed myself silly. It was a *wonderful* idea.'

During the third week of filming, Bette and Joan's respective autobiographies were released. 'Sisters under the celluloid . . . Hollywood's most bona-fide dazzzlers,' was how Bob Downing of *Variety* described them. The books were accurate reflections of the two stars' personas, the reviewer believed. Crawford's was sleek and shimmering 'with scarcely a jarring note,' while Bette's had 'flashes of venom . . . It is the truer reflection of a human being.'

Joan had the makings of a good book in her, said Bette, 'but this *isn't* it'; and Crawford observed that her rival's memoirs were depressing – due largely to the lack of men in her life. 'Poor Bette,' said Joan, 'it appears she's never had a happy day – or night – in her life.'

'*Whaaaatt*!' said Bette on hearing that. 'I've had affairs; not as many as her, but outside of a cathouse, who has?'

During a joint interview with reporter Joe Hyams, when Joan appeared with her book under her arm and placed it on the table in front of her, Bette excused herself, went to her dressing room, and returned with her book. When the Hyams piece appeared, he was obliged to feature both books, on either side of his column. Joan then proceeded to get herself booked, solo, on a local TV show. The afternoon it was scheduled to be shown, she asked Bob Aldrich if she could watch it at work. 'Bob Aldrich had a portable TV brought to the soundstage,' said Bob Gary. 'We all sat around this big oval table to watch the show. There was a chair for Joan, and one for Bette, and in between them Bette placed a chair for her *Baby Jane* doll. When the show began, Bette got up and went to a corner of the room where a phonograph was set up. As soon as Joan appeared on the TV, Bette turned on the phonograph and began to play her *Baby Jane* song ('I've Written a Letter to Daddy'). While Joan was trying to watch herself on TV, Bette was dancing and singing in the corner, as loud as she could. I've never seen her be that far-out rude to Joan before. Bob Aldrich is sitting there,

being quiet. He is walking on eggs the whole time. And Joan is a
model of control. Anyone else would haul off and belt Bette.'

'Mother would have *loved* a confrontation with Joan. But Crawford was too smart for her games,' said B.D. Hyman.

'You could never lay a glove on Joan Crawford,' Bob Sherman
believed. 'She came from MGM and Louis B. Mayer. When she
didn't like someone on a picture she would go to Uncle Louis and
say, "Cut his balls off, Uncle Louis. Or else I'm going to be
unhappy." And he would do her dirty work.'

By the fourth week of shooting, Bette had had it up to her
famous eyeballs with Joan's ladylike posturing and her pretense of
infinite patience. 'Bette came from Warner Brothers,' Bob Sherman
continued. 'Unlike Joan she was a very straight-on lady who
wouldn't go behind your back. She'd kill you right upfront. Once
during the movie she took off on me and hit me real hard.'

This was the day Bette filmed the sequence standing in front of
the rehearsal mirror. 'She sees herself for the first time as Baby
Jane and realizes what a hideous mess she is and screams,' said
Sherman. 'When it was over, she seemed upset, a little uptight.
We were standing outside her dressing room and, to comfort her,
I decided to remind her that the next day she was going to work
on the scene where she grabs a hold of Joan and batters her in
the music-room. I threw my arm around her and said, "Oh, don't
worry about it, Bette, tomorrow you'll get the chance to kick the
brains out of Joan." Suddenly she pulled back and said to me: "Oh
you think I'm *pretending* to be upset? You think that I'm being a
phony like *that* cunt?" And she proceeded to call me every dirty
name she could think of.'

The door to Crawford's trailer was open during Bette's tirade.
'Joan was in there listening,' said Sherman. 'And then I realized
what Bette was doing. She was yelling at me but tearing off in a
tangential way at Crawford. She couldn't do it directly to Joan
because Joan never gave her a chance. So I got it with both barrels
blasting, and while she was screaming at me, out of the corner of
my eye I could see Crawford's door slowly closing. Joan heard
everything. Eventually, to stop Bette, I said, "I'm sorry you feel
this way, because I like you." If I said, "I respect you," she would

have cut my head off. But like was a better word because how can you yell at someone who likes you? She said, "Oh, come on in," and we went into her trailer and had a drink.'

At home, as in previous times of vocational stress, Bette unleashed her repressed fury on her nearest and dearest. But, lacking a husband to fly at, and with daughter B.D. already grown to five feet ten inches ('I towered over Mother; she wouldn't touch me'), Bette had to aim her punches at her real-life sister, Bobby.

Recovered from two nervous breakdowns, Bobby was apparently still a source of irritation to Bette. 'She's *jealous* of me,' said the star. 'She's always *tried* to drag me down. But she's never won. Ha! Even her bouts in the loony bin were kept from the press and didn't hurt me. But they sure cost me a pretty penny, she was in the rubber room at Payne Whitney more than once . . . and what I went through visiting her I can't describe.'

Parallel to Blanche in *Baby Jane*, Bobby was dependent on her sister, Bette, for sustenance and survival. During the making of the film, she lived in a room above the garage at Bette's estate, and for her keep she worked as her sister's cook and housekeeper. But apparently she spoiled the children and spent too much money on food. One night, at dinner, she ruined the roast beef. Knocking the serving plate out of her sister's hand, Bette was 'actually about to kick her' when B.D. intervened. The brawl continued in the kitchen. 'Mother let go with one hand and hit her in the face. In an instant they were pulling each other's hair, kicking at each other, and screeching like a pair of alley cats.'

Banished to her room over the garage, Bobby told B.D. she forgave Bette. She was scared to be on her own, she said, and she understood Bette. 'She has pressures that she has to vent sometimes, and I'm a convenient target . . . but underneath it all I know she loves me.'

'I *do*,' said Bette. 'She's a tough customer, but she knows how to behave in my house, or I'll kick her out on her ass.'

'In the scene where I was supposed to imitate Joan over the phone, I wasn't able to do it. Joan had to dub in her voice for me. She was very pleased about that.'
Bette Davis

*'Nobody can imitate me. You can always see impersonations of Katharine
Hepburn and Marilyn Monroe. But not me. Because I've always drawn on
myself only.'*

Joan Crawford

To save time and money, while one unit was filming the exteriors of
the Hudson house on McCadden Drive, a second cameraman, strapped
to the front of the car, was filming Bette, driving her beat-up Lincoln
Continental along Wilcox Avenue and at Sunset and La Brea. At the
McCadden Drive house that evening, Bette arrived in time to witness
Joan being photographed through the iron bars of her upstairs bedroom
window. Set up on a huge crane outside the window, the camera was
supposed to zoom in on the imprisoned Blanche, clinging to her iron
bars, feebly calling out for help. As Aldrich yelled for action, Joan
wheeled herself to the window and lifted herself to the bars; as the
lens moved in for its horrifying close-up, the director, looking through
the viewfinder, saw a frightened but *fabulous*-looking Crawford. 'Joan
was wearing *lipstick* and ludicrously long *eyelashes*,' said Bette. 'It was
sooo funny. In her cry for help, my terrified co star insisted on looking like she was posing for the cover of *Vogue*.'

When *Life* magazine visited the *Baby Jane* set, Bette, in the name
of vanity, got to compete with Joan. A team had been assigned to
photograph various Hollywood stars, when Crawford and Davis
were added to the list. Assisting on the shoot was New York illustrator, Joe Eula.

'We needed an old-time but classy background for Bette and
Joan,' said Eula, 'so we decided to photograph them sitting on the
front of a vintage Rolls-Royce. I set it up. We rented the car in
Hollywood and drove it right up to the studio gates. Those doors
swung up like an airplane hangar, and we rolled that mother onto
a section of the soundstage. We had the lights set, and we were
ready for the two dames. It was fairly early in the day, and they
arrived wearing formal gowns, furs, and diamonds, behaving like
they always dressed like this for breakfast. Bette arrived first, and
Miss Crawford was late. So we sat and waited, and Davis was a
little miffed. But once Crawford arrived, the two pros got in there
and did their stuff. They arched their backs, threw their heads

back, and we were back in the golden days when these two superstars ruled the town.'

There were no pleasantries or dialogue exchanged between the two, Eula recalled. 'Not a word. That's why we had them sitting on the headlights, one on each side of the Rolls. We couldn't put them within arm's reach or the fur would really fly. It was over in twenty minutes. Then one went off with her Pepsi bottle full of vodka, and the other one muttered, "She's so fucking unprofessional." But somehow you could sense that deep down they respected one another.'

When filming ran behind schedule, the stars agreed to come in on a Sunday to rehearse the physically difficult scene where Baby Jane brutalizes her sister, Blanche. In rehearsals, Crawford agreed that there would be no stand-in involved. When the time came to shoot, she changed her mind. 'She amused *me*,' said Bette. 'Joan was really *not* my kind of actress. In one simple scene where I was supposed to slap her, I knew how to do it without hurting her. It's an old theatrical trick. All you do is cup your hand as you touch someone; the one being hit throws her head back, and the sound is added later. But she had her double play the scene, which made it very tense and awkward for me.'

The prelude to the terror – where Joan as the crippled Blanche lifts herself downstairs by the banister, then crawls to the phone to call the doctor – had been shot previously, and edited by Michael Luciano. 'We used a close-up of Joan on the phone, then cut to a long shot of Bette standing in the doorway behind her, watching. The next frame was of Joan. She senses she is being watched. She turns her head slowly, sees Bette and begins to babble incoherently. Then the violence begins.'

Crossing the hallway, Bette hangs up the phone, raises her foot, and viciously kicks Joan in the head with her shoe. She keeps on kicking her, savagely, across the hallway and into the living room.

'When it came to the actual filming of that scene, Crawford became afraid again. She said, "I'm not doing it. I don't trust Miss Davis. She's going to kick my teeth in." And she may have been right,' said Bill Aldrich.

A dummy was used for the close shots. While the hand-held camera stayed on Bette's face and upper body, her flying feet were kicking a mannequin, not Joan, across the room. 'She was kicking so hard and so viciously, we were all afraid she would break her foot,' said a cast member. 'And all the while, Joan Crawford is watching this from the side of the soundstage, not with fear or revulsion, but with fascination, pleasure almost, as if she enjoyed the thought of being abused by Bette.'

For the long range two-shots, Joan had to lie on the floor and keep rolling over, as if propelled by the kicking from Bette. As staged, Bette's right foot, encased in the familiar ankle-strapped shoe, was supposed to whizz past Joan without touching her. On one take, however, it was reported that she did indeed manage to make contact with the royal Crawford noggin.

Crawford screamed.

'I barely touched her,' Bette said without apology.

'She raised a fair-sized lump on Joan's head,' said Hedda Hopper.

'Her scalp was cut and required three stitches,' another writer reported.

'I don't believe that Bette ever hurt her,' said Bob Sherman. 'If she did, it was an accident. She was too much of a pro for that kind of behavior.'

'To my credit I have never indulged in physical punches, only verbal ones,' Bette claimed.

'There are those with the scars who would claim otherwise,' said Bob Downing of *Variety*.

Joan would of course be avenged. On Friday morning, August 24, the last scene in Blanche's bedroom was shot. Bound and gagged and strung up underneath a spotlighted portrait of herself, Joan was to be united, then carried from the room by Bette. Because of the camera setup, Crawford knew no double could be used. She was determined that Davis experience her full star weight, and more.

'There is a way of making it easy on the actor who is doing the carrying,' said Bob Aldrich, 'but Crawford wanted Bette to suffer every inch of the way.'

To add to the burden, it was said that Joan had weights strapped on underneath her long gown.

'I was told it was a special weightlifter's belt, lined with lead,' said author Hector Arce.

'I'm not sure just what she had on, but you could clearly see that when Bette lifted Joan off the bed, she was straining herself,' Bob Gary recalled.

'It was a long, difficult scene,' said Lukas Heller. 'Bette had to lift her from the bed, carry her across the room and into the hallway.'

In the first try, halfway across the room, Joan, who was supposed to be unconscious, began to cough and opened her eyes, which meant that the scene had to be done over.

'There was no break in the shot,' said Heller. 'It was one continuous take. Bette carried her from the bed across the room and out the door. Then, as soon as she got in the hallway, out of the camera's range, she dropped Joan and let out this bloodcurdling scream.'

'It was the most terrible scream I have ever heard,' said Bob Gary. ' "My back! Oh, God! My back!" she screamed as Joan got to her feet and strolled contentedly back to her dressing room.'

'AND STILL NO FEUD'

'With one more week to go on the filming of What Ever Happened to Baby Jane?, *the film is on schedule and there is still no feud between the stars. Bette feeds her lines off-camera to Joan for her close-ups.'*
                                    A press release from Warner Brothers

'Tomorrow we're going to do that goddamn beach scene, my big scene, but just watch. She'll find a way to steal it. She always does. When you play crazy ladies you always walk away with the honors.'
                                    Joan Crawford to writer Roy Newquist

The final sequence of the movie took place on the beach, where Baby Jane brings her crippled and battered sister to die. According to Bette's memoirs, *This'n That*, the filming at the beach was canceled because Joan was drinking heavily and could not stand the heat of the outdoor sun. 'Alcohol in the body makes one perspire freely,' said Bette.

'Joan wasn't drinking at the beach,' said Adelle Aldrich, confirming that the shots were done outdoors.

'We worked three days at Zuma Beach,' said Peggy Shannon.

'It was two days, near Paradise Cove,' Bob Gary believed.

'All I remember is that it was hot,' said Phil Stern, 'and Bob Aldrich had a hell of a time trying to keep the dolly tracks on the sand.'

According to the production logs, Bette stayed at a motel in Trancas, while Joan commuted by limo. Both stars were accompanied by their daughters, Bette with B.D., Joan with her daughters, Cindy and Cathy. But again no socializing was allowed between the girls. Joan's daughters, clad in long shirtwaist dresses, strolled on the beach a respectable distance from the filming, while fifteen-year-old B.D. stayed near the action, wearing a white two-piece bikini to perpetuate her tan and titillate the young males on the crew (who stripped down on their lunch break and cooled off in the ocean).

The sequence where Baby Jane, totally unhinged, sits on the beach making sand castles while her sister lies dying beside her was vital for the plot, and for Crawford. This was her big acting scene. It ran for four pages. Lying in the sand, emaciated and near death, Joan was to look up at Bette and confess that it was she who had caused the long-ago accident that crippled her legs and drove her sister half mad with guilt. 'You mean, after all this time, we could have been friends?' was Bette's one-line reaction. The rest of the time she was supposed to shut up and listen to Joan.

For days, Joan was sure that Bette would do something to steal the scene. 'Oh, she'll roll her eyes, or blow her nose. She'll think of something to bring the attention to her,' said Crawford.

But during the first take of the scene, Bette was a pro. She made no effort to upstage her co star. With parched lips and wide eyes, Joan gave a flawless delivery of the lengthy dialogue. When it was over, Bob Aldrich clapped his hands and yelled, 'Wonderful!' Ignoring Joan, Bette turned to the director and said, 'Thank *you*, Bob.'

'It was a tough scene to shoot, because Aldrich wanted different camera angles,' said Bob Gary. 'It was also harder on Joan than on Bette. Bette could get up and move about, but Joan had to lie there in the hot sun. Bette was also wearing white, while Joan wore a long dark robe, which absorbed the heat.'

'They had two guys standing over her, holding these huge scrims to shield her from the sun,' said Hector Arce, 'but the alcohol in her system was dehydrating Joan.'

'As soon as Bob Aldrich yelled "Cut," ' said Bob Gary, 'Joan would get up from the sand and get into her limo, which took her to her dressing room, parked a hundred yards away.'

In one setup, when Joan came back from her trailer and resumed her prone position on the beach, Bob Aldrich turned to script supervisor Gary and said, 'Bob, do you think she's getting younger?'

'It was a subtle change,' said Gary. 'Every time Joan went to her trailer, Aldrich suspected she was making herself more glamorous. She was supposed to be dying, but when it came right down to it, Joan had been such a glamour queen all her life that it was hard for her to look bad. She kept taking off her dying makeup, bit by bit, adding softer makeup.'

Bette Davis told of another Crawford metamorphosis. Dying on the beach, Joan decided to wear her largest falsies. 'Let's face it,' said Bette, 'when a woman lies on her back, I don't care how well endowed she is, her bosoms do not stand straight up. And Blanche was supposedly wasted away after twenty years. The scene called for me to fall on top of her. I had the breath almost knocked out of me. It was like falling on two footballs!'

'In the very last shot of What Ever Happened to Baby Jane? *Bette Davis goes off to buy an ice-cream cone for her sister. Almost magically, the grotesque makeup and wrinkles disappear from her face as she does a dance of liberation.'*

Ciné Fantastique magazine

Although the battle of the Hudson sisters was settled with Blanche's dying confession, the combat between Bette and Joan continued straight through and beyond the end of filming. To compete with the expiring, glamorous Joan, there was considerable speculation that Bette added some cosmetic improvements to her appearance for the famous waltz-of-liberation scene that ended the movie.

'This may be spurious,' said Bob Gary, 'but Bob Aldrich believed that when Bette saw what Joan Crawford was doing, she decided to pretty herself up a little for her final shots in the picture.'

On the last day at the beach, Bette went to lunch and was unusually late in returning. 'What Bob Aldrich suspected was that Bette went to her motel and had her own makeup man, Gene Hibbs, drive over from the Valley. He was a master at those instant face-lifts, of using tapes and hair clips to pull back the loose facial skin. He worked on her face in the motel. There was no way she was going to let the movie end with Crawford looking better than she.'

On returning two hours later, Bette told Aldrich she had been in a car crash. 'She told this long, involved story that she had to bring B.D. to the hospital,' said Bob Gary.

'But we *were* in a car crash,' B.D. said in 1988. 'Mother was a very nervous driver. She was always crashing into people on the highway. Gene Hibbs may have been at the motel, but I never saw him. And I was there for most of the filming.'

The beautification of Bette in the final scene was 'a photographic phenomenon,' said Joan Crawford's makeup artist, Monte Westmore. 'When Bette came back late, the sun had shifted to the west, over the ocean. In order to balance out the light on Bette, who had her back to the beach, the cameraman brought in an arc, facing her. The key light was so intense it burned out every wrinkle on her face and made her look like a little girl again.'

'Baloney!' said Bette, refusing to share any artistic credit. Her transformation had nothing to do with the cosmetic or technical expertise of *others*; it was *her* genius, her acting talent. Script girl Adelle Aldrich agreed. 'I was at the beach, playing cards with Bette, and twenty minutes before the scene was shot she asked for some time by herself. She walked down the beach alone, and when she came back there was this glow on her face. It was the most amazing thing I've ever seen. It came from within her and reflected on her face.'

Bette's genius also reflected on Joan Crawford's ego. After watching the rushes the following day, the star called Bob Aldrich to her dressing room. She told him the final shots in the picture didn't match. It was apparent that Bette's lighting was better than hers, and she insisted that her dying scene be redone.

'My dad had to agree with Crawford,' said Bill Aldrich. 'The lighting for her last scene wasn't good enough. But we couldn't bring sixty people back to the beach.'

'So a set *had* to be built at the studio and *tons* of sand brought in,' said Bette Davis.

'The retakes added sixty thousand dollars more to the budget,' said Bill Aldrich. 'And for that the studio took away some of my dad's profit points. But he felt it had to be done. If that scene didn't work, the entire picture didn't work.'

On Wednesday, September 12, 1962, after thirty-six days of shooting, *What Ever Happened to Baby Jane?* was finished. The total cost was $980,000. On Friday evening the traditional wrap party was held on the soundstage at Melrose Avenue.

'I don't remember seeing Miss Crawford there,' said Joe Eula.

'As far as I know, Joan had already returned to New York, to do something for Pepsi,' said Peggy Shannon.

'Joan was smart,' said a cast member. 'She knew that when the picture was finished, Bette would be lying in ambush for her. At the party, with a few drinks, Bette might attack. So Joan skipped the proceedings.'

Actress Ann Barton, who played the mother of Jane and Blanche Hudson, recalled Bette coming over to her table during the evening. 'In her definite intonations she said, "You know, Blanche resembles your side of the family." There was no great love between Bette and Joan, we all knew that. And Bette's last words to us were: "That *woman*. That *woman* should be here tonight. That *woman* should not have gone to New York. That *woman* owes it to Bob Aldrich to be here tonight!" She took a deep drag on her cigarette and regally moved on, murmuring, "That *Woman* . . . That *Woman* . . ." '

'She was mouthing at Crawford all the way through the party,' said Joe Eula. ' "Look at that," she'd say. "The bitch didn't even show up. *That's* professional?" We all thought she'd be happy that the movie was over and she wouldn't have to look at Joan again. But no. It seemed that Miss Davis wasn't quite through with Miss Crawford. There was still some unfinished business to attend to.'

THE SELLING OF BABY JANE

'Maybe they should put us in cages when they promote the picture.'

Joan Crawford

'If Bette Davis and Joan Crawford come to blows during the promotion of their film What Ever Happened to Baby Jane?, *it is now possible to make book on the probable winner, Bette Davis. Each of these movie queens has a good right cross and left hook, and both are formidable in-fighters. But Bette Davis is the more aggressive. She can take out an opponent with one punch.'*

Brooks Atkinson, *The New York Times*, September 8, 1962

When filming was completed, Bob Aldrich was asked by Warner's to do a very fast edit of the picture. The studio had signed a deal with The Theater Owners of America. A new exhibition concept was about to go into effect. *What Ever Happened to Baby Jane?* was chosen as the first movie to inaugurate the new 'Showcase Premiere' policy. Instead of booking the film in first-run city theaters, Warner's would open it in four hundred neighborhood theaters throughout the country. To meet the November date, the film had to be edited and scored in thirty days.

'It was a tough schedule,' said Michael Luciano, 'but we met it, because the stuff Bob shot was all good. He was a rare talent and a gentleman. The man could direct anything.'

On October 20 the first preview was held in Long Beach, California. The audience, enticed by a movie ad that read, *'A new thriller – starring Bette Davis and Joan Crawford'* – relished the film, applauding five scenes. Some young patrons wanted to sit through a second showing. 'They're going to have a hard time hiding the profits from this one,' said Bob Aldrich.

The following Monday the producer-director flew to New York to show the picture to the Warner's East Coast executive and publicity staff. Again, the reaction was positive. That Thursday evening Aldrich attended a press party at the 21 Club, with his stars, Bette Davis and Joan Crawford.

Bette, accompanied by her secretary and daughter B.D., was

dressed in pearls and a dark-blue satin evening coat. Joan, with four male escorts, wore a full-length mink, rubies, an aqua turban, and an aqua cocktail dress.

By careful design, the Warner's press officer placed the stars at opposite ends of a long table. 'At one point, Crawford was getting all the attention,' said a reporter, 'so Davis climbed atop a table and bawled: "Everybody down here." ' Crawford, according to Davis' daughter, then 'gave a haughty wave of her hand towards Mother and called "Hello darling Bette. Bless you". Mother leaped out of her seat, thrust forth her arms as though to embrace the multitude and emoted: "Jesus! Look at that broad! The turban matches the blouse which matches the jacket which matches the skirt which matches the shoes and gloves. Shit!" She threw back her head and gave vent to a wild cackle, slapped her thighs and finished, "Can you believe her? She looks like she just came from a fire sale in Macy's basement!" '

On Friday evening, October 23, 1962, a special invitational preview of *Baby Jane* was held at the RKO Eighty-sixth Street theater on Manhattan's Upper East Side. Jack Warner attended with producers Elliot Hyman and Ray Stark. Joan Crawford showed up with a contingent of Pepsi executives and their children. Bette Davis was missing.

'This was the official preview for the press,' said Crawford, 'so naturally I was apprehensive.'

'For months, the word in the industry was that Bette and Joan had thrown what was left of their careers down the toilet by doing this B movie,' said a New York critic. 'No one expected it to be any good.'

'The preview was a smash,' said Crawford. 'It took me thirty minutes to get through the lobby to reach my car.'

On November 3, Election Day, the film opened nationally. The major reviews were glowing and spicy.

'A brilliant tour-de-force of acting and film-making,' said *Time*.

'A superb showcase for the time-ripened talents of two of Hollywood's most accomplished actresses,' said *The Saturday Review*. 'Scenes that in lesser hands would verge on the ludicrous simply crackle with tension.'

'Fine, horrific fun . . . Take it straight, and you'll recoil from a murderous duel of snarls, shrieks, moans and rattlesnake repartee by Bette Davis and Joan Crawford,' said *The New York Times*.

Some of the critics took sides, praising Bette while panning Joan, and vice versa.

'As an ugly old hag, Bette Davis with her ghastly layers of makeup and her shuffling-clump walk, is rather appealing. And Joan Crawford is – oh, just Joan Crawford,' said *Newsweek*.

'Joan is such a sweetly smiling fraud. Such an artless helpless ninny, that one feels virtually nothing for her. No wonder her crazy sister finds her a deadly bore,' said *The Nation*.

'Miss Davis, with the mind of an infant has something of the force of a hurricane. Miss Crawford could be described as the eye of that hurricane, abnormally quiet, perhaps, but ominous and desperate,' said the *New York Telegraph and Sun*.

'Crawford wisely underplays with Davis,' said *Variety*. 'In one superb bit, she reacts to herself on television making her face glow with the remembrance of fame past . . . A genuine heartbreaker.'

'My absolutely *favorite* notice came from the *New Yorker*,' said Bette. 'They had this cartoon of two women standing under a marquee of the theater. "I like Bette Davis," said one woman, "and I like Joan Crawford. But I don't think I'd like Bette Davis and Joan Crawford *together*." '

'Sure, she stole some of my big scenes, but the funny thing is, when I see the movie again, she stole them because she looked like a parody of herself, and I still looked liked something of a star.'

Joan Crawford

It had been announced that Crawford and Davis would make a cross-country tour of theaters showing the film, but a week before the tour Crawford canceled, without apology or explanation. 'She was afraid to share the stage with me,' said Bette, who also attempted to drop out midway through the tour.

'Somewhere along the way Davis got upset,' said Bill Aldrich. 'She said she was walking out and coming home. My dad had to get on a plane and go to her.'

'Mother was having one of her usual star tantrums,' said B.D. Hyman, who joined Bette onstage at theaters in New York.

'We had *terrific* fun,' said Bette. 'I sang my song and gave out dolls to people in the audience. Sometimes a fan would shout out, "Where's your sister? Where is Joan *Crawford*?" And I would answer, "She's *dead*! On the beach at Malibu." And everybody laughed and laughed.'

Appearing on Jack Paar's TV show, Bette told the story of how Jack Warner had initially turned down the movie, refusing 'to put up one nickel for us two old broads.' The following morning, at her hotel, Bette received a telegram. It read, 'Dear Miss Davis, Please do not continue to refer to me as an old broad. Sincerely, Joan Crawford.'

'Oh for chrissake!' said Bette. 'I was only referring to what the moneymen said.'

THE OSCARS

In January 1963, during the preliminary canvassing for Oscar nominations, Warner Brothers pushed Bette and Joan as Best Actress for *Baby Jane*. In February when the nominations were released, only Bette made the list (with Anne Bancroft for *The Miracle Worker*, Geraldine Page for *Sweet Bird of Youth*, and Lee Remick for *The Days of Wine and Roses*).

When asked to comment on her loss, Crawford said, 'But I always knew Bette would be chosen, and I hope and pray that she wins.'

'That's so much *bull*!' said Bette. 'When Miss Crawford wasn't nominated, she immediately got herself booked on the Oscar show to present the Best Director award. Then she flew to New York and deliberately campaigned *against* me. She told people *not* to vote for me. She also called up the other nominees and told them she would accept their statue if they couldn't show up at the ceremonies.'

Dorothy Kilgallen reported that Anne Bancroft, acting in *Mother Courage* on Broadway, had requested Patty Duke accept for her. 'But Patty is also up for an award and will not be allowed to accept for Bancroft. So Joan Crawford will do the honors if she wins,' said Kilgallen.

'I received a lovely note of congratulations from Miss Crawford,' said nominee Geraldine Page. 'And then she called me. I was tongue-tied, very intimidated in talking with her. To me she was the epitome of a movie star. I always loved her movies. In fact, the character I played in *Sweet Bird of Youth* was said to be based partly on Joan Crawford. That's what I heard. In the movie I also used certain things I admired about her, and about Bette Davis. When I walked down the stairs in the filming of the movie scene – I had seen Bette do that in one of her movies. And later when I'm in the theater watching that scene, I lowered my glasses and looked over the rims at the image of myself on the screen. I had seen Joan Crawford do that in a photograph from one of those old movie magazines. Growing up, I was a big fan of Bette Davis and Joan Crawford. As a teenager, I had seen almost all of their movies. But when Miss Crawford called, I told her nothing of that. I was tongue-tied. All I could manage was, "Yes, Miss Crawford. No, Miss Crawford." When she mentioned about accepting the Oscar for me if I won, I said yes. Actually I was relieved. That meant I wouldn't have to fly all the way to California, or spend a lot of time looking for a new dress to wear. I was happy and honored that Joan Crawford would be doing all of that for me.'

On the evening of April 8, the thirty-fifth annual Oscar cere-monies were held at the Civic Auditorium in Santa Monica. That entire day, Crawford prepared for her dazzling appearance. Her silver-beaded gown had been designed by Edith Head. Her diamonds, for her wrists, ears, and neck, were on loan from Van Cleef and Arpels. Her hair, which had been washed and set and curled by Peggy Shannon, was dusted with a fine silver powder to match the rest of her combative glitter.

In her new Colonial-style house on Stone Canyon in Bel Air, Bette Davis was also giving special attention to her appearance for the Oscar show. Her dress was likewise by Edith Head. Her face had been rejuvenated by minilift expert Gene Hibbs, and the evidence, the adhesive tapes and clips, was covered over by a fetch-ing auburn wig with bangs. Before leaving the house, Bette 'had a long talk with my two tarnished Oscars on the mantelpiece. And I promised to bring them home a baby brother.'

That she would win was a foregone conclusion to Bette. 'I was positive I would get it, and so was everybody in town.'

Escorted by Cesar Romero, Joan Crawford was the first arrival at the Civic Auditorium and 'made a beeline for the fans, getting down on her knees to sign autographs for some of the blocked-off people.'

When asked by a TV reporter whom she had voted for in the Best Actress category, Joan deftly answered, 'The winner!'

Bette arrived with daughter B.D., son Michael, and Olivia de Havilland, who told reporter Amy Archerd that she had flown in from Paris for this important occasion. 'Bette deserves to win. She's the greatest and the industry owes her this,' said Olivia.

'Yes, I want that Oscar,' Davis told Archerd. 'I *have* to be the first to win three.'

Backstage, Crawford once again held court. In the main dressing room, she had a wet bar set up, with Pepsi coolers filled with bourbon, Scotch, vodka, gin, champagne – 'plus four kinds of cheese and all the fixings.' She also had a large TV monitor installed, so her guests could watch the show as it unfolded on stage. 'Look at that Eddie Fisher, giving newcomer Ann-Margret all the camera angles,' said Joan. 'He sure has a way with the ladies.'

Down the hall, in Frank Sinatra's dressing room, Bette sat holding hands with Olivia de Havilland.

As the final top five awards came up, Crawford, Bette, and Olivia moved from backstage to the wings. Joan looked radiant and to show her admiration, Bette Davis went up behind her to kiss her on the back of the neck. 'Thank you, dear,' Joan whispered. 'It was the nicest thing a human being could do,' Crawford told reporter Len Baxter, 'so dear of her, so gentle, and I was deeply touched. I really thought we were friends.' ('That *nevah* happened,' said Davis when she was told of the report.)

To the strains of 'Some Enchanted Evening,' Joan swept onstage to present the Best Director award, to David Lean for *Lawrence of Arabia*. As Lean and Joan exited arm in arm, Bette Davis came onstage, to present the award for Best Original Screenplay. In an aside to the audience, she said that the writers she had known during her long career 'were among the surliest in Hollywood.' After stumbling over the pronunciation of the foreign names, she ripped the envelope open and said the winners were 'Those three difficult Italian names, for *Divorce Italian Style*.'

Then the big moment arrived – the category of Best Actress. Contender Bette and surrogate receiver Joan stood in the wings, three feet apart, chain-smoking. As Maximilian Schell stood onstage, reading the names of the five nominees, Bette handed her purse to Olivia de Havilland. Opening the envelope, Schell paused, then announced: 'The winner . . . Anne Bancroft for *The Miracle Worker*.'

'I almsot dropped *dead* when I heard Miss Bancroft's name,' said Bette. 'I was *paralyzed* with shock.'

'Joan stood instantly erect,' said TV director Richard Dunlap, 'shoulders back, neck straight, head up. She stomped out her cigarette butt, grabbed the hand of the stage manager, who blurted afterwards, "she nearly broke all my fingers with her strength." Then with barely an "excuse me" to Bette Davis, she marched past her and soared calmly on stage with the incomparable Crawford manner.'

'Bette bit into her cigarette and seemed to stop breathing,' said Dunlap. 'She had lost the award. Joan was out *there* – suddenly it was *her* night.'

'*I* should have won,' said Bette. 'There wasn't a doubt in the world that I wouldn't. And Joan – to deliberately upstage me like that? She was actually preening on stage. Like *she* was the winner. Her behavior was despicable.'

'Disloyalty never entered my mind,' said Crawford. 'If Geraldine Page had won, I'd have been glad for her. I'm working for an industry, not an individual.'

'The triumph of the evening,' said *Time*, describing Joan Crawford as she posed backstage with the winners.

'She kissed Gregory Peck, she kissed Patty Duke, she kissed Ed Begley. She would have kissed the doorman and the limo drivers too, if it meant she could get another photograph taken,' said Sidney Skolsky.

In her column the next day, Hedda Hopper summed up the event. 'I was rooting for Bette. But when it comes to giving or stealing a show, nobody can top Joan Crawford.'

19

BETTE BOUNCES JOAN FROM CANNES

In February 1963, to launch the film in Europe, Elliott Hyman, president of Seven Arts, instructed Bob Aldrich to invite Bette Davis and Joan Crawford to attend the showing of *What Ever Happened to Baby Jane?* at the Cannes Film Festival, then fly to London for the British premiere.

In the aftermath of the Oscars, one invitation was rescinded.

'Basically Mother didn't want to go to Cannes,' said B.D. Hyman. 'She preferred to stay home. I was the one who bulldozed her into going. I was sixteen, I wanted to see Cannes. Mother gave in and issued an ultimatum to Bob Aldrich. She said, "I'll go, but *not* with Joan Crawford. I won't share it with her." '

Bette Davis was a bigger draw in Europe, and it was up to Aldrich to tell Joan that she was disinvited.

Crawford, in 1973, said it had been *her* decision not to go. 'Those festivals are a zoo, a real zoo,' she said. 'And I didn't care to subject myself to any more unpleasantness from Miss Davis.'

The producer's files at the American Film Institute told another story. When her invitation was rescinded, Crawford threatened to bring legal action against Bob Aldrich and Bette Davis, whom she felt was maligning her reputation.

'Mother was telling these silly stories about how Joan took the Oscar to bed with her on the night of the awards,' said B.D.

'She wouldn't give the damn thing up,' said Bette. 'She packed it in her luggage the next day and carried the award with her on a trip around the world for Pepsi Cola. It was six months before she even let Anne Bancroft *see* her Oscar.'

On May 5, 1963, Crawford's lawyers in New York, Seligson and Morris, dispatched a telegram to Bob Aldrich Associates. It read in part: 'On behalf of our client, Joan Crawford, we hereby advise you that you will be held liable and accountable for all loss, damage, and injury sustained by her in connection with your actions relating to her attendance at the Cannes Film Festival and further that you and Miss Davis will be held strictly accountable for any false or misleading statements or publicity concerning the circum- stances under which you have canceled arrangements for Miss Crawford to attend the aforesaid Festival.'

On May 6 Aldrich's law firm, Prinzmetal of Beverly Hills, responded. They advised Crawford's lawyers that their client could not 'be respon- sible for any false or misleading statements or publicity which may be issued by Miss Davis, have no reason to believe that such statements were or will be made by Miss Davis, or by Mister Aldrich.'

A copy of the wire was sent to Davis' lawyer, Tom Hammond, who was told, in short, to advise Bette to put a lid on it when it came to the topic of Joan Crawford. On arriving in Cannes, with Aldrich, Davis told the packed press conference at the Carlton Hotel that she had no idea why her co star wasn't along for the trip. 'Certainly she was *invited*,' said Bette, 'but Joan is a busy, *busy* woman. And I know we will all miss her *terribly*!'

THE FEUD ROLLS ON

When the profits from *Baby Jane* were tallied that July, another dispute arose. The gross on the income statement from Warner's-Seven Arts was $3.5 million, and not the ten or twelve million dollars that was widely mentioned. After the negative and distri- bution costs were deducted, Crawford received approximately $150,000 and Bette, seventy-five thousand dollars minus thirty thou- sand for repayment of a loan Aldrich Associates had advanced to her as a down payment for the purchase of Honeysuckle Hill, her new Colonial-style home in Bel Air.

Dissatisfied with her share from *Baby Jane*, Bette requested that her lawyer be allowed to examine the books at Warner's, but the figures were confirmed by Bob Aldrich and, close to broke again, Bette had to solicit work. The previous September, when *Baby Jane* wrapped and no other scripts were forthcoming, she had placed a 'situation wanted' advertisement in the employment section of *Variety*. All of Hollywood, and Joan Crawford, expressed amazement that the great Davis would openly ask for work. 'I would pack my bags, get on a bus, and work as a waitress in Tuscon, before I would belittle my name by begging in public for a job,' said Joan.

'Every time the goddamn widow Steele holds up a bottle of Pepsi Cola they give her a thousand bucks,' said Bette, lashing back. 'I am *not* Joan Crawford. I am *Bette Davis*, a working mother.'

The ad was a joke, Davis later claimed, as were some of the offers it produced. She was offered the role of Dick Van Dyke's mother in the Vegas production of *Bye, Bye, Birdie*. She declined, but agreed to guest-star on TV's *Perry Mason* and to sing and dance on the Andy Williams variety show. Bob Aldrich then hired Bette to play the supporting role of a madam in *Four For Texas*, a western starring Frank Sinatra, Dean Martin, and the Three Stooges. She was being fitted for her brothel costumes when Jack Warner called with a better deal. He had a project, *Dead Ringer*, set to go with Lana Turner playing dual roles. But Lana, it was said, didn't want to play twins, figuring, and rightly so, that one edition of her gorgeous self was enough for the general public. When she turned down the film, Warner presented it to Davis, who got a release from Aldrich. She played twins before, she said, but the special effects were more complex and frustrating this time. A visitor to the set agreed. 'It was hardly the apex of comfort for an artist like Bette Davis to play a scene where, as twins, she must put a gun to her head and blow her own brains out.'

Crawford had toiled earlier that year in *The Caretakers*, playing Lucretia Terry, the tough head nurse in a psychiatric institution. With steel-dusted hair and individual key-spot lighting, Joan taught judo to the younger nurses and got her own mad scene, though it was cut from the final picture. 'I was changed from a cameo part to just an angry woman,' said Joan. 'The director's excuse was that some of my scenes made me look cheap. But every woman who's rejected by the man she loves looks cheap. I should know, I'm a woman.'

After washing the silver out of her hair ('I found I was throwing away all my beige clothes – because they were designed for a redhead. And, mentally, gray hair dampened my spirits'), Crawford, as a russet brunette, descended further into the pit of the not-so-Grand Guignol with her next alliance, with producer-director William Castle.

An independent producer-director specializing in horror and terror films, William Castle had none of the style or talent of Robert Aldrich. Fond of showing up at his own premieres in a coffin and hearse, and suspending twelve-foot skeletons on wires over the heads of the audiences, Castle scored his first box-office success in 1959, with *The Tingler*. His trademark was a decapitated head that appeared in many of his films. 'We used the same old dead head in every movie,' said the producer proudly. 'We bought it for $12.50. That was the head that was used in *Psycho*. They rented it from us for a hundred dollars a day.'

After seeing *What Happened to Baby Jane?* fifteen times, Castle dreamed of hitting the big time, of working with stars like Bette Davis and Joan Crawford. One evening, at a party in Beverly Hills, he had the good fortune to be introduced to Crawford. 'He almost fell at her feet,' said writer Hector Arce. 'He told her he had a script that he had written specifically for her. It was called *Straitjacket*. It was written by the man who wrote the Hitchcock classic, *Psycho*.

'I'm listening, Mister Castle,' said Joan.

Castle told her the story. It was a psychological murder mystery about a deranged woman who finds her husband in bed with his mistress and chops their heads off. She spends twenty years in a mental institution, is cured, and then released to the care of her loving daughter. She is happy and readjusted to society when a fresh series of beheadings occur in the town.

'Ummm,' said Joan.

'She is the suspected killer,' said Castle. 'She believes it herself.'

'And?' said Joan.

'She is arrested. But she's not the killer; it's her twisted daughter.'

'The little bitch,' said Joan. 'When can I see the script?'

After Crawford read *Straitjacket*, she called the director. The woman was supposed to age from thirty to fifty. Joan wanted to make the character younger, to lop off five years at each end. Castle agreed. He also said yes to her salary, percentage, and contract demands.

When she was announced for the picture, she was immediately blasted by Bette Davis and Louella Parsons.

'*Straitjacket* was supposed to star Joan *Blondell*,' said Bette, 'until Crawford stepped in and *stole* the role.'

'Joan Blondell was set for the lead and had been fitted for her costumes,' Parsons confirmed. 'Then out of the blue, producer William Castle signs the other Joan. And then he proceeds to turn his picture upside down to please her. Even the crew has been revamped, with a new cameraman, makeup man, hairdresser, costumer – even a switch in the publicity man. No one involved is talking.'

'It stinks, I tell you,' said Bette. 'There is an unwritten *law* in this town. Once an actor is signed for a part, it's *his* until they die or drop out voluntarily. Miss Crawford *knows* this and should be ashamed of herself.'[1]

The following February photographs of Bette and Joan appeared side by side in *Time* with reviews of *Dead Ringer* and *Straitjacket*. Both films were panned. 'A trite little thriller. Exuberantly uncorseted, her torso looks like a gunnysack full of galoshes,' said *Time* of Bette and *Dead Ringer*; while her rival received a flip *New York Times* notice: 'Joan Crawford with an axe. Tennis, anyone?'

Of the two competing films, *Straitjacket* took in the most money, helped somewhat by Joan's charismatic in-person tour of theaters. Using the Pepsi jet, the star flew cross-country to give the press and her public one 'last look at the old tradition of Hollywood hoopla.'

Her entourage included her maid, Mamacita; public-relations

1 In 1977 Joan Blondell confirmed that she was signed for the film, but she withdrew because of an accident. 'I stepped through a glass partition in my home and had to have sixty stitches in my leg. Nothing was said in the newspapers, because of the insurance, but Joan Crawford did not steal the role. Someone had to do it.'

man Bob Kelley; a girl photographer; and two Pepsi pilots, who
flew the plane from city to city; plus twenty-eight pieces of luggage,
including food hampers, two knitting bags, and an axe with a three-
foot haft, which Joan would carry onstage from theater to theater.

'She criticized *me*, for raffling off dolls onstage for *Baby Jane*,'
said Bette Davis, 'and she's got a goddamn axe under her skirt?'

STAR WARS – PART TWO

*'The second time around, Bette wanted vengeance. It was Elizabeth the First,
all over again. A mere apology from Joan wasn't enough. Bette wanted her
head.'*

George Cukor

*'I have always believed in the Christian ethic, to forgive and forget. I looked
forward to working with Bette again. I had no idea of the extent of her hate,
and that she planned to destroy me.'*

Joan Crawford

In the winter of 1963, when Bob Aldrich's follow-up film *Four for
Texas* failed to attract a wide audience, he turned his thoughts to
the idea of reteaming Bette and Joan. He asked *Baby Jane* novelist
Henry Farrell to write a new story featuring the two stars. Farrell
came up with a tale of malice and murder set in the Deep South.
Bette would play an ageing eccentric Southern belle, whose wealth
and sanity are threatened by a visiting cousin. Also figuring prominently would be a domineering father, an unsolved murder, a
buried body, and the razing of the family mansion. The working
title of the story was *Whatever Happened to Cousin Charlotte?*

Bette read the first draft of the script and agreed to play Charlotte.
Meeting with Aldrich, she asked whom he had in mind to play
Cousin Miriam. He said Ann Sheridan was a possibility.

'Good choice,' said Bette.

'But most of the studios have requested Joan Crawford,' the
director stated.

'I wouldn't piss on Joan Crawford if she were on fire,' Bette replied.
Aldrich then talked *money* with Bette. With Crawford as part of

the package the budget would be larger and Bette would get $120,000 upfront, which was double the sum she got for *Baby Jane*; and he would give her a percentage of the profits. 'Forget the percentage,' said Bette. 'I got screwed on *Jane*.'

Aldrich raised his offer to $160,000, pushing Joan and advocating the script. It was Oscar material, he felt, 'a much more difficult, narrow-edged part, with the Gothic bravura of Jane.' As Cousin Charlotte, Bette would rule the plantation, dominate the story, *and* at the finish have the pleasure of crushing Cousin Miriam (Joan) to death with a massive concrete flowerpot.

'I *will* accept Crawford if you will change the title of the picture to *Hush . . . Hush, Sweet Charlotte*,' Bette replied, referring to the name of the title song, composed by Frank DeVol and Mack David.

With Davis amenable to working with her rival again, Aldrich had to persuade Crawford to come aboard. He had not met or spoken with her since the unpleasantness over the rescinded Cannes Festival invitation. 'Taking no chances on writing or phoning, the director sent the script to Joan in New York, then showed up on her doorstep,' said reporter Len Baxter.

'You got a problem, Bob?' said Joan, when an awkward lull came up in their conversation.

'Yes,' said Aldrich, 'I was wondering . . . would you . . . could you . . .?'

'You wasted time and money, coming to see me,' said Joan. 'The answer is yes.'

She liked the character of Miriam – a bitch, but a stylish one. Unlike Blanche in *Baby Jane* in the new film she would be ambulatory, *and* in one scene she would get to slap Bette repeatedly across the face, then push her down a ravine locked in the arms of a dead Joseph Cotten.

She told the director she would also accept the fifty thousand dollars in salary, with twenty-five percent of the net profits, plus five thousand dollars in living expenses for the duration of the nine-week shoot.

'There is just one request I have to make,' Joan concluded firmly.

'Name it,' said Aldrich.

'In the billing for *this* picture my name comes first, *before* Miss Davis.'

'In a *pig's* eye,' Bette shouted when Aldrich called her from New York with Joan's request. 'I will *not* have my name come *second* to Joan Crawford, not now, not ever.'

Back in Los Angeles, further sweetening was offered to Bette by Aldrich. To get her to agree to take second billing to Joan, the director had to raise her salary another forty thousand dollars, to two hundred thousand. 'That is the same amount I am getting for producing and directing,' he told her, 'so that makes us partners on this picture.'

'*Partners*, all the way down the line. I will hold you to *that*,' said Bette.

On December 28, 1963, the announcement appeared in *The New York Times* that the stars of *Baby Jane* would be reteamed for *Whatever Happened to Cousin Charlotte?*

'Yes, we are making *another* picture together,' Bette told reporter Wanda Hale. 'I like to work with Joan. She's a *real* pro, serious about her acting, always on time, always *prepared*. So different from some of these new young people, some of whom are stars but still not pros.'

Budgeted at $1.3 million, 20th Century-Fox agreed to finance and tribute the new film, with Aldrich and the studio equally dividing all future profits, after negative and distribution costs and the payment of profit participation to the players were paid. Scheduled to begin production in April, Crawford requested a postponement of one month. 'April is no good for me,' she informed Aldrich, 'because I am due to attend the Pepsi sales convention in Hawaii that month.'

'Miss Crawford was *not* thanked for this delay,' said Bette. 'With the heat of summer on location, she made us suffer greatly for her silly business appointments.'

In preproduction, during the postponement, according to the director's files, it was Bette who then threatened to jeopardize the film, by quitting completely. Early in May, in an eight-page hand-written letter to Aldrich, she said her promised partnership on the film was being ignored. She expressed her bitter disappointment that the title had not yet been changed, a cinematographer had not yet been chosen, and the original writer, Henry Farrell, had been replaced without consulting her.

'I feel I know and understand you as well as anyone,' Bette wrote to the director-producer. 'You are stubborn and have to be solely in charge. You do not function well with someone of my type. That was obvious throughout the filming of *Baby Jane* – and the suicidal desire this put me into many times, was almost more than I was able to bear.

'The machinations of the new film from the very beginning have been tricky. And therefore most discouraging. I do not wear well with tricks designed to make me do what someone else decides I will do. We have not been partners – and you do not intend that we will be.'

Repeating her lament on the change in writers, Bette said it was done surreptitiously, without advising her ('It is incredible that you forget I have friends who care for my welfare and keep me informed'), and she found the new script appalling. She knew what the director was up to; he was trying to trick her into playing a repeat of their last film. 'You will do your best to do a remake of *Baby Jane*. No matter what I look like on the set – you can order the cameraman to "Fix me up".

'I could never trust you again,' she concluded. 'There is no going back. I truly do not feel I can work with you again. If you are wise for the good of the film you will re-cast and pay me off. It will be cheaper in the long run.'

Responding with flowers and an apology, Aldrich quickly induced Davis to stay but again he was forced to make some adjustments in her contract. Early in May he confirmed in writing that the billing of the film would show her name on the same line as Crawford. 'Both the same size. Yours on the right. Joan's on the left, with an asterisk to show "In alphabetical order" the producer promised, and to validate her worth as a consultant and an official partner, he would give her an additional fifteen percent of 100 percent of net profits [the same cut as Joan], with Twentieth Century Fox assuming ten percent of that payment.'

On May 14, with a firm start-date agreed upon, Fox held an open party to reintroduce the stars and the director to the press. Bette arrived on time, with Bob Aldrich. Joan arrived precisely fifteen minutes late.

'This isn't going to be *Baby Jane* strikes back. It's altogether a different picture,' Aldrich told the assembled reporters.

'Yes,' said Bette, 'it's a whole new story. Miss Crawford and I are not doing an Andy Hardy series.'

'I am not in a wheelchair this time,' said Joan. 'I will be very active and appear more attractive I might add. My character works in public relations in New York, which means I will get to wear some beautiful, expensive clothes. Right, Bob?'

'Certainly, Joan.'

'And I will be singing the title song in the picture,' said Bette, 'accompanied by a harpsichord. It will be *quite* lovely.'

'What about the billing?' a reporter asked.

'We tossed a coin and Miss Crawford won,' said Aldrich.

'There will be an asterisk beside Joan's name and one beside Bette's,' a publicist hastily spoke up. 'The asterisk reads "in alphabetical order".'

According to *Motion Picture*, the enmity between the two stars erupted anew on day one of the costume fittings, when Joan arrived and found she was barred from the set where Bette was testing her wardrobe and makeup. 'Comparative testing is important for contrast,' said the magazine. 'If one star is wearing her hair down, the other will probably wear it up. If one wears pink, the other certainly is not going to wear pink.'

When Joan complained to Aldrich, he asked his 'partner' Bette to call and mollify her co star. 'What does it *matter*, Joan?' said Bette, attempting to ease Joan's paranoia. 'I am going to be a *mess*, and you are going to look your usual gorgeous self.'

'Dear Bette,' said Joan, comforted for the moment.

On May 18 the cast showed up for the first day of rehearsals, on stage six at Fox. For an opening-day gift, Joan gave Bette a huge box of kitchen matches tied in ribbon, the kind that Bette liked to strike on her shoe or rear end. Bette sent Joan a thank-you note.

At the first reading, closed to the press, Bette was sitting at the round table, hunched over, with her glasses perched on her nose, when she noticed that '*Madame*' (Joan) was preening unduly. Up in the flies, in the catwalks overhead, the star had sensed there was a photographer recording the proceedings.

'I asked Aldrich if I could take some shots,' said Phil Stern. 'He said, "No way, you son of a bitch. I have enough trouble with the two dames." I kept pleading. I told him my coverage of the *Baby Jane* rehearsals brought him good luck. He said, "OK, but, damn it, keep out of our way and don't let the ladies see you." '

Using a long lens, Stern was up in the flies, confident that no one could spot him. 'Except for Joan. The woman had radar up her ass. Maybe she heard the clicking of my camera, because she straightened her spine and started smiling and acting very gracious to Bette and Joseph Cotten and the rest of the cast. Then she began to inch her Pepsi bottle towards the middle of the table, so it would be in the shots. Bette noticed this and leaned forward, blocking the Pepsi bottle. When Joan pushed the bottle out further still, Bette moved forward again. It was a riot. They were competing for space, with the Pepsi bottle between them.'

During the rehearsals, it was said, Davis held up the proceedings by questioning every line. There *were* problems with the script, Lukas Heller recalled. 'Bob Aldrich had originally hired Henry Farrell to write the story and script of *Charlotte*. They had a disagreement over protocol. Aldrich had kept Farrell waiting, and he walked out. I was called in to rework the script. Aldrich was a great director, but story was not his strongest point. He wanted a bit of *Diabolique*, a bit of this, a bit of that. We didn't have the time we had on *Baby Jane*, which was reworked over a period of six months.'

Bette Davis made only the usual actor's comments about lines, 'which is the object of rehearsals,' said Heller. Joan Crawford then insisted that she have her say. 'She would query lines with absolutely no concept of the emotional or dramatic content – but purely on the grammatical or logical element. She argued for hours, being very literal in her interpretation, and always putting it in this beautiful, modulated voice. She was giving a performance. She wanted to establish her authority on the picture and everyone had to go along with her.'

Rehearsing a scene where Cousin Miriam had to help poor mad Charlotte into bed, *Motion Picture* reported that Bette slapped Joan's hands away from her. ' "I'm not going to do the scene until it's written right," said Davis and strode off the set.'

'We leave for Baton Rouge, Louisiana, this weekend, for ten days of location shooting,' said Bob Aldrich at the end of rehearsals. 'I hope we live through it.'

CANNIBAL TIME IN DIXIE

'You're a vile, sorry little bitch! What is it you say you do? Public relations?
It sounds like something pretty dirty to me.'
                        Cousin Bette to Cousin Joan in *Sweet Charlotte*

On Sunday May 31, traveling in a chartered plane, the *Hush . . . Hush, Sweet Charlotte* company arrived at the airport in Baton Rouge. Posing for a group photograph for the *Louisiana News*, it was noticed that Joan Crawford was not with the troupe. 'Why? I don't know why,' said unit publicist Harry Mines. 'Bette went both ways – round trip with the gang. I guess Joan wanted to travel on her own.'

The entire company were put up at the Belmont Motel, a mile outside the city. 'The accommodations were always first-class with Aldrich,' said Bob Gary, on hand again as script supervisor. 'No one had to double up. Everyone had their own bungalow.'

Three locations were chosen for filming: an office on Government Street in Baton Rouge; a house in Oak Valley, Vacherie (where Mary Astor's character would reside); and a moss-covered ante bellum mansion near Burnside, Louisiana, overlooking the Mississippi River. It was here that the next duel between the leading stars would be played out, before and behind the motion picture cameras.

With Crawford not scheduled to arrive until the fourth day of filming, Bette used that time to make friends with the local and visiting press. 'Never overly partial to giving interviews, Bette called in all the reporters and entertained them for an hour with the best copy she'd ever given,' said Hedda Hopper. She also became tight with the *Charlotte* crew. 'Her trailer was parked at the front side of the mansion,' said Harry Mines, 'but Bette was seldom there. She set up this huge mirror in the hallway of the house and she put on her makeup there. At lunchtime she had her meals outside, with Aldrich and the grips.'

On Wednesday, June 3, Crawford; her maid, Mamacita; her hairdresser, Peggy Shannon; her makeup man, Monte Westmore; and her luggage arrived at the Baton Rouge airport. Expecting a VIP welcome, perhaps the mayor or a marching brass band, the star was chagrined to learn that no one, not even a member of the *Charlotte* production company, was there to meet her. 'There was a foul-up in the schedule,' said Harry Mines. 'Everyone was filming at the plantation house, and somehow Joan's arrival was not relayed to the proper driver.'

When she reached the Belmont Motel, Joan found her rooms were not made up, and she had to sit for an hour in the motel's lobby. Then she was put in a bungalow next to the garbage disposal unit. That evening, as soon as the unit had returned from filming, Joan complained to the wrong person – Bette Davis. 'Oh Joan! Pull yourself *together*. This is Baton Rouge, *not* Beverly Hills,' said Bette, who was settled in the slightly larger, more luxurious bungalow across the way from Crawford.

'The trouble between the two was still there,' said publicist Harry Mines. 'We were the wave that followed the wave. Aldrich was the referee, and all of us knew we were going to have to work around the unpleasantness.'

On location the wakeup call for the entire company was 7:00 A.M., except for Joan Crawford, who was up an hour earlier. 'It was a regular three-hour routine,' said Monte Westmore. 'I'd wake her up at six. She'd exercise a little bit while I set out her makeup. Then she'd make breakfast, which I had to eat.' Under the special lights at her makeup table, while Joan sat and worked on her face, Westmore stood by her side for two hours and worked on her obligatory false eyelashes. 'They always had to be just right. Trimmed perfectly in line, then curled in a circle. I would lay out six pairs for her on the table. She would then inspect them. "This one's good, that isn't," she would say, going down the line. When I glued them on her eyelids, and she was finished spitting and putting the mascara on them, they'd be uncurled and looked right. We went though a gross and a half of eyelashes per picture, and later, when she was traveling for Pepsi, she'd send me more to work on. I'd clean 'em and set 'em and roll 'em and curl 'em, and send them back to her in Europe or wherever. She was very particular about her eyelashes, and so was Bette Davis.'

Neither Westmore nor Bob Schiffer, Bette's makeup man, ever touched the stars' faces. 'Joan did her own face and mouth,' said Westmore.

'And they were welcome to their mouths,' said Schiffer. 'I didn't believe in all that heavy lipstick, or the thick pancake around their eyes. On *Charlotte* I had my own makeup concept for Bette, which lasted about five minutes. She would say to me, 'Don't fuck with my face.' But she was a pro, with a great sense of humor. Once she gave me an eight-by-ten photograph of herself, with her face superimposed on the body of a *Playboy* cover girl. It was a very erotic pose. Some people thought it was really Bette. "If this gets out it's your ass," she told me. She was very funny and was always a trouper, but inflexible about the look of her face and lips. Crawford wouldn't listen to you either. All you did was work on the eyelashes, then hold the mirror for her between setups. It was a servitude position, and Joan made the slaves look like Boy Scouts.'

Arriving for her first day of shooting at the Mississippi mansion, Crawford let it be known that, unlike Bette, she didn't intend to become too chummy with the film company. 'She had her trailer set up at the back of the house, with her own golf cart to take her back and forth when we were filming,' said Harry Mines.

'While Crawford rides around in her golf cart, Bette walks,' Hedda Hopper reported.

'Bette lets her hair down but Joan surrounds herself with the aura of a great of yesterday. Times have changed and she doesn't seem to realize that,' said Sheilah Graham.

'Bette was crazy in some areas, but she stayed a human being,' Bob Gary recalled, 'but Joan always had "the act" going. She expected obeisance from everyone. When you approached her it was almost like you had to genuflect.'

It was in Joan's contract that her trailer be placed so many yards away from Bette, 'which was understandable,' said Harry Mines, 'but it caused difficulties for all of us.'

'Whether by design or accident, every time a shot was set up for the two stars there would be a sweltering delay in the sun waiting for Joan Crawford to emerge from her ice-cold trailer,' said writer Gail Cameron for *McCall's.*

There was only one scene involving Bette and Joan at the mansion, and that was deliberately delayed by Aldrich. 'First we shot all of Bette's scenes with Agnes Moorehead and Cecil Kellaway,' said Bob Gary, 'then we did Joan's scenes with Joseph Cotten and the other actors. Bob Aldrich wanted to put off the moment when the two war horses got together.'

It was publicist Harry Mines who had the arduous task of bringing the two ladies together for interviews. Working with temperamental and tormented stars was not unusual for him, he claimed. A few years before he had been the unit publicist in Nevada for *The Misfits*, Marilyn Monroe's last picture. He remembered: 'She was in bad shape, overweight and on pills. When she arrived in Nevada, she said she wasn't going to see any press. She was rude. I became angry. I told her, "OK, we'll close the set to everyone. You can work and I'm leaving." She acted surprised. She said, "No one ever spoke to me like that." I said, "Well it's about time someone did." She looked at me a long time and said, "All right. I'll work with you." I said, "If you don't like any reporter or photographer, we'll use the old dodge of stroking your ear or something, and I'll get rid of them." She said, "No, I'll go through with it." But even then it was tough getting her together with the press. You always had to go look for her. Clark Gable saved the situation many times for me. He was a wonderful human being. He would say, "Look, when you have these people out here and you have trouble finding Marilyn, just call me. I'll keep them entertained until she shows up." He was a magnificent man.'

Working with Crawford and Davis on *Hush . . . Hush, Sweet Charlotte* was 'double trouble' for Mines. 'The two stars didn't want to pose for pictures, not even for the still photographer. Then *Life* magazine decided to do a piece on the filming, and that made it a little easier for me, because neither Bette nor Joan could say no to *Life*.'

The photographer assigned to that story was Flip Schulke. 'Bette was fantastic,' he said, 'but Crawford was a bum. Bette joked around a lot, wearing blue jeans and carrying a big box of matches and a Coke bottle. Crawford had Pepsi machines installed around the place; she was a very cool customer. She never seemed to show consideration for anyone. She always arrived three or four minutes late for her scenes. Bette would turn to me and say, "She's making a grand entrance just for you." I wanted to photograph the two of them making up. Bette started from scratch in her dressing room. When I got to Joan's trailer, she was already made up, and she posed very grandly with an eyebrow pencil, as though she was just beginning. Everything was posed with her. Nothing could be candid, and she would tell me when to take the picture.'

The idea of having the two ladies pose for photographs sitting on tombstones in a cemetery came from director Bob Aldrich. 'Bob appreciated the publicity value of the feud between the two stars,' said Harry Mines, 'but he never took sides as far as I knew. He had a fake cemetery built on the plantation property and when he suggested the two pose sitting on the tombstones, I thought, "What a great shot, but who is going to ask them to do it?" Aldrich wouldn't. The photographer wouldn't. I suggested it to Bette first, and she roared with laughter. She was all for it. Joan was a little reluctant at first, but it was for *Life* magazine, so she went along with it.'

When it came time to do the tombstone photographs, the session lasted for hours due to the stars' egos and conflicting schedules. 'There were three or four different sessions,' said Mines. 'It was done between filming. Joan would be ready when Bette would be called away. When Bette returned, Joan would be gone, back in her trailer, with her clothes off, resting. She would take a long time getting ready. Eventually, the last time, when Bette came back to do the shots and Joan was missing, she said, "I'm going to settle this once and for all, because I know you guys have a job to do."

She went to the back of the house to Joan's dressing room. She rapped on her door, then stood outside and yelled, "Joan Crawford! Get your clothes on and come and do these photographs, right away!" Joan said, "Oh, Bette. I'm coming. I'm coming." She came hurtling out the door. They did the photographs, and when it was all over, the photographer who was just as nervous as I was, said, "My God! I forgot to take some color." I said "Oh, Jesus!" He said, "We've got to get them together again." "Not on your life, or mine," I told him. I wouldn't ask them, even if it was for a cover. As it turned out, *Life* never used any of the shots. They were only interested in Bette and Joan as a team, so when Joan left the film they killed the story and the tombstone photographs were never published.'

'*Miss Crawford always says good morning when she walks on the set. Miss Davis seldom answers her. Three hours later she may say "Hi", and Miss Crawford looks around to see if she's addressing her or someone else.*'

Lily May Caldwell

According to Joan Crawford, she tried very hard to reconcile her differences with Bette Davis during those first days and nights in Baton Rouge. 'It was a challenge to try and make her my friend,' she told *Motion Picture* reporter Len Baxter. 'Crawford obviously wants to clear the air,' said Baxter, 'but Davis is not able to kiss and make up. She doesn't know how to say I'm sorry and Crawford doesn't feel *she* has anything to be sorry for.'

Forgiveness was never one of Bette's weaknesses, her friends agreed. She could not easily forget the humiliation she had suffered because of Crawford's behavior at the Oscars the previous year. 'Perhaps if Joan had prostrated herself in front of Bette, and the entire company, and begged her forgiveness in front of the Louisiana State Assembly, then Bette would have considered a pardon with qualifications,' said a cast member. 'But Joan wouldn't offer a crumb of contrition, so the major games of revenge began.'

'Bette told me that Joan was terrified of her on the second film,' said Vik Greenfield, 'and with good reason. After the business with the Oscar, this was *war*.'

Vengeance in the movies was always sweet, and, short of spiking Joan's Pepsi with cyanide, or tampering with the brakes of her car (which had been done in *Queen Bee*), in real life Bette loathed the obvious. Her retaliation on *Hush . . . Hush, Sweet Charlotte* had to be inconspicuous, and final.

'She wanted to make a basket case out of Joan, and she almost succeeded,' said George Cukor.

Censuring Crawford for her heavy drinking and star posturings would not be enough. This second time around, Bette intended to attack Joan's more vulnerable area – her advancing age and appearance.

Having turned sixty that April, Crawford was more sensitive than ever that her true age be kept from the press and public. She insisted on going with the lower figure of fifty-six, the same age as Bette. But in a joint story for the *Birmingham News*, Davis told the reporter, Lily May Caldwell, that if their ages were printed Lily May should note that Joan was four years older. 'She's sixty, and I have witnesses who can prove it,' said Bette.

In her story, Caldwell, an old friend of Joan's, omitted all mention of age. 'Each is a Hollywood star of first magnitude,' the reporter wrote, 'but it's Joan, not Bette, who is the queen of this Bayou Country plantation, where the murder mystery is being filmed.'

When the two stars were invited to the governor's mansion for a reception, they arrived in separate cars and held court on opposite sides of the room. 'The wives were enchanted by Joan, by her softspoken voice and manners, while the men seemed more taken with the outspoken more bawdy Bette,' said Caldwell. During the evening, when another reporter approached Bette and began to speak about 'the lovely Joan Crawford,' her co star spoke up promptly. 'Yes! She *is* lovely, isn't she?' said Bette. Then, in a voice loud enough to be heard across the Mississippi River, Bette added, 'She is *quite* a dame for her age. She's over *sixty*, you know.'

Bette was also publicly derisive of Joan's extensive location wardrobe. 'For a goddamn week in Baton Rouge, she brought twenty pieces of luggage. It was a black-and-white movie but she had color-coordinated outfits for the daytime scenes, and for the night shots all of her evening dresses were chiffon, which meant that the wardrobe lady had to spend hours ironing them in the one-hundred-degrees weather.'

There was also the matter of Joan's thinning hair, become finer with advancing age, as had Bette's ('Both stars wore wigs in *Baby Jane* and *Charlotte*,' said Monte Westmore). 'She brought *mounds* of hairpieces to Louisiana,' said Bette. 'Maggie Donovan, who had been my hairdresser for years, said to me one day, "We're up to our asses in Crawford's hairpieces." '

> '*Most Aries are inclined to forgive and forget all but the most cruel encounters. If one Ram is stronger, and insists on butting away, the weaker Ram gradually turns into a neurotic sheep.*'
>
> Astrologer Linda Goodman

Off the set, at the Belmont Motel, Bette continued to ostracize Joan. Socially she made sure that it was she, and not Crawford, who was the leading hostess of the *Sweet Charlotte* film company. Each evening she held court in her larger bungalow, across the way from her rival. She entertained Joseph Cotten, George Kennedy, Cecil Kellaway and his wife, and Bob Aldrich. One night she hosted a get-together for Mary Astor. 'That was Astor's last picture,' said Harry Mines. 'She was there for three days. She didn't want to see me. She had closed herself away from everyone. It made my job a little difficult. I mentioned that to Bette and she said, "Do you need to talk to Marry?" I said I'd like it, if I could. She said, "My dear, let me take care of it. I'll have Mary over tomorrow night for drinks, and you can come in and meet her." '

Drinks for Miss Astor became a party, with all of the cast on hand except Joan Crawford.

'Bette didn't invite her,' said Harry Mines.

'Why should I?' said Bette. 'Miss Crawford and I never socialized.'

'Joan was staying in the bungalow across the way,' said Mines, 'and during the party I looked out the window and saw her drive off for dinner with Mamacita.'

Bette also organized several social evenings in Baton Rouge, including a trip to a local nightclub to see ex-housewife turned comedian, Phyllis Diller. Agnes Moorehead was Bette's special guest that evening, and two nights later, she hosted a dinner for Bob Aldrich at a nearby restaurant. Again Crawford was not invited, but left to herself in her bungalow, where the empty vodka bottles were beginning to pile up outside her door. Socially and psychologically, the star was beginning to crumble.

'Bette does not play a part, she attacks it. She comes on hungry. And Joan began to worry. She too was coming on hungry; but when she entered the dining room instead of devouring her dinner, she began to feel she was the dinner.'

Joseph Cotten

As a 'partner' on the film, it was said that Bette used that leverage to codirect the picture.

'She and Aldrich were very tight,' said Harry Mines. 'She was always by his elbow.'

'Unlike Joan who when she's through with her scene retires to her dressing room, Bette remains on the set, like a spy. She sits in her canvas chair watching every scene,' said Paul Gardner in *Action* magazine.

'What I remember is how helpful Bette was to the other actors,' said photographer Flip Schulke. 'One day this old guy [Cecil Kellaway] had trouble with his lines, and Bette kept walking him back and forth outside the house, going over his lines with him.'

'Bette was a formidable presence on the set, and I think she intimidated Joan,' said Bob Gary.

When asked in 1987 to respond to reports that Crawford was scared to compete with her on this second film, Bette replied, 'Things were quite different from *Jane*. She had quite a lot of people to contend with. There was Kellaway, and Mr. Joseph Cotten, and Agnes Moorehead. I think it was a combination of all those people.'

'Joseph Cotten and Agnes Moorehead would hardly seem to be a problem for Joan Crawford,' said Bill Aldrich. 'Joan could have taken them with one hand. Bette was something else. She worked the company, the crew. She was a very strong lady who was still carrying on a one-way feud with Crawford. It began at rehearsals of *Jane*, went through that picture and through *Charlotte*. In Bette's mind, to this day, it has never stopped.'

In the last three days in Baton Rouge, the shots involving Bette and Joan were completed. In the first sequence there was no dialogue involved. Joan was to arrive at the plantation mansion in a cab, then exit, carrying a small case, pay the driver, and lowering her sunglasses, look up at a balcony of the house where Bette, in pigtails and a nightgown, was standing in the shadows, holding a shotgun.

The scene was designed to be photographed in a wide continuous shot, and, thanks to Crawford's proficient technical skill, it was completed in one take. Later that evening, when Harry Mines called on Bette in her motel bungalow, he found her standing in the middle of the room practicing Joan's scene. 'My God!' said Bette. 'I'm imagining getting out of a cab and trying to do that whole business in one gesture. How *did* she do it?'

That praise was apparently never conveyed to Crawford; nor was Bette regressive in her criticism of her co star. On the next day, during the filming of a Crawford scene on the veranda, according to *Motion Picture*, Bette positioned herself in front of the camera. 'This is strictly unusual,' said Len Baxter. 'A director doesn't permit an actor to sit in front of the camera, directly in another actor's line of vision, unless the actor is part of the scene.' During one of Joan's close-ups, Bette turned to director Aldrich and said in a loud voice. 'You're *not* going to let her do it like *that*, are you?' Trembling, but a pro, Crawford finished the scene and returned to her dressing room.

Late that night, concerned about her work, the actress said, she called Aldrich in his motel room. It was past midnight, and Crawford apologized for waking him up. 'I was worried,' said Joan. 'I wanted to explain how I felt about those scenes. I urged that they be redone. He said I was overreacting, that my work was fine. But then I heard this second voice, talking loudly beside him. I knew immediately who it was. It was Miss Davis. She was *there*, in Mr. Aldrich's bed.'

'I wouldn't put it past Mother to let Joan Crawford *believe* that she was having an affair with Bob Aldrich,' said B.D. Hyman, 'but I don't think there was ever a physical relationship between them. Certainly Mother was always adoring of her directors when they got along, and hated them when they didn't. She would always concoct these fantasies that this director or that was madly in love with her. But I think the last thing in this universe that Bob Aldrich would ever consider was a relationship with either Mother or Crawford, and certainly not with Mother.'

On June 12, the last day of shooting in Louisiana, further ignominy was served on Joan. After some late-afternoon shots, she was relaxing in her trailer, on hand if needed for additional scenes. She apparently dozed off, because when she woke up it was dark. When she sent Mamacita to check when shooting would be completed, she found the place empty. The crew had packed up and left, leaving Joan at the rear of the house in her trailer with no transportation back to the motel.

'There were a lot of mishaps on location,' said Bob Gary. 'We had a production manager who drank a lot. He would get drunk and forget to schedule things. When we were ready to leave Baton Rouge the next day, Aldrich found out we had no plane. The one we normally used wasn't scheduled; it was off someplace else.'

'They brought us back to Los Angeles on this old beat-up World War II plane. We were almost killed in transit,' said Peggy Shannon.

'It had trouble taking off,' said Gary. 'When we got back in L.A. we found a lot of shrubbery and branches stuck to the wheels of the plane. These were the tops of trees we cut off when clearing the runway. Everyone laughed, but if we had gone down the headline would have read, "Bette Davis killed in crash. No survivors reported."

Except for Joan Crawford, who flew back to Los Angeles first-class on a commercial air-line, that evening. The privacy and distance from the company gave her time to pacify her rage and come up with a solution to combat the winning Bette.

'The fight was much fiercer the second time around. And Joan did not enjoy losing,' said Monte Westmore.

'She was facing the same situation as with *Baby Jane*,' said Bill Aldrich. 'When she accepted the film, she knew her part was subordinate to Bette's. When shooting started, she realized she was playing second banana again, and she wanted no part of that.'

There were few options for the losing star. In Baton Rouge, Crawford had called her agent, who spoke to Bob Aldrich about fattening up her part. The answer was no. The script was set, along with the shooting schedule, Aldrich replied. There could be no rewrites for either actress at this late date. Crawford then called Leonard Rosen, her lawyer in New York. She wanted him to find a legal out in her contract. There was none, he told her. If she quit the picture she could be sued for breach of contract. Her only recourse was to bow to Bette and finish the picture. But this was *Joan Crawford* – conqueror of men and idol of millions. She could not, would not, allow herself to be vanquished by *anyone*, especially Bette Davis. As long as she had the spirit to fight and the ability to scheme, she knew the battle was not yet over.

By the time she arrived at Los Angeles International Airport that Saturday evening, Crawford had her defense strategy in order. Leaving the airport in her limousine, the star tapped on the dividing window and instructed her driver that there was a change in directions. She did not want him to go to her apartment on Fountain Avenue. They were to proceed directly to Cedars Sinai Hospital, where she checked herself in as a patient.

'As happens in times of stress, Crawford became ill,' Bob Thomas reported.

> *'I can't tell you what I went through during those weeks that shooting stopped, waiting for Crawford to get well. It was sheer torture.'*
>
> Bette Davis

The following Monday, June 15, with Crawford in the hospital, her stand-in, E.M. Jones, substituted for the star on the first day of filming. 'It was just a matter of days, we were told, and Joan would be back,' said Bob Gary.

Bette Davis, who knew a few things about faking illnesses from her battles with Jack Warner, advised Bob Aldrich not to cater to Joan's tricks. On June 16, 17, 18 and 19, Aldrich rescheduled scenes and shot around the missing actress. That Friday, he requested a medical report from the hospital, and was told that Crawford had a bad case of dysentery and an excessively high blood count. The following day, the hospital reported that the patient had developed a sore throat and 'intermittent cough.'

'It is no wonder she has a cold,' said Bette Davis. 'She insists on having the soundstages frozen at fifty degrees. Grown men were wearing lumber jackets and the ladies had long underwear under their dresses. We were freezing our asses off.'

At the end of the second week, when Aldrich had completed the scenes with the other actors, Joan Crawford was still in the hospital. By then it was Davis' belief that her opponent wanted out of the picture. But Crawford's lawyer turned down a settlement offer on her behalf. This confused Aldrich and his star-partner. 'Just what *is* her angle?' Bette asked. A possible answer came from Hedda Hopper's column that weekend. 'I am bedded with the script,' Joan told the columnist. 'It will be a much better movie when I've recovered.'

On day twelve of her illness, the director spoke to Crawford. She confirmed she had some 'wonderful new script ideas' for him. For starters, she felt that the audience should know more about Miriam, her character. There was a considerable amount of background on Bette's character as a young woman, etc., and none on hers. Aldrich agreed that a flashback scene could be inserted, showing the *two* characters as young women. Joan also felt, that inasmuch as Miriam had been and was still a very beautiful woman, it didn't seem authentic that she had only one gentleman caller (Joseph Cotten) in the entire script. 'She should have more beaus,' said Joan.

'How many more beaus?' the director asked.

'At least two . . . perhaps an attorney and a politician,' the star recommended.

Major idea number three was the inclusion of a good old-fashioned Southern ball at the mansion. A formal party, welcoming Cousin Miriam back to Louisiana, would give a dandy decorative and dramatic boost to the story. It would enable Joan to dress up and make a spectacular entrance down the grand staircase. 'Charlotte [Bette] could be there, of course, under the staircase, or watching from her bedroom,' Crawford suggested. 'That would increase the conflict between the two and make Cousin Miriam seem like more of a threat.'

'There will be no *goddamn* ball or any changes in the script,' said Cousin Bette when Aldrich went over Crawford's suggestions with her on Monday, June 29.

On Tuesday, June 30, Joan's cold suddenly became worse and developed into pneumonia.

On Thursday, Aldrich was forced to inform the cast and crew of *Hush . . . Hush, Sweet Charlotte*, that production was temporarily closing down.

A week later, Crawford was still in the hospital. 'No one could figure out what was wrong with her,' said Bill Aldrich.

'Doctor Kennamer, Elizabeth Taylor's specialist, has diagnosed Joan's mystery ailment as a rare form of pneumonia,' reported Hedda Hopper. 'The cause of it has the specialists and the insurance company stumped.'

'They thought perhaps it was hair spray that got into her lungs,' said Peggy Shannon. 'But I told them I never use hair spray.'

On July 10, with her health improved slightly, Joan was able to sit up, take calls and fully appreciate the attention that at last was being paid. The flowers, cards and notes came in abundance from the *Sweet Charlotte* company. 'We love you,' said the giant card, signed by each member of the crew. 'Come back, we miss you,' wrote Agnes Moorehead.

'Well . . .' said Sidney Skolsky, 'what do you hear from Bette?'

'Nothing.'

'No flowers?'

'No flowers.'

'No telegrams?'

'No telegram.'

'No card?'

'No card.'

'No call?'

'No call.'

* * *

'Dear Mr. Aldrich,' said a letter found in the director's files, 'I read about Miss Crawford's respiratory illness, and I feel positive it is "psychosomatic." Joan "wants a little more depth in her role," and her subconscious mind is holding out for the change. Give her what she wants, and mark my words, Mr. Aldrich, her illness will disappear. Believe me it's worth a try. Most sincerely, Mrs. Betty Clark.'

On Monday, July 20, Crawford returned to work. Arriving at Fox at 6:30 A.M., she spent three hours in makeup, then accompanied by her retinue stepped on the soundstage to applause and hugs from the cast and crew. Bette Davis also joined in the welcome. She handed Joan, 'one perfect red rose, with, surprise! – the thorns removed,' said Dorothy Kilgallen.

Upon going through the script and counting the revised pink pages, Joan seemed content, assuming her role had been magnified; but on the afternoon of the second day she learned that her part was going to be diminished further, by Bette. Resuming her position of authority behind the camera, Davis announced, during a scene between Crawford and Joseph Cotten, that she wanted some lines eliminated. 'I am cutting some dialogue,' said Bette, wielding a large red pencil and excising large chunks of dialogue from Joan's scene. 'Miriam doesn't need them, and you, Mr. Cotten, I hope you don't mind. These lines hold me up.'

This time Joan abandoned her professionalism. She turned on her heel and went to her dressing room, Len Baxter reported.

'It was just a matter of each wanting something, and Davis kind of won out,' Monte Westmore said.

'Not quite,' said the party of the second part.

According to the insurance reports for the next day, 'a weakened Joan Crawford reported to work and left at noon.' On Thursday, July 25, she left at 11:00 A.M.; on Friday she departed for home at fifteen minutes past noon.

Sceptical of her condition, Robert Aldrich, at the urging of Bette, decided to have Crawford followed that weekend by a private detective. His report was found in the director's files:

'Case No. 5229. Date of Report: July 27th, 1964. Subject: Joan

Crawford, 8313 Fountain Avenue. Apt D. In compliance with instructions from Mr. Aldrich, a stakeout and surveillance was maintained on the above location in an effort to determine if the named subject departed the premises over July 24, 25, 1964. The following information is submitted as a result of observations made at the times indicated.'

According to the private detective, no activity of interest was reported on Joan's apartment house on Friday evening or all day Saturday, 'except for the spotting of Loretta Young, who also resided in the building.' On Saturday at 5:00 P.M., 'a late model Rolls-Royce, two-tone brown, was observed to depart and proceed west on Fountain Avenue. Vehicle displayed License No 071–483 and was driven by a woman appearing to be the subject. She wore a bandana with her hair and dark sunglasses. There is little or no doubt that this was Miss Crawford and she was alive at the time [sic].'

Detailing the streets that Joan drove along, 'mostly in Beverly Hills,' the sleuth confessed that at the intersection of Wilshire and Santa Monica Boulevard he lost the subject. Circling the streets in the area and 'the garage and parking lot of the adjacent Beverly Hilton Hotel,' he could not locate the car or Miss Crawford. Returning to her building he checked the open parking spaces, to determine if the Rolls-Royce had been returned. It hadn't. 'At 6:10 P.M. until 11:00 P.M., stakeout was resumed at the entrance to the garage area so that subject could be observed returning. 'At 11:30 P.M., when the car had not been observed, surveillance was discontinued.'

'She gave the *fool* the slip,' Davis blared with amazement and approval when Aldrich gave her the sleuth's report.

On Monday, July 27, Joan came to work but quit at 12:55 P.M., complaining of fatigue again. That afternoon an 'insurance meeting' was held at the studio, attended by Bob Aldrich, his lawyer, and the vice-president of production at Fox, Richard Zanuck. During the meeting the lawyer placed a call to Crawford's lawyer, Leonard Rosen, in New York. He explained to him 'in minute detail the seriousness of the situation and that if Crawford was unable to daily extend her working period, the insurance company would force us into taking some drastic action.'

When asked for a definition of drastic action, Aldrich's lawyer replied '(a) cancel the picture (b) replace Crawford. In either case, it would probably resolve itself in Crawford's future uninsurability [for future pictures].'

The following day, Tuesday, July 28, when Crawford showed up for work, Aldrich met with her in her dressing room and 're-phrased' the warning. 'It was quite obvious that she and her lawyer had talked,' the director wrote in a memo to Dick Zanuck. 'She went on to state that her point of low energy seemed to be right after lunch. I suggested we take a 2–2½-hour lunch and that she come back and work after that. That was done and the total of Tuesday's work was five hours and twenty-five minutes, which all things considered wasn't too bad.'

On the set on Wednesday, Joan worked until one-thirty, then informed Aldrich she 'had over-taxed herself the previous day, and that reluctant as she was, she would have to return to a less strenuous shooting schedule.' Aldrich in turn informed the star that he wanted her examined by the company's insurance doctor. Resenting his suspicions and the harassment, Joan said she was returning to her dressing room and would no longer talk directly to the director.

'The only way they communicated was through me,' said the star's makeup man, Monte Westmore. 'Joan would tell me something, then I'd go and tell Aldrich. He would give me a reply to take back to Joan. It was an unpleasant, awkward position for me to be in.'

That same afternoon, Aldrich spoke to Dick Zanuck, and the two agreed to give Crawford the benefit of the doubt. They would declare a short hiatus in filming. Production would shut down for three more days, from Wednesday afternoon, July 29, until Monday morning, August 3, to give the ailing star a chance to recover.

'I returned to the stage and informed Crawford, in the plainest and simplest language, that the situation was so serious we could not continue in this matter,' said Aldrich.

He also called her lawyer.

An hour later Joan emerged from her trailer and went to Aldrich's office.

'She asked if she could rehearse on the stage during her days off,' he said. 'I told her I thought this would be contrary to the spirit of the hiatus since we wanted her to get total rest. And I doubted if this would put us in very good light with the insurance company to have her parading around the stage while we maintained she was incapable of shooting.'

Crawford then changed her approach. She told the director that her apartment was so hot during the daylight hours it was uninhabitable, 'and would we allow her to spend those hours in her Fox dressing room. I replied that anything that would speed and help her recovery would be to our collective advantage and of course this would be okay.'

Meanwhile, Bette Davis began to feel she was entitled to equal angst time. On the following day, Thursday, she had been scheduled to report to Fox to record dialogue with the other cast members. That morning she called the director and begged off. She was 'filled with despair and despondency,' Aldrich told Dick Zanuck, 'and truly sad. Her point was that she was so depressed at not knowing when and if the picture was ever going to be finished, and she seriously doubted her capacity to contribute much to the pre-recording.'

Feeling that 'understanding was the best part of economics,' the director excused Bette, and the recording was canceled. 'Perhaps you should be advised,' Aldrich told Zanuck, 'that it is Davis' belief that after this serious warning, Crawford will return to work and give full time for one or two days and then revert to being "too tired". Whether there is any validity in this I no longer know.'

On Friday morning, upon the advice of her lawyer, Crawford agreed to submit to a medical examination by the insurance doctor. To validate her fragile respiratory condition she requested that a portable X-ray machine be brought to her air-conditioned dressing room. She 'also insisted that "Doctor" Prinzmetal [Aldrich's lawyer] be in attendance.' Her willingness to cooperate in the examination naturally aroused the suspicions of Bette, who said that she wouldn't 'put it past Joan to sit up all night in front of her air-cooled system, puffing away on a carton of cigarettes to - - - - up her lungs.'

Immediately after the examination, Dr. Gourson of the insurance company gave his report to Aldrich. Joan had a temperature of 99.2, her white blood cells count was a little over eleven thousand. But he minimized the importance of the star's ailment 'and felt that many people walk around in far worse shape than this.' Therefore he could see no reason why the actress couldn't return to work for 'reasonably full time.'

Crawford argued with this diagnosis. She complained of 'fatigue, etc. etc.' She told Aldrich she would return only if she would work 'no more than two hours a day.' Discussing the matter with Davis and Dick Zanuck that afternoon, the director estimated that at that slow pace, it would take forty-five more days to complete the film, adding an additional $525,000 to the budget. His solution was to find out once and for all if Crawford was really sick. He wanted to call in a specialist the next day to re-examine Joan. If the specialist agreed with the diagnosis of the insurance doctor, Aldrich would then schedule Crawford 'for a full day's work next week, and if she failed to perform, declare her in breach of contract.'

The stage was set; the specialist was called for the next morning; and Crawford agreed to a second examination. But the super-canny star knew she was being set-up. She also knew how to give the slip once more to Bette and the director. She called her own doctor. She was feeling much weaker, she told him. Even as they spoke she could feel her pulse fading. Concerned, the doctor called an ambulance and at seven that night, with all sirens blaring, the critical patient was rushed to Cedars Sinai Hospital. Protected and isolated, she would remain there for the next thirty days, safe from the rage and suspicions of her wily co star and director.

> *'I feel terrible. This is the first time I ever held up a picture.'*
> Joan Crawford to columnist Mike Connolly

On Tuesday, August 4, production on *Hush . . . Hush, Sweet Charlotte* was suspended indefinitely, with the cast and crew retaining full pay. 'We sat on our butts for weeks, drawing full pay, waiting for Joanie to get well,' said Bob Gary.

'She was a very, very sick girl,' said Peggy Shannon.

'She was sick all right, sick of Bette Davis,' said Bob Schiffer.

'They are using the *wrong* doctors to diagnose Miss Crawford,' said Bette. 'They should send for Dr. Menninger.'

'Joan couldn't take any more of Bette's intimidation,' Harry Mines believed. 'This was the only way she could make a positive retreat.'

But on this retreat, Crawford intended to take the enemy with her. During this relapse it wasn't her plan merely to hold up production on *Hush . . . Hush, Sweet Charlotte*, she wanted to close the picture down. That way she would save face and Bette Davis would lose her role *and* the balance of the hundred thousand dollars due to her in salary, plus all potential profits.

'Fox had closed down my last movie [*Something's Got To Give*],' said George Cukor, 'because no actress wanted to take over for Monroe. The picture was covered [by insurance] and I think Joan figured they would do the same thing for her.'

'They approached Loretta Young and Barbara Stanwyck. Both are friends of mine and wouldn't dream of taking a job away from me,' Crawford told Louella Parsons when her infirmity entered its second week.

Wearing a $110,000 sapphire necklace over a hospital gown by Dior, she also posed for an Associated Press photographer. 'With her meals catered from Chasen's Joan Crawford is the most glamorous and popular star at the Cedars celebrity hospital,' wrote Edith Gwynne, 'The doctors and nurses line up each day for the privilege of taking care of her.'

'I kept up with her condition by reading Hedda Hopper, who received frequent bulletins from Joan under her oxygen tent,' said Bette Davis.

'No one was sure what was going on,' said Bob Gary. 'Aldrich felt that Joan was doing a job on him. But he couldn't prove it, because she had those doctors at the hospital who claimed otherwise.'

Crawford's friend Vincent Sherman spoke of visiting the star in the hospital. 'She called me the second or third week and said she was dying for company. When I got to her room, she jumped out of bed, and locked the door. "I'm not sick," she said. "I just couldn't stand working another minute with that Bette Davis." '

Cautioning Bette Davis to say nothing publicly about Joan's 'mystery illness', lest they lose their insurance ('If she'd been faking, the insurance company would have never paid the claim,' Aldrich told *Sight and Sound*), the director embarked upon his own strategy to combat Joan and save his picture. In a memo to Dick Zanuck dated August 5, he discussed the possibility of replacing her. 'To re-do the work involved with another actress would cost us roughly $285,000, plus the cost of the actress, plus the carry before said actress was able to commence,' said the director.

Zanuck agreed to the extra cost. A replacement should be sought immediately, without consulting Crawford.

The choice of replacement, however, had to please Bette Davis, who had co star approval in her contract.

'Obviously the ideal candidates would have been Vivien Leigh and Katharine Hepburn, but there are deep-seated personal and historical reasons why she didn't want them,' said Aldrich. 'I had a strong feeling that she didn't really want Hepburn to do it. And I knew Hepburn would probably turn us down, no matter what we offered her.'

The Fox studio wanted Vivien Leigh, but it was said that Bette, still sensitive over the loss of *Gone With the Wind*, some thirty-seven years before, argued that Vivien could not play an authentic Southern character (Scarlett *and* Blanche Du Bois be damned).

'Dear Bob,' said Bette in a handwritten letter to Aldrich on the matter of Vivien Leigh, 'I will not do Charlotte with the very British Miss Leigh. For Fox to suspend me is nonsense. This is wrong casting. The part is for an American actress and there are many. You have consulted me all along the line – this answer is *no*. Why go from the frying pan to the fire? That is what you would be doing. Trust my lousy female instincts. They have been known to be right every now and then. My roses are divine. Thank you so much. Bette.'

(Vivien Leigh reportedly did not want to work with Bette either. In London, when called by a Fox executive about the role, she declined by saying: 'No, thank you. I can just about stand looking at Joan Crawford's face at six o'clock in the morning, but not Bette Davis.')

Selection number three was Olivia de Havilland, who hesitated because of a film she made the previous year, *Lady in a Cage*. In the first fifteen minutes of that movie, her co star Ann Sothern was thrown in a closet, then strangled by some hoods, while the usually genteel and *soignée* Olivia spent the rest of the film on her hands and knees, tormented in a hot suspended elevator. 'Add Olivia's name to the list of movie actresses who would apparently rather be freaks than forgotten,' said *Life*, commenting on her ordeal.

When the script of *Hush . . . Hush, Sweet Charlotte* arrived by courier at Olivia's home in Switzerland, followed by a transatlantic call from Bette Davis and Bob Aldrich, Olivia said, 'Bette, thanks, but no thanks.'

'But, Olivia, you *must* do this picture,' said Bette. 'We need you *desperately*.'

'Darling,' Olivia replied firmly, 'you know how much I hate to play bitches. They make me *so* unhappy.'

'Get her to change her mind,' Bette said to Aldrich when they had hung up.

'How?' asked Aldrich.

'The same way you got Crawford into this mess,' she stated. 'Get on a plane and *make Olivia change her mind*.'

Two days later, after taking three planes, a train, and a taxi up a goat trail, Aldrich arrived at Olivia's summer home in the Swiss mountains. They spoke for an entire day and night, until 'the shrewd director' made the actress see the character of Miriam in a different light. Instead of being played as a hard, conniving bitch, she should be portrayed as a cool but devious sophisticate. 'It's always the charming ones of evil intent who are the dangerous ones,' Olivia agreed. 'The others you can see coming. But you can't see Miriam coming, and she's really dangerous.'

The added lure of the hundred thousand dollars in salary, plus living expenses of a thousand dollars a week for ten weeks, and first-class air transportation for her, her two children, and a nurse-maid, also helped, and Olivia finally said yes to Aldrich.

She and the director then called Bette Davis in Los Angeles and gave her the good news. Aldrich requested that Bette keep the news a secret until he returned to Los Angeles in two days, when he would legally inform Crawford and her lawyer by letter. But, according to the director, further 'confusion and treachery' then occurred, this time initiated by Bette. She had no intention of waiting two days to tell the world that she was finally rid of Joan Crawford. She called her press agent, Rupert Allen, who immediately leaked the story to the press.

'I heard the news of my replacement over the radio, lying in my hospital bed,' said Joan. 'I wept for thirty-nine hours.'

Regretting 'the tactless, aggressive self-serving efforts' of Bette and her staff, Aldrich dismissed the premature announcement with: 'C'est La Goddamn Vie!'

'I still believe in this business, but there should be some gentleness,' Joan wept further to the press the next day. 'I think it takes a lot of guts to make pictures, and I'm going to make a lot more of them. But I am going to make them with decent, gentle people.'

'She made all these statements from underneath her oxygen tent,' said the unsympathetic Bette. 'The widow Steele even took a crack at Olivia. She said, "I'm glad for Olivia, she needs the work." '

'I still get chills when I think of the treachery that Miss Davis indulged in on that movie,' Crawford told this writer in 1973, 'but I *refused* to ever let anger or hate enter my heart.'

'Years later, Mother would only have to *hear* the name of Bette Davis mentioned to start a tirade,' said Christina Crawford. 'Bette Davis was the consummate match for my mother's storehouse of tricks and intimidation. She was as shrewd a professional and every bit as indomitable.'

Producer-director Robert Aldrich would also be showered with scorn by Crawford in the years to come. 'He is a man who loves evil, horrendous, vile things,' she said.

'If the shoe fits, wear it,' said Aldrich, 'and I am very fond of Joan.'

TheWorks.co.uk

What will you discover?

The Works Stores Ltd B46 1AL
Twickenham(908) 02087440119
VAT Reg No: 135597879

SALE   908 2 195652 03/04/2019 10:35

You were served by LANIE

Qty Description	Amount
1 Bette and Joan The Divine F	1.50
Total	1.50
Total To Pay	1.50
Cash	£1.50

VAT INCLUDED IN ABOVE TOTAL AMOUNT

RATE Z	0.00%	0.00 OF	1.50

*** *** *** *** *** *** *** *** *** ***

You could have earned 5 points with a
Together Rewards card. Forgotten your
card? Bring your Together card and
this receipt within 90 days to collect
these points.

*** *** *** *** *** *** *** *** *** ***

Thank you for shopping at The Works

20

'People who wanted to be nice about my looks always would say – "You remind me so much of Bette Davis." Very nice, except I can't stand Bette Davis.'

Jeanne Moreau, 1965

On September 9, 1964, when production resumed on *Hush . . . Hush, Sweet Charlotte*, it was said that Bette Davis and Olivia de Havilland bid goodbye and good riddance to Pepsi queen Joan Crawford by raising their bottles of Coke in a toast to a fresh start and a future triumph.

As filming proceeded, even though de Havilland and Davis were close friends, Bette attempted to reassert her position as first star and partner of the production. She was in her usual position of authority, sitting in front of the camera, when Olivia appeared in her opening scene on the mansion stairs. But de Havilland refused to be intimidated by the assertive Bette. She stated: 'I am not a competitive person. If I am attacked, I simply refuse to fight back. I never said a word to her. I just did my scene, with a look that said "I will not fight you; I will not accept your challenge." Bette understood.'

When *Charlotte* was released early in 1965, critics with a yen for violence applauded the film. Kenneth Tynan said the piece was 'yanked to the level of art by Miss Davis' performance as the raging, aging Southern belle; this wasted Bernhardt, with her screen-filling eyes and electrifying vocal attack, squeezes genuine pathos from a role conceived in cardboard. She has done nothing better since *The Little Foxes*.' Judith Crist also sanctioned the movie. 'The blood is on the cleaver, the madwoman is on the loose, the headless corpse is on the prowl and the Guignol is as grand as it can get,' said Crist, praising 'the succulent expertise of Bette and the exquisite refinement of Olivia,' while nothing that Agnes Moorehead as 'the whining po' white trash just almost walks off with the show'.

To help the box office, Bette and Olivia made a personal tour of theaters in the East and Midwest. The two stars were squared off evenly, said *World Telegram* reporter William Peper, with 'two Oscars each, separate limos, entourages and personal eccentricities.' In one interview Olivia sweetly told Bette it was a pity she did not get the chance to work with Vivien Leigh. 'That would have given you a chance to forgive her for getting *Gone With the Wind*,' said the former Melanie, while Bette 'roared and spouted cigarette smoke.'

Skillfully avoiding questions on Joan Crawford ('We don't want to give her more ammunition than she already has, do we, dear?'), Bette told John Gruen that she was happy that Crawford had left the picture. 'Those repeat duo appearances never really work out,' she said. 'Look at those Doris Day–Rock Hudson films. They're getting worse by the minute.'

In Chicago, at a press luncheon, while Olivia sipped on 'a whisper of gin and a whisper of soda,' Bette drank straight Scotch and puffed on endless cigarettes, 'inhaling with a finality that seemed to defy the smoke to seep out.' Mourning the recent death of Errol Flynn – 'I was almost *hysterical* when I heard the news,' said Bette – Olivia smiled and suggested that Bette and Errol had hardly been bosom buddies during their professional days at Warner's.

'Shut *up*, dear,' Bette hissed at de Havilland.

'How would you like to make this tour with Joan Crawford?' Olivia replied.

'And how would you like to make it with Joan Fontaine?' said Bette, as reporters hastily scribbled the testy jabs in their notepads.

In Hollywood that same month, while she was being followed by a team from *Look*, Bette was approached in a disco by a young girl. 'Excuse me,' said the young girl, 'but are you Miss Joan Crawford?' Bette laughed uproariously and the girl fled. A short time later, spotting the girl crying in a corner, Bette rose and went to her. Putting her arm around her shoulder, the star explained, 'We weren't laughing at you, my dear. Miss Crawford is my oldest and bitterest rival. My name is Bette Davis.'

Angling for another Oscar nomination for *Sweet Charlotte*, Bette appeared on the Los Angeles talk shows in late January. When the nominations were released, the film received seven mentions, including Best Song, Best Editing for Michael Luciano and Best Supporting Actress for Agnes Moorehead. Bette Davis was not included in the final citations.

A recovered Joan Crawford was delighted, of course. With Bette out of the running for Best Actress, she was now relieved of the duty of soliciting permission to accept for the other nominees. She had already secured a major spot on the show, to present Best Director, and that enabled her to reign supreme backstage on the night of the big show. She told the press she was 'thrilled to death to meet Patti Page,' who was chosen, in lieu of Bette, to sing the title song from *Hush . . . Hush, Sweet Charlotte* on the Oscarcast. That night Joan also had to grapple with the weighty decision of which of two gowns she should wear. Deborah Kerr was scheduled to appear before Crawford. She told the Academy she was wearing white. 'I don't trust her. I think she might change at the last minute,' said Joan. She told Edith Head to make up the same gown twice, one in white, the other in black, at three thousand dollars a pop. 'Miss Kerr wore white and Joan switched to the black gown. She was the hit of the evening when she presented the award to George Cukor for *My Fair Lady*,' said Miss Head.

QUEENS OF HORROR

Throughout the sixties, to a new generation, the names of Bette Davis and Joan Crawford were synonymous with horror movies. Of the two it was Crawford who caused the most damage to her reputation, by appearing in a series of cheap, exploitative films which were many watts away from the days of *Mildred Pierce* and *Grand Hotel*.

Stabbed between the ribs, she expired early in her second film for William Castle, *I Saw What You Did*. For four days' work she received top billing and fifty thousand dollars. When asked by Harrison Carroll why she was doing the role, Crawford replied, 'Because I think the film will have a terrific identity with parents and audiences.'

'Of course she rationalized what she did,' said George Cukor.

'Joan even lied to herself. She would write to me about these pictures, actually believing that they were quality scripts. You could never tell her they were garbage. She was a star, and this was her next picture. She had to keep working, as did Bette. The two of them spawned a regrettable cycle in motion pictures.'

In 1967, when the offers ran out in Hollywood, Joan Crawford went to England to make *Circus of Blood*, later retitled *Berserk*. Dressed in a scarlet ringmaster's jacket and black leotards (designed by Edith Head), she played the owner of a traveling circus whose staff are stabbed and garroted to death. Again, the true villain of the story was her troubled daughter (Judy Geeson). When asked by a British interviewer why her real-life actress-daughter, Christina, wasn't asked to play the latter role, Joan snapped, 'Because she is much too old for the part.'

> *'Bette Davis says: "My name goes above the title. I am a star." Yes, she is a star, and a great one. But is it worth playing all those demented old ladies to maintain that status?'*
>
> Myrna Loy

In England that year, Bette also found employment, but she bristled loudly when it was suggested that, like Joan Crawford, she seemed to be specialising in horror films.

'*Hush . . . Hush, Sweet Charlotte* was *not* a horror film,' said Bette. 'It was the study of a very sad woman who had a terrible thing happen in her life.' *The Nanny*, her new picture, in which a British governess knocks a ten-year-old boy unconscious and then tries to drown him in a bathtub, was described by the actress as 'a problem between a nanny and a young boy. That's the contretemps.'

During the late 1960s, Davis did make repeated attempts to escape the low-budget horror mold. When Warner Brothers bought the screen rights to *Who's Afraid of Virginia Woolf?*, she campaigned vigorously for the role of the virago, Martha. 'I must *have* it,' she told Wanda Hale. 'I love those gutty words. I told Mr. Abee that I would *kill* for the part.'

When she didn't get the role, Bette said she was shaken. 'Though not as shaken as when I learned that Elizabeth Taylor would play it. That's when I really went into shock. Miss Taylor is a *darling*, but, my dear, they must be obviously making *another* picture.'

In 1967 Angela Lansbury was starring on Broadway in the musical *Mame* when Bob Aldrich considered her for the lead in his new movie, *The Killing of Sister George*. 'We met with her in her hotel suite,' said Lukas Heller. 'When Bob offered her the part of the lesbian, Miss Lansbury became quite offended. "No, I think not," she told him, "I have my fans and reputation to think of." '

Bette Davis was then approached. 'I have no qualms about playing a lesbian,' she told Leonard Lyons. 'I have been married four times so I think my track record speaks for itself.'

In November 1966 Sheilah Graham reported that Davis was also up for a lead role in *Valley of the Dolls*. She would play Helen Lawson, the tough, neurotic, boozy Broadway star, who was said to be an amalgam of several women, including Ethel Merman and Joan Crawford. Jacqueline Susann, author of the trash novel, dismissed that speculation. 'Ethel Merman was a lady and a philanthropist compared to Joan Crawford,' said Susann. 'If I had known Joan when I was writing *Valley of the Dolls*, Helen Lawson would have been a monster.'

She was still a bitch (Helen Lawson) and a strong part, Bette believed, and eager to land the movie role, she became good friends, temporarily, with author Susann. A shrewd quid-pro-quo dealer, Susann also used Davis as her *entrée* into what was left of Hollywood society. The two posed for magazine photographs at Bette's rented Malibu beach house. Susann also used Davis to push her book in media circles closed to her. Barred from appearing on the Johnny Carson TV show, Susann got Bette to plug her book for her. 'You know, John,' said Bette on the air to Carson, 'I just read the most marvelous book. It's called *Valley of the Moon*.'

In March 1967, when Bette lost out on *Valley of the Dolls* and *The Killing of Sister George*, she went back to England to make *The Anniversary*. 'Another horror exercise for faint-hearted horror fans.' The role of the fiendish one-eyed mother of three sons, one of whom 'likes to wear ladies' underthings,' came to Bette courtesy of Hammer Films, which was co-owned by her British son-in-law's family, the Hymans. 'They were Jewish, and Mother still had an aversion to Jews,' said B.D. 'She even tried to get me to change my last name after I married my husband, Jeremy. I refused. I told her there was nothing wrong with Jews; they were God's chosen people. And the Hymans were good enough to employ her when no one else would.'

> *'An affair now and then is good for a marriage. It adds spice, stops it from getting boring . . . I ought to know.'*
>
> Bette Davis advising B.D. to cheat on her husband

> *'Christopher is twenty-five now and is in Vietnam. He's in Saigon, that's all I know. He's been running ever since he was five; this is the one place he can't run from. It will make a man of him.'*
>
> Joan Crawford to the *New York Post*, 1967

By 1968, Bette and Joan had forsaken Hollywood and were living on the East Coast but in separate states. Davis bought a house in Connecticut, near her married daughter. Crawford moved to a smaller apartment at 150 East Sixty-ninth Street, where by a wry coincidence, Bette's dentist was also located. 'Every time I went there with Bette, I was hoping we'd bump into Crawford in the lobby,' said Vik Greenfield, 'but it never happened.'

Greenfield had met Bette in California a few years before. When he relocated to Connecticut, he rented her garage apartment, and eventually became employed by her for five years. 'I was her secretary, and I mean secretary,' he said. 'That means you baby-sit. All stars are children. They can't be left alone for a minute. Bette was the first to admit that. They are totally impossible to cope with – when it comes to reason and logic. I was fired about once a month, but I was always *for* her. I liked Bette. It's very difficult to dislike her. She was an Aries, with her moon in Gemini, which gives you her mind as twins. Professionally she was a completely different woman to the one we privately knew. When she was at work she was always perfect. On the set she seemed to know everything by osmosis. Without looking, she knew exactly where the camera was. So did Crawford and Turner and Taylor. They were pros, and that was their job.'

In May 1968, both stars officially turned sixty. 'The years are just numbers,' said the outwardly complacent Crawford, as Bette recalled she 'screamed and stayed in bed all day' on her birthday.

Old age could be less desperate with a man around the house, Davis agreed, but one who came without a marriage certificate. Since her divorce from Gary Merrill, she had been adamantly opposed to the legal aspects of marriage. 'I'd only marry again if I found a man who had fifteen million dollars and would sign over half of it to me before the marriage and guaranteed he'd be dead before the year,' she stated.

But a more thorough review of her life during this time found her less rigid in her criteria for a spouse. She was lonely and considered marrying three men during the mid to late 1960s. One was Bob Taplinger, the former head of publicity for Warner's in California, now employed with a corporate public-relations firm in New York. The two met on a plane bound for New York, and it was Bette's idea to resume their old romance. They attended the premiere of *The Sound of Music*, danced every dance at the party afterwards, then spent long weekends together in Connecticut. When Phyllis Battelle of the Hearst syndicate reported that a wedding might be in the offing, Taplinger skipped around the issue but Davis said the idea had occurred to her. 'Bob asked me to marry him twenty-seven years ago,' she told Battelle. 'He's so great. When I've mentioned marriage it's been more or less in kidding form. But it could be fun. Besides, think of the loot. Bob would never *dream* of getting married without the loot!'

Taplinger, a bachelor for fifty-six years, preferred to remain that way, and Bette cast her imposing eyes on other candidates. One suitor had money and social position, she said, but he was a Catholic. His mother sent a priest to her hotel room to talk to Bette about converting. She got the holy man drunk, sent him staggering on his way, and 'that was the end of my attempt to become a Catholic.'

Another 'fiancé' visited her in England while she was filming *The Anniversary*. She was suspicious about his mercenary intentions, so, while discussing their forthcoming nuptials, she told him her lawyer insisted he sign a premarital agreement. The next day, when she returned from the film studio, she was informed that her betrothed had packed up and left that afternoon, leaving no word of farewell. 'It was a terrible blow to my pride,' said Bette. 'But that didn't stop her from proposing to men,' said Vik Greenfield, 'all of whom declined, because her reputation had obviously preceded her.'

Publicly, Joan Crawford was also inclined to downplay her desire for another husband. She told one reporter, 'Every time I say I hope to remarry I get letters from retired colonels, telling me they understand I am very rich, which I'm not, and that they still have all their teeth, and why don't we get together?'

During the mid-sixties she had a discreet but intense affair with an executive at Pepsi Cola. He promised to leave his wife and children for the star-spokeswoman. Instead, under the pressure of an ultimatum from Joan, he left Pepsi for a better position at another company, where he refused to take her calls.

Joan was subsequently linked with Nelson Rockefeller, but he wed another. She then proposed to two men; dubious partners for passion, but perfect escorts. One was George Cukor, who displayed a 1966 photograph of Joan in his California home, endorsed with her signature and her offer of marriage. The other candidate was acting guru Lee Strasberg. A recent widower, Strasberg was placed next to Joan at a dinner party at the home of Jennifer Jones and David Selznick, in 1967. The next day she sent him a letter. 'At dinner last night at Jennifer's you were very sweet to me, and I meant what I said when I asked you to marry me,' wrote Joan. 'I think we'd make a wonderful couple.' Strasberg kept the letter, married a younger woman, and thereafter, to paraphrase actress Ruth Gordon, Crawford 'drew the veil,' retiring reluctantly but gracefully from the war of the sexes. In one of her last interviews, when pressed by *New York Times'* interviewer Patricia Bosworth for some spicy quotes to match the recent sexual confessions of the older Gloria Swanson, Crawford countered with: 'She was talking about the past, wasn't she?' 'No,' said Bosworth. 'She wasn't?' said Joan. 'Well, I think it's rather shocking. I'd rather listen to a good poem.'

'Warner Brothers asked me to play Paul Newman's mother in Cool Hand Luke. *They offered me $25,000 for one day's work. I said "No." I would have been on and off the screen in three minutes. That would be a cheat to the audience.'*

Bette Davis

'Sure, I'd play an ape if they asked me. Maurice Evans did.'

Joan Crawford

Without a spouse or other kindred interests to pursue, all that remained to fill the lives of Bette and Joan was their careers. 'Work is all there is,' said Bette. 'Family doesn't last . . . they all go off. Human relationships – ha! – they're a joke.' After making another tepid film in England, she went to California to play a retired safe-cracker 'with arthritic fingers' opposite Robert Wagner in the TV series, *It Takes a Thief.* In Los Angeles that November she was asked to attend a farewell dinner for studio boss Jack Warner. Not long before, she had castigated Warner for selling her old films to TV ('He received five million dollars for the rights to our old movies, and we will not see a *penny*'), but as the former First Daughter she felt it was her duty to salute Papa Jack at his sendoff. Among the thousand guests who attended the formal sit-down dinner on stage seven at the Warner studio, were Ruby Keeler, Edward G. Robinson, Joan Blondell, Miriam Hopkins, Claire Trevor, Governor Ronald Reagan, Rosalind Russell, and Frank Sinatra. Missing from the alumni lineup was Joan Crawford. 'She didn't show because she knew that Bette would be up on the dais ready to slit her throat,' said Bette's escort, Vik Greenfield.

As it happened, Bette tried to bounce Rosalind Russell from the spotlight. 'They were both on the dais together, and Bette said to Roz, "I want a photograph taken with Mr. Warner." And she pushed her out of the picture,' said Greenfield.

Jim Watters was an entertainment reporter for *Time-Life* when he saw Joan Crawford perform one of *her* competitive star performances at a New York restaurant that year. 'There was a reception at the 21 Club for Ingrid Bergman and Goldie Hawn, who were in New York to make *Cactus Flower*,' said Watters. 'As I was going in, Crawford was getting out of a limo. She apparently had not been invited to the party, because in a loud voice she said to the doorman, "What is this? Whose do is this?" He explained that there was a reception in progress upstairs for Ingrid Bergman and Goldie Hawn. Crawford headed straight for the elevator and went upstairs. She made a grand entrance into the party, and the first person she came face to face with was her old enemy Gloria Grahame, whose husband, Tony Ray, was the assistant director on *Cactus Flower*. Joan's face dropped when she saw Grahame, but she quickly recovered and proceeded to sweep through the room, taking over the party; which wasn't hard, because Goldie Hawn wasn't a star yet, and Ingrid Bergman looked rather dowdy wearing a dress that looked as if she made it.'

> '*Warner Brothers sent me a letter saying they wanted to use a clip from* Now Voyager *in* The Summer of '42. *They implied that they wanted to use it as a laugh. My lawyer wrote back saying, if they wanted a clip to laugh at, why didn't they choose a scene from one of their current films.*'
>
> Bette Davis

As the sixties segued into the seventies, the drastic cultural changes confused and irritated many, including Crawford and Davis. The hippies, free love, and the political protesters especially annoyed Joan. 'Peace and love and all of that is just fine,' she said, 'but there are limits to be observed. When I was young, I also broke some of the stuffy conventional rules. But, damnit, we obeyed the laws, respected our elders, and we always earned our own way. The kids today say they don't trust anyone over thirty. Does this apply to their parents, who seem to be paying for their freedom and rebellion?'

Bette Davis favored the legalization of marijuana. 'It is the forbidden fruit element that attracts,' she said. 'If pot is legalized, I think the young might fall away from it.' She also decried the lack of personal grooming on some of the new generation. 'I think the parents of the revolutionaries have given up,' she told *Show* magazine. 'For example, if my son ever grew his hair to his shoulders

and did not bathe, and he's about six foot and I'm a shrimp, I'd
cut his hair off in the middle of the night and I'd dump him in a
tub.'

The Great Unwashed were not the audience Joan Crawford
had in mind either, for her 1970 book *My Way of Life*. 'Entertain,
decorate, be sexy for your husband,' Joan advised, with tips on
posture ('Sit on hard chairs – soft ones spread the hips'); cooking
('A red vegetable next to a yellow one looks unappetizing); how to
pack for a trip ('Stuff the sleeves of your dresses with tissue, so they
won't wrinkle'); and how to be a perfect houseguest in the country
('Have breakfast in your room and never see your hosts until lunch').

In the book, Joan the Pepsi board member published her work
schedule, opening new bottling plants, from San Diego to Copen-
hagen to Sao Paulo. The timing and precision were that of a West
Point cadet officer. 'Arrive at the plant at ten,' the schedule stated.
'At ten-ten we have the invocation. At ten-fifteen platform guests
and speakers are introduced. At ten forty-five we start touring the
plant, and from eleven to twelve I'm on the platform, signing autographs. On the dot of noon I head for the airport, for our next
destination.'

'The old bitch just wants everyone to know how busy she is,'
said Bette Davis. 'She's like a *goddamn* robot!'

Keeping her cannon well oiled, Joan then fired off her rebuttal
to Bette. 'I'm the quiet one and Bette's explosive,' she told *Life* in
1971. 'I have discipline. She doesn't.'

'My head is high as to my discipline as an actress. I can provide
witnesses,' Davis shot back, which led Crawford to disparage her
rival's following. 'She has a *cult*,' said Joan, 'and what the hell is
a cult except a gang of rebels without a cause. I have *fans*. There's
a big difference.'

THE LADIES WHO LUNCH

Although the two women claimed repeatedly that they preferred
the company and friendship of men, both stars had a steady circle
of female friends over the years. Crawford had more than Davis,
retaining a steady acquaintanceship with dozens of other actresses

by phone but mostly through her voluminous correspondence. Her contacts included Vivien Leigh, Myrna Loy, Marlene Dietrich, Rosalind Russell, Nancy Kelly, Virginia Grey, and such diverse talents as Barbara Stanwyck and Debbie Reynolds.

Reynolds became friends with Joan at the start of the 1950s, during her early days at MGM. 'It wasn't a close friendship,' said the musical-comedy performer. 'It was superficial in that respect, but it was consistent and endured.' They had the same masseuse, Nancy Gianno, and Joan was one of the first to call Debbie when Eddie Fisher left her for Elizabeth Taylor. 'She offered her home to me and the children, if we wanted to get away from the press.' When Reynolds married shoe tycoon Harry Karl, she and Joan frequently lunched at the 21 Club in New York. 'It was always on the second floor, the same corner table at the front of the room, so Joan could see and be seen by everyone who entered.' On those occasions Crawford wore a big hat, drank Russian vodka ('so you couldn't smell it on her breath'), and was always warm and amiable. 'I never knew the bad side of her,' said Debbie. 'She was always very sweet and kind to me.'

Visitors to Crawford's New York apartment commented that the only photographs displayed in the star's living room were one of President John F. Kennedy and one of Barbara Stanwyck.

Approximately the same age, the two began as 'hoofers' on Broadway in the mid-1920s and went to Hollywood to star in silent movies not long after. In the early 1930s, when Stanwyck was married to actor Frank Fay, she lived in Brentwood, close enough to Crawford to find refuge in her house when Fay went into his alcoholic rages.

'Joan really liked Stanwyck. She never had anything but wonderful things to say about her,' writer Carl Johnes recalled. 'It was always a kind of bond between them that the crews on their pictures used to call Stanwyck "Missy", and Joan Crawford was always "Miss C." ' In 1935, when newcomer Robert Taylor was making MGM's *The Gorgeous Hussy*, the sight of the gorgeous young actor with the coal-black hair, the blue eyes and double eyelashes sent the star of that picture, Joan Crawford, into spasms of ecstasy. But it was a 'look, but don't touch' situation for Joan, because Taylor was the steady boyfriend of the slightly older Barbara Stanwyck

('He's got a lot to learn and I've got a lot to teach'), who, according to one reporter, 'would kick Joan right in the butt if she even so much as touched a hair of Taylor's fine head in private.'

On a visit to New York in the early 1970s, Stanwyck had lunch with Crawford at the 21 Club. Also at the table was Stanwyck's close friend, reporter Shirley Eder, who wrote up the meal in a book. Dispensing with menus, Joan ordered calves' liver for all three. 'She also chose our vegetables, and the salad, leaving the choice of our dessert to us,' said Eder. When Joan got up to greet someone in another part of the room, Stanwyck said, 'I hate calves' liver.'

'Why didn't you tell her?' Eder asked.

'I wouldn't dare,' said the star.

On a subsequent occasion, prior to one of her work trips to California, Eder said Crawford made plans to see Stanwyck for dinner when she arrived. At noon that day Joan's secretary, Betty Barker, called Stanwyck. Miss Crawford was on a plane, en route from New York to L.A., Barker told the star, and she planned to see her at Don the Beachcomber's for dinner at 5:00 P.M.

'Five P.M.?' Stanwyck asked. 'Who eats dinner at that ungodly hour? Why do we have to meet so *early*?'

Because of the time difference, the secretary replied: 'Miss Crawford's stomach will be on Eastern Standard Time.'

'Well you tell Miss Crawford that Miss Stanwyck's stomach is on California time and has been for the past thirty years,' the classy silver-haired legend replied, declining to dine with Joan on that trip.

'It's a strange friendship, but nevertheless it's real,' said Shirley Eder.

'And every year, on Joan's birthday, there was a big floral gift from Stanwyck,' said Carl Johnes. 'It was always signed "From Missy to Miss C."'

BETTE AND OLIVIA

'In my day the most beautiful actresses in Hollywood were Hedy Lamarr and Rita Hayworth. And the most liked were Carole Lombard and Jean Harlow. But I never did pal around with actresses. Their talk usually bored me to tears.'
                                                            Bette Davis

In December each year a select group of actresses received a Christmas card from Bette. They included Agnes Moorehead, Joan
Blondell (both on Crawford's list), Claire Trevor, and Deborah
Kerr. 'She was also friendly with Marlene Dietrich, without sending
cards or letters,' said secretary Vik Greenfield. 'Once they were in
the same hospital in Philadelphia, on the same floor, and Marlene
sent a note that said "Dear Bette, Get well soon. But please, *no*
visitations. Love, Marlene." '

There was also her 'best friend,' Olivia de Havilland.

'They were never really that close,' said B.D. Hyman. 'In later
years Olivia always visited Mother when she was in the States, and
if Mother was in the mood she called Olivia when she was in
Europe.'

'I think they're as close as actresses can be,' said Vik Greenfield.
'Olivia has a great admiration for Bette. It is not returned. Since
they were girls at Warner's together, Bette always had the upper
hand, so she – I hate to use the word – tolerates Olivia. And Olivia
really, really likes Bette.'

BETTE AND KATE

'I wanted to be the first to win three Oscars, but Miss Hepburn has done it.
Actually it hasn't been done. Miss Hepburn only won half an Oscar. If they'd
given me half an Oscar I would have thrown it back in their faces. You see
I'm an Aries. I never lose.'

Bette Davis

She was a fan of only two actresses, Davis said repeatedly. One
was Garbo; the other was Katharine Hepburn.

She always wanted to have Hepburn's face, 'with its hollows and
high cheekbones,' she told entertainment reporter Robert Osborne.
'When I hit forty, I screamed every time I saw a mirror. But Miss
Hepburn with her bone structure could look good at a hundred.'

'She's awfully good,' Hepburn said in a sparse tribute to Davis,
who occasionally acknowledged she was amenable to working with
the Great Kate. Early in 1936, at RKO, when Hepburn had been
cast as Mary, Queen of Scots, Davis wanted the role opposite her,

Elizabeth the Tudor Queen. One report claimed Jack Warner refused to loan her out, while another said it was director John Ford who booted her off the set, because Bette 'talked too damn much.' ('I always thought Mary was an absolute *jackass*,' said Hepburn, regretting that she hadn't played Elizabeth herself.)

In the decades to come, Hepburn and Davis were considered as co stars for other projects, including *The Great Lie, The Night of the Iguana*, and *Ship of Fools*; but the kinetic pairing never occurred. In March 1977 *The New York Times* reported that the two actresses were scheduled to work together in *Whitewater*, a film based on a novel about two spirited women in a small Texas town during the 1940s. The scheduled director was Jan Kadar, who said there would be a pivotal confrontational scene between the two, but which of the two formidable stars would win the showdown, and first billing, was not announced.

Whitewater was never made. In 1985, *Life* attempted to bring the two legends together for a photo layout. Entertainment editor Jim Watters was in charge of the magazine's special movie issue. For the cover he persuaded the current female powers – Jane Fonda, Barbra Streisand, Jessica Lange, and Sally Field to pose for a group portrait; for the closing shot he wanted Katharine Hepburn and Bette Davis seated side by side. 'I felt it would be an historic picture,' said Watters. 'The two didn't know each other, but they represented all that was great about Hollywood.'

Watters sent a letter to each actress, outlining his concept. Bette answered first, with a telephone call. 'This is a fantastic *idea*,' she said, 'truly inspiring.'

Hepburn did not respond. 'I wrote her a second note,' said Watters, 'saying "Why are you ignoring me?" In the meantime, Davis kept calling me. "I am coming to New York, to do these photographs with Miss Hepburn," she said, "but apparently Miss Hepburn doesn't *want* to do them. What is *wrong* with her? She *must* do this. Contact her *again*." '

The third note apparently moved Hepburn. Watters answered his phone one day and heard a familiar voice bellowing at him from the other end. 'This is Kate Hepburn, and why are you making my life miserable?' she barked.

She wouldn't pose with Davis, she declared. 'Oh, I can see your mind just clicking away, that this is one of those things where you get two old dames together and we'd be embarrassed to back out because one would blame the other. But I am saying no because it is a shitty idea and because I have done enough for *Life* magazine. The last time you didn't even put me on the cover.' ('We had a wonderful private look at Kate's domain in Connecticut, and a strong Mick Jagger story, but the photo editor went with an embryo on the cover,' said Watters.)

Hepburn could not be swayed by the historical significance of the photograph or the fact that Bette Davis was hot for the idea. 'Well, I'm not going to do it,' said Kate. 'I did enough shit for *Life*.'

'She kept using that word twenty times in two minutes,' Watters recalled.

'Forget the shitty idea, and don't write again, and don't call me,' said the intractable one.

'Then she hung up in my ear by slamming down the receiver,' said the editor, who had to tell Bette Davis that Hepburn wouldn't pose with her.

'Is she *crazy*?' Bette roared. 'The woman is *nuts*!'

'Davis was not happy, to say the least,' said Watters. 'But I managed to calm her down by assuring her that *Life* would be very happy to photograph her on her own, which we did.'

> *'The camera doesn't know how to lie. There is a thing, God help us, called close-ups. There is no place to return to when you retire from the movies.'*
> Alexandra del Lago in *Sweet Bird of Youth*

By 1972 the movie careers of Bette and Joan were apparently over. Joan had made her last feature two years before, playing an anthropologist in *Trog*. Her leading man was an eight-foot troglodyte monster, but the star behaved as though she was appearing opposite Cary Grant or Clark Gable. She supplied her own wardrobe, arriving on location on the gray English moors with thirty-eight pieces of luggage. She had her face taped back by 'gifted hairstylist, Ramon Guy,' and divulged one of her special beauty secrets to a woman's magazine writer: 'There's a trick, Claudette Colbert taught me years ago,' said Joan. 'Dump a tray of ice in your wash basin and splash ice water on your bazooms. It keeps them firm.'

In 1971 Bette Davis made her last film for five years, *Bunny O'Hare*. Wearing a hippie dress, a long blond wig, and a floppy granny hat, she played a bank robber bored with her family and retirement. 'Silly, a gimmick . . . dreadful,' said Vincent Canby, panning the film and the star, whose career, 'which began forty years ago, has been recycled more often than the average rubber tire.'

With no offers for features, Davis and Crawford grabbed whatever work they could in TV. 'I want to do more guest spots,' Crawford told *TV Guide*. 'I was dying to do a *Daktari* or an *I Spy*. I was desperate to work with Judy [the chimp in *Daktari*] and with Gentle Ben. When I read that Clarence the Cross-Eyed Lion died I sent a telegram to the producer, Ivan Tors.'

Lucille Ball used Crawford in one of her revivified comedy series on TV. The script, not written for Joan, exploited one of her fetishes – her mania for cleaning. The plot had Lucy and her sidekick, Vivian Vance, with a broken-down car, stopping at a Hollywood mansion and finding the occupant, a once great star, down on her hands and knees scrubbing the floors. Assuming the star was destitute, Lucy and Ethel then arranged a charity auction to help her.

Gloria Swanson was being talked of for the role of the star when Stan Kamen, Crawford's agent at William Morris, said, 'Why not give it to Joan?'

'She won't sue us?' said Lucy.

'She loves your show,' said Kamen. 'She'd be delighted to play herself.'

During rehearsals, Crawford, terrified of appearing before a live studio audience, frequently forgot her lines and came close to being fired by Lucy the coproducer. But Lucy the actress tried to relax the great star. Between breaks, as Joan sat in her chair 'with her nose in her purse,' Lucy, no shy violet, went over and teased her with: 'What'cha got in there?' Then she snapped open Crawford's purse. 'The star was drinking 100-proof vodka from a brown paper bag – with two straws. And all these years she's been so refined,' said the item in *McCall's*.

Bette Davis also clashed with Lucille Ball, but not over a mere TV-guest-star job. At stake was the multi-million-dollar musical *Mame*. When Warner's bought the movie rights, Bette asked her agent to submit her name. 'I wanted the lead,' she said. 'I had agreed to test and pay for my own wardrobe. Then, when Lucy was signed, I said, "What about the other role? As Vera Charles, the close friend to Mame?" Everyone thought it was a *divine* idea. After all I *knew* Miss Ball. We were old *buddies*. We attended the same dramatic school in New York many years *before*. Then the word got back to me that Miss Ball didn't want two stars in the same picture. I said, "Forget the star billing. Put me in a special box at the end of the credits. Or leave my name off entirely. I could be a *mystery* guest." But no, Miss Ball would have *none* of that. It was her show and she was determined to sink it *alone*.'

In August 1972 Davis and Crawford were working at the same TV studio, Universal. Bette was starring in a pilot film for a potential series, *The Judge and Jake Wyler*, Joan was a guest star in a segment of *Sixth Sense*. Of the two, Bette had the larger salary and assignment, scheduled for ten days' work. Joan was there for three days, and was paid a paltry two thousand five hundred dollars, but she was given her customary perks – a studio limousine, her own bungalow, and fresh flowers each day. 'That shows the difference between the two,' said Vik Greenfield. 'Bette had this little dressing room and she took her meals alone, as she preferred.'

One day, Davis instructed her secretary to 'Go and see what Crawford was up to.'

'After lunch I went off and watched Joan come out of her bunga-low,' he said. 'She had five men as escorts, and she had her hands on each one of theirs. They escorted her like this fragile queen down to her limousine, and then they all drove off to the lot, which was a block and a half away. I didn't follow, because if someone pointed out who I was, there would have been a scene.'

Each afternoon of her three-day stay, Joan was visited by such studio notables as Lew Wasserman (Bette and Joan's former agent, now president of the studio), Alfred Hitchcock, Rock Hudson, and producer Aaron Spelling, who invited Joan to dinner to meet his new bride, Candy. 'This was before Aaron made it big,' said *Dynasty* designer Nolan Miller. 'And Candy wore a pair of wispy diamond earrings at dinner. Crawford quickly took Mr. Spelling aside and told him, "Until you can afford to buy your wife important pieces of jewelry, don't buy her anything." '

Photographer George Hurrell was also called to the set, to photograph Joan. He recalled the occasion for *Interview* magazine. 'How she ever got through or how she remembered her lines, except when they held up a card, I don't know.' Crawford started the morning off with 100-proof vodka over ice, and was partial to complaining to the veteran artist. 'She was "Oh-George"-ing me and all that, asking "Why don't they give me a series, why don't they . . ." All she wanted to do was work as a star. The producers were sore as hell about it, but they had to cater to her or else.'

At the conclusion of filming, Joan attended the Friday-night wrap party. 'Slightly drunk,' she gave gifts to each member of the cast, shook hands with the crew, then departed in her limousine. 'As she was driven out of the studio, the irony of the situation was not evident,' said writer Hector Arce. 'This would be her very last job in Hollywood. She was ending her career playing a small part in a TV film at the same studio where Bette Davis began her career forty years before. And the title of the last film was "Dear Joan, We're Going to Scare You to Death." '

> *'Women's Lib? Poor little things. They always look so unhappy. Have you noticed how bitter their faces are?'*
>
> Joan Crawford

> *'Gay Liberation? I ain't agin it, it's just that there's nothing in it for me!'*
>
> Bette Davis

Strangely enough, at the same time the studios stopped making new Davis and Crawford features, the demand for their old movies increased. Classic pictures such as *All About Eve* and *Mildred Pierce* were becoming cult favorites at revival houses and on college campuses across America. Part of the renewed interest was due to a national nostalgia craze that began in 1971 with the opening of *No, No, Nanette* on Broadway. The fascination with the past was described by *Life* writer Loudon Wainwright, as 'A longing for the irrecoverable to stave off preoccupation with a future in which there is only one predictable entirely unsentimental outcome.'

Coupled with their renewed popularity from the nostalgia boom, Bette and Joan also learned they were the favorite leading icons of another growing public force – the Gay Liberation movement.

In March 1953 James Quirk, author of *The Films of Joan Crawford* and writer, editor, and publisher of his own newsletter, offered his timely thesis – THE CULT OF BETTE AND JOAN. The True Reasons Why They Drive Homosexuals Wild.

Analyzing the 'frenzied, high-camp' element involved in the gay preoccupation with Davis and Crawford, Quirk said the stars 'mirrored certain frenzied, posturing, arrogant, primadonna-ish, ego-deifying, self-projective, super-compensating principles that psychologists and psychiatrists have spotted in the more aggressive and flamboyant homosexuals, especially those in show business.'

Using multiple metaphors, similes, and parallels, Quirk pointed to Bette in *Now Voyager*. In that she was mother-dominated, fat, and unattractive, *but* she transformed herself into a swan and landed herself a beautiful man, which was exactly the same scenario as 'many a gay gone New York-way via Florida or some godforsaken hinterland.' Then there was Joan Crawford in *The Damned Don't Cry*, busting out of a dull small town and using a ladder of men to get 'a plushy pad, groovy duds, etc., culminating in a Gotterdammerung of masochistic hell-let-loose [sic] with a fast fall back to the gutter.' Many a homosexual could identify with that too, Quirk opined; and with Joan in *Possessed*, when she shoots the man she can't have, offering gays vicarious purgation, because, 'being essentially non-violent,' they prefer to watch Joan Crawford do the killing for them. Men, money, and power – these were the three things the two actresses were in aggressive, intent pursuit of, the author said in summation, and that was why the typical cross-section homosexual got a bang out of old Bette and Joan movies.

'Your article was *very* informative,' Joan Crawford told Quirk, whilst Bette Davis was more expansive for *Playboy*. 'Homosexuals are probably the most artistic and appreciative human beings who worship films and theater,' she said. 'Certainly, I've been one of the artists they admire very much. It was always said that Judy Garland and I had the biggest following, but I don't think it's fair to say it's because I'm flamboyant. I'm not flamboyant. In my personal life, I've never been known as flamboyant. Joan Crawford was flamboyant.'

THE RACE GOES ON

In May 1970 Joan Crawford was presented with an award of achievement from her old alma mater, Stephens College, which she had attended for a grand total of two months in her youth. The college, eager to get as much coverage as possible from the star's return, held a press conference for newspaper and TV reporters from St. Louis and Kansas City. Among those present was future author Alanna Nash, then a sophomore at the school. Weeks after the event the student-writer was surprised to receive a typewritten, personally signed letter from Miss Crawford, thanking her for attending the press conference. 'I soon learned,' said Nash, 'that everyone in the room had received a similar thank you. This was my introduction to the incredible Crawford efficiency.' Nash responded by sending Joan her story on the star's visit to Stephens. 'And thus began a correspondence and a friendship that would last for the next eight years,' said the young writer.

In 1972, Carl Johnes was an assistant story editor at Columbia Pictures, when he too became friends with the star. One day at work he was assigned to go and help Crawford pack her books and papers, for dispatch to Brandeis University, where her collection was stored. 'I beat Bette Davis in *that* department,' Joan crowed to Carl, pleased that her bestowal had preceded Bette's donation to Boston University. 'This was the first of a series of wry outbursts on the subject of their famous rivalry that I was treated to over the next five years,' Johnes recalled.

One favorite tale, delivered by Joan in a flawless imitation of

Bette Davis, recounted the time in 1943 when the two rivals met at Warner Brothers. 'When she first went to the studio, Joan told me she tried very hard to make peace with Davis,' said Johnes. 'She went to her one day and said, "Bette, we are now at the same studio. We have the same boss, the same friends in New York. We've had a similar career." And Davis listened to all this, then, waving her arms and popping her eyes, she said, "So *what!*" – which Crawford mimicked perfectly.'

In November 1971 Davis was honored with a day at the prestigious Players Club in New York. 'She arrived looking very chic,' said Sanford Dody, co-author of her book *The Lonely Life*. 'At one o'clock in the afternoon she was wearing a little suit and sables. She was every inch Miss Margo Channing.'

The following year Joan Crawford had her day at the Gramercy Park Club. 'She arrived in a peekaboo dress, fuck-me shoes, and her hair was blown out. She looked like a dress manufacturer's lay for the night,' said Dody.

For sustenance, the star carried a huge handbag, which housed her usual bottle of vodka. 'We showed her movie *A Woman's Face*,' Dody recalled. 'And afterwards, across the room, she gave me the eye and beckoned to me. I went over with a guest and introduced myself. After I had mentioned that I had written Bette's autobiography, Joan looked at me and said, "Oh!" Then she fled to the john with her handbag and we didn't see her sober for the rest of the afternoon. She was truly wild.'

The marked difference between Crawford and Davis, the author believed, was that 'Joan never truly knew who she was – ever. She was very insecure as a person. She never had that center of gravity that Bette Davis had. From the minute Bette came out of the womb she screamed her name to the moon. She was also a very great artist. That artistry gave her a very strong center. Whereas Crawford, although I think she's underestimated as a movie actress, was never a great performer. Some of her old movies are excellent, but she never had the acting ability of Bette.'

Film critic Judith Crist agreed. 'Bette was an actor who was also a movie star. She had the impact, the gestures, and everything else. She was unique, complete; her only equal today is Meryl Streep.

Joan Crawford, on the other hand, was a product of the movies. She was created shot by shot. She could not have a life of her own upon a stage. That's the difference. The ultimate test.'

A CALL FROM BETTE AND JOAN

In 1973 veteran publicist John Springer launched his popular series Legendary Ladies of the Movies, at Town Hall in New York City. The series featured clips of movies, followed by a personal appearance and question-and-answer period with the featured star. The first Legends announced were Bette Davis, Myrna Loy, Sylvia Sidney, and Jean Arthur. Arthur, terrified of *any* appearance, withdrew, and Springer asked Ginger Rogers to step in. Ginger accepted, then canceled when the news was prematurely announced by a columnist. 'Could I possibly approach Joan Crawford?' Springer asked, knowing her fear of live audiences. 'If it means a lot to you . . . I'll do it,' said Joan.

But first on the bill, as always, came Bette Davis. On the night of February 4, 1973, a medley of her greatest film hits opened the series at Town Hall. 'Swamp fevers, gunshot wounds, bubonic plague, the deaths of countless lovers, the brain tumor to end all brain tumors, car accidents, shipwrecks, beatings at the hands of the syndicate and suicide on the Chicago train tracks – she has survived them all,' said columnist Rex Reed. 'Fasten your seat belts, it's going to be a bumpy night,' said Bette in the last clip, from *All About Eve*. The frame faded, the houselights came up, and the star swept in from the wings. Halting mid-stage, she threw a wave towards the balcony, then bowed from the waist at the roar of acclaim from her fans. 'I will never *forget* that welcome as long as I live,' she told them, before sitting down to answer questions from her audience.

Where did she get her famous walk?

'I never planned it that way, it's part of my zest for life.'

Would she marry again?

'No, my dear. The point is, who'd consider marrying me?'

And what is your professional opinion of Joan Crawford?

'I would not presume to answer that,' said Bette, cutting the topic short.

Eight weeks later, on April 5, it was Crawford's turn at Town Hall. 'She had prepared herself,' said Springer. 'A Crawford spy was at all the preceding shows. She knew exactly how Bette Davis entered, how Myrna Loy took her bows.' Following clips from her greatest hits – *Grand Hotel, The Women, Mildred Pierce, Sudden Fear* and *What Ever Happened to Baby Jane?*, Joan was pushed from the wings into the spotlight onstage. The volume and length of her ovation (greater than Bette's she would boast) stunned then dissolved the legend. 'Grateful tears dripped from her eyes to the floor,' said *Village Voice* reporter Arthur Bell. 'But somehow the mascara stayed intact. So did the famous shoulders, the mouth, the shoes.' Responding to written questions, Joan was asked if she knew the name for her famous ankle-strapped shoes. 'It starts with an F,' said Crawford, 'and I think if you remember, they held me up a goddamn long time.' She said she enjoyed playing mean women, 'because there's a little bit of bitch in every woman, and a lot in every man.'

And what was it like to work with Bette Davis?

'It was one of the greatest challenges I ever had,' said Joan seriously. Pausing to allow the laughter from the audience to taper off, she added, 'I meant that kindly. Bette is of a different temperament than I. Bette had to yell every morning. I just sat and knitted. I knitted a scarf from Hollywood to Malibu.'

'It was probably the most threatening scarf since Madame Defarge's,' said Beth Fallon of the *Daily News*.

'Put up your dukes, Bette,' Addison Verrill advised in *Variety*.

The following Saturday morning the phone rang in this writer's apartment. On the other end was Bette Davis, calling from her home in Connecticut. She was responding to an interview request I had made, to talk about *The Catered Affair*, one of her favorite movies. After discussing the film, she segued easily to other topics – Hollywood, her other films, her advancing age. Like Margo Channing, Bette loathed the march of time and the inevitable aging process. 'I turned sixty-*five* a week ago,' she said. 'It was a tragedy! I thought sixty was *bad*, but this is the *pits*. There is *nothing* good about growing old.'

As the conversation was drawing to a close, I wondered if it would be prudent to talk of Joan Crawford, whom I had seen at

Town Hall the previous week. First, I had assumed that Davis had already heard about the event; second, I was sure that when the subject of Crawford came up she would offer her usual terse 'No comment.' But when I mentioned the evening to her, it was apparent that this was her first feedback. '*God!*' said Davis, her voice rising with interest. 'I would have given anything to have been a *fly* on the wall at that thing. Tell me how *did* it go?'

I mentioned that Miss Crawford had been nervous at first, but eventually rose to the occasion and fielded the questions and answers quite well.

'And the *clips*? Were there *enough*?' Miss Davis asked, as if to suggest that her rival didn't have that many good films to fill an evening.

'The clips were sensational,' I said, 'very entertaining.'

'*Oh!*' said Bette, 'and which ones were *those*?'

'*Mildred Pierce, Sudden Fear*, some of the musicals, and *What Ever Happened to Baby Jane?*'

'Yes, *Jane*. A *good* film,' said Davis.

'She spoke about working with you,' I ventured.

'Of course she did,' said Bette. 'And what did Joan *say*?'

Without mentioning the long-scarf-to-Malibu crack, I repeated the quote Crawford had given about it being the greatest challenge of her life to work with her.

'A *challenge*?,' said Bette, leaping into the fight ring again. 'Did she *tell* the audience how she gave *everyone* such a hard *goddamn* time on *Jane*? How she held up production day after *day* because she didn't like the way she *looked*? That she was frequently so drunk she had to *stop* the cameras, and put her glasses on to read her cue cards. When we were finished, she *refused* to help me publicize the *picture*, and *then*, when I was nominated for an Oscar for *Jane* and she wasn't, Miss Crawford went to New *York* and began to campaign *against* me.'

After pausing to light a cigarette and take a swig from whatever she was drinking at that early hour, Davis told how Joan had had the 'absolute gall' to solicit permission from the other nominated actresses to accept the award, should they win. 'And *then*, on the night of the Oscars, she was *determined* to steal the show from *me*.

When Anne Bancroft's name was announced Joan almost *laughed* in my face. She went out onstage and took that statue as if it were her own. Then she wouldn't part with it. It was a year before she even let Miss Bancroft take a look at her prize.'

Winding down, Bette laughed at her anger, then spoke of the major difference between her and Crawford. 'We were completely different kinds of women. She was – women like Crawford – they're the ones that first *made* the town like it was. Let's face it, there were *two* groups. There were the theater people who came out, but we didn't have that same kind of Hollywood *thing*. If we only had that, the town would never have been what it became. And Crawford was definitely one of *them*. But we must hand it to her. Where she came from and all that – she accomplished *much*. She became a movie star, and I became the great actress. There is of course a need for both in this business, but you have to know *when* to put a stop to the nonsense that goes with the job. Stars are people *too*. They have to eat, sleep, and go to the bathroom too, without applause or a standing ovation. But I don't *think* Joan Crawford ever sleeps. She never *quits* being Joan Crawford. I find that tedious *and* quite insane. Yes, in that area, Joan is *not* too bright.'

That evening, after transcribing the interview with Bette, I had dinner with a writer-friend from California, Hector Arce, who at the time was working with George Cukor on his autobiography. During the dinner I mentioned Davis and repeated some of her quotes on Joan Crawford. A former entertainment reporter for *Women's Wear Daily*, and well grounded on Hollywood history, Hector offered some of his insights on the star-crossed duo. He also, I later learned, passed along some of Bette's remarks about Joan to her good friend George Cukor. Three days later, on Tuesday night, I received another call. The voice on the other end this time belonged to – Joan Crawford.

My acquaintanceship with Miss Crawford was slight. She wrote to me once for a story I was working on; and later we were introduced in the back room of P.J. Clarke's restaurant on Third Avenue, New York. That meeting was pleasant and brief, but Joan Crawford remembered. On the phone, after some preliminary small talk, she got to the critical item. She had heard I was doing a story on Bette

Davis and that Miss Davis had made some 'slanderous remarks' about their working relationship. Before I could explain that my story wasn't on Bette Davis, Crawford (also in her cups, I suspected) had launched her own defense. As far as she was concerned, it wasn't proper etiquette to badmouth a professional colleague to the press. 'Those in a position of influence who possess any semblance of class or ethics should never talk ill of anyone in the same industry,' said the star. 'Unfortunately, Miss Davis chooses to abuse that standard, time and time again.'

She had no intention of descending to Miss Davis' level of disclosure, except to say that she admired her enormously, 'as an actress, but not as a human being.' How could she, when Bette was so contemptuous of her fellow actresses? 'She loathes most women,' said Joan. 'She thinks like a man, talks like a man. On the set of *Baby Jane*, after one of her many unpleasant outbursts, she said, out loud, "Boy, if I had been born with a penis, my life would have been different." '

Without a link, Crawford jumped tracks, from flailing at Davis to praising the talents of actress Lee Grant. 'She's got it, hasn't she,' said Crawford. 'I went to see her on Broadway last year in the Neil Simon play [*The Prisoner of Second Avenue*]. It was an exciting experience. The audience stood up and applauded when I arrived. People can be so kind. Can you hold on a minute, dear.'

I held on, while Crawford spoke to someone in the background or on another line. When she returned, she thanked me for calling her. 'My pleasure,' I replied, thinking it a moot point to remind her that *she* had made the call, and who would argue with Joan Crawford anyway? In closing I did manage to slip in a word of appreciation for *Mildred Pierce*, which had been shown on TV some weeks before. That compliment brought another fifteen minutes with the Legend. 'Did you see it too?' Joan asked warmly. 'I received so many calls and letters from friends about it. It was on at such an ungodly hour that I thought no one would watch it. Also, the last time it was shown on TV, the commercials came every eight minutes. I dropped a note to the station owner about that, and it worked. This time they shut up with the interruptions and let us do our stuff. It pleases me so much that the movie still holds up.'

'*What Ever Happened to Baby Jane*? also holds up,' I volunteered.

'Yes, in a strange way it does,' said Crawford. 'It was a good movie, but not as good as it could have been. They tricked me, you know?'

'They?'

'Bob Aldrich and Bette Davis,' she said. 'But let's not open that can of worms again.'

Oh please, *let's*, I thought, looking for a way of getting the old feud train rolling again.

'Mr. Aldrich found the book . . .' I offered.

'No, he did *not*,' said Joan. '*I* found the book.'

Crawford explained that a friend had sent her the book when it was first published, in 1961. 'I read it and went out and bought three copies. I sent one to Nicholas Ray, one to Alfred Hitchcock, and the third to Bob Aldrich. He was the first to option it. He wanted me for Blanche, and he suggested Katharine Hepburn for Jane. I insisted on Bette Davis. I also brought Mister Aldrich and Miss Davis together. Then later, for their own selfish, neurotic reasons, they teamed up against me.'

Furthermore, Bette's story about her hijacking Anne Bancroft's Oscar was an outright lie. 'I never campaigned against Miss Davis. The Oscar went to Anne Bancroft because she deserved it. After it was engraved, I presented the statue to Miss Bancroft in New York. It was a week or two later, and not six months or a year, as Miss Davis has claimed. And I would appreciate it if you would set the record straight on this in your story.'

The next day a letter, with 'JOAN CRAWFORD' embossed on the back, arrived. Inside the blue envelope was a clipping of a newspaper photograph. It showed the star presenting the Oscar to Anne Bancroft backstage at the Royale Theater in New York, after a performance of *Mother Courage*. Over the clip, marked in ink, was the inscription – 'Taken in New York, one week after the Oscars.'

I forwarded the clipping to Bette Davis in Connecticut, together with an original illustration of her by artist Michaele Vollbracht, for possible use as an insert for a book she was working on. The illustration appeared, on the hardcover jacket of the book (*Mother Goddamn*) but Bette preferred to ignore Crawford's clip and correction. In the years to come she would continue to tell the Oscar hijack story until it became the established version. 'It plays better that way!' said Hector Arce. 'Bette is a legend and a star and she feels she's entitled to rewrite the facts as she sees fit. After all, it's life; her picture show.'*

* AUTHOR'S NOTE: In 1987, after Davis put the story in *This'n That*, her second book of memoirs, and repeated her version on numerous tv shows, I asked actress Anne Bancroft if she could set the record straight. Miss Bancroft responded: 'Crawford is right. She brought the award to me, sometime shortly after the awards, while *Mother Courage* was still playing on Broadway.'

21

THE TWILIGHT YEARS

In 1973, the success of the Legendary Ladies at Town Hall series brought offers of work for Bette and Joan. Producer Morton Gottlieb asked Crawford to appear in his hit play *Sleuth*. It would be revised, rehearsed, and performed in a lengthy out-of-town tour before bringing Joan to Broadway. She turned it down, saying she preferred to do 'the O'Neill plays . . . the mothers . . . I'm anxious to do something like that.' She was also asked by NBC to appear as the guest-target on a Dean Martin TV celebrity roast. When told that Governor Ronald Reagan, Kirk Douglas, and Jimmy Stewart had gamely appeared and been lampooned on the show, Crawford scowled: 'No! I don't think an hour of insults is funny. I don't have that much of a sense of humor about myself or my work.'

Bette Davis was not as touchy about her legend. She agreed to be roasted by Dean and his guests. She also accepted a bit part as the alcoholic mother of a psychopathic killer in a TV suspense movie, *Scream, Pretty Peggy*.

In March 1974, with no other offers to accept, Davis decided to play herself on a tour of theaters and auditoriums across America. She and John Springer took her one-woman question-and-answer tour to Saratoga, Princeton, Denver, and twenty-six other cities; then on to Australia, New Zealand, and England. 'Is that your real hair, Miss Davis?' one fan asked in Scotland. 'Yes it is' (it wasn't), said Davis, 'and these are my real eyes, my real teeth, and my real tits.'

Traveling with Bette as her hairdresser was Peggy Shannon,

who performed the same duties for Joan Crawford for many years. 'I was with Joan for fifteen years and with Bette for twelve,' said Shannon.

Bette seemed not to remember that Shannon had worked with Crawford on *What Ever Happened to Baby Jane?*

'In 1974 she needed someone for her tour, and a makeup man from *Green Acres* told her about me,' said the hair stylist. 'Then, when we were in London, the newspapers said that I had been with Miss Crawford for a long time.'

'You never mentioned it,' said Bette.

'It was work. Who cares? Why should I mention it?' said Shannon in 1988, proud to recall that she had worked on the heads of some of the most famous women in Hollywood. 'I was with MGM and 20th Century-Fox during the 1950s,' she said. 'Stars were really stars back then. Not like the kids today – they work on one television series and they think they're stars. They don't know what a star is.'

Lana Turner was a star, and Ava Gardner, Grace Kelly, Marilyn Monroe, Cyd Charisse, and Kay Kendall, all of whom Shannon helped to beautify ('We *never* used hot rollers like the stylists today; we iron-curled'). But the pinnacle for Peggy, the absolute zenith in stars, was Joan Crawford and Bette Davis.

'Joan was the love of my life . . . a great, great person,' said Shannon. 'We began together on *The Best of Everything* at Fox in 1959. We were together on *Baby Jane, Sweet Charlotte,* and throughout the 1960s. I did her for premieres, the Oscars, and for TV shows. Every Sunday when she was in Hollywood she had her facials and I would color her hair. She was very disciplined. The lady took very good care of herself. She had gorgeous skin and very good hair.'

Bette had fine hair and a different personality. 'She could be *firm*. But when Miss Davis wanted to have fun, she was a ball. We pulled a lot of practical jokes on people. She never spoke about Miss Crawford. And I never brought her up. I knew they didn't like each other – that was obvious. Bette said a few things about Joan to the press that weren't true; and maybe Joan spoke about Bette too. It was none of my business. When reporters would ask, "What about their feud?" I would say, "What feud?" I had nothing bad to say about either one. I saw none of that child abuse that

Christina wrote about. The people at Paramount called me when they were doing the *Mommie Dearest* movie. They wanted to see some photographs of hairstyles I had done for Joan. I said, "No way!" To me Joan was a walking saint. Bette was wonderful too. Both of them were very kind, very thoughtful; they made you feel like part of the family. Once, when my back was broken on a movie set, Bette flew into town and insisted that I see her specialist. When I got out of the hospital, she moved in with me, to take care of me. Joan was very generous too. That's the kind of people these two ladies were. So when anyone asks me what they were like, I always say, "They were the greatest. The best. I was very lucky to know them." '

'A feud? Oh, no. I couldn't ever be bothered with anything like that. Let's just say Joan's not someone I would have any cause to see socially. Or ever did.'
                                                     Bette Davis to *McCall's*, 1974

On Bette's tour through New Zealand, John Springer was putting together an all-star cast for the movie version of the Broadway musical *Follies*. The concept was to be changed from the closing of a Broadway theater to that of a Hollywood studio. Set for the leads were Elizabeth Taylor, Henry Fonda, Shirley MacLaine, and Gene Kelly, with a stellar supporting cast to be played by Debbie Reynolds, June Allyson, Joan Blondell, and Bette Davis and Joan Crawford.

'Joan agreed to do the Yvonne De Carlo part although her song would have been "Broadway Baby," ' Springer told columnist Liz Smith. 'Bette Davis was set to sing "I'm Still Here," and she was thrilled, even though she had some misgivings about working with Crawford again. All through the trip to Australia and New Zealand she would play the *Follies* album, learning the song, and you haven't heard anything until you've heard Bette sing "I'm Still Here." '

The project was set to go at MGM when producer Hal Prince had a falling-out with the studio. 'He felt they were going back on promises,' said Springer, 'and he withdrew the whole project. He was too hurt and bitter to try another studio, and it died. But wouldn't it have been a beauty?'

Eager to resuscitate her career, in August of 1974 Davis opted to return to Broadway, as the star of a big-budget musical, *Miss Moffatt*. Based on her original film, *The Corn Is Green*, the role was first offered to Mary Martin. When she declined the director, Joshua Logan, persuaded Bette to do it.

'Thank God for this play,' Bette told Logan. 'It's going to save me from those flea-bitten films. The last one I read they had me hanging in a closet.'

During the rehearsals in New York, Logan, who had experienced that abject lesson in 'planned frustration' when he tried to get Crawford to appear on Broadway in 1953, was now at the mercy of Bette's fears and belligerent defenses. Describing herself as 'a klutz,' when it came to intricate dancing, she asked that her choreographed steps be kept to a minimum, and that her singing voice, aged and abused from forty years of smoking and yelling at her ex-husbands, be limited to performing no more than three songs in the show. 'During the rehearsals while the rest of us were dancing and singing our little hearts out, Miss Davis preferred to stand by the piano and talk her way through the songs. I don't believe she intended to let anyone hear her sing until we opened in Philadelphia,' said one of the other performers.

Out of town, faced with an inordinate amount of rewrites at rehearsals, the star lashed out repeatedly at the director. 'She had an aversion to the soft, a loathing for the sentimental,' Logan said. 'It's as though whenever she enters a room, she is compelled to use her favorite silver screen expression, "What a dump!"'

'Logan and Emlyn Williams [the writer] were cowards,' said Davis' assistant, Vik Greenfield. 'She was scared and getting older and they didn't know how to handle her.' During the preview performances in Philadelphia, Bette began to forget her lines and was inaudible at times. She blamed her lapses on the bad material. 'I am too *big* a star to give a bad performance,' she railed at Logan. Then her 'system cracked,' and she entered the hospital 'with an old back injury.' She recovered in time to perform for opening night, but the critics panned her and the play and, after more changes and rewrites, Bette decided to quit. 'One night I went backstage and I saw her standing in the dressing room. I said, "Oh, no, this is it," ' said Greenfield. 'She went to bed that night, and the next morning she called me in and said, "I'm not doing it anymore." I said, "Bette, you can't do this. You can't put all these people out of work before Christmas." She looked at me and said, "You're fired." '

When she lost the use of her legs, Bette entered the hospital again. After submitting to tests by the show's insurance doctors, they confirmed that she was indeed paralyzed from the waist down. 'Everyone seemed to forget that Mother was one of the most convincing actresses alive,' said daughter B.D.

'She behaved mischievously,' said Joshua Logan, who was threatened with libel when he spoke out against the actress. 'How could I damage her career,' he asked, 'when she's been doing that for thirty years?'

Joan loved to travel for Pepsi-Cola. Once on tour she needed a vitamin shot. A doctor was called to the airport. There was nowhere for them to go but the men's room, which was empty. Joan bent over. "Can you imagine," she told me, "if a man had come in and seen my bare ass?"

Sheilah Graham

In the spring of 1973, although she was finished in movies and television, Crawford was still an active board member of Pepsi-Cola. Her popularity and association with the soft-drink company were so established that every day stacks of mail were delivered to the company headquarters addressed to Joan Crawford, President of Pepsi-Cola. She had her own office, press representative, a secretary at home, her limo in New York, and the company jet always at her disposal when she traveled out of town. But that April the job and the benefits ended abruptly. When she turned sixty-five she was involuntarily retired by Pepsi.

She said she learned the news from the financial pages of *The New York Times*. She would continue to draw her fifty-thousand-dollar salary as a lifetime pension, but forty-thousand-dollar expenses, her car, her New York secretary, and the use of the company jet were discontinued.

Because of the cutback in funds, Crawford moved to a smaller apartment in her building, making do with five rooms instead of nine. The corner of one room was converted into an office, with a table and a typewriter, so the retired star could devote herself to the one remaining task that would occupy her time, the dispatch of the notes and letters to her legion of fans, friends, and new acquaintances.

'There are probably more signed and framed notes from Joan Crawford in the bathrooms of New York apartments, than there are hampers,' said reporter Arthur Bell.

'She always sent out her Christmas cards the day after Thanksgiving,' said Sheilah Graham. 'When she received your card she sent you a thank-you note.'

'Yes, those letters were very important to Miss Crawford,' said Florence Walsh, her New York secretary, who continued to work part-time for Crawford. 'They gave her enormous pleasure. It didn't matter if you were famous or not; everyone who wrote to her always received a reply. She felt that was their due.'

In September 1974, Crawford agreed to act as a co-hostess, with actress Rosalind Russell, at a book party for John Springer in New York. Wearing red chiffon, diamonds and a light-brown wig that seemed slightly askew, the star stationed herself at the door of the Rainbow in Rockefeller Center. With Rosalind Russell at her side, she personally greeted each guest, including this writer. When my name was given to Joan, she shook my hand but the tone of her voice was cool. Turning to Rosalind Russell, she said, 'This is a good friend of Miss Bette Davis.' I waited for the punch line, thinking she was joking. She wasn't. Grasping my hand in introduction, Rosalind Russell smiled warmly; then, raising one eyebrow she gave a signal that suggested, 'Don't pursue this right now, dear.' Since Crawford had already turned to greet other arrivals, I paid my respects to Miss Russell and moved into the room.

Crawford was angry because I never wrote up her rebuttal to Bette, I was told. But I never printed Davis' account of their feud either, and later that evening, when I attempted to seek Crawford out to explain, I learned that she had left the party shortly after the last of the guests arrived. She was tired, said John Springer. She was angry, said columnist Jack O'Brien, 'because her name had been put on the invitations *before* she agreed to co-hostess.' Rosalind Russell had another explanation. 'Joan is one of the most glamorous creatures God ever put on this earth. But she gets nervous in a crowd. And she was upset because we weren't seated at the same table.'

The following morning in her hotel suite, Rosalind Russell looked at the newspaper coverage of the previous night. Suffering from crippling arthritis, her face appeared swollen from the cortisone injections she was taking. 'Dear God!' said Russell to visiting *Newsday* reporter Jerry Parker. 'Just look at that picture of those two old broads.'

'Wait until you see the *Post*,' her husband, Frederick Brisson, said.

'No, no, don't show it to me,' said Russell, shrieking with laughter. 'I can't bear it.'

'You look very vivacious and animated,' Brisson said gallantly. 'But it's not very flattering of Joan.'

Crawford, ten blocks to the north in her own apartment, agreed. Staring at the photographs of herself and Russell in the newspapers she said with finality, 'If that's how I look, they won't see me again.'

That same week Crawford went through her date book and canceled all public appearances for the remainder of the year. That December she had been scheduled to receive a special award at the Pepsi convention in San Francisco. A short time before, she called Mitchell Cox, their PR chief, and refused to attend. 'I worked my ass off for the company for almost twenty years and now they have washed me up. Well, screw 'em. I'm not going,' said the star.

Jack O'Brien reported another reason for the Pepsi cancellation. 'Joan had fallen down and blackened her beautiful eye,' he said in his column.

'Have you looked in the mirror lately? You're a drunk, Mother, nothing but a broken-down drunk.'

					B.D. Hyman, *My Mother's Keeper*

'Alcohol preyed on mother's mind, distorting reality, causing her to blame others for her mistakes and personal weaknesses. It also preyed on her own ego, eating away at her self-respect and good looks.'

					Christina Crawford, *Mommie Dearest*

During the same period of time, according to their daughters, Bette Davis and Joan Crawford became reclusive alcoholics.

After the closing of *Miss Moffatt*, and the insurance claims were settled, Davis regained the use of her legs and returned to Connecticut, where she remained in semi-seclusion for the next ten months.

Crawford, according to Christina, also began to live a progressively more solitary life, without seeing many people, but Carl Johnes, a frequent visitor, said the perception of the star being a recluse in her ivory tower was 'just a load of horseshit.'

'She had a problem about going out,' he recalled, 'because Joan always wanted to be the movie star. Still, she entertained all the time, with lots of people around. But Christina was never there. In her book she said they had reconciled, but they hadn't. In 1974 I brought up Christina's name, and Joan said, "I hear she's found a new home. I hope she's very happy. All she and Christopher ever wanted was my money." And I said, "Gee, that's awfully hard. Can't you do something about that?" And she said, "Yes, I can. I can cut them out of my will." '

Alanna Nash, who also visited and spoke to Crawford frequently, recalled the same interdict. 'I had been warned never to bring up the name of Christina or Christopher. I never heard of any reconciliation between them. Later, when *Mommie Dearest* came out, I interviewed Christina for the Louisville *Courier* and I asked her about that. She became evasive, and at the end of our conversation she said she would appreciate it if I didn't mention it in my story.'

Nash said she could understand the breach between mother and daughter, after she experienced some icy behaviour from the star. Describing her visits to Joan as 'electrifying, terrifying, unnerving, and even demeaning,' the writer said she never understood why Crawford pursued a friendship with her. 'I would go to her house and she would greet me with polite tolerance. She usually had other people there so she could ignore me. If I attempted to make conversation with her, she would cut me off with a sarcastic retort.'

Looking for a reason for the star's hostile behavior, Nash wondered if it was because she was female and younger; or because she had been an honor student at Stephens College, where Joan had once failed. 'Billie Cassin still existed within Joan Crawford,' the author believed, 'and perhaps I was her chance to get back at those other girls who shamed her into running away from school so long ago. I didn't know. But I found my visits with her demeaning and painful. Once she invited me to dinner, then insisted I eat alone while she played backgammon with her friend Mary Jane Raphael. I wasn't halfway through my meal when she asked me what time my first class was in the morning. On the way home that night, sharing a cab with Mary Jane, I told her I felt so humiliated that I didn't intend to visit Crawford again. "You've got to go back," she said. "Joan is awfully fond of you. She thinks you're very bright. And besides, she's terribly lonely." '

Carl Johnes also stated that his friendship with Crawford wasn't always easy. 'She wasn't sweet and perfect all the time, which was fine with me, because I've never been attracted to wimps either. She could be great fun and very frank. Once she told me that she and actor John Ireland made two movies together. During their love scenes he would always get a huge erection. 'Now, John,' she would caution him, 'we can't have *that* in our close-ups.'

'It was as if she wanted me to know that in her day she was a very hot number,' Johnes continued, 'and Bette Davis *wasn't*. Joan was very specific about that. "You see, Bette is disappointed in life," Joan would say, "and that's why if you look at her mouth carefully, darling, you'll see that over the years it has turned down." '

There were frequent nights when Crawford could be found at home, alone, drinking and talking back to her television set. When her old movies were shown, if the movie was real bad she would yell at the TV and say, 'Joan Crawford, you stink, you really stink.' If the film was good, she cut telephone callers short. 'Hang up,' she told her daughter Cindy, 'I'm watching *Flamingo Road* and it's enchanting.'

Joan also kept track of Bette Davis' exposure on TV. 'The night Bette appeared on Dick Cavett's show, Joan called me,' said Alanna Nash. 'I asked if she watched the show. "Yes," said Joan, "and Cavett made a fool out of himself." It was as if she was actually defending Davis. She thought Cavett's questions were silly and not worthy of Bette.'

Illustrator Tim Scott recalled similar signals from Joan. 'She would call me early in the morning at work, and she'd say, "Watch Channel Nine tonight. *Special Agent* with Bette Davis is on at eleven. It's a real stinker. You'll love it." '

When Bette's cult classic *All About Eve* was shown, Joan took the phone off the hook. 'She must have seen it ten times,' said Scott. 'She told me she always watched it because of the script and the director, Joe Mankiewicz.'

'She never told *me* she liked it,' said Mankiewicz.

In Connecticut, Bette Davis could also be found parked in front of a TV set. In the afternoon, according to Vik Greenfield, she watched soap operas and the occasional Joan Crawford movie. '*Christ*, that dame had a face,' Bette would say in baleful tribute. 'She admired Joan up to a point,' said Greenfield. 'She always said she was a professional, and Bette also recognized that Joan was a star.'

The possibility of the two ageing actresses burying the hatchet and becoming friends at this time was remote. 'Mother felt they had nothing in common,' said B.D., 'and at that time she couldn't be friends with herself. She was full of self-pity and hatred.'

'She's antagonized every - - - - ing person she's come in contact with,' said Gary Merrill. 'She had no friends left, because nobody would put up with her.'

'High on vodka, demanding, neurotic and imperious,' Lawrence Quirk described Joan Crawford calling him at three and four o'clock in the morning. 'I felt for her loneliness and unhappiness, but she was just too much.'

'It was a period of sheer terror for Joan,' said George Cukor, who was also on the receiving end of late-night calls from the star. 'One night she would call and say she was so happy to be out of the business, that this was the first time in her life that she was free from the pressures and the stress. And why wasn't I living in New York, how could I stand living in Hollywood? Two nights later she would call again, begging me to assure her that she would work again. She needed what we all needed – another job, another movie – the chance to create, to keep busy, to stop thinking of ourselves and what we had in the past.'

According to her agent, Stan Kamen, there were jobs for Crawford during this period, but she had lost her self-confidence. 'Joan's career and life had been built on two things – her looks and her glamour. When her looks began to go, the foundation crumbled. If she couldn't retain the image of the movie star she cherished, she didn't want to work anymore. She called one day and told us not to bother submitting her name for parts anymore.'

'Today, after more than a quarter of a century of being all roles to all fans, Joan Crawford doesn't know who she is,' columnist Sidney Skolsky reported in 1975.

Bette Davis also had vanity, but *her* foundation was her acting talent. Tougher and more resilient as long as she could walk and talk, she felt she was eligible for work. In June 1975, with bills to pay, she stopped drinking and went to Seattle to appear in a minor role in a horror film entitled *Burnt Offerings*. On location, the legendary matriarch displayed little affection for her co stars, Oliver Reed and Karen Black. Reed got drunk one night and fell down a mountainside while playing the bagpipes, she told Rex Reed. Karen Black 'changes her makeup in the middle of the scene, so nothing matches on the screen. She sleeps all day, never goes to rushes and you can't hear a bloody thing she says on the set. When I made movies you could hear me in a *tunnel*.'

The next year Davis played the mother of Faye Dunaway in the TV film *The Disappearance of Aimee*. Dunaway, who would later play Joan Crawford in *Mommie Dearest*, was, according to Joan, the only actress in the 1970s crop who 'has the talent and the class and the courage to become a real star.'

Naturally, Bette Davis disagreed.

While filming in Utah during the summer heat wave, Bette censured Faye for 'riding around town all night in a chauffeur-driven limousine, sipping champagne in the backseat,' then holding up production the next day. 'Compared to Miss Dunaway, Joan Crawford was a real pro,' she observed.

'The biggest disaster in my years in the business,' Bette's hair-dresser, Peggy Shannon, concurred. She was on the set the afternoon the dynamic but tardy Dunaway made fifteen hundred people stand around in 110-degree heat. 'The girl was so stoned all she did was read cue cards, which her makeup man held down in front of her,' said Shannon. 'The director got so mad he threw a bottle of Coke at her. It hit the floor and splattered all over her white dress. I was standing stage right and walking towards me, she said, "Get the *hell* out of my way." I stood there and let her walk around me. Later, thinking that Miss Davis had returned to the big double dressing room, I went in. Dunaway was sitting there, alone, with her hairdresser doing her hair. When she saw me enter, she jumped out of her chair and put her face in front of mine. "When I tell you to move, Goddamn it, you move!" she said. "I have work to do," I replied. She said, "I haven't seen you do *any* work on the set." "No," I said, "because my work is so perfect I don't have to change a thing." Her hairdresser then grabbed her and, I swear, I had to run like hell, because she was going to belt me.'

'I absolutely will not allow anyone to call me grandmother. They can call me Auntie Joan, Dee-Dee, Cho-Cho, anything but grandmother. It pushes a woman almost into the grave.'

Joan Crawford

In 1975, Joan Crawford renewed her faith in Christian Science and gave up drinking. 'We were all amazed,' said daughter Christina. 'She had been drinking since I was a baby.'

'She lost weight and began to relax,' said Tim Scott. 'She even developed a sense of humor about herself. I remember I called her up one morning and invited her to the opening of the New York Film Festival. She seemed pleased by the invitation. "But Tim, dear," she asked, "who do you want to go with? Me or Joan Crawford?" I said, "What's the difference?" "Thirty days," she said. "That's how long it would take to varnish the face and make *her* presentable." '

Kathleen Carroll, the film critic for the *New York Daily News*, was at home one Sunday evening when her phone rang.

'*Kathleen?*' the husky voice inquired. 'This is *Joan Crawford*.'

'Yes, Miss Crawford,' said Carroll, a little nervous.

'Call me *Joan*,' the star commanded.

'Yes, Miss Crawford,' said Kathleen.

Crawford proceeded to invite the critic and her predecessor, Wanda Hale, to her home for drinks the following Wednesday night.

'Naturally, we accepted,' said Kathleen, who was excited at the prospect of seeing the star in her own home. 'Wanda and I arrived promptly on the appointed evening. The door to her apartment opened, and there stood this elderly woman in a house-dress and rubber-thonged flip-flops. It was Joan, looking as if she had just stepped out of the shower. Her hair was pulled back and she wasn't wearing any makeup, just a little lipstick, which made her look surprisingly young, but not like the Joan Crawford we knew. Miss Hale and I were taken by surprise. We thought we had the wrong date, but Joan said, "Come in, I've been expecting you." She showed us her apartment, then we sat down in the living room. Drinks were served in plastic glasses, but Joan didn't have a drink. She told us she had not taken hard liquor in nine weeks. She pulled her housedress around her waist to show off her girlish figure. Apparently she had made a deliberate decision not to dress up for us, but she gave no excuses or an explanation. We figured she just couldn't be bothered with the glamour anymore.'

The visit lasted about an hour. 'Joan talked about Hollywood, how she seldom went out there anymore and when she did she never left her hotel. "All my friends are out of work," she said. "It's so sad. They never leave their house." She could have been speaking about herself, or Bette Davis, but no names were mentioned, and she preferred to give the impression that she didn't really care. And then she disappeared into the kitchen and came out with some frozen quiche, which she served on paper plates. I never got to eat mine, because her little dog jumped up on my lap and finished it off. We spoke some more, and then it was time to leave. Saying goodbye she seemed bravely self-sufficient. Wanda and I felt so sad that we headed straight to a restaurant and had a few stiff drinks. It hurt us to see someone we had admired for so long to be so desperately lonely.'

'I have never been so content in my life. I think one had to earn that in life: "Contentment" – and it's a beautiful feeling.'
                    Joan Crawford to Alanna Nash, September 21, 1976

A LAST CALL FROM JOAN

In December 1976, while researching a story about cinematography, I wrote Miss Crawford a letter. In a career spanning five decades she had worked with some of the leading cameramen, including George Folsey, Robert Planck, and Ernest Haller. In the letter I mentioned the story and wondered if she would care to talk about these craftsmen. I delivered the letter to the doorman of her building. The doorman said that Miss Crawford was in residence, but not seeing anyone.

Two days passed, and on the morning of the third day, Crawford called. She was enthusiastic about the article I was doing. 'It's about time someone wrote about our wonderful cameramen,' she said. 'They are the real magicians of this business, and they are so seldom mentioned in reviews or articles.'

Her voice was soft and she spoke very slow. I asked if she wanted to set up an appointment, to talk at a later time. 'Can we do it now?' she said. 'My mind is clear, and I have business meetings all week.'

Speaking of her early days at MGM, she said she knew nothing about the camera. 'It was there. I was told not to look into it. In time I grew less awkward, but my primary concern was that I looked good. My nose always seemed to be too big, and I hated my mouth. I seldom smiled, because there was a space between my teeth; it was slight, but on the screen I thought it looked enormous. I was vain and silly, like any young actress who thinks that the entire world is looking only at her.'

During the 1930s, she said, it was cameramen Oliver Marsh (*Possessed*) and William Daniels (*Grand Hotel*) who taught her about camera lighting and how the close-up lens could catch her slightest emotion. 'I was constantly told not to give so much, especially with my eyes and features. I listened, and I learned. Some early critic once said something to the effect that Joan Crawford was an effective actress but only in front of the camera. That upset and confused me. Movies are *made* by cameras. Where else should I project? Into the scenery? Down to the floor? Yes, it seems funny today, but back then I was a very serious young girl about my work.'

Crawford proceeded to talk about the differences between working at MGM and Warner's. At her old studio they would spend hours lighting the sets and the stars, whereas at Warner's the emphasis was on time and cost. 'It was the war. Film was scarce. They had to do so many setups within a work period. If they missed too many, Jack Warner would call down to the set.' She spoke about Ernest Haller and his work on *Mildred Pierce*, and on *Humoresque*, when the leading star of the studio, Bette Davis, stole the cameraman's services. On her last film with Haller, *What Ever Happened to Baby Jane?*, Crawford said she couldn't recall any specifics on the camera work, because the shooting schedule was so tight.

'One of the few scenes of mine that required an elaborate setup was the one when I found the dead rat on my luncheon tray. It wasn't enough that I screamed. Mister Aldrich needed action with my reaction. I couldn't run from the room, because I was playing a cripple. It was Ernie's idea to shoot me from overhead, circling in a frenzy in the wheelchair. He used two cameras. One was placed at waist level in the doorway. The second camera was ten feet above my head, in the crosswalks. When they yelled "Action" I was to scream and spin myself around and around in the wheelchair. We did so many takes that my arms were ready to drop off from pushing myself in the chair. It was very hard work. I remember later, at the beach, Miss Davis was supposed to wheel me from the car to the water's edge, but she couldn't push the chair in the sand. "You can see how tough it was on *my* arms," I told her, and she agreed.'

During this part of the conversation there was no animosity in Crawford's voice when she mentioned Davis' name. She gave the impression that Bette was just another actress she had worked with, until, unprompted, she began to talk about seeing a final cut of *Baby Jane* in California, in October 1962. 'I attended a screening at Warner and I became totally immersed in the movie. I thought it was a powerful film. Everyone – Ernie Haller, Bob Aldrich – did a marvelous job. And Bette Davis was superb as Jane. I sent her flowers and champagne that evening. She never acknowledged the gesture or even bothered to call the next day, when she saw the movie.'

'This was in 1962?'

'Yes,' said Joan, 'in October of 1962. Two weeks before the picture was released.'

But according to Davis, she never saw the completed film until the following year, at the Cannes Film Festival, in May 1963.

'That's a *lie*,' said Crawford. 'She saw the picture, fully edited, the day *after* I saw it. It was complete except for part of the credits, and one short scene with Jane as a young girl, which was being redubbed. The rest of the picture was there. I saw it with Mister Aldrich at Warner Brothers. Bette was to have joined us for that screening, but she never showed up. Despite some initial misgivings about the way I looked, I thought Bob did a terrific job, and Bette was magnificent. That afternoon I sent her the flowers and champagne, and later that night I called her at home. "You were wonderful, darling," I told her. "I *heard*," she said. She told me she had no intention of seeing the film. "But you must," I urged her. After all we were supposed to go out, to tour together, to promote the film. How could she talk about a picture that she hadn't seen? You've got a *point*," she said. So, the next afternoon, Bob Aldrich set up another screening for her. I waited all that evening and that night to hear from her. She never called. The next morning I called her.'

'Well, Bette, what did you think?' Joan asked her co star.

There was a pause; then Bette answered, 'You were *so* right, Joan. The picture is good. And I was *terrific*.'

'That was it,' said Joan. 'She never said anything about my performance. Not a word.'

Not once in her entire career, it seemed, had the great actress Bette Davis ever acknowledged that her rival Joan Crawford had any talent. And, presumably, it was that last denial of approval that led Crawford to cancel the *Baby Jane* publicity tour with Davis; and to upstage her, in another round of competitive tit-for-tat, at the Oscars the following year. But before I was allowed to harbor a thought that any star of Crawford's stature would hold a grudge or stoop to malice, Joan rushed in with a tactful and concluding assessment of her trials with Bette. 'Of course that was a long, long time ago, and I've forgotten most of the unpleasantness. Certainly I continue to admire Miss Davis. She is one of our finest dramatic actresses. Her movies will remain beacons of achievement forever.'

In January 1977 it was reported that Crawford was getting ready to return to movies. 'She has found a script she likes and is coming out here for story conferences,' said Hollywood publicist Joe Hoenig. There was also a report in *Variety* that the star was set for a TV series entitled *The Silver Fox*. That same month, actress Mamie Van Doren said that Crawford had the hotel room next to her at the Ambassador East Hotel in Chicago. 'She was seldom seen outside her room,' said Van Doren, 'but I could hear her up at all hours of the night, watching television and moving about like a phantom.'

According to Crawford's secretary, the actress never left New York in 1977. She couldn't work or travel because she was dying of stomach cancer. Carl Johnes had visited the ailing star that December. 'She still talked of working, but it was obvious something was very wrong. She looked as if she was disintegrating right in front of me. "I'm getting down to picture weight, darling," she said, but I didn't buy that.'

BETTE RISES, AGAIN

By an ironic twist of fate, during the last few months of Joan Crawford's life, Bette Davis resurrected her life and career. She left Connecticut and bought a condominium apartment in Los Angeles, 'because, let's face it, this is where the industry is.'

In January 1977, she traveled to Washington to attend the inauguration of Jimmy Carter, and took a poke in the press at the President's mother ('Miss Lillian doesn't like any women,' said Bette. 'She was perfectly terrible to all of us at the inauguration. She only wanted to see the men. When any women came up to her, she just glared at us like *this*!'); and at Elizabeth Taylor, who declined to have Davis as a co star in the film of *A Little Night Music* ('She is such a *fool*,' said Davis. 'One would think that after all her years in the business she would want to work with a professional').

That month it was also announced that Bette Davis would be the first woman to receive the Lifetime Achievement Award from the American Film Institute in Los Angeles. The attendant press leading up to the March event was plentiful and most of it was seen by the ailing Joan Crawford. Interviews with Bette appeared in *The New York Times*, the *Los Angeles Times*, *Time*, *People*, and *Women's Wear Daily*. 'She is another Di Maggio, another Einstein, the best there is,' said Robert Aldrich, not mentioning his other *Baby Jane* co star, Crawford. 'I am thrilled to be back in Hollywood,' Bette told the *Los Angeles Times*, and mentioned that at long last she would be making *Ethan Frome* with Henry Fonda as Caleb and Liv Ullman in the role that her rival had once coveted.

In New York, as the AFI event approached, Bette Davis retrospectives were held at revival houses and on television. 'I am happy for Bette,' Crawford was quoted as saying. 'She deserves this most prestigious honor.'

Director Vincent Sherman recalled a different reaction from Joan. Having directed Bette in *Old Acquaintance* and *Mr. Skeffington*, Sherman was asked to attend and speak at the AFI tribute to Davis. He considered declining because she had recently been 'particularly nasty and vicious towards an old friend and colleague of mine, Irving Rapper.'

'It was gratuitous cruelty,' said Rapper. 'Bette kept giving these interviews saying I was not responsible for any of her good moments in *Now Voyager*. She claimed that her most famous scene, the one with the two cigarettes, was thought up by her and Paul Heinreid, when in actuality it came from a 1932 movie with Ruth Chatterton.'

'I was writing to Joan,' Sherman continued, 'and I told her I had doubts about going to the AFI tribute for Davis. A few days passed and I had a call from Betty Barker, her secretary. She asked if I would be at home to take a call from Joan. I said, "Of course." Joan called and said, "Darling, don't go to the Davis dinner. She's really not worth the trouble."'

'I didn't go,' said Sherman.

And Crawford didn't watch the ceremony, she said, when it was shown on television in late March.

'If you've earned a position, be proud of it. Don't hide it. I want to be recognized. When I hear people say, "There's Joan Crawford!" I turn around and say, "Hi! How are you?"'

Joan Crawford – *My Way of Life*

Up until the last week of her life, the seventy-three-year-old Legend did not expect to die. Her faith in Christian Science made her believe that her body would cure itself of the pancreatic cancer that had spread through her system. As the pain increased and her weight kept dropping, she asked Mrs. Markham, her Christian Science practitioner if she was dying. 'With God, the spirit was eternal,' she was told, and Crawford accepted that. She didn't complain or tell anyone, not even her children, that she had cancer because that was how stars behaved, and Joan Crawford was one, of the first order.

'I am so at peace with the world that I'm even thinking good thoughts about Bette Davis,' Crawford wrote on one of her Christmas cards that last season. To special friends she sent a recent photograph taken by John Engstead. The false eyelashes were in place, the famous mouth was painted, and her posture was erect as she held her beloved dog, Princess, in her lap. But her hair was turning white and her face was taut with pain. 'She knew she didn't look good,' said Vincent Sherman. 'She sent me a note with the photograph. It read: "Darling, if you don't like the picture, please throw it away. I'll understand."'

Early in May, as her weight dropped to ninety pounds, Crawford could no longer lift her small dog, and she gave it away. 'She called me that same week,' said Monte Westmore. 'Her voice was very weak; she spoke very slow and wasn't her usual bright and cheery self. When she mentioned she was giving the dog away, I knew something had to be drastic. I tried to get Peggy Shannon and Joan's friend, Vivian Walker, to find out what was wrong. None of us knew she was dying.'

*   *   *

On Tuesday morning, May 10, the ailing star insisted on getting out of bed to make breakfast for her housekeeper and a fan who had stayed over. While they were eating the meal, Crawford returned to her bedroom and died. At noon the medical examiner was already there when her secretary, Florence Walsh, arrived for work. 'She died of a heart attack,' said Walsh. 'It was cancer,' said Betty Barker, her long-time secretary in California. 'That's what the lawyer told us.'

'I never bought that story,' said Debbie Reynolds, who was one of several people who believed that Crawford committed suicide. 'There were too many coincidental events leading up to it,' Reynolds believed. 'I just feel Joan found some way to exit this life before she looked too bad, before she had to suffer the ravages of decay anymore.'

'Suicide wasn't her style,' said Harry Mines, who had just picked up his mail that morning when he heard the news over the radio. 'I stood there with a letter from Joan in my hand. It was a terrible shock, because I had no warning.'

Bette Davis was on a movie set when she learned of the death of Joan Crawford. 'We were at Disney Studios working on *Witch Mountain*,' said Peggy Shannon. 'I was doing her hair at the time, in the makeup van, when Joan's secretary, Florence, called me from New York. She had made arrangements for me to fly to New York to attend the funeral services. I thought it so strange. Joan was gone, and here I was working on Bette. I am sure she would have given me the time off, but I didn't ask and she said nothing.'

'Bette Davis is more evasive on the subject of Joan Crawford than Richard Nixon is with David Frost,' said reporter Arthur Bell when he covered the services that Friday at Campbell's Funeral Chapel in New York. 'It was a mob scene outside, with the fans and celebrities swapping tears and autographs,' said Bell. 'Myrna Loy was there, and Van Johnson, and Joan's daughter Christina, who nobody recognized or seemed to care about. When Andy Warhol arrived with his flock and his Polaroid camera, he came over to me and said, "Arthur, is Bette Davis here?" I said, "Hardly." That evening I called Bette's press agent to get a quote for my column. But I was told she wasn't talking to anyone. That was understandable. What could she say? "The bitch is dead; long live the bitch." '

'The memorial service in Hollywood was beautiful,' said Peggy Shannon.

'Each branch of the union was represented,' Harry Mines recalled.

'We read telegrams from every director and star she ever worked with,' said George Cukor, 'but there wasn't a word from Bette Davis.'

A year would pass before Davis would offer a comment on the death of her most faithful and formidable rival. The occasion was the Academy Award ceremonies in Hollywood, which featured a special tribute to the stars who had died the previous year. As Sammy Davis, Jr., sang 'Come Light the Candles', Bette was backstage watching the tribute on television, in a dressing room with Greer Garson, Barbara Stanwyck and Olivia de Havilland. As the song was ending and photographs of the deceased – Charles Chaplin, Groucho Marx, Bing Crosby and Elvis Presley – appeared on the TV monitors, Bette stood up and prepared for her appearance as a presenter. Suddenly the sound of a tumultuous ovation filled the entire auditorium. Appearing on the giant screen and monitors was the luminous face of the ultimate movie star, Joan Crawford. Looking up at the wide lustrous eyes of Crawford, Bette Davis paused, nodded, then clipping each syllable, bestowed a final benediction on her long-time rival. 'Poor Joan,' said Bette, 'gone but *not* forgotten. *Bless* you!' And then she exited the room to seize the stage for her appearance.

22

'I'm the nicest goddamn dame who ever lived!'

Bette Davis to Rex Reed

There was '*nevah*' a feud between them, Bette stated repeatedly in the years that followed her rival's demise. In London, when reporter Nancy Mills asked about the enemies she had made in the motion picture business, Davis replied, 'Enemies? I have no enemies? Who?'

'Joan Crawford?' said the brave Miss Mills.

In a tone of 'sugared innocence,' Bette replied, 'Miss Crawford and I weren't enemies. We made one film together. We didn't know each other at all."

'Most of her rivals are now dead,' said the reporter, 'and Miss Davis would like to present herself as just another little old lady in tennis shoes.'

The myth and legend of Joan Crawford were also magnified after her death. In 1978 her personal effects – hats, sheets, monogrammed pillowcases – were auctioned off at Sotheby's and Christie's in New York. Appraised at eight thousand dollars, the small cache of Crawford memorabilia brought in $42,850. Among the bidders was Andy Warhol, who purchased several pairs of Crawford's false eyelashes, and pieces of her costume jewelry, which the Pop artist would wear under his suits and ties when he ventured forth on his own peripatetic rounds of self-promotion.

The 'camp element' of the auction was a source of shame to Crawford's daughter Christina, who said she was 'embarrassed by my association with her.' Christina, of course, did not share in the proceeds of the sale, or in her mother's will. But in November

1978 she remembered Mama with the release of her book *Mommie Dearest*. 'It's a love story, a very sad love story,' said the authoress.

'Tina cared about that bitch. She still cares,' said the other disinherited member of Crawford's family, her son Christopher. He recalled a meeting in Florida in 1962 when he had brought his newborn daughter to see her famous grandmother. 'Joan Crawford summoned me to her suite at the Fontainebleau Hotel. She took one look at my child and said, "It doesn't look like you. It's probably a bastard." I walked out. It was the last time I saw her.'

'She was tough on us, sure,' said daughter Cathy in her mother's defense. 'You'd get a swat once in a while, but none of that physical beatings – the coathangers. I think Christina must have been in another household.' Her sister Cindy recalled the time she was attending Dubuque University and had a romance with a student. She became pregnant and told Joan, who at first offered to arrange for an abortion. 'But I wanted the kid and Mother gave her full approval.'

'I think Christina was jealous,' Cindy believed. 'She wanted to be the one person she couldn't be – Mother. I think she'll use Joan until she can't get anymore out of it. Then she'll dump her.'

With *Mommie Dearest* selling ten thousand copies a day, some of Crawford's Hollywood friends and co stars came forward to protect the memory of the star they knew. 'It's lies, all lies,' said Van Johnson. 'No one I know ever saw any child abuse,' said *Mildred Pierce* daughter Ann Blyth.

When Paramount Pictures bought the film rights to the book, Marlene Dietrich wrote an angry letter to one of their executives. 'I am shocked that Paramount bought that filthy book, and made the frightful bitch who wrote it rich – and that rhymes,' said Marlene. 'I did not know Joan Crawford but nobody deserves that kind of slaughter. Too bad she did not leave her where she found her, so she could now spit her poison in the slums of some big city. I hate her with a passion and I know the public will.'

Bette Davis bought an early copy of *Mommie Dearest*, then called her daughter. 'I am reading the most terrific book. You must read it,' she told B.D.

'I read that book in a state of shock,' Bette confessed to Elliot

Surkin of the *Chicago Tribune*. 'It didn't make me feel the least bit sorry for Joan. She was clearly not disciplined personally, and her problem was obvious. Drink.'

'The book makes her a monster, but one gets the feeling Christina couldn't have made it up, could she?' Bette told *The New York Times*; and in *Playboy* she stated that Christina had every right to publish the book. 'I don't blame the daughter, don't blame her at all. She was left without a cent, living in a motor home in Tarzana. One area of life Joan should never have gone into was *children*.'

MOTHER BETTE

While endorsing the merits of *Mommie Dearest*, Bette Davis frequently told the press that her children would never write a book about her. 'Boy! You could really do a number on me. But you won't, will you, dear?' she warned her daughter, B.D. But in 1985 Davis was awarded the same filial dishonor as her rival when the personal accounts of her drinking and domestic tirades were put on public display in *My Mother's Keeper*.

This was the latest in a series of dire misfortunes for the ageing star. She had just undergone a mastectomy ('My God! I always thought cancer would never *dare* come near me'), and suffered a stroke ('I was furious,' she said; 'I did not think I deserved it. Of all the human afflictions a stroke is about the worst. I wouldn't wish it on Adolf Hitler!'), and then the book by B.D. Hyman was released.

'Scathing!' said the Philadelphia *Inquirer*. 'So moving!' said *The New York Times*. 'So what?' said Ed Baker of the Seattle *Times*. 'Aren't there a few other imperfect mothers in the world?'

'Epic characters have epic torments,' said Neal O'Hara in *Christopher Street*, 'and Christina Crawford, as leaden as her little heart may be, at least made a decent stab at the epic. Christina knew she was dealing with a mythic figure whom she did not purport to understand. B.D. on the other hand, is heavy into amateur psychology. I know what she would have deserved. Joan for a mother. That would have given her something to write about.'

BETTE AND HELEN AND LILLIAN

Davis survived the cancer, the stroke and the book, and in the dogged pursuit of her art, she went on to demolish a few other living legends. Her 1983 co star in an Agatha Christie TV movie was Helen Hayes. She and Miss Hayes had met a few times before, once at a party in Bette's New York townhouse. When daughter B.D. referred to Miss Hayes as the leading actress of the stage, Bette replied, 'First Lady of the Theater, my ass! *I'm* the first lady.'

'When I heard Miss Hayes was going to work with Mother on the Agatha Christie movie, my heart went out to her,' said B.D. 'She was a dear, sweet lady. I felt she didn't deserve this.'

On the first day of filming, Davis 'started by snapping at me,' Miss Hayes told Pat O'Haire of *The New York Daily News*. 'I said, "Good morning," and she looked right through me. Later when the cast gathered for introductions, our eyes met, and I waved. "What's *that* mean?" Bette snapped. "I was saying good morning," I answered. "You already did that," she snapped back.'

'I was never so scared in my life. And *I* was in the war,' said another actor on the film, John Mills.

Miss Lillian Gish did not glow in the warmth of Bette's embrace either. When the two seasoned stars met at the National Board of Review awards in 1984, Miss Gish went onstage and made a lovely but lengthy speech about D.W. Griffith. 'Bette was sitting in the front row and she became annoyed because Lillian was talking too much,' said a New York writer. 'As Miss Gish went on and on, Bette began to mutter out loud, "The silly bitch, get her off, get her off."'

In Maine, two years later, on the first day of shooting for *The Whales of August*, Miss Gish went over to Bette and welcomed her. 'If you want to talk about the work or the script,' Bette growled at the frail Lillian, 'fine. Otherwise, we have *nothing* to talk about.'

On the set another day, it was reported that when director Lindsay Anderson complimented Lillian Gish on a lovely close-up, Bette barked from the sidelines, 'Of course, it's a lovely close-up! The bitch *invented* close-ups!'

'She made mincemeat out of poor Lillian,' said Helen Hayes.

'Lillian swears she'll never act again. So first she drove me from the screen, now she's driven Lillian. She's making a clean sweep of everyone our age.'

THE MAIN CONTENDER

In 1987, ten years after her death, it was Joan Crawford who remained as the number one nemesis of Bette Davis. That spring Bette's second set of memoirs, *This'n That*, became a best-seller. The book was anticipated as a blistering retort to her disloyal daughter, but she was mentioned only in the afterword, in a letter euphemistically addressed to 'Dear Hyman' ('She couldn't very well call her "Dear C-t," could she?' asked one irreverent scribe). The letter took up two short pages, while another, older, more formidable foe – Joan Crawford – received an entire chapter.

'Did Bette Davis and Joan Crawford feud during the filming of *Baby Jane*? No!' said the author-star, answering her own question. With that settled, the magnificently virulent Bette marched on, blithely disclosing that Joan was a skilled sexual politician who drank too much vodka on the job, wore three sets of falsies (at different times), and was in general a silly, vain old fool who stole the Oscar that rightfully belonged to Davis.

That November, Miss Davis agreed to talk for this book, devoted entirely to her and Miss Crawford. Again she said there was no feud, and she had nothing further to say about her rival. She then proceeded to talk about Aries women; Joan's background; her unrequited crush on Joan's second husband, Franchot Tone; the making of *Baby Jane*; and other Crawford related topics (the quotes on which are in those chapters).

At the end of the conversation Davis declared it was fascinating that the public still linked her name with Crawford. 'I have never been *anywhere*, all over the world, they haven't asked about Joan and me. I don't mind it. I find it interesting. But I have always wondered. What do people *think* they see in us together? After all, we had *nothing* in common.'

23

'Indestructible. That's the word that's often used to describe me. I suppose it means that I just overcame everything. But without things to overcome, you don't become much of a person, do you?'

Bette Davis

In 1988, when the original edition of this book was near completion, Bette Davis was still very much alive, emotionally and intellectually, though her physical health was not as robust as her tumultuous will desired.

At age eighty, the after-effects of the stroke had left one side of her face paralyzed and her legendary stride was impeded by a limp. That, however, did not curb the most important force in her life – 'the work' – the zest to find, then lose herself in the next great role, which in turn would provide her with her next glorious honor. 'I wanted to be the first to win three Oscars,' she said. 'But Miss Hepburn has done it. Actually it hasn't been done. Miss Hepburn only won half an Oscar. If they'd given me half an Oscar I would have thrown it back in their faces. You see, I'm an Aries. I never lose.'

In our conversation the previous November, Davis revealed that she had found her next perfect character – that of the aging, cantankerous Southern woman in *Driving Miss Daisy*. She had read the finished script and though other established Hollywood stars were also vying for the part, including Katharine Hepburn and Angela Lansbury, Miss Davis concurred that she should have it: the producer was Richard Zanuck, and she had rescued his father, mogul Darryl Zanuck, from a critical situation during the early 1950s. 'He was desperate for someone to replace Claudette Colbert in *All About Eve*,' she said. 'And I did him a *huge* favor, by taking over the role of Margo Channing.'

That bountiful gift aside, it was payback time, Davis decided. She called Zanuck Jr and requested a meeting. She also contacted Steve Ross, the CEO of Warner Brothers, who were financing and distributing the film – with the huge revenue they were receiving from the sale of her classic films on home video, Davis believed.

Memorizing the script, she practiced key scenes, using the brisk Southern cadences mastered for her Oscar-winning role in *Jezebel*. And then she waited. Waited. Waited. But alas, was given no opportunity to perform for the producers.

The role of Miss Daisy went to Jessica Tandy, one year younger than Davis. Tandy also got the Oscar, and Robbie Lantz, Bette's long-time agent in New York, got the abuse. When he heard Davis was talking to other representatives in Hollywood, he wrote her a lovely note, suggesting they part professionally but keep their enduring friendship intact. Bette never responded, choosing instead to put her signature on an exclusive pact with the ICM agency in Los Angeles.

THE LAST FILM

At the same time the young turks at ICM were looking for suitable projects for their senior star, Bette was busy, beating the literary bushes on her own. A script arrived, created exclusively for her by Larry Cohen. He had written independent non-cult films such as *Women of San Quentin* and *It's Alive 3*, an original story about mutant babies starring Karen Black. His tailored offering for Bette was a black comedy, the story of an elderly witch who marries an older man and proceeds to wreak metaphysical havoc on his stepchildren. Bette, who adored ghoulish props, (remember the dead parakeet and rat in *Baby Jane*?), was delighted with those whipped up for her in *The Wicked Stepmother*. When her stepdaughter starts to wither under the stress, and wishes her stepmom were as kind and beautiful as her dead mother, the camera pans to a framed photograph of . . . Joan Crawford. (But not the one from Bette's private scrapbook, which had Joan's front teeth blacked out.)

Her fee of $250,000 was agreed, and Bette's live-in companion, Kathryn Sermak, was hired as a co-producer – a good investment as she would be the production liaison and ensure that her boss got to work on time. Taking care of her interests, however, soon stretched the budget of the modest independent film. Bette had to be consulted on everything, from the camera angles to her wardrobe, no expense spared. She insisted that her clothes be fitted and made by Western Costume, who outfitted her for *All About Eve*. Her red wigs were also custom-made, but the cost to the producers was cut substantially when Davis called the manufacturers and told them that she was wearing the wigs, so they better be perfect and come wholesale. Her make-up was also custom-blended, and her false eyelashes purchased in bulk. There again money would eventually be saved, because during filming no one was allowed to touch the star's face. Final makeup credit: Bette Davis.

Filming began on April 25, 1988. In advance everyone was told not to treat Miss Davis as old. She was not to be helped or catered to. If she forgot a line or walked out of the camera range, she or the director would be the ones to correct this, not the script girl or cinematographer. On the way to the set when she fell and couldn't get up, rather than embarrass or anger her, the crew were told to walk around her.

With time, Bette grew accustomed to the pace and was proud to be part of an independent unit. Then problems developed. The soundman had trouble when her dialogue became garbled, due to a broken dental bridge in her mouth. For the scene where she was to show her quintessential artistry with a cigarette, she whipped one out, placed it in her mouth, whereupon her character's demonic power was supposed to light it automatically. But the prop man goofed. Too much air was propelled into the cigarette and the flames scorched Bette's nostrils.

Paranoia and insecurity crept in after that. Fearing that it was she who was being used as the ultimate prop, to bolster and strengthen an inferior script, Davis asked that the complete footage be screened for her. She was horrified by what she saw. Akin to Joan Crawford's situation on *Hush . . . Hush Sweet Charlotte*, Bette knew the only way she could save her stature and sanity was by ditching the picture. That weekend she called the director and told him she was ill and would not be returning to complete his film.

Similar to Joan, she hoped the entire production would now be disbanded. And even if they recast her part, her filmed scenes would never be shown. She was wrong. The fifteen minutes of her footage were edited into the revamped film, which was then released with her name above the title. And though she went on *Entertainment Tonight* TV, to denounce this, *The Wicked Stepmother* would be forever known as Bette Davis's last movie.

> *'The role Bette Davis played best was herself, and it was the one everyone could identify with. She simply acted as if she were an irresistible force, and she got away with it.'*
>
> The New York Times

With no further film offers, to fill the void and keep her legend alive, the indestructible Bette would borrow another page from Joan Crawford's star survival manual. She would use herself to sell and sustain interest in her image and incredible career.

At eighty, and out of work, it was important to be seen. When her co star Ann Sothern was nominated for an Academy Award for *The Whales of August*, which Bette had refused to promote, she nonetheless called Sothern and said she would accept for her if the actress was unable to attend the ceremonies. She also called Johnny Carson and other late night TV hosts, asking when they intended to give themselves the substantial pleasure of having her on their talk shows as a guest. The blunt tactics worked. Offers came in and she decided it was now time to give the world a brand new Bette.

Previously conservative and modest in apparel, she met with a good friend of Kathryn Sermak – Patrick Kelly, a whimsical, cutting-edge designer from Mississippi, now based in Paris. Grace Jones and Madonna wore his clothes, so he knew a few things about strong independent women. When he met the prototype Bette, once he got over his initial shock and awe, he told her he was going to re-invent her, sartorially, from head to toe.

With the figure and weight of a twelve-year-old boy, she was to be his cartoon homage to what he thought an iconic Hollywood star should look like. And Bette, forgetting that she had frequently rapped Joan Crawford for her exuberant color-coordinated outfits and flashy ornamentation, went along with the zany metamorphosis.

'I want to die with my high heels on, still in action,' she said, appearing on TV in a form-fitting black dress with oversized rainbow buttons. Her custom-made red dress with black question marks splayed across the front was also a splendid distraction. As was the jewelry – rings, bangles, brooches, large hoop earrings, with assorted sorority pins stuck to her Archie Andrews beanie hat.

Which is not to say that the new Bette Davis forgot how to look serious. For a literary event she wore a chic black suit, red and black wide-brimmed hat, red and black reading glasses, with gloves, handbag and shoes to match.

The best fun of all was getting styled for the numerous award shows that were being hustled up for her. In January of 1989 she and Clint Eastwood were singled out for the American Cinema Awards in Los Angeles. Decked out in a white brocade gown with white fur cuffs, white fur pillbox and ash-blonde wig, Bette puffed and drank her way through the dinner, then passed out at her table.

Carried supine by the staff, from the banquet room to the hotel manager's office, she was placed on a couch, where she remained for close to a half hour. Minutes before her award was announced, she re-entered the room, fully refreshed and touched up. Escorted to the podium by Robert Wagner, she accepted the trophy, then proceeded to talk and sing at length, until Clint Eastwood gallantly cut in and helped her off the stage.

That spring, following her eighty-first birthday, the really big tribute would come, from New York's prestigious Film Society of Lincoln Center. Previous honorees were Charlie Chaplin, Sir Laurence Olivier, Billy Wilder, and Alfred Hitchcock. When asked how she felt about adding this respected prize to her war chest, Bette said: 'Greedy, greedy. Can't have too many awards. I've gotten just about every award there is to get.'

Looking forward, never back, she said that Lincoln Center would be the best memory, and until then she would be 'very nervous'. And busy. Every step, on stage and off, had to be planned. She asked that a map be drawn and photos made of each entrance, exit and in-between area at Avery Fisher Hall, where the award ceremonies were to be held. She wrote the acceptance speech, adding, subtracting and reinserting key lines from her movies. Timing the speech she then performed it, in full dress, standing in front of a full-length mirror in her living room.

On the day before the event, wearing a David Kelly black wool dress and a vivid red wrap, Bette met with selected reporters in her suite at the Plaza Athénée in Manhattan. The following evening, after her blonde wig was brought back reset and restyled from the hairdressing salon, she proceeded to don her extremely tasteful tribute outfit. Black slip, black stockings, black jeweled embroidered gown, black shoes, one string of white pearls, and a brilliant diamond clip placed crown-like on the top of her little black mink hat.

At 7:30 P.M. promptly, she emerged from the hotel, escorted by Harold Schiff, her lawyer. Waiting for them at Lincoln Center was the dutiful and vigilant Kathryn Sermak. All was in order and ready. Escorted by three security guards, they made their way to the royal box. Upon entering, the star stood for a moment, waved to the applauding mob below, then sat down and, on cue, the lavish tribute began.

Following the mandatory intro by the society's chief, one by one the guest presenters appeared – Geraldine Fitzgerald, Ann-Margret, James Stewart, and *All About Eve* writer-director Joseph L. Mankiewicz – to talk of Bette and introduce clips from the momentous passages in her extraordinary motion picture career. All edited magnificently, with bracing economy, and no overly intrusive on-screen competition from co stars like Joan Crawford, thank you very much. 'What a dump!' said the honoree, standing on stage 95 minutes later. Thanking the presenters and the film society, she proceeded to toss aside any trace of humility by behaving as if this night was long overdue. But she was grateful, and in closing, peering out into the audience of 2700 people, the great actress paused, wide-eyed, then with each syllable dramatically measured, she cooed and gave them her saucy benediction: 'I'd like to kiss ya, but I just washed my hair.'

The standing ovation was timed at one minute and 47 seconds, all of which the teary-eyed old-timer embraced like a warm spring breeze. It was tiring, too, and when Bette made it to the wings she was told the decision was hers. If the long ceremony had exhausted her, she could skip the supper party at Tavern on the Green and return to the hotel in the wheelchair sitting nearby.

'We will go to the party,' she said, 'standing.'

When her limo arrived at the Central Park restaurant, this writer was walking towards the entrance. When I saw Kathryn Sermak emerging from the car, I stopped and watched as she made her way to the TV press assembled on our left. Addressing them, Sermak said: '*Entertainment Tonight?* Cable TV?' Each nodded yes. She returned to the limo, opened the back door and extended her hand. As Bette Davis emerged the TV camera lights were automatically switched on. Ignoring her companion's hand, the elderly star, akin to Norma Desmond in *Sunset Boulevard*, weaved her way slowly towards the camera lights. Stopping before the reporters, she bade them to begin.

Not wanting to miss a moment of this, I circled around, stood next to the *ET* cameraman, and listened. The questions were the usual. Mostly mush. Until, believing that Bette Davis deserved more, I opened my mouth and heard myself saying: 'Miss Davis. Do you think Joan Crawford is up there tonight, looking down at you and smiling?'

'*Whaaatt?*' said Davis.

I repeated the question.

With a mischievous, slightly askew grin, she looked straight at me, and as the TV cameras kept rolling she said: 'Well, I'm not sure Joan is "up there". And if she is, she certainly is *not* smiling.'

Pure Bette. Fast. Wicked. On target.

Inside the restaurant, when I found my friends, many of them contemporary film critics, I sat and listened as they, rather blasé, summed up the evening as a swan song to the old/old Hollywood. At the same time, each chance they got, surreptitious glances were being cast towards the far corner of the room, where the grand honoree was sitting, smoking and drinking and revelling in the attention she was receiving from the swellegant parade of people that kept trooping towards her table. Later, when I noticed an extended gap in the line, I decided to pay my respects. I went over to Miss Davis, crouched by her chair and said I wanted to apologize, for asking that impertinent question outside about Joan Crawford.

'No, no. That was fine,' said Bette, looking down at me with the largest blue eyes and longest false eyelashes I had ever seen on anyone.

Freed from the tease of the famous eyes, I reminded her that I was the author of the forthcoming book about her and Joan Crawford.

'Oh,' she said, no longer completely happy. 'The book.'

'Yes,' I said.

'Does it have a title?' she asked.

'Bette and Joan,' I said.

She mused on this.

'In alphabetical order,' I added. 'Like Elizabeth the First and Mary Queen of Scots.'

With her mouth curled towards me, and the faint trace of a smile, she said: 'Yessss! I see.' At the same time a slight 'ummmm' was emanating in her larynx, which if released, I was sure, was going to explode into a loud laugh or, at least, a wild cackle.

But at that precise moment her companion Kathryn Sermak returned to the table, with three people in tow.

I stood up.

Bette looked at Sermak; then at me.

'I will send you a copy when it's published,' I said to her.

'Yes. Please do,' she said, then turned to receive her new guests.

'I'm back 100 percent . . . Now, we must go out and find another script. There is one rolling around but it's not at the point where we can say anything about it. Just yet. But I do love very much to work.'

Bette Davis, April 1989

Returning to California, Bette kept active, giving occasional interviews and posing for photographs. When it was remarked how thin she was, she said her health was fine, that her weight was perfect for future screen work. In July, when it was reported that the magazine rights to my forthcoming book, *Bette and Joan – The Divine Feud*, had been sold to two major publications, a week later, by an odd coincidence, the news came that Bette Davis was updating her 1962 memoir, *The Lonely Life*, to include her relationship with Joan Crawford.

That she had already written about this at length two years before in the bestseller *This'n That*, might have raised the question of redundancy. But who knows? Maybe our last conversation stirred dormant memories and new feelings about Crawford. Also, in a way I felt relieved. This would give her the chance to respond to my book, due to be released in November. That she would not be overjoyed with some of the disclosures, I also anticipated, sensing that Queen Bette would take to the airwaves and demand my head.

Till then, I felt it was best to keep busy, with a new totally different work, a biography of Paddy Chayefsky, the most daring and prized screenwriter in Hollywood's history. He had written three Oscar-winning scripts: *Marty*, *The Hospital* and *Network*. He also created the original TV play, *The Catered Affair*, the film version of which starred Bette Davis, giving what she told me was her favorite and most under-acknowledged performance.

On Friday October 6, after spending the day at the Museum of Broadcasting in Manhattan viewing kinescopes of Paddy Chayefsky's old TV plays, I was at home when a news flash came on TV. The legendary Bette Davis had died in France at the age of eighty-one.

Over the next few hours more details came in. The cancer she had conquered so valiantly had returned. She received treatment for this in California and the final prognosis was not good. But she insisted on travelling 6000 miles, to Spain, to receive another award, from the San Sebastian Film Festival. After the ceremonies she became ill. Too weak to return to the U.S. she was flown to the American Hospital outside Paris. At her side when she died was her companion, Kathryn Sermak.

The following morning, as newspapers around the world featured her death on their front pages, television producers and reporters were scrambling to put their coverage together. At noon I received a call from Cindy Adams, a New York columnist and co-host of *A Current Affair* on Fox TV. Another call was from a casting assistant for the Jonathan Ross program in London. Both asked if I would appear on their shows that Monday. The timing didn't seem right, I said. 'But your book – *Bette and Joan* – was published here only last week,' said the Jonathan Ross assistant excitedly. 'And Bette Davis just died,' said Cindy Adams. I mentioned something old fashioned, like having respect for the dead, and preferring to wait until after Miss Davis was buried, before flogging the book on TV or anywhere else.

Meg Blackstone, my New York editor, understood this. As did the publicist for the book, due in stores in the U.S. on November 15. Any and all interviews for radio, TV and newspapers would be timed for that date, it was agreed.

Wrong move, publicity-wise, we soon learned. Because the wicked side of Bette Davis' turbulent spirit was apparently still hovering.

On the afternoon of October 31, a purge swept through the halls of my respected and long-time New York publishing house. Described within the industry as the 'Halloween Bloodbath,' the executive publisher, editor-in-chief, and numerous staffers including my editor and most of the publicity department, had been fired.

The fate of *Bette and Joan – The Divine Feud,* set for release two weeks hence, was now in limbo.

But then a funny thing happened on the way home from the funeral services.

In mid-November the reviews for the book began to appear. Included were positive assessments from serious but humorous critics as author Luc Sante and Irish playwright Hugh Leonard. Other sprightly coverage trickled in from columnists and reviewers in Great Britain and the U.S. Followed eventually by the most important axle – the spinning, gleaming word-of-mouth from readers, which included established writers and performers from both sides of the Atlantic. Until it seemed as if most of the British theatrical investiture of knights and Dames, including the sublime, aristocratic Diana Rigg, were reading the book.

That December among the holidays cards was one from Bette Davis's daughter, B.D. Hyman. Sporting the direct frankness and humor of her mater, she wrote: 'I hear *Bette and Joan* is terrific. I wish you the best. So . . . where's my copy?' In an afterthought, referring to her recent loss, the death of her mother, she added: 'Your timing turned out to be superb, did it not? A nice bonus. Love B.D. and Jeremy.'

> *'I do not regret one professional enemy I have made. Any actor who doesn't dare to make an enemy should get out of the business.'*
>
> Bette Davis, *The Lonely Life,* 1990

With her demise, and the many tales of the protracted strife between her and Joan Crawford exposed, other stellar figures began to step forward to tell of their encounters with the formidable pair.

In *Second Act,* volume two of her memoirs, actress Joan Collins, who was named after her mom's favorite film star Joan Crawford, met the legend in London during the late 1950s. It was at a party, and Crawford, 'with eyebrows as thick and dark as Groucho's,' was disdainful and dismissive of the younger, sultrier English beauty.

Not long after Collins was in Hollywood, working with Bette Davis, on the set of *The Virgin Queen.* This was the starlet's first film for 20th Century Fox. Davis played the queen and Collins was Beth Throgmorton, her lady-in-waiting. On this particular day, Bette was 'ratty with everybody,' snapping at the other court handmaidens for chewing gum. When her scene was ready to roll, Collins was to kneel at the queen's feet and tie the satin bow on her one of her shoes. Understandably nervous, Collins began to tremble and fidget, wherein Bette raised her foot and kicked her viciously, sending the young ingenue 'flying across the set, petticoats over my head, much to the amusement of the crew.'

Bette Davis didn't actually do that, it could be argued. It was the royal character, displeased with the inefficiency of her servant, who levelled that punt. Same polemic could be applied to the incident when she kicked Joan Crawford in the head during the filming of *What Ever Happened to Baby Jane?* For actors, serious actors, who become so immersed in the roles they play, often get carried away by the unquenchable transferral of emotions.

The alchemy of higher 'art' aside, in real life, away from the soundstages, the same theory would not apply. Especially in a civilized society where laws against battery and physical abuse exist.

Which takes us back to the mysterious death of Bette's second husband, Arthur Farnsworth.

Details on this were given in chapter 10 of this book, with added input from Farnsworth's two sisters, and director Vincent Sherman, who was having an affair with Davis when her husband was killed. When interviewed, Sherman was reluctant to disclose the full details of what he knew, because he planned to write his own book. Graciously, he did agree to discuss the data and information I had assembled; repeated in part below.

Farnsworth, or 'Farney' as Bette called him, had fallen on Hollywood Boulevard in August of 1945 and died of a cerebral haemorrhage shortly thereafter. There was an autopsy, followed by an inquest, when it was revealed that a previous head injury caused his death. Testifying, Bette Davis recalled that he had fallen the previous month, on the stairs of their house in New Hampshire. In the witness stand she was asked if their relations were 'pleasant', and if anything in their home life could have contributed to his injury. 'No,' Bette replied tersely to the second question, revealing nothing to the jury about their frequent fights, or that she was in love with another man.

In our discussion, Vincent Sherman confirmed the affair, and that Bette asked him the previous spring to join him in Mexico, where she planned to vacation, without her husband. Before she left, she and Farney were at home, drinking, when they began to argue and she told him she was in love with Sherman. The following day, Farney went to see the director in his office at Warner Brothers and pleaded that he do the decent thing: not join Bette in Mexico. Farney, 'a gentle soul' said Sherman, was assured there would be no meeting in Mexico and that the future relationship between him and Bette would be strictly professional.

In 1996, in his book *Studio Affairs*, Sherman disclosed what had happened after his meeting with Farney, as told to him by Bette Davis. The day she left for Mexico, Farney escorted his wife to the train station in Los Angeles. In her compartment he 'taunted' her and told her that her lover would not be meeting her in Mexico. They quarrelled. The train started to move. She pushed him towards the platform. He stepped off the speeding train and fell on to the platform, where he hit his head. Bette, concerned and brave, confessed to Sherman that she 'ran down to the bottom step, held on to the bar on the side to look back and see if he was all right. He had fallen and was holding his head.' She wanted to stop the train and get off, she cried, but she was so unnerved she just stood there 'frozen, unable to utter a sound or to make a move.'

A chilling confession, for sure. And one kept from the examiner at the inquest. With good reason – it would have destroyed the career of Bette Davis, who was the number one female box office star in 1945. Also, it might not have entirely satisfied the coroner. The train incident happened in March. Farney collapsed on Hollywood Boulevard in late August, five months later. At which time the autopsy report stated a more recent 'basal skull fracture' occurred, estimating that this happened no more than two weeks before. Which confirmed what I had been told. That Bette and her husband had fought again, in the sleeper-coach room of the train from New York to California the first week in August. The journey took sixteen hours. They were both drinking. Harsh words were exchanged. She pushed him out of their room. He fell.

In any event there did seem to be a lot of screaming and pushing. But again, none of this was brought up at the inquest, where in a stunning about-face, the coroner who performed the autopsy, said he could have been wrong, and that the original injury could have happened months earlier. Which, if fully investigated, could have been traced to the day when Davis left Los Angeles for Mexico. For surely there was someone at Union Station who saw Farney fall from the train and land head first on the platform?

Whether Davis' studio, the mighty Warner Brothers, used their influence to discourage any further probing of the sensitive matter could not be determined, because the voluminous legal record concerning Bette Davis, now stored at the University of Southern California, reportedly shows nothing for the months of August and September, when the tragedy and investigation occurred.

Further protection, or paving over what actually happened, resulted in a few subplots being added, the intricacies of which would have encouraged the writers-producers of her next picture, the renowned Epstein brothers (*Casablanca*), to throw their type-writers out the window.

Again, as previously documented, here's a recap of the 'B' melodramas:

Farney apparently worked for a highly classified government agency and might have been killed for the secret documents he was carrying. He was also seeing that other woman, whose husband discovered them together in a motel and hit Farney over the head. Then there was the tender tale of the little urchin boy, who showed up at the studio gates looking for Bette Davis: he wanted to give her Farney's briefcase, which he had swiped from the injury scene. Bette received the boy and gave him a dollar for returning the briefcase to her. But when she opened the case she was overcome with sadness, because all it contained was empty whiskey bottles. Never mind, as stated, that the police and doctor at the hospital where his injured body was delivered, made written reports that there was no odor of alcohol on his breath.

Farney was a drinker, Bette said frequently, with remorse. And furthermore all of her husbands abused her. That included number one, her childhood sweetheart, Ham Nelson. He was the one who had the audacity to spy on her in their bedroom when she was making out with Howard Hughes. And then Ham blackmailed the reclusive millionaire. An entirely fabricated story, his second wife, Ann, said decades later. She also called Bette, who commiserated with her, blaming the distortions on the tabloid press and those salacious biographers. Yet in all subsequent interviews and memoirs, Davis never corrected the fictional accounts.

And let's not forget husband number three – artist William Grant Sherry. Highly disciplined, he seldom drank and was surprised to read (in this book) that Bette spoke such bad language. 'She never used it around me,' he said in a letter dated December, 1989. That same month, when asked to verify what Bette told him about the guilt she felt after pushing Farney on Hollywood Boulevard, Sherry repeated the story, on TV, and for another biographer.

Obviously, everybody was out of step but our Bette. Including her sister, Bobby, who, as told, was also belted and booted when she fell short of Bette's domestic standards.

But that was also family stuff, and as a popular song of the 1940s said – we always hurt the ones we love. The only irony perceived from the distance of time was that while Davis has been permanently enshrined as noble and exemplary, her most faithful rival, Joan Crawford, has been branded as verbally and physically abusive to her family. A grossly inaccurate indictment, her younger daughter Cathy recently told *Vanity Fair* magazine.

As a mother Joan Crawford, though strict and a disciplinarian, was the best and most loving single parent that she and her twin sister could have wished for, said Cathy.

PAX DEORUM

'She is taller than me? Then she is too high. For I myself are neither too high nor too low.'

Elizabeth I on Mary Queen of Scots

In the decades that followed their deaths, the legends of Bette and Joan continued to flourish, helped considerably by the release of their classic films on home video. Then the digital revolution kicked in, encouraging their staunchest fans all over the world to create websites, blogs and YouTube videos devoted to their legacies and their differences.

Befitting the imperial countenance of Davis, her 'official' site concentrated solely on business, including the marketing of her name, for hard cash upfront.

Joan on the other hand outdrew her with the sheer number of websites and fan pages freely glorifying her career and aesthetics. Quality sites include: *bestofeverything*, *legendaryjoancrawford* and *filmsofcrawford.com*, with significant essays and sumptuous photographs, from on-screen and off, that confirmed, in the parlance of her prime, what a hot number this luminous star really was. Especially during the late 1930s and early 1940s, when Bette Davis and other prominent Hollywood ladies feared for the virtue of their husbands and young men when Joan was on the prowl in their neighborhood.

As the speed and ease of computers grew, heated forums on Bette and Joan began to appear, questioning who was the greater star and better actress. New York writer Liz Smith, who knew both, made a brave statement when she stated in her column that 'Crawford was very much underrated, primarily because of her legendary glamor.' And Bette? 'I believe she overrated herself in terms of what she was capable of as an actress.' But that was part of her greatness, Smith added. 'She had an epic, staggering tunnel vision concerning "Bette Davis" and her own work.'

From time to time their epic feud was also questioned in published hypotheses, some gushingly vague, others feverishly far-out.

One ardent hagiographer implied in her 'personal' biographies that the two imperishable icons were above such mortal emotions as envy and anger. Apparently, from their respective pinnacles, each had read so much about their feud they started to believe it. Hard to swallow since the major studios during the 1930s and 1940s had enormous power over the entertainment press. This included the hugely popular movie magazines, who were strongly encouraged to write chirpy, uplifting and patriotic copy about the gods and goddesses of Hollywood. Hence Bette and Joan were seldom given the chance, or the joy, to read about the inside spats and sophisticated power plays they both excelled at.

Taking the opposite approach, another biographer implied that Bette Davis, in her relative youth, indulged in a precipitous carnal act. In 1935 she was supposedly seen giving Franchot Tone 'a blow job' in her dressing room. Tone was engaged to Crawford at the time, but apparently that was OK (the BJ, that is). Because Joan was 'really bisexual and always wanted a piece of Bette,' said the scholarly author. But Bette wanted 'no part of a lesbian affair,' and so the 'Homeric feud' began. Salty stuff, for sure. Except if Crawford ever made a sexual pass or overture at Davis, then or later, the latter, seldom shy, would have told someone, if not the entire world, about it.

> *'Just because someone is dead does not mean they have changed!'*
> Bette Davis after Joan Crawford had died

As this update was being written, preparations were underway for the centennial of the gloriously mismatched pair. And though Bette, born in April 1908, always swore that Joan was 'five years older, if she's a day,' the Hollywood marketeers have stuck to their own charts.

In March, 2008, Warner Brothers released volume two of Joan Crawford's films on DVD. A month later they came forth with volume three of Bette Davis' work. The following week, 20th Century Fox scheduled their DVD salute – *The Bette Davis Centenary Celebration* – highlighted by her infallible performance in the rapturously fluid *All About Eve*.

At that juncture it seemed that Bette was far ahead in the birthday sweepstakes. Except, in the final sprint, the spectre of Joan threatened to trip her up again.

Included in the Fox collection was *Hush . . . Hush, Sweet Charlotte*, starring Davis and Olivia de Havilland. Among the extras on the DVD was a documentary, tantalizingly entitled: 'Hush . . . Hush, Sweet Joan', which according to *Variety* magazine was going to feature the never-shown-before footage of Bette's original co star – Crawford.

The fans were ecstatic. Anticipated amount of rare footage: at least thirty minutes' worth, including the seven days of scenes Joan completed in Baton Rouge, Louisiana. Motion picture historians were also keen, because this would finally enable them to assess Crawford's performance in the film, which over time had acquired renewed attention. Though she had become 'ill' while making the movie, Crawford apparently was in prime condition where it mattered most – on camera. Screen veteran Mary Astor, who won an Academy Award in 1941 for her performance opposite Bette Davis in *The Great Lie*, had likewise benefitted from working with Joan – in *Hush . . . Hush, Sweet Charlotte*, which was Astor's last film. 'She was just marvellous with Crawford,' said Patricia Medina, wife of Joseph Cotten, the male lead. 'She gave a much better performance with Joan than with Olivia,' Medina told writer-historian Jimmy Bangley. 'Even Bette agreed that Astor was great with Crawford.'

Crawford apparently also brought out the primal creative force in Bette, and 'it was a shame that she left the film,' Medina said further. 'Bette and Joan, despite everything, had good chemistry.'

Cut to the centennial spring of 2008, when the final testament of their unusual chemistry would be seen in the *Sweet Charlotte* DVD documentary. Except when it was released in April 2008 there was no footage of Crawford. 'Hush . . . Hush, Sweet Joan', whatever its intention, silenced the great star, by showing none of her performance in that film.

Whether the rare footage would appear on a future disc, the producer of the documentary and the studio's publicity department declined to comment. It was 'permanently lost', the attentive fans and bloggers mourned, as the underlying rumour of previous sabotage spread. That dire conjecture replayed the tragic and much abused Crawford leaving the original production because of ill health, wherein the honorary producing 'partner' of the film, Queen Bette, ordered that all existing footage of her completed work be destroyed immediately. Better that than having her locked up in a prison cell for the rest of her life, before being decapitated, one could only speculate.

As with the real-life Elizabeth Tudor and Mary Queen of Scots (who never actually met), the legend of Bette and Joan – Hollywood's consummate film actress versus its ultimate movie star – will undoubtedly continue to flourish. Recently, when this seasoned commentator was asked what qualities, if any, the dynamic, constrasting monarchs shared, I pondered, then replied: 'Spirit, talent, strength, discipline, perfectionism, vanity, territorialism and stubbornness.'

For this update I would like to add: 'God bless them both.'

And wherever they are: 'Settle down ladies and try to make peace.'

Otherwise, as my friend Liz Smith commented: 'It's going to be a bumpy eternity.'

WHATEVER HAPPENED TO THE
WHAT EVER HAPPENED TO BABY JANE?
CLASSIC, ORIGINAL, PHOTOS?

In 1998, when the original edition of this book was being edited, a search was underway for the right photo for the cover. The image ardently sought was one of those taken on the set of *What Ever Happened to Baby Jane?*, by photographer Milton Greene, for *LIFE* magazine. The magazine, however, did not publish the photos, and subsequently Greene's entire Bette and Joan archive mysteriously vanished, for twenty-five years. This is the story of what happened during that amazingly labyrinthine period, starting with the legendary sitting, and detailing how later, the gifted photographer, with his illustrious career and credits mainly forgotten, came close to being buried with his extraordinary work.

PART ONE

THE PHOTO SESSIONS

It all began with Joan Crawford. In the late spring of 1961, after persuading producer–director Robert Aldrich to buy the rights to *What Ever Happened to Baby Jane?* and to cast Miss Bette Davis opposite her, Miss Crawford, a pro at marketing, turned her attention to the major publicity for the film. Top of her list, *LIFE* magazine. Photographer of choice, Eve Arnold, who three years before had captured the Pepsi executive and supporting performer (*The Best of Everything*) in a riveting seven-page photo story published in the same magazine. But the London based Miss Arnold was busy that summer of '62 and in her stead Milton H. Greene was chosen.

Renowned for the elegance of his fashion work and his celebrity photos – which appeared on twenty-five covers of *LIFE* and *LOOK* – the New York photographer also had a natural ease with formidable females. Such as Judy Garland, Marlene Dietrich, Anna Magnani and his ex-film partner, Marilyn Monroe, who had collaborated with him on an unprecedented fifty of her photo sessions. Hence working with Davis and Crawford should be relatively easy, especially since director Aldrich, a trite weary from refereeing the brilliant upstaging of his two leading ladies, arranged for the *LIFE* team to be there only for the last three days of shooting.

On September 5, 1962, with the majority of sensitive scenes completed, the first photo session was held on the soundstage of the Producers Studios in Hollywood, with both stars dressed in character. Gathered in Blanche Hudson's bedroom, to visually capture the confinement and despondency of the scripted situation, Greene asked that the two actresses pose in front of the foreboding window with iron bars. Bette, as Baby Jane, with garish white makeup and brassy blonde curls, stood grimly by her mark. Joan, in wheelchair (not visible), supposedly emaciated and abused, adopted the usual star approach to her dramatic interpretation. Cosmetically flawless, with sculpted crimson lips, and wide eyes fringed with false eyelashes, to integrate glamour with terror, she reached up and clung desperately to the iron bars. An arduous repetitive process, which necessitated frequent breaks, allowing the star to go to her dressing-room, for rest and her usual restorative libation. 'Pepsi spiked with vodka,' said Bette, remaining seated on Blanche's bed, playing gin rummy with Greene's partner, Joe Eula.

Photo session two was easier for Joan as she was no longer crippled, enabling her to stand by the window, which, with iron bars removed, was now draped with gaily patterned curtains. Aquamarine, the dominant hue of the drapes, matched the sash of the pretty, all- white, little-girl dress that Bette was now wearing. Taking the left position this time also enabled Miss Davis to be listed first in the photo captions. Which encouraged Miss Crawford to further elevate her visual impact. In her dressing-room, dispensing with the flat shoes her invalid character wore, she replaced them with personal footwear. A pair of her sexier, everyday, sling-back shoes, which though unseen under her monk's robe, empowered her to stand taller and slimmer than the hunched glum Bette positioned far left.

The next assembly, number three, was for Milton, the main event, the one where his landmark sense of personal style would dominate. Given their ages and lengthy careers, he also knew that Bette and Joan required a special tableau. The initial photo concept was that they be portrayed as Queens of the Silver Screen. Not a good idea, Harry Mines, the *Baby Jane* publicist, stated. Because twenty years before, Bette, the top box-office star and Queen of Warner Brothers, had refused to acknowledge recent arrival, Joan Crawford, was working at the same studio – let alone possessed the same degree of talent or star stature

At that point, Green's partner and stylist, Joe Eula, offered his concept. With the entire world infatuated with the current U.S. President's wife, Jacqueline Bouvier Kennedy, he suggested, why not adopt her honorary sobriquet? Presented to Mary Leatherbee, *LIFE*'s movie editor, she readily agreed, and came up with the title for the historic Hollywood Bette and Joan pairing: *New Film Brings Two Former First Ladies Together*.

At that juncture the budget for the photo project was increased and approved by *LIFE*. Meticulously supervised by Eula, early on the morning of their third day in Los Angeles, racks of expensive furs and designer gowns from Norman Norrell, James Galanos and others were wheeled into the climate controlled studio on Melrose Avenue. Costly accessories, including emeralds and rubies from posh jewelry stores on Rodeo Drive were delivered separately, by armed security staff. With the fabulous clothes and baubles, the ultimate background prop was chosen for the two imposing stars – a gleaming, vintage, Rolls-Royce convertible, leased and driven to the soundstage, where the key lights were blueprinted, then arranged.

Bette Davis showed first, alone and fully made up. Crawford, refining her appearance in her dressing-room, was precisely ten minutes late. In a regal swoosh, with an entourage, including her hairdresser, Peggy Shannon, publicist Harry Mines, and a personal assistant, when Joan arrived she by-passed her co-star and went directly to Milton Greene. The question of which star would sit behind the wheel of the Rolls Royce was no longer a factor. For maximum visibility and stylish impact, he requested they position themselves at the front of the Rolls, sitting on the polished grille, but apart. Davis automatically took the left spot. Crawford, with the help of Peggy Shannon and her assistant, placed herself on the far right. Arranging her gown and fur, she arched her back and famous shoulders, beckoning the photographer to begin.

Totally aware that glamour and swank were not part of her majestic countenance, Bette, refused to wear furs or any of the precious jewels, which allowed Joan, the quintessential movie star, to bedeck herself with the finest of the luxury items. Diamonds of every size adorned her neck, ears, left wrist and fingers, and over the slinky white satin gown, only the most expensive fur was allowed to envelop her well-kept body: Chinchilla, floor length, impeccably structured as the final resting place for 150 dead South American animals.

Thrilled by what he was capturing, and that each legend was giving him her undivided attention, upon loading roll five the photographer asked that they not look at him, but at each other. A silence of at least eight seconds ensued. Until Bette, apparently deciding – *why the hell not?* – slowly turned her head and looked at Joan. Who was not looking back at Bette, but at herself, in the hand mirror she was now holding. While Peggy Shannon, with the tip of her solid silver comb (a gift from Joan), proceeded to gently prod and raise the hairpiece concealed in the top of the star's chignon. The effect of which, again, enabled Miss Crawford, though seated, to appear taller and more magisterial than her co-star, who, wise to the ruse, reverted attention to her coiffure. Without mirror or comb, Bette began to pluck at her carefully set hair (all her own). Grasping the outer strands she then began to twist and extend them, until they she looked like she was wearing a crown of pre-punk barbed wire. Milton Greene got the message. Dispensing with his profile request, he fired off a few more face-forward shots. Then handing the camera to Joe Eula he bowed before his two subjects and said: 'We're done, ladies. Thank you very much!'

The Haute Couture Rolls Royce sitting was completed. As was the entire assignment, Greene and Eula believed. Except during lunch they were told that a vital scene in the film was being redone that afternoon. This was the controversial beach sequence, where Joan, as the dying Blanche, despite a brilliant performance, had discovered while watching the rushes closing that the lighting on her face was lousy. All the more inappropriate as Bette's closing performance, as Baby Jane, with the guilt removed of having crippled her sister years before, she looked twenty years younger.

Greene and Eula, welcoming the opportunity to capture the two stars in an actual scene, accepted the invitation to photograph the re-shoot of the beach sequence.

Crawford, lying on the two tons of imported sand, repeated her first-class performance. Kneeling beside her, Davis was once more a pro. Her face, a canvas of unspoken emotion, displayed none of the derision she felt about the accoutrements her co-star had added to her dying performance. Namely the false breasts, which, as the Milton Greene photos would attest to, were as firm and taut as that of a nubile fifteen-year-old girl. Silence was golden, Bette felt. Especially as she knew retribution would soon be secured, at the completion party to be held that evening. Except Joan knew of Bette's planned verbal ambush. So she skipped the party. Which is not to say she didn't acknowledge the significance of the event. Flushed from the experience of creative fulfillment, and her own 110 per cent proof spirits, later that night Miss Crawford called photographer Eve Arnold in London. Referring to the discomfort and abuse she suffered during the two months of filming, the triumphant star told the photographer: 'You would have been so proud of me. I was a lady, not like that c—t Bette Davis.'

PART TWO

ACCEPTANCE. BETRAYAL. OBLIVION. GLOBAL LARCENY AND RESTITUTION

The following week in Manhattan, when the film was processed, the best frames were enlarged and shown to the editors of *LIFE*, who were thrilled. Five were chosen for the back of the magazine. For the cover, one of the portraits of the two stars, sitting on the Rolls Royce grille was selected. As was the publication date, December 10, 1962, a week prior to *Baby Jane* opening in New York and Los Angeles. Except a few days after the photos were accepted, it was announced that the film had been chosen to inaugurate the new revolutionary system of 'Saturation Booking'. Instead of opening exclusively in New York and Los Angeles, *Baby Jane* was being released in 400 theaters, on November 3, a full month before the original date. *LIFE* magazine, caught off guard, was nonetheless prepared. They simply moved their exclusive story forward. At the same time they drastically altered the theme of their story. The 'First Ladies' concept was junked, and Bette and Joan, in ghoulish close-ups, were depicted as the elderly harridans they played in the film. Hence all of Milton Greene's classy photos, including the cover, were pulled and replaced with garish black-and-white shots taken surreptitiously on the movie set by a Los Angeles stringer.

The film became a huge success, promptly resuscitating the careers of Bette and Joan. Milton Greene was not as fortunate. His photos was filed away and forgotten. During the rest of the 1960s, while continuing to contribute to *LIFE*, he had only one significant credit – the cover and a dazzling six page fashion feature on the star of *Bonnie and Clyde*, Faye Dunaway. The latter session was once more brilliantly styled and staged by Joe Eula, who unfortunately left Milton shortly thereafter. Four years later when *LIFE* suspended publication, the photographer drifted, between minor assignments and marketing his former work. None of which attracted the acclaim or revenue he once enjoyed. Disillusioned, he withdrew. In 1980, separated from his wife, he was a semi-recluse in his east side townhouse when he was visited one day by Joanna Thorman, a beautiful blonde model, with her portfolio.

Thorman said she was 'Shocked to see an old man.' Further bewilderment came when Greene, looking at her folio, slammed it shut and rasped at her to: 'To give it up. It's all *crap*.' Uncertain if he was referring to her photos or the current fashion industry, she left. But by invitation, she returned the next day, to see his work, which was a revelation to the artistically imbued young woman. 'His talent seemed like a gift from God, like that of a Michelangelo, a Goethe, a Dante,' she said.

Thirty years his junior, Joanna became his creative supporter and lover. With photography now slowly being recognized as fine art, she was determined that he receive the same respect and renewed acclaim as his contemporaries Irving Penn and Richard Avedon. Assignments from *Harper's Bazaar* followed. One of the final ones was with Farrah Fawcett, looking surprisingly harsh and de-illuminated. Reflecting perhaps the state of Milton's physical state. He had a massive coronary, recovered, moved with Ms. Thorman to Los Angeles, where he was later diagnosed with cancer. He died in California on August 8, 1985; aged 63. Undeterred, Joanna, confirmed her commitment to continue to have his life's work fully recognized.

Shortly thereafter, working on the book, *Bette and Joan*, I called Ms. Thorman about purchasing one of the Rolls Royce photos for the cover. Amiable and enthusiastic, she said she knew of them, but didn't know where they were – in New York or Los Angeles. But she would look into this and get back to me.

Time passed, and as the deadline for the *Bette and Joan* cover was getting closer, I looked for the photos elsewhere. *LIFE* magazine had commissioned and accepted the images. But when I visited their office, they were surprised to discover they had nothing in their files. No photos, memos, telexes, shooting schedule or invoice, which I had been previously told was paid in full by the magazine. Leading me to question if the photos had been destroyed. Or if they ever existed? A briefly deranged theory shot down when I recalled seeing two of the photos, and that I had interviewed Joe Eula, who co-directed the Hollywood sessions.

With no alternative, the art director of *Bette and Joan* used a composite photo on the cover. The book was released and despite a rather bumpy start it became very successful. Resulting in other editions, the covers of which prompted renewed attempts to find the Milton Greene photos, all of which failed. However, in March of 1993 the matter of his estate was documented by reporter Stephen Fenichell in a story in *American Photographer* magazine. Entitled 'A Tangled Affair,' with a plot that 'Sizzles with a volatile mixture of greed, pride, infidelity, and jealousy,' Fenichell delivered.

Flashback to 1985 and Milton's last days. Terminally ill in a Los Angeles hospital, his estranged wife, and family, refused to allow Joanna Thorman, his mistress and professional partner to visit. Upon his death, his family were further saddened to learn that Ms. Thorman was the co-executor of his will, and had been left the entire estate.

The family sued. Two years passed, whereupon it was agreed that a Milton Greene Trust would be established, with Joanna as a trustee and his two sons, Joshua and Anthony, as co-trustees and 'primary beneficiaries' It was additionally sanctioned, since the lengthy legalities had bankrupted the estate, which was now held as collateral by a New York bank, that Thorman would raise the money to pay off the bank and to market Milton's work.

Joanna evidently tackled that part of the mission. The financial saviour, according to *American Photographer*, was a Chicago businessman, Dino Matingas, who 'knowing nothing about photography, or of Milton Greene,' said he was persuaded by the former model to spend $350,000 in helping them save the photo archives from bankruptcy. As collateral the original prints, transparencies and negatives were transferred to him. But when he declared his intentions to reproduce and sell some of the new prints, the newly incorporated Trust sued him. Until he offered them another $600,000, to form a Milton Greene licensing company, which would employ Thorman and the late photographer's sons. The trustees said yes to the second infusion of cash. Matingas then stalled, for reasons not fully explained in the magazine story. But when revealed, the details would make the previous experiences and altercations, including the *Baby Jane* star-crossed collisions, seem like a like a soothing nursery tale.

In 1989, when Dino Matingas saved the Greene archives from bankruptcy, he was quietly rescuing a far larger concern – the government of Poland. The former Soviet state, on the road to democracy and a free market, had enormous foreign debt on their hands. Hence, Grzegorz Zemek the chief of FOZZ, the government agency, devised a financial plan. He would would use the hordes of American dollars sitting idly in their Treasury to buy back their foreign debt bonds in the U.S., at a lower price. This would require special sub-agents in the U.S., one of whom was his good friend, Dino Matingas, who agreed to help. In May of 1989 the agreement between the two was signed and the purchase money was sent to Matingas in Chicago. An impressive sum it was revealed a year later – $15.5 million, which Dino did not use to buy the Polish debt bonds. Instead the money was allegedly funneled through 22 different tax haven corporations that he owned, one of which had financed the purchase of the Milton Greene photo archives.

In August of 1992 Matingas was sued in Chicago by a law firm representing the FOZZ litigator in Poland. The litigator won, whereupon Dino, ordered to return the money, declared that the only assets he owned was the Milton Greene archives. Under court order he transferred the archives to the City National Bank in New York, where they would be held pending instructions from FOZZ. Except by this time the agency in Poland had been dissolved and the investigation of corruption was allegedly being stalled by its former chief, Grezegorz Zemek, good friend of Dino Matingas, who likewise, was not what the angel of egalitarianism and financial relief that he seemed to be.

Nor was he a mere civil servant. During Soviet Russia's occupation of Poland. Zemak was a KGB agent and General in their military. Aware that democratic freedom was on the political horizon, he devised a series of schemes that would strengthen their intelligence and financial agencies. The boldest was using FOZZ to buy back their debt bonds in the U.S., at a lower price. And since the Security and Exchange system in Washington considered this illegal, the purchases had to remain secret, he told the FOZZ board, who knowing little of where the money was going, accepted

Zemek's assurance that his calculated return of $500 million each year would eventually erase Poland's $40 billion debt.

In 1990 when the return cash didn't materialize, and the Polish Treasury was being further depleted, an investigation was made. Zemek was jailed and indicted for corruption and embezzlement. The prosecution, however, had a hard time setting a trial date, due to a series of accidents. Amongst the casualties, an independent publisher in Warsaw, who, following a meeting on 'secret' testimony, was in his car when he was stopped by the police. Beaten with truncheons and jailed, two days later when he returned to his car, he found it was broken into and the 'incriminating documents removed'. Far more tragic incidents occurred. The chief state investigator was 'found dead in mysterious circumstances', and his boss, the head of the Supreme Chamber of Control, 'was killed in a car cash'. All quotes and details courageously reported by Polish reporter Marek Matraszek in *The Spectator,* January, 1992.

The prosecution persisted, and nine years later, Zemek was brought to trial. Found guilty, he was sentenced to nine years in prison and a fine was imposed, plus interest. In March of 2013 the fine was reduced and he was released for 'good behaviour', at which time, according to a recent email from reporter Mr. Matraszek, Mr. Zemek, the former General and KGB agent, was 'looked after financially' by the Starak family, whose head, Jerzy Starak, a pharmaceutical billionaire, is the fourth richest man in Poland.

Meantime none of the many millions embezzled in Zemek's notorious U.S. transfer scheme (estimated at $85 million) were recovered. The only compensation seems to have come from Dino Matingas, who soon vanished. In 2012 the Milton Greene photo archives were finally sent to Warsaw. The treasury employees, not knowing what was there, upon opening the first of two crates, yelled: 'moj Boz!' ('my God!'). The folder on top, marked: 'Pulling off Stockings' 'Legs Spread,' 'Hat in Lap,' revealed illustrious archival prints of Marilyn Monroe, from the renowned 'Black Sitting'. Further down in the crate were other remarkable blow-ups, of Marlene Dietrich, Brando Brando, Ava Gardner, Elizabeth Taylor and Frank Sinatra.

That November the Treasury auctioned the prints in Poland, The gross, $740,000. Thus enriched they decided to sell the rest of the archive, in sunny, wealthier California. The announcement in May of 2012 brought added excitement and consternation, as this time they weren't merely offering prints. They were selling the original Milton Greene negatives and transparencies, with the copyrights, which meant the purchaser could print and license the images for whatever commercial products they choose.

With skepticism but lingering hope that the Bette Davis and Joan Crawford portraits might be part of the auction, I purchased and went through the $65 catalogue. Past the bountiful Monroe images (eighty separate lots), and those of Audrey Hepburn, Gary Grant, Doris Day and Jane Fonda, there it was. Lot 102, featuring the original 1962 Bette and Joan photos, created on the set of *What Ever Happened to Baby Jane?* Over eighty colour transparencies, including those from the opulent Rolls Royce session.

Estimated to sell at $800 to $1,200, the Davis and Crawford lot went for $5,000, purchased by Theo Pouros, a London bookseller and devout Bette Davis and Joan Crawford collector.

Total gross of the Los Angeles auction – $1.8 million. At which time it was assumed from the vastness of the collection, 3,700 prints, negatives and transparencies, that this was the entire collection. Not quite. In June of this year there was a third auction, in Poland. Over 3,000 more prints were sold in one unit for $1.6 million, to a software manufacturer in Wroclaw. This was also 'the final' sale, the auction house stated. There were no other images left, it was assumed. Except upon checking the catalogue and listings I noticed there were some some important items not featured in the three auctions. Amongst them the original negatives of the aforementioned 'Black Sitting' with Marilyn Monroe. And though one vintage print from these had been sold in Warsaw for $16,000; and another thirty different enlargements were being marketed on the Milton Greene U.S. website, managed by his son, Joshua, apparently there was no record of who had the original negatives. From which additional enlargements could be made. Were the negatives lost? Misplaced? Did the 1950s film nitrate fade? Disintegrate? Or combust from the heat of Marilyn in so many extraordinarily sensual angles?

A puzzlement and dangling mystery, best left perhaps for another Sherlock Holmes photo sleuth to solve.

This one now retired from the case. Albeit contented. Because the cover of the book you are now holding has finally been graced with the long-sought portrait of Bette Davis and Joan Crawford, created by Greene–Eula. Hand printed from the original transparency, in rich color and detail. Befitting the twenty-fifth Anniversary of the original edition, and the singular, unquenchable sovereignty of the two Hollywood Empresses, whose impact today remains as vigorous, unyielding and imperishable as when they ruled the Silver Screen.

Acknowledgements

Together with Bette Davis and Joan Crawford, I am indebted to many people who helped with this project. It began as a magazine article in 1978 and was eventually put aside due to the bulk of material accumulated. In 1987 the material was expanded for a book outline, augmented, and finally completed twenty-one months later. During the entire time span, hundreds of people were contacted. Many contributed interviews, anecdotes, leads, further insights and confirmed or denied existing quotes and facts, when necessary. Some of these contributors are no longer living; others asked that their names be withheld. My respect and thanks extend to everyone, including: Adelle Aldrich, William Aldrich, Hector Arce, Anne Bancroft, Ann Barton, Arthur Bell, Joan Blondell, Barbara Briggs, Larry Carr, Kathleen Carroll, Judith Crist, George Cukor, Mrs. Jon De'Besche, Sanford Dody, Joe Eula, Dale Eunson, Douglas Fairbanks, Jr., Dore Freeman, Bob Gary, Sheilah Graham, Vik Greenfield, Lukas Heller, B.D. and Jeremy Hyman, Carl Johnes, Stan Kamen, Norma Koch, Michael Luciano, Joe Mankiewicz, Gary Merrill, Harry Mines, Alanna Nash, Geraldine Page, Jerry Parker, Irving Rapper, Nicholas Ray, Peggy Shannon, William Grant Sherry, Marian Richards Sherry, Vincent Sherman, Bob Schiffer, Flip Schulke, Adela Rogers St. Johns, Liz Smith, Phil Stern, Bob Taplinger, Phillip Terry, Linn Unkefer, Jim Watters and Monte Westmore.

Special thanks to Eileen Tuohy for her important research in Los Angeles; and to Kathy Judge for the same in Vermont. I am also especially grateful to the American Film Institute in Los Angeles, who provided access to the files of the late Robert Aldrich;

to Russ Butner at that Institute; to Michael Kelly; to the staff of the Billy Rose collection at Lincoln Center; to Ron Magliozzi in the Film Department at the Museum of Modern Art, New York City; to the library staff of the Academy of Motion Pictures Arts and Sciences in Los Angeles; the Screen Actors' Guild; the American Society of Cinematographers; the Directors' Guild of America; the Publicists' Guild; the Hairdressers' and Makeup Union; and to Cindy Adams, Dennis Ferrara, Robert Osborne, and to the agents and staff at William Morris, ICM, CAA, and the Barry Douglas Agency.

For assistance in tracking down photographs over a twelve-month period, I am especially appreciative of the efforts and generosity of Lou Valentino, who gave from his own collection and provided other leads. Thanks also to Maryam Garahan for her photography; to Mary Corliss at the Museum of Modern Art; to Fred Cantey at Wide World; to Neal Peters; to William Chapman and Phil Stern in Los Angeles; and to Flip Schulke in Florida.

For the original British hardcover edition, I would like to thank Editorial Director Paul Sidey, Rowena Webb, and Caroline Freyer.

For this updated edition: thanks to Theo Pouros for steadfastly suggesting it; to Donna Nowak for helping to track down the original photograph for the new cover; to Viki Ottewill at Little, Brown for designing it; and to Emma Stonex for editing and guiding the entire new edition through production.

For this 25th Anniversary edition, thanks to publisher David Shelley, who enthusiastically endorsed it. To Rhiannon Smith, who edited the new essay and ably shepherded the changes and new artwork through production. To Theo Pouros, again, who agreed to contribute the original Milton Greene photos. And to Helen Surman who designed the new cover.

Last and first as always, top honors go to a special patron, Saint Jude, who always delivers, no matter how minor the request.

Source Notes

1

3   'Crawford is five years older': Bette Davis to publicist Linn Unkefer on set of *What Ever Happened to Baby Jane?*

3   'Damn you! I'll get you for this': Bette Davis with Sanford Dody, *The Lonely Life.*

3   'Sounded more like an entrance . . .': Alexander Walker, *Stardom.*

4   'He ran off with a stripper . . .': Bette Davis with Michael Herskowitz, *This'n That.*

4   'Being abandoned so often . . .': author's interview with Adela Rogers St. Johns, 1978.

4   'Cut in scallops': *Time*, March 28, 1938.

5   'Mother shacked up . . .': Joan Crawford to Roy Newquist.

5   'They led such adventurous lives': author's interview with Joan Crawford, 1976.

6   'I always felt special . . .': Davis, *The Lonely Life.*

7   'She stole money . . .': David Houston, *Jazz Baby.*

7   '. . . I'll teach you how . . .': Joan Crawford with Jane Kesner Ardmore, *My Way of Life.*

8   'I lived for those words . . .': author's interview with Joan Crawford.

9   'Often or not, ending upstairs': Houston, *Jazz Baby.*

10   'I was carrying her up the stairs . . .': Henry Fonda, *My Life.*

11   'She robbed us blind . . .': Houston, *Jazz Baby.*

12   The account of Crawford's alleged first marriage to James Welton appeared in Patricia Fox-Sheinwold, *Gone But Not Forgotten* (Bell Press, 1981). The date or place, however, were never substantiated.

13   in a series of soft-core porn movies: *Viva*, August 1978.

13   Joe Mankiewicz said he thought the meeting . . .: Alexander Walker, *Joan Crawford: The Ultimate Star*.

14   'We acted in a few school plays . . .': author's interview with Joan Blondell, 1978.

2

17   'Italianate *Padre-Padrone*': Walker, *Ultimate Star*.

17   'Look, I've got certain things . . .': Gary Carey, *All The Stars in Heaven*.

18   'My skirts were a trifle shorter . . .': Joan Crawford, *My Way of Life*.

19   'That's not true . . .': author's interview with Joan Crawford, 1973.

19   In the opening shot: Ethan Mordden, *Movie Star*.

20   'She refused dates . . .': Charles Higham, *Bette*.

20   'a very interesting actress . . . She was a stubborn young lady . . .': author's interview with George Cukor, 1978.

21   a few legal skirmishes: Joan Crawford's file at Lincoln Center, and Walker, *Ultimate Star*.

24   'vital, energetic, very pretty . . .': Douglas Fairbanks, Jr., *Salad Days*.

25   The accounts of their exclusion: interview with Douglas Fairbanks, Jr., 1988.

25   Joan was 'on the toughie side': from *Sweetheart* by Roland Windeler.

3

29   'This was the period . . .': Bette Davis, *The Lonely Life*.

30   picked up some beauty secrets: Frank Westmore, *The Westmores of Hollywood*.

30   'There was a bunch of us . . .': interview with Joan Blondell.

31   After altering the shape of her face: Barry Norman, *The Hollywood Greats*.

32   '. . . most exotic pieces of affectation . . .': Cecil Beaton, article at Lincoln Center.

33ff   Details on the filming of *Grand Hotel* are from files at Lincoln

Center, from books on George Hurrell, Edmund Goulding, Greta Garbo, and John Barrymore, and from *Time, Newsweek, Modern Screen*, and *Photoplay*.

4

41   'Hollywood in the early days . . .': telephone conversation with Joe Mankiewicz, 1987.

41   'That's the way Warner's worked . . .': interview with Joan Blondell, 1978.

42   Stopped twice for speeding: Bette Davis file at Lincoln Center.

42   learned how to smoke and talk dirty: ibid.

43   His salary: interview with Douglas Fairbanks, Jr.

44   'Bette Davis seems convinced': *Garbo and the Night Watchman*, edited by Alastair Cooke.

45   '. . . bad timing for Bette . . .': interview with Adela Rogers St. Johns.

45   'There was an inordinate amount': interview with Douglas Fairbanks, Jr.

46   'I've never been at Buckingham Palace . . .': Edward G. Robinson, *All My Yesterdays*.

48   'Don't talk to me . . .': Joan Crawford files at Lincoln Center.

48   'Chiseling with an extra girl . . .': *Motion Picture* magazine, January 1932.

49   'Yes, Clark and I had an affair . . .': Roy Newquist, conversations with Joan Crawford.

49   'accommodated anyone important . . .': interview with Hector Arce, 1978.

49   'silk shirts and underwear . . .': Lyn Tornabene, *Long Live the King*.

50   'With his wife sitting . . .': Myrna Loy, *Being and Becoming*.

50   'Joan was aggressive . . .': interview with Adela Rogers St. Johns, 1978.

51   Doug began to notice: Douglas Fairbanks, Jr., *Salad Days*.

52   'I was on my way to . . .': interview with Adela Rogers St. Johns.

53   'This was a big scoop . . .': Ezra Goodman, *The Fifty Year Fall and Decline of Hollywood*.

54   'Right under my surprised hostess' eyes . . .': Louella Parsons,
         The Gay Illiterate.

5

57   'Garbo had her Gilbert . . .': press book for *The Big Shakedown*
         at Lincoln Center.
57   'Jack Warner seldom . . .': interview with Joan Blondell.
57   'Any number of actresses . . .': Cromwell to Leonard Maltin,
         Action magazine, 1973.
58   'Yes, I *was* offered that part . . .': interview with Bette Davis,
         1973.
59   their faces were blank . . .: Bette Davis, with Sanford Dody,
         The Lonely Life.
61   'was a drunk, not a doper . . .': interview with Bette Davis.
61ff   The account of the relationship between Joan Crawford and
         Franchot Tone is from their files at Lincoln Center.
64   'He was a most charming . . .': interview with Bette Davis,
         1987.
64   'I was on the lot . . .': interview with Joan Blondell.
64   'I didn't know Davis . . .': interview with Adela Rogers St.
         Johns.
69   'How much is Joan making?': interview with Sheilah Graham,
         1988.
70   'Joan resembles MGM . . .': Sidney Skolsky, in *Motion Picture*,
         September 1965.
72   'We build stars around here . . .': Warner Brothers files at the
         University of Southern California.
73   'Jimmy was always complaining . . .': interview with Joan
         Blondell.
73   'I was a woman . . .': interview with Bette Davis.
73   'There was a principle at stake . . .': Charles Higham, *Bette*.

6

76   when the Eunsons lived in Connecticut: interview with Dale
         Eunson, 1987.
76   'In her bedroom . . .': *Liberty*, May 1938.

77   'Don't be *ridiculous*! . . .': interview with Bette Davis.

78   'That story is just another . . .': interview with Joan Crawford.

78   'That was pure hype . . .': interview with George Cukor.

79   'Clark was not even *remotely* interested . . .': interview with Joan Crawford.

80   'Gable and Bette Davis? . . .': interview with George Cukor.

80ff   The making of *Jezebel* is taken from press book and files at Lincoln Center, and books on Bette Davis, director William Wyler, Henry Fonda, and producer David Selznick.

83   'The picture is permeated . . .': from *The Making of 'Gone with the Wind'* on TNT Network, 1988.

83   'with tennis court, swimming pool . . .': *Time*, March 28, 1938.

85   'Thank God I'm in love again . . .': Joan Crawford file at Lincoln Center.

85   'In ten minutes . . .': Joan Fontaine, *No Bed of Roses*.

86ff   The account of Crawford's affair with Spencer Tracy is taken from Sheilah Graham and Adela Rogers St. Johns interviews, and from books by Alexander Walker, Bob Thomas, and Roy Newquist.

86   'Cold hearted . . . a high-class thief . . .': *Screenland*, 1938.

88   'Bette had the fantasies . . .': interview with Adela Rogers St. Johns.

89   'Her biggest concern was that Wyler was Jewish . . .': interview with B.D. Hyman, 1988.

90   After dinner: *Life*, September 1938.

91ff   Details of Davis' affair with Howard Hughes were confirmed by B.D. Hyman and by William Grant Sherry.

91   'preference for oral sex': Lana Turner, *Lana*.

91   He suffered from 'recurrent ejaculatory impotence': Charles Higham, *Bette*.

92   'After listening . . . potency problems': ibid.

92   Hughes considered hiring a professional killer: *International News Alliance*, November, 1981.

93   'I was in a sovereign state . . .': Bette Davis, with Sanford Dody, *The Lonely Life*.

7

95   'I'd like to slap their faces . . .': Joan Crawford file at Lincoln
         Center.

96   'I designed my own hair styles . . .': press book of *No More
         Ladies* at Lincoln Center.

96   It was the perfect facsimile . . .': Melvyn Douglas, *See You at
         the Movies*.

96   'You'd have to watch . . .': Kenneth Geist, *Pictures Will Talk*.

97   '. . . telling difference . . .': interview with Irving Rapper, 1987.

97   'I was out scouting . . .': interview by Guy Flatley, *New York
         Times*, 1976.

99   'multilingual snatches of songs . . .': Alexander Walker, *The
         Ultimate Star*.

101   'They knew all that . . .': Crawford to Katharine Albert.

101   'Sensitive husbands . . .': Joan Crawford, *My Way of Life*.

103   'I like Bette Davis . . .': John Kobal, *People Will Talk*.

104   'Christ, she really rode . . .': Joan Crawford files at Lincoln
         Center.

104ff   The preproduction and filming of *The Women* from interviews
         with Joan Crawford and George Cukor, and from files at
         Lincoln Center.

108   'I let it be known . . .' Rosalind Russell, *Life is a Banquet*.

108   'Shearer would look . . .': Lazslo Willinger to John Kobal in
         The Art of The Great Hollywood Portrait Photographers.

8

110   Although a tent: New York *World Telegram*, January 3,
         1940.

113   'She began to talk . . .': interview with Harry Mines, 1987.

113   'She went out of her way . . .': interview with Joan Blondell.

115   'You don't have to be beautiful . . .': *Cosmopolitan*, November
         1937.

115   'He was the longest real romance . . .': Bette Davis to Nancy
         Collins, *Women's Wear Daily*, 1976.

116   'Current gossip . . .': Joan Crawford file 1674 n.c. at Lincoln
         Center.

116	'. . . He was an *actor* . . .': Bette Davis to Phil Donahue, June 15, 1987.
116	'Sitting at a ringside table . . .': Clifford Odets, *The Time is Ripe.*
117	As a wedding present: B.D. Hyman, *My Mother's Keeper.*
118	'To Arthur Farnsworth . . .': Rutland (Vermont) *Herald,* August 1943.
118	'That plaque ended up . . .': interview with Mrs. Jon De'Besche, 1988.
118ff	The account of the filming of *Strange Cargo* is from the file and press book at Lincoln Center.
119	Telegrams were sent: Alexander Walker, *The Ultimate Star.*
120	She gave him her virginity: Lana Turner, *Lana.*
121	'But I didn't go . . .' Jackie Cooper, *Please Don't Shoot my Dog.*
123	'I never quite believed her . . .': Douglas Fairbanks, Jr., *Salad Days.*
123	'Jesus! Look . . .': Roy Newquist, *Conversations with Joan Crawford.*
124	'based on personal interviews': Christina Crawford, *Survivor.*
125	'The little girl . . .': Melvyn Douglas, *See You at the Movies.*
128	'I knew what kind of a marriage . . .': Crawford files at Lincoln Center.
128	'. . . "Forever!" . . .': ibid.

9

Material for 'The War Years' was gathered from video cassettes at Lincoln Center, from *City of Nets* by Otto Friedrich, *The Story of Hollywood* by Barry Norman, and from *Look, Life, Colliers, Photoplay, Modern Screen, Motion Picture,* and other publications.

135	'It's cut too close . . .': Doug Warren, *James Cagney.*
136	'Nobody but a mother . . .': Brian Aherne, *A Proper Job.*
136	'It could be marvelous . . .': Larry Carr, *Four Fabulous Faces.*
137	'He went fishing and fucking . . .': Viveca Lindfors, *Viveka . . . Viveca.*
138	'Bette has a lot of mannerisms . . .': Wyler interview in *New York Times,* 1941.

142   'wanted very much . . .': interview with Bette Davis, 1973.

142   'I'd rather work with Jack Barrymore drunk . . .': Davis files
           at Lincoln Center.

143   'That was a first for black people . . .': Whitney Stine with
           Bette Davis, *Mother Goddamn*.

144   'There is something frenetic . . .': John Huston, *An Open Book*.

144   'reading favorite passages from the Holy Bible . . .': Charles
           Higham, *Sisters*.

145   'When I can't sleep . . .': George Eells, *Ginger, Loretta and Irene
           Who?*

146   'It was a grand entrance . . .': from *Collier's*, November 25,
           1955.

146   thirty-six days behind schedule: Rudy Behlmer, *Inside Warner
           Brothers*.

10

148   'The studio no longer cared . . .': Myrna Loy, *Being and
           Becoming*.

151   Raging at Crawford . . .: Alexander Walker, *The Ultimate Star*.

152   'Jack Warner was a *wonderful* man . . .': author's interview with
           Bette Davis, 1987.

153   'That was my dream . . .': author's interview with Joan
           Crawford, 1973.

154   'He's full of shit': from Dore Freeman, 1987.

154   'It's possible . . .': interview with George Cukor, 1977.

156   'My mother requested . . .': author's interview with Mrs.
           De'Besche, 1988.

156   The chief coroner, Frank Vance: *Los Angeles Times*, August 28,
           1943.

157   'When the hotel maids . . .': Bette Davis, *This'n That*.

158   'I was not aware . . .': author's interview with Vincent Sher-
           man, 1987.

159   'At the last minute . . .': ibid.

159   'To my chagrin . . .': Bette Davis, *This'n That*.

159   'There was a stairs . . .': author's interview with Mrs. Roger
           Briggs, 1988.

160   'He and Bette . . .': interview with Mrs. De'Besche.

160   In Los Angeles, on the day he collapsed: from *Photoplay*, November 1943.

161   'Rising from her sickbed': *Los Angeles Times*, August 28, 1943.

161   'The details of their conversation . . .': interview with Hector Arce, 1981.

162   'No role of tragedy . . .': *Los Angeles Times*, September 1, 1943.

162   'A basal skull injury . . .': Charles Higham, *Bette*.

162   Meanwhile her lawyer: interview with Hector Arce.

163   'It is impossible for me . . .': *Los Angeles Times*, September 1, 1943.

163   On Saturday, September 4: *New York Times*, September 4, 1943.

163   'I was outraged . . .': interview with Mrs. De'Besche.

163   'It was a very difficult . . .': interview with Mrs. Roger Briggs.

163   Details of the funeral are from Rutland (Vermont) *Herald*, September 6, 1943, courtesy of Kathy Judge.

164   'The remains *were* moved . . .': from Mrs. De'Besche, with date of re-internment from town clerk at Pittsford, Vt.

164   'She told me he was epileptic . . .': interview with Joan Blondell.

165   '. . . "El Portal motel" . . .': interview with Bob Gary, 1988.

165   'The subject was off-limits': interview with Sheila Graham, 1988.

165   'Bette turned white': interview with William Grant Sherry, 1988.

11

166   'when we found out . . .': Lee Server, *Screenwriter*.

166   'She wants her name mentioned . . .': Warner Brothers files at University of Southern California, courtesy of Michael Kelly.

167   'Guilty? Bette Davis? . . .': interview with George Cukor.

167   'She made it very difficult for me . . .': interview with Vincent Sherman.

167   'I avoided her . . .': ibid.

168   'Hints on how to treat wounded vets . . .': Stage Door Canteen files at Lincoln Center.

172   'A very pleasant pile of shit . . .': Roy Newquist, *Conversations with Joan Crawford*.

173   'I think Joan felt . . .': interview with Vincent Sherman.

173ff   The account of the filming of *Mildred Pierce* is taken from interviews with Joan Crawford, the files at Lincoln Center, and from Roy Hooper, *Cain*; *Mildred Pierce* the script, with introduction by Albert J. La Valley; *Genius of the System* by Thomas Schatz; *The Hollywood Professionals*; *Inside Warner Brothers*; *Screenwriter*; and *American Film* magazine.

12

188   'She spent an entire day auditioning dogs . . .': Charles Higham and Joel Greenbaum, *The Celluloid Muse*.

188   'There was some resistance . . .': interview with Harry Mines.

189–190   Reports of the accidents are from Warner Brothers files at USC.

191ff   Details of his meeting and marriage with Davis are from an interview with William Grant Sherry, 1988.

192   'Mister Sherry? . . . I want you to come to dinner': ibid.

194   shortly thereafter Philip Terry left home: Christina Crawford, *Mommie Dearest*.

194   'I have no recollection . . .': Phillip Terry by phone, 1988.

195–6   Details of Lindfors' meeting with Davis and Crawford are from Viveca Lindfors, *Viveka . . . Viveca*.

197   'In this outline I am going Italian . . .': Rudy Behlmer, *Inside Warner Brothers*.

198   'a Mexican schlemiel': Larry Swindell, *Body and Soul*.

198   'So you're Joan Crawford . . .': Bob Thomas, *Joan Crawford*.

199   'I wasn't being generous . . .': author's interview with Joan Crawford, 1976.

200   'Guess who just got on the train? . . .': Jerry Parker in *Newsday*.

200   'There was a terrible row . . .': interview with Irving Rapper, 1987.

201   fifteen costume changes: press book of *Deception*; Whitney Stine with Bette Davis, *Mother Goddamn*.

202   'It became a knock-down . . .': Jimmie Fidler to Hector Arce.

205   'It was a softer, gentler Bette . . .': *Photoplay*, January 1947.

205   'All is hearts and flowers . . .': Joan Crawford file 1675 n.c. at Lincoln Center.

13

206   'It was not difficult . . .': Charles Higham and Joel Green-baum, *The Celluloid Muse*.

209   'She liked men who gave her . . .': interview with Adela Rogers St. Johns.

209   'She certainly knew how . . .': Fred De Cordova, *Johnny Come Lately*.

213   'Coming in with a swirl of skirts': James M. Cain in *Modern Screen*, September 1946.

214   'She was a miserable little kid . . .': interview with Joe Mankiewicz, 1987.

214   'I was there when Christina': interview with Larry Carr, 1978.

215   In her book, *Child Star*, Shirley Temple Black claimed the incident with Crawford and her children happened in 1938, but Christina and Christopher were not born until 1940 and 1942. When contacted through her agent in November and December 1988, Miss Temple Black declined to be interviewed or to provide a corrected date for her story.

216   'Crawford immediately leaned . . .': Barry Norman, *The Holly-wood Greats*.

217   'Just imagine Bette Davis . . .': Neal O'Hara in *Christopher Street* magazine.

217   'Wrong fucking sex': Gary Merrill, *Bette, Rita and the Rest of My Life*.

220   'There is a wonderful story . . .': interview with George Cukor.

220   'Mrs. Lincoln . . .': interview with Irving Rapper, 1987.

222   'Robert still has to prove . . .': interview with William Grant Sherry.

223   'Neither Bette nor Joan . . .': interview with Vincent Sherman.

224   'I used to hear her . . .': interview with Marian Richards Sherry.

224   'Oh, I wouldn't do that . . .': Bette Davis to Arkadian in *Sight and Sound*, 1965.

224   'It was dirty pool . . .': Whitney Stine with Bette Davis, *Mother Goddamn*.

225   'My agent, Charles Feldman . . .': interview with Irving Rapper.

226   'Miss Jane Wyman': Bette Davis file at Lincoln Center.

14

227   'Predatory and possessive': Barry Norman, *The Hollywood Greats*.

228   '. . . "You're so clean" . . .' Kirk Douglas, *The Ragman's Son*.

229   'I wasn't afraid for my mother . . .': Christina Crawford, *Mommie Dearest*.

230   'I am sorry that Joan and I . . .': Hector Arce.

231   'I was looking at guys . . .': interview with William Grant Sherry.

232   'Yes, that happened . . .': ibid.

234ff   Details of Davis and Sherry's marital breakup are from an interview with William Grant Sherry; Bette Davis, *The Lonely Life*; Dorothy Kilgallen columns; and *Modern Screen* and *Motion Picture*, June, 1950.

234   'Any amateur student . . .': *Motion Picture*, June 1950.

237ff   The account of the casting and filming of *All About Eve* is from conversations with Joe Mankiewicz, Bette Davis, Gary Merrill, Marian Sherry, and from Gary Carey's transcript of his interview with Mr. Mankiewicz for *More About All About Eve* (transcripts on file in the film department of the Museum of Modern Art in New York City).

245   'I met Joan . . .': author's interview with Vincent Sherman, 1987.

246   '. . . "someone who was superior" . . .': ibid.

15

249   'I had a production company . . .': interview with Douglas Fairbanks, Jr., 1988.

250   'He's been a favorite of mine . . .': Gary Merrill with John Cole, *Bette, Rita and the Rest of my Life*.

251   'They were so *right* . . .': interview with Irving Rapper, 1987.

252   '. . . Joan threw me out . . .': interview with Vincent Sherman.

256   'That was our starting-off point . . .': interview with Dale Eunson, 1987.

259   'It was as though . . .': Joshua Logan, *Movie Stars, Real People and Me*.

261   'Hitler's diaries . . .': Fred De Cordova.

261   'Why don't you take her outside . . .': Cheryl Crane, *Detour*.

262–3   Porfirio Rubirosa: interviews with Sheilah Graham and Hector Arce.

264   'I barely got out of there . . .': Eddie Fisher, *Eddie*.

264–5   Details of Jeff Chandler's affair with Joan Crawford from fan magazines and clips in Crawford's file at Lincoln Center.

265   Story of Crawford's night with Rock Hudson from various sources. In 2009, actor Robert Wagner, 22 years younger, said he was the toy boy who played with Joan in her pool.

267   'You get paid . . .': *Starstruck* by Robert Heido and John Gilman.

268ff   Details in the Crawford–Monroe passage came from numerous sources, including interviews with Sheilah Graham, George Cukor, Harry Mines, Hector Arce, and from Fred Guiles, *Norma Jean*; Mamie Van Doren, *Playing the Field*; Bob Thomas, *Joan Crawford*; Marilyn Monroe, *My Story*; Randall Riese and Neal Hitchens, *The Unabridged Marilyn*.

16

272   'She wanted Barbara Stanwyck . . .': interview with Nick Ray, 1978.

273   '. . . He had picked me . . .': Mercedes McCambridge, *The Quality of Mercy*.

275   'Joan was drinking a lot . . .': interview with Nick Ray, 1978.

277   'It *was* a mistake . . .': interview with Joan Crawford, 1973.

282   'Come on now! You're Joan Crawford . . .': interview with Vincent Sherman, 1987.

283   Details of Crawford's road trips are from Hector Arce and from Louella Parsons' columns at Lincoln Center.

284   '. . . You have such a sweet face . . .': Mamie Van Doren, *Playing the Field: My Story*.

286   'Aldrich asked me . . .': interview with Bob Sherman, 1988.

17

288   'They're all fatter and richer . . .': Gary Merrill.

288   'I had been warned . . .': Joan Collins, *Past Imperfect*.

289   'Keep it in your pants, Harry . . .': interview with Arthur Bell, 1978.

290   At a 'Hello London' party: from Sheilah Graham column, *New York Daily Mirror*, August 2, 1956.

291   'Make it brief, boy . . .': *Variety*, May 14, 1958.

292   'You're cruel . . .': Charlotte Dinte, in *Screenland*, January 1960.

292   'morally insane . . .': Associated Press, May 10, 1958.

293   'She ran over to him . . .': *Modern Screen*, November 1959.

294   'I told myself . . .': Hal Boyle, AP, October 5, 1959.

294   'Would you mind . . .': *Life*, October 5, 1959.

295   '. . . Burt Lancaster's mother . . .': AP, March 16, 1960.

296   'That's nonsense . . .': interview with Gary Merrill, 1988.

296   Inscribed 'Fuck you': Gary Merrill, *Bette, Rita, and the Rest of My Life*.

297   ' "Hey, William Buckley . . ." ': interview with Phil Stern, 1988.

298   'I heard Rita screaming Bette's name': from *Associated Press*, 1962.

298   'My son, Michael': interview with Gary Merrill, 1988.

298   'Talk about life imitating art': Joe Mankiewicz, 1987.

299   'None of us . . .': Audrey Wood.

18

301   'There was never a thought . . .': interview with Lukas Heller, 1988.

301   'Let's make this quick': interview with Bette Davis, 1973.

302   'I took a lot of time composing . . .': Arnold Miller, *The Films and Career of Robert Aldrich*.

302   Joan tried to seduce Aldrich: interview with Bob Sherman, 1988.

304   'Joan and I . . .': Bette Davis, *This'n That*.

304   'So I had no great beginnings . . .': Roy Newquist, *Conversation with Joan Crawford*.

305   Details of the stars' contracts are in the directors' file at the American Film Institute, Los Angeles, courtesy of Eileen Tuohy.

305   'I must have been going through . . .': B.D. Hyman, *My Mother's Keeper*.

306   '. . . "Color scheme?" . . .': Bette Davis, *This'n That*.

306   'There were two distinct changes . . .': interview with Norma Koch, 1978.

307   'He had a problem with the wig . . .': interview with Peggy Shannon, 1988.

307   'The camera was on a track . . .': interview with Bob Gary, 1988.

308   'The bitch could cry on demand': from Judith Crist, 1988.

310   'Mother liked to be thought of . . .': interview with B.D. Hyman, 1988.

311–2   Details of the dinner with Hedda Hopper are in her column of September 16, 1962, New York *Sunday News*.

312   'My dad had to spend . . .': interview with Bill Aldrich, 1988.

312   'Mother was on the phone . . .': interview with B.D. Hyman, 1988.

313   'Crawford never reacted . . .': interview with Lukas Heller, 1988.

314   'We would give them . . .': interview with Peggy Shannon, 1988.

314   'She loathed the makeup . . .': interview with Monte Westmore, 1988.

314   'Miss Crawford was a *fool* . . .': interview with Bette Davis, 1987.

314   'I am aware of how . . .': interview with Joan Crawford, 1973.

315   'She started crying . . .': interview with Vik Greenfield, 1988.

316   'She used to drink "white water" . . .': interview with Bob Sherman, 1988.

317   'Joan came to my house . . .': interview with George Cukor, 1978.

318   Details of Miss Crawford's falsies were reported by Bette Davis, B.D. Hyman and Joe Eula.

318   'I am not sure . . .': interview with Lukas Heller.

319   'Bob Aldrich had a portable TV . . .': interview with Bob Gary.

320   'You could never lay a glove . . .': interview with Bob Sherman.

320   'She sees herself . . .': ibid.

321   'I towered over Mother . . .': interview with B.D. Hyman.

321   'In the scene where . . .': interview with Bette Davis, 1987.

322   'Nobody can imitate me . . .': Lillian Ross, *The Player*.

322   'We needed an old-time . . .': interview with Joe Eula, 1988.

323   'We used a close-up of Joan . . .': interview with Michael Luciano, 1988.

323   'When it came to the actual filming . . .': interview with Bill Aldrich.

324   'Her scalp was cut . . .': interview with Hector Arce.

324   'There is a way . . .': *Show*, 1974.

325   'I'm not sure . . .': interview with Bob Gary.

325   'It was a long, difficult scene': interview with Lukas Heller.

326   'Joan wasn't drinking at the beach': interview with Adelle Aldrich, 1988.

326   'Oh, she'll roll her eyes . . .': interview with Joan Crawford, 1973.

327   'It was a subtle change . . .': interview with Bob Gary.

327   'Let's face it . . .': Bette Davis, *This'n That*.

328   'But we *were* in a car crash . . .': interview with B.D. Hyman, 1988.

328   'a photographic phenomenon . . .': interview with Monte Westmore, 1988.

328   'I was at the beach': interview with Adelle Aldrich, 1988.

329   'My dad had to agree with Crawford . . .': interview with Bill Aldrich.

329   'In her definite intonations . . .': letter from Ann Barton to author, 1987.

329   'She was mouthing at Crawford . . .': interview with Joe Eula, 1988.

331   'This was the official preview . . .': interview with Joan Crawford, 1973.

332   'Somewhere along the way . . .': interview with Bill Aldrich.

333   'Mother was having . . .': interview with B.D. Hyman.

333   'We had *terrific* fun . . .': interview with Bette Davis, 1973.

333   'But I always knew . . .': letter from Joan Crawford to author, 1964.

333   'That's so much *bull*! . . .': interview with Bette Davis, 1973.

334   'I received a lovely note . . .': interview with Geraldine Page, 1978.

336   'Joan stood instantly erect . . .': Mason Wiley and Damien Bona, *Inside Oscar*.

19

337   'Basically Mother didn't want . . .': interview with B.D. Hyman.
337   'Those festivals are a zoo . . .': interview with Joan Crawford, 1973.
337   'She wouldn't give the damn thing up . . .': interview with Bette Davis, 1973.
338   'On behalf of our client . . .': directors' files at American Film Institute.
341n   'I stepped through . . .': interview with Joan Blondell, 1978.
342   'The second time around': interview with George Cukor.
342   'I have always believed . . .': interview with Joan Crawford.
343   Details of Davis' salary in American Film Institute files.
343   Details of Crawford's contract: ibid.
345   'I feel I know and understand you . . .': ibid.
347   'I asked Aldrich . . .': interview with Phil Stern, 1988.
347   'She would query lines . . .': interview with Lukas Heller.
348   Bette slapped Joan's hands away from her: *Motion Picture* magazine, September 1965.
348   'Why? I don't know why . . .': interview with Harry Mines, 1987.
348   'The accommodations were always first-class . . .': interview with Bob Gary.
349   'The trouble between the two . . .': interview with Harry Mines.
349   'It was a regular three-hour routine . . .': Monte Westmore.
350   '. . . "Don't fuck with my face . . ." ': interview with Bob Schiffer, 1988.
352   'Bette was fantastic . . .': interview with Flip Schulke, 1988.
353   'It was a challenge': *Motion Picture* magazine, September 1965.
353   'Bette told me . . .': interview with Vik Greenfield, 1988.
354   '. . . a basket case out of Joan . . .': interview with George Cukor.
356   'Things were quite different . . .': interview with Bette Davis, 1987.
356   'Joseph Cotten and Agnes Moorehead . . .': interview with Bill Aldrich.
358   'I wouldn't put it past Mother . . .': interview with B.D. Hyman.

358   'They brought us back . . .': interview with Peggy Shannon.

359ff   Details of Crawford's illness, the revised schedule, the surveillance by detective, and the memos from Aldrich to Richard Zanuck are from the directors' files at the American Film Institute.

366   '. . . a very, very sick girl': interview with Peggy Shannon.

366   'She was sick, all right . . .': interview with Bob Schiffer.

367   'Fox had closed down my last movie . . .': interview with George Cukor.

367   'She called me . . .': interview with Vincent Sherman.

368   'Obviously the ideal candidates . . .': memo in directors' files at American Film Institute.

368   'I will not do Charlotte . . .': letter from Davis in American Film Institute files.

20

371   'I am not a competitive person . . .': Charles Higham, *Sisters*.

372   'Excuse me . . .': *Look*, March 9, 1965.

373   'Of course she rationalized': interview with George Cukor.

375   'We met with her in . . .': interview with Lukas Heller.

375   'They were Jewish . . .': interview with B.D. Hyman.

376   'Every time I went there with Bette . . .': interview with Vik Greenfield, 1988.

377   'The years are just numbers . . .': interview with Joan Crawford, 1973.

377   'Bob asked me to marry him . . .': *New York Journal American*.

378   'But that didn't stop her . . .': interview with Vik Greenfield.

378   'At dinner last night . . .': *New York Times*.

379   'ready to slit her throat': interview with Vik Greenfield.

381   'She has a *cult* . . .': Joan Crawford to Jane Allen Wayne.

382   'It wasn't a close friendship': Debbie Reynolds, *My Life*.

382   '. . . It was always a kind of bond . . .': interview with Carl Johnes, 1988.

383   'She also chose our vegetables . . .': Shirley Eder, *Not This Time, Cary Grant*.

383   'And every year on Joan's birthday . . .': interview with Carl Johnes, 1988.

384   'She was also friendly . . .': interview with Vik Greenfield.

384   'They were never really that close . . .': interview with B.D. Hyman.

385   '. . . Mary was an absolute *jackass*': TV series *The RKO Years*.

385   '. . . a historic picture . . .': interview with Jim Watters, 1988.

388   '. . . I had agreed to test . . .': interview with Bette Davis, 1973.

388   '. . . what Crawford was up to . . .': interview with Vik Greenfield.

390   'The Cult of Bette and Joan . . .': from *Quirk's Reviews*, March, 1973.

391   In May 1970: interview with Alanna Nash, 1988.

391   'I beat Bette Davis . . .': interview with Carl Johnes, 1988.

392   'She arrived looking very chic . . .': from Sanford Dody, 1988.

392   'Bette was an actor . . .': interview with Judith Crist, 1988.

399n   'Crawford is right . . .': in note from Anne Bancroft, 1988.

21

401   'I was with Joan . . .': interview with Peggy Shannon, 1988.

403   'She had an aversion to the soft . . .': Joshua Logan, *Movie Stars, Real People and Me*.

403   'Logan and Emlyn Williams . . .': interview with Vik Greenfield, 1988.

407   '. . . She had a problem about going out . . .': interview with Carl Johnes.

407   'I had been warned . . .': interview with Alanna Nash.

408   'She would call me early . . .': interview with Tim Scott, 1978.

409   '*Christ*, that dame had a face . . .': interview with Vik Greenfield, 1988.

409   'She's antagonized every . . .': interview with Gary Merrill, 1988.

409   'It was a period of sheer terror . . .': interview with George Cukor.

410   'The biggest disaster . . .': interview with Peggy Shannon.

411   'She lost weight . . .': interview with Tim Scott.

411   '*Kathleen*? . . .': interview with Kathleen Carroll, 1988.

413   'I have never been so content': letter to Alanna Nash, September 21, 1976.

413 'It was there . . .': interview with Joan Crawford, 1976.

416 'She still talked of working . . .': interview with Carl Johnes.

417 'It was gratuitous cruelty . . .': interview with Irving Rapper.

417 'I was writing to Joan . . .': interview with Vincent Sherman.

419 'She died of a heart attack': interview with Florence Walsh, 1987.

419 'It was cancer . . .': interview with Betty Barker, 1988.

419 'We were at Disney Studios . . .': interview with Peggy Shannon, 1988.

419 '. . . It was a mob scene . . .': interview with Arthur Bell, 1978.

420 'Poor Joan . . .': interview with Hector Arce, 1978.

22

421 'Enemies? . . .': interview of Bette Davis by Nancy Mills, London, 1979.

421 '. . . embarrassed by my association with her': Christina Crawford, *Survivor*.

422 'Joan Crawford summoned me . . .': *People*, 1981.

422 'She was tough on us . . .': ibid.

422 'I am shocked that Paramount . . .': Marlene Dietrich letter, dated August 7, 1981.

424 'First Lady of the Theater, my ass!': interview with B.D. Hyman, 1988.

424 'She made mincemeat out of poor Lillian . . .': reported by Pat O'Haire, *New York Daily News*, 1988.

425 'I have never been *anywhere* . . .': interview with Bette Davis, 1987.

425 'After all we had *nothing* in common': ibid.

23

426 'Indestructible . . .': Bette Davis to Glenn Collins, *New York Times*, April 20, 1989

426 'He was desperate . . .': author's interview with Bette Davis, November, 1987.

430 'Greedy, greedy . . .': Glenn Collins, *New York Times*, April 20, 1989

432   'Miss Davis. Do you think . . .': author to Bette Davis, Tavern on the Green, April 24, 1989

24

434   'I'm back 100 per cent . . .': Glenn Collins, *New York Times*, April, 1989

435   'And Bette Davis just died . . .': telephone conversation with Cindy Adams, October 7, 1989

435   'The Halloween Bloodbath': *New York Post*, November 1, 1989

436   'I hear *Bette and Joan* is terrific . . .': Christmas card from B.D. Hyman, December 17, 1989

436   'With eyebrows as thick . . .': *Second Act*, Joan Collins, St. Martins Press, 1997

437   'Flying across the set . . .': ibid

438   She pushed him towards the platform: *Studio Affairs*, Vincent Sherman, University Press of Kentucky, 1996

439   Legal records . . . stored at University of Southern California: *More Than A Woman*, James Spada, Bantam Books, 1993

440   Ann Nelson details: *Bette Davis: A Biography* by Barbara Leaming, Simon & Schuster, 1992

440   Cathy Crawford on Joan as a mother: *Vanity Fair*, March, 2008

Pax Deorum

441   'Crawford was very much underrated . . .': Liz Smith column, November, 1989

442   Joan was 'really bisexual . . .': *Dark Victory*, Ed Sikov, Henry Holt, 2007

443   'It's going to be a bumpy eternity!': Liz Smith review of *Bette and Joan – the Divine Feud*, November, 1989

Bibliography

Agee, James. *Agee on Film*. New York: Grosset & Dunlap, 1981.

Aherne, Brian. *A Proper Job*. Boston: Houghton Mifflin, 1969.

Alpert, Hollis. *The Barrymores*: Dial Press, 1964.

Allyson, June, with Frances Spatz Leighton. *June Allyson*. New York: Putnam 1982.

Arden, Eve. *Three Phases of Eve*. New York: St. Martin's Press, 1985.

Arnold, Eve. *Marilyn Monroe: An Appreciation*. New York: Knopf, 1987.

Behlmer, Rudy. *Inside Warner Brothers*. New York: Viking, 1985.

Brown, Peter and Pamela Ann. *The MGM Girls*. New York: St. Martin's Press, 1983.

Burchill, Julie. *Girls on Film*. New York: Pantheon, 1986.

Canham, Kingsley. *The Hollywood Professionals*. London: A.S. Barnes, 1973.

Cagney, James. *Cagney by Cagney*. New York: Doubleday, 1976.

Carey, Gary. *All The Stars in Heaven*. New York: E.P. Dutton, 1981.

Carey, Gary. *More About All About Eve: A Colloquy with Joseph L. Mankiewicz*. New York: Random House, 1972.

Carr, Larry. *Four Fabulous Faces*. New York: Galahad Books, 1970.

Clurman, Harold. *All People Are Famous*. New York: Harcourt Brace Jovanovich, 1974.

Collins, Joan. *Past Imperfect*. New York: Simon & Schuster, 1984.

Cooke, Alistair (ed.). *Garbo and the Night Watchman*. McGraw Hill: New York 1974.

Cooper, Jackie, with Dick Kleiner. *Please Don't Shoot My Dog*. New York: William Morrow, 1981.

Cotten, Joseph. *Vanity Will Get You Somewhere*. San Francisco: Mercury House, 1987.

Crane, Cheryl, with Cliff Jahr. *Detour*. New York: Arbor House, 1988.

Crawford, Christina. *Mommie Dearest*, New York: William Morrow, 1978. *Survivor*. New York: Donald Fine, 1988.

Crawford, Joan, with Jane Kesner Ardmore. *A Portrait of Joan*. New York: Doubleday, 1962.

Crawford, Joan, with Jane Kesner Ardmore. *My Way of Life*. New York: Simon and Schuster, 1971.

Crist, Judith. *Take 22*: Viking Press, 1984.

Crowther, Bosley. *The Lion's Share*. New York: E.P. Dutton, 1957.

Crowther, Bosley, with Sanford Dody. *The Lonely Life*. New York: Putnam, 1962.

Davis, Bette, with Michael Herskowitz. *This'n That*, New York: Putnam, 1987.

De Cordova, Fred. *Johnny Come Lately*. New York: Simon and Schuster, 1988.

Dody, Sanford. *Giving Up the Ghost*. New York: M. Evans and Co., 1980.

Douglas, Kirk. *The Ragman's Son*. New York: Simon & Schuster, 1988.

Douglas, Melvyn, with Tom Arthur. *See You at the Movies*: University Press of America, 1986.

Eames, John Douglas. *The MGM Story*. New York: Crown, 1979.

Eder, Shirley. *Not This Time, Cary Grant*. New York: Doubleday, 1973.

Edwards, Anne. *Vivien Leigh*. New York: Simon & Schuster, 1977.

Eells, George. *Ginger, Loretta and Irene Who?* New York: Putnam, 1976.

Eells, George. *Hedda and Louella*. New York: Warner Books, 1973.

Fairbanks, Jr., Douglas. *Salad Days*. New York: Doubleday, 1988.

Farber, Stephen, and Green, Mark. *Hollywood Dynasties*, New York: Putnam, 1984.

Fisher, Eddie. *Eddie: My Life, My Loves*. New York: Harper & Row, 1981.

Flynn, Errol. *My Wicked, Wicked Ways*. New York: Putnam, 1959.

Fonda, Henry, with Howard Teichmann. *My Life*. New York: NAL, 1981.

Fontaine, Joan. *No Bed of Roses*. New York: William Morrow, 1978.

Freedland, Michael. *The Warner Brothers*. New York: St. Martin's Press, 1983.

Freedland, Michael. *The Two Lives of Errol Flynn*. New York: William Morrow, 1979.

Friedrich, Otto. *City of Nets*. New York: Harper and Row, 1986.

Geist, Kenneth L. *Pictures Will Talk: The Life and Films of Joseph L. Mankiewicz*. New York: Scribners 1978.

Goodman, Ezra. *The Fifty-Year Decline and Fall of Hollywood*. New York: Simon and Schuster, 1961.

Graham, Sheilah. *Confessions of a Hollywood Columnist*. New York: William Morrow, 1969.

Grandlund, Nils. *Blondes, Brunettes and Bullets*. New York: Van Rees Press, 1957.

Guiles, Fred. *Norma Jean*. New York: McGraw-Hill, 1969.

Harris, Warren G. *A Touch of Elegance*. New York: Doubleday, 1981.

Higham, Charles. *Bette: The Life of Bette Davis*. New York: Macmillan, 1981.

Higham, Charles. *Sisters: The Story of Olivia de Havilland and Joan Fontaine*. New York: Coward, McGann, 1984.

Higham, Charles, and Greenbaum, Joel. *The Celluloid Muse*. New York: NAL, 1969.

Hirschorn, Clive. *The Warner Bros Story*. New York: Crown 1979.

Hopper, Roy. *Cain: The Biography of James M. Cain*. New York: Holt, Rinehart & Winston, 1982.

Hopper, Hedda, with James Brough. *The Whole Truth and Nothing But*. New York: Doubleday, 1963.

Houston, David. *Jazz Baby*. New York: St. Martin's Press, 1983.

Houston, John. *An Open Book*. New York: Alfred A. Knopf, 1980.

Hyman, B.D. *My Mother's Keeper*. New York: William Morrow, 1985.

Hyman, B.D. and Jeremy. *Narrow Is the Way*. New York: William Morrow, 1987.

Jerome, Stuart. *We Ran Warner Brothers*. Secaucus, N.J.: Lyle Stuart, 1983.

Kobal, John. *The Art of the Great Hollywood Portrait Photographers*. New York: Crown, 1987.

Kobal, John. *People Will Talk*. New York: Alfred A. Knopf, 1985. *Damned in Paradise*. New York: Atheneum, 1977.

Kreidl, John Francis. *Nicholas Ray*. Boston: Twayne Publishers, 1977.

Lamarr, Hedy. *Ecstasy and Me: My Life as a Woman*. New York: Bartholomew House, 1966.

La Valley, Albert J. Introduction to *Mildred Pierce*. *Warner Bros. Screenplay Series*. Wisconsin: University of Wisconsin Press, 1983.

Leigh, Janet. *There Really Was A Hollywood*. New York: Doubleday, 1984.

Levant, Oscar. *The Memoirs of an Amnesiac*. New York: Putnam 1965.

Lindfors, Viveca. *Viveka . . . Viveca*. New York: Everest House, 1981.

Logan, Joshua. *Movie Stars, Real People & Me*. New York: Delacorte, 1978.

Loy, Myrna, with James Katsibilas-Davis. *Being and Becoming*. New York: Knopf, 1987.

McCambridge, Mercedes. *The Quality of Mercy*. New York: Times Books, 1981.

McClelland, Doug. *The Unkindest Cuts*. New York: A.S. Barnes, 1972.

McGilligan, Pat. *Backstory*. Los Angeles: University of California Press, 1986.

Madsen, Axel. *John Huston*. New York: Doubleday, 1981.

Marx, Arthur. *Goldwyn*. New York: Norton, 1976.

Merrill, Gary, with John Cole, *Bette, Rita, and The Rest of My Life*. Augusta, Maine: Lance Tapley, 1989.

Miller, Arnold. *The Films and Career of Robert Aldrich*: University of Tennessee Press, 1986.

Mordden, Ethan. *Movie Star: A Look at the Women Who Made Hollywood*. New York: St. Martins Press 1983.

Newquist, Roy. *Conversations with Joan Crawford*. Secaucus, N.J.: Citadel Press, 1980.

Niven, David. *Bring On the Empty Horses*. New York: Putnam, 1975.

Norman, Barry. *The Hollywood Greats*. London: Hodder & Stoughton, 1979.

Norman, Barry. *The Story of Hollywood*. New York: NAL, 1987.

Odets, Clifford. *The Time is Ripe*. New York: Grove Press, 1988.

Parish, James Robert, with Ronald L. Bowers. *The MGM Stock Company*. New Rochelle, N.Y.: Arlington House, 1973.

Parsons, Louella O. *Tell It to Louella*. New York: Putnam, 1961.

Quirk, Laurence J. *The Films of Joan Crawford*. New York: Citadel Press, 1968.

Reynolds, Debbie, with David Patrick Columbia. *My Life*. New York: William Morrow, 1988.

Riese, Randall, and Hitchens, Neal. *The Unabridged Marilyn*. New York: Congdon & Weed, 1987.

Ringold, Gene. *The Films of Bette Davis*. New York: Citadel Press, 1970.

Robinson, Edward G., with Leonard Spiegelgass. *All My Yesterdays*. New York: Hawthorne Books, 1973.

Russell, Rosalind, with Chris Chase. *Life Is a Banquet*. New York: Random House, 1977.

St. Johns, Adela Rogers. *Love, Laughter and Tears*. New York: Doubleday, 1978.

Schatz, Thomas. *Genius of The System*. New York: Pantheon, 1988.

Server, Lee. *Screenwriter*. Pittstown, N.J.: Main Street Press, 1987.

Stine, Whitney, *The Hurrell Style*. New York: John Day Co. 1976.

with Bette Davis. *Mother Goddamn*. New York: Hawthorne, 1974.

Swindell, Larry. *Body and Soul: The Story of John Garfield*. New York: Morrow, 1975.

Temple Black, Shirley. *Child Star*. New York: McGraw-Hill, 1988.

Thomas, Bob. *Joan Crawford: A Biography*. New York: Simon & Schuster, 1979.

Thomas, Tony. *The Films of Olivia de Havilland*. Secaucus, N.J.: Citadel Press, 1980.

Thompson, Howard. *The New York Times Guide to Movies*. Chicago: Quadrangle Books, 1970.

Tornabene, Lyn. *Long Live the King: Clark Gable*. New York: Putnam, 1976.

Truffaut, François. *Films in My Life*. New York: Simon & Schuster, 1975.

Turner, Lana. *Lana: The Lady, The Legend, The Truth*. New York: E.P. Dutton, 1982.

Van Doren, Mamie, with Art Aveilhe. *Playing the Field: My Story*. New York: Putnam, 1987.

Walker, Alexander. *Joan Crawford: The Ultimate Star*. New York: Harper & Row, 1983.

Walker, Alexander. *Stardom*. New York: Stein & Day, 1970.

Warner, Jack, with Dean Jennings. *My First Hundred Years in Hollywood*. New York: Random House, 1965.

Warren, Doug. *James Cagney*. New York: St. Martin's Press, 1983.

Westmore, Frank, with Muriel Davidson. *The Westmores of Hollywood*. Philadelphia: B. Lippincott, 1976.

Wiley, Mason, and Bona, Damien. *Inside Oscar*. New York: Ballantine Books, 1987.

Wilkerson, Tichi, and Borie, Marcia. *The Hollywood Reporter: The Golden Years*. New York: Coward, McCann 1984.

Wilkie, Jane. *Confessions of an ex-Fan Magazine Reporter*. New York: Doubleday, 1981.

Windeler, Robert. *Sweetheart: The Story Of Mary Pickford*. New York: Praege, 1974.

Winters, Shelley. *Shelley: Also Known as Shirley*. New York: William Morrow, 1980.

Index

MORE THAN
A WOMAN
A Biography of Bette Davis

James Spada

From bestselling author James Spada, here is the first truly definitive biography of one of the few genuine Hollywood legends – Bette Davis. Revealing a life replete with scandal, sex, violence, courage and sacrifice, *More Than A Woman* is the fruit of three years of painstaking research, including in-depth interviews with Davis' relatives, colleagues and friends.

It is a portrait of one of the most complex and misrepresented women in Hollywood history, and details many of the trials and traumas that were to shape her troubled life: her strangely close relationship with her mother; her ambivalent attitude towards sex; her possible role in the brain damage of her adopted daughter and her stormy, roller-coaster marriages.

Balanced and hugely readable, *More Than A Woman* finally tells the complete story of one of the most enduringly popular movie stars.

'Spada has certainly done his homework, and charts
Davis' climb to fame . . . without ever losing sight of
the woman who motivated the actress'
Time Out

'Absorbing and thoroughly documented'
Sunday Telegraph

'Spada's irresistible, revelatory biography . . . bursts with film
lore, gossip, countless affairs and family secrets'
Publishers Weekly

ROSEBUD
The Story of Orson Welles

David Thomson

Rosebud is a riveting and powerful portrait of the rise and fall of one of Hollywood's greatest innovators – the man who brought us *Citizen Kane* and then lost himself to obesity, small talk and conjuring tricks on daytime television.

With humour, pace and the twists of a mystery story, acclaimed film critic and writer David Thomson probes the essential questions surrounding Welles, exploring the ferocious energy and demonic intellect behind the boy genius. Challenging, idiosyncratic, compelling: *Rosebud* understands Welles as no other study has, and in a way that leaves the reader breathless, amused and deeply moved by the wonder that was once Orson.

'Masterly . . . full of fresh insights'
Observer

'The glory of Thomson's superb book is that he never tries to resolve the questions raised; he just makes you want to rewind this bewildering newsreel back to the beginning and puzzle out those questions all over again'
Guardian

978–0–349–10909–1

Other bestselling titles available by mail:

☐ Bette Davis: More Than a Woman   James Spada   £10.99

☐ James Dean   Paul Alexander   £8.99

☐ Rosebud: The Story of Orson Welles   David Thomson   £12.99

☐ Elizabeth Taylor   Donald Spoto   £7.99

The prices shown above are correct at time of going to press. However, the publishers reserve the right to increase prices on covers from those previously advertised, without further notice.

— sphere —

Please allow for postage and packing: **Free UK delivery.**
Europe; add 25% of retail price; Rest of World; 45% of retail price.

To order any of the above or any other Sphere titles, please call our credit card orderline or fill in this coupon and send/fax it to:

Sphere, P.O. Box 121, Kettering, Northants NN14 4ZQ
Fax: 01832 733076   Tel: 01832 737526
Email: aspenhouse@FSBDial.co.uk

☐ I enclose a UK bank cheque made payable to Sphere for £ . . . .
☐ Please charge £ . . . . . . to my Visa, Delta, Maestro.

☐☐☐☐☐☐☐☐☐☐☐☐☐☐☐☐

Expiry Date ☐☐☐☐   Maestro Issue No. ☐☐

NAME (BLOCK LETTERS please) . . . .

ADDRESS . . . .

. . . .

. . . .

Postcode . . . . Telephone . . . .

Signature . . . .

Please allow 28 days for delivery within the UK. Offer subject to price and availability.